Portrait of
Jennifer

A biography of
Jennifer Jones

By
Edward Z. Epstein

Simon & Schuster
New York   London   Toronto   Sydney   Tokyo   Singapore

SIMON & SCHUSTER
Rockefeller Center
1230 Avenue of the Americas
New York, NY 10020

Designed by Hyun Joo Kim

Manufactured in the United States of America

1   3   5   7   9   10   8   6   4   2

Library of Congress Cataloging-in-Publication Data

Epstein, Edward Z.
Portrait of Jennifer : a biography of Jennifer Jones / by Edward Z. Epstein.
p.   cm.
1. Jones, Jennifer. 2. Motion picture actors and actresses—United States—
Biography. I. Title.
PN2287.J59E67   1995
791.43'028'092—dc20

[B]

94-38641
CIP

ISBN 0-671-74056-3

With love and thanks to my mother, Rose, my sister, Vivian, and my brother, Steve. And to my late father, Leonard, whose passion for reading and writing set a wonderful example for all of us.

PROLOGUE

"*Jennifer, good luck!" exclaimed Ingrid* Bergman.

"I'm sure you'll win," said producer William Perlberg.

"You look divine, darling!" Gene Tierney declared, grinning.

A glittering battalion of Hollywood's elite were out in full force this March evening of 1944, in part to wish the newest addition to their tight-knit clan the best of luck at tonight's Oscar ceremony, individuals whose secret thoughts were not quite as elegant as their dress or their manners.

Here was a classic Hollywood scene: wildly cheering fans held back behind barricades by police, photographers' flashguns exploding around Jennifer, their blinding glare disorienting.

Jennifer, radiant and regal, didn't enjoy being subjected to public scrutiny. On one level she reveled in the attention, but on another she felt overwhelmed by it.

Once inside the ornate lobby of Grauman's Chinese Theater it was another kind of mob scene, elbow to elbow as celebrities, press agents, and power brokers eyed each other and edged their way into the auditorium.

Jennifer, usually cool, calm, and collected, had taken on the color of her own emotions. All at once she seemed tense, anxious, oblivious of almost everything but the ordeal facing her: the Academy Awards ceremony, a very public turning point in her newly troubled life.

Powerful gossip columnist Hedda Hopper, gowned and bejeweled like a queen, coolly appraised the twenty-five-year-old newcomer, a virtual unknown less than a year ago and now a leading contender for the Best Actress award.

Jennifer was smartly dressed in simple black taffeta. At five feet seven, she was considerably taller than the petite candy-box cuties usually favored by the front offices (most movie executives at that time were short, stocky, and intimidated by women taller than they were).

"Jennifer seemed self-conscious about her height. She was the most insecure girl," recalls fellow contract player Joan Fontaine. "She was such a beautiful girl—maybe she felt a little tall, a little robust, perhaps, maybe she felt gangly, I don't know, but she certainly felt inadequate. . . ."

Jennifer's doubts and fears hadn't proven a hindrance in pursuing her career. With her scrubbed-clean, flawless complexion, her looks were pure all-American. "She's the only actress I've worked with who didn't wear makeup on camera," notes Charlton Heston. Jennifer's enormous eyes, dark at times, more gray or green at others, were fringed with long black lashes. Her gleaming shoulder-length brunette hair was parted in the middle with a dip on each side. "We all wanted to look like her, do our hair like her," recalls Gwen Verdon, who was then a teenager married to the best friend of Jennifer's estranged young husband, Robert Walker.

"To be a film star of enduring quality, an actress must be not only admired, but also imitated by women fans," actress/author Louise Brooks once observed. And fans all over the country were imitating Jennifer Jones.

Jennifer also possessed that intensely desired quality so rare in the Hollywood community: class. It couldn't be bought or acquired; one simply had it or one didn't.

Top insiders knew that Jennifer's powerful and volatile mentor, *Gone With the Wind* producer David O. Selznick, had taken a very personal interest in the girl. Knowledgeable reporters like Louella Parsons and her arch rivals, Hedda Hopper and Sheilah Graham, were nibbling eagerly on the edges of the story. "Louella was Jennifer's bête noire," recalls the star's lifelong friend and confidante, Anita Colby.

Selznick talent executive Henry Willson was "the beard"—the front for Selznick—who, to quote Joan Fontaine, "was safe in every way. Evidently Henry was simply attracted to his own sex."

Jennifer's birthday was today. ("Talk about luck!" exclaimed director Edmund Goulding.) Obviously the lush new sable coat the actress wore was a daring, ultraexpensive, and very visible token of David Selznick's affections.

Remarkably, Jennifer and David's relationship was still a closely guarded secret, but the couple's pairing was a potential bombshell, ripe for scandal. Jennifer, a Catholic, was not only married, but a mother with two very young sons. Selznick, who was Jewish, also had two young children and a highly respected wife, Irene, who was powerful in her own right.

"Poor Irene," was the hypocritical lament of current behind-the-scenes gossip; Marlene Dietrich and others took a different view: "Poor Jennifer," they quipped.

A great deal was at stake. Selznick was a fanatic on maintaining all levels of his hard-won reputation as the Tiffany of Hollywood's independent filmmakers—of *all* filmmakers. Yet regarding Jennifer Jones, he was exhibiting supreme indifference to public opinion.

Jennifer was concerned about *her* reputation. Her upbringing, her background, her very personality, precluded the kind of situation she now suddenly found herself enmeshed in as the object of *two* men's desperate passion. The contrast between ladylike Jennifer and the bombastic Selznick was astonishing. He was unlike anyone she'd ever known, "like a force of nature." As different from her husband as a lion from a cocker spaniel.

Jennifer had changed all her priorities on Selznick's account. The producer was, indisputably, a legend in his own time, the equivalent today of Francis Ford Coppola, George Lucas, and Steven Spielberg combined.

Jennifer, in contemporary terms, was on a par with Julia Roberts, a girl launched into superstardom after only one picture. In Jennifer's case the vehicle was a religious epic, *The Song of Bernadette,* in which she portrayed not a whore, but a saint.

The compulsive forty-two-year-old Selznick was a man who said yes to life, who reached out and took what he wanted, including Jennifer. Selznick's appetite for the best of everything was already, in Hollywood's inner sanctums, notorious.

Taft Schreiber, fifteen-year-old Shirley Temple's powerful MCA agent, had recently warned the teenager about David Selznick, "not as a producer, but as a man." She'd signed a long-term contract with the mogul anyway.

There'd been nobody to warn Jennifer. "David was, to me, a voluptuary of the most revolting sort," Joan Fontaine states. "You know, he'd try to rip your clothes off."

"David was an *adorable* man," declares Anita Colby, one of the few beautiful, famous females other than Jennifer who worked for Selznick and sang his praises on a personal level. "We were like brother and sister," states Colby. She described Jennifer and David's relationship as one of the great love stories. "He was wonderful with her and she was crazy about him, and it was *fun* to be with them."

Colby, then virtually the only highly successful female executive in the movie business ("That was David's doing—he's the one who thought of it") notes: "Jennifer seemed so young and naive, not at all the 'usual' movie star. You can't make her out to be somebody mean or indifferent," says Colby, "because she's not. She loves her family, and she loves her privacy."

There are other points of view. Iron-willed, highly neurotic, cold, calculating, austere, and selfish are other descriptions that have been applied to Jennifer Jones. But one fact is unassailable: The young Jennifer had turned her life inside out for David Selznick. An intense and passionate, serious young woman, she was not a person to play second fiddle with her emotions or her affections.

"Look at Jennifer's face," said Anita Loos, observing her on Oscar night, "fresh as a cherub. This year's Cinderella story, but with the real drama yet to unfold. . . ."

"Over here, Jennifer!" Hymie Fink, one of the most enterprising photographers in Hollywood's omnipresent press corps, clicked his shutter. Editors were demanding plenty of pictures of Jennifer Jones, the newest golden girl next door to capture the public's interest. Access had been almost impossible, and Oscar night was the occasion to stockpile shots.

For the first time in its seventeen-year history, the Academy Awards were taking place in a theater rather than a hotel ballroom. It was March 2, 1944, and the world was engulfed in war. On this glamorous evening in Hollywood, however, movie fans could vicariously enjoy lighthearted, live moments of distraction thanks to a local radio hookup to broadcast the ceremonies.

In these pretelevision days, studio newsreel cameramen, their lights and equipment whirring away, hovered everywhere. It seemed everywhere Jennifer looked she saw a famous face—Humphrey Bogart, Bette Davis, Gary Cooper, Ginger Rogers, Loretta Young, Lana

Turner, Myrna Loy, Rosalind Russell, Linda Darnell, Hedy Lamarr. Twenty-two-year-old Judy Garland was on hand, as was the striking titian-haired Greer Garson, the jewel of MGM, who would be presenting the Best Actress award.

With a single breathtaking leap, Jennifer had become one of them. Thirty-three-year-old army air force lieutenant Ronald Reagan arrived in full uniform. His beaming thirty-year-old wife, actress Jane Wyman, was swathed in silver fox. Unlike Jennifer, Wyman had been struggling in movies for eight years, with more to go before she'd hit it big. Wyman's huge fifty-two-carat amethyst engagement ring—"only a *semi*precious stone, darling," observed Roz Russell to pals—sparkled brilliantly on her finger.

Edith Mayer Goetz, top dog on the Beverly Hills social circuit and a gossip of Olympian proportions, perused the crowd and zeroed in on Jennifer Jones. "Edie" was Irene Selznick's sister and David Selznick's sister-in-law. Edie's producer husband, William ("Bill") Goetz, had, ironically, been instrumental in casting Jennifer in the role for which the actress was in the limelight this evening.

Edie had observed and evaluated Jennifer like a scientist studying a specimen under a microscope. She'd been pleased to discover a flaw: if Jennifer smiled too broadly, she showed too much gum. But otherwise her beauty was unassailable: "She's an American Vivien Leigh," remarked Alfred Hitchcock.

Edie certainly knew what was going on between Jennifer and David, even if her sister, Irene, ostensibly didn't.

"Surely Irene had to know," Joan Fontaine states authoritatively. "How could she not? Although," adds Fontaine, "having been married, I know *I* was always the last to know." At one point a furious Selznick thought Fontaine had told Irene, which she hadn't.

As the Oscar ceremonies were set to begin, Jennifer sat chatting with her good friend, fellow contract player Ingrid Bergman (a girl even taller than Jennifer). "The complexions on *both* those girls was unbelievable," recalled New York film reporter Wanda Hale.

Shirley Temple sat nearby, alongside an attentive David Selznick. Joan Fontaine sat with her actress pal Jean Arthur and Arthur's husband, Frank Ross (himself a nominee for Original Story and Best Screenplay for Jean's vehicle, *The More the Merrier*).

Incredibly, three of the five actresses nominated for Best Actress—Jennifer, Ingrid, and Joan Fontaine—were under personal contract to Selznick. Jennifer was certain Bergman would win, for

For Whom the Bell Tolls (Ingrid was star of another current block-buster, *Casablanca,* in contention with *The Song of Bernadette* for numerous Oscars).

Fontaine, a recent Best Actress winner (for Alfred Hitchcock's *Suspicion*) was in the running for *The Constant Nymph.* Jean Arthur, expertly playing young leading ladies although she was forty-three years old, was nominated for *The More the Merrier,* the only "comedy" performance in the group. Greer Garson, last year's winner for *Mrs. Miniver,* was nominated for *Madame Curie,* in which Jennifer's husband, Robert Walker, had a featured role.

Robert Walker, one of the fastest-rising young talents on the Hollywood scene, was not present on this evening. His absence was a stinging comment on the state of his relationship with his wife. "In the thirty years I've written Hollywood history, I've never known a case like this," exclaimed the dean of the Hearst sob sisters, Adela Rogers St. Johns. "Too much ambition under one roof," ventured another film reporter.

The Hollywood press corps had been lied to from the beginning about Jennifer's personal life. Other than Selznick, no one at the Oscars was aware of the stunning news that the actress's "perfect" marriage was about to end in divorce.

There were other secrets soon to be revealed, including the fact that *The Song of Bernadette,* widely ballyhooed as Jennifer's first picture, really wasn't.

The host for the evening, comedian Jack Benny, observed how the only thing that depressed an actor more than losing an accolade was having his or her best friend win one! An easy laugh of self-recognition swept through the auditorium.

As the hour grew late, the prognosis for Jennifer began to look bleak. *Bernadette,* up for twelve Oscars, hadn't yet won in any of the major categories, while *Casablanca* was proving a surprise winner ("Maybe I've been nominated for the wrong movie," quipped Bergman).

When it came time for Greer Garson to announce Best Actress, Jennifer sat motionless—after this critical moment she would never again view herself or her career in the same way.

Selznick was watching her covertly. If she turned her head suddenly, she would have observed in his eyes that familiar, speculative look, a look almost embarrassingly revealing of the intensity and complexity of his feelings.

Greer Garson took center stage and read the list of Best Actress nominees. Laughter and applause erupted briefly when she read her own name. Then there was a sudden hush as Garson tore open the envelope and announced the winner: Jennifer Jones.

Jennifer's jaw dropped. Astonishment and joy were written plainly on her face. Seemingly in a daze, she proceeded to the stage to collect her award. "I was just numb," she recalled later. "It had all happened to me so fast, I couldn't digest it mentally. . . ."

Flash forward thirty-five years. I wrote to Jennifer Jones to see if she was interested in cooperating on a book I was planning to write about her.

Her handwritten reply was done in a childish scrawl in red ball-point ink on gray notepaper, imprinted discreetly "Mrs. Norton Simon." "Dear Mr. Epstein," she wrote. "Thank you for your interest in me as a subject for a book. However, I think I prefer not to join the ranks of 'show and tell,' or should I say 'kiss and tell'! Even were I so inclined, my schedule would not permit. Nonetheless I am flattered and appreciative of your proposal. Sincerely, Jennifer Jones Simon."

No false modesty in her note—no ludicrous protest along the lines that her life was simply nothing out of the ordinary. Indeed, of the great Hollywood star sagas, Jennifer's is one of the most dramatic and compelling of all—one girl's journey from the plains of Oklahoma to the lofty heights of international success and achievement. A life played out on a broad canvas, encompassing the star-studded worlds of New York and Hollywood, the playgrounds of Europe and drawing rooms of high society. A fascinating, charismatic woman around whom controversy has swirled, Jennifer, by virtue of these very qualities, represented the kind of epic tale that would have appealed to her Svengali, David O. Selznick. . . .

Part I

*J*ennifer Jones was born Phylis Lee Isley on Sunday, March 2, 1919, in Tulsa, Oklahoma ("Where they knoweth little of the grapes of wrath, but much of the grapes of wealth," wrote one ex-Tulsan). Located on the Arkansas River about 120 miles northeast of Oklahoma City, in the center of oil- and gas-producing areas, desertlike Tulsa was not, in those days, a culturally rich town. For people who dreamed of a career in the arts, particularly one in the glamorous faraway world of "the theater," Tulsa might as well have been on the moon.

Philip Isley, a native of Tulsa, was an ambitious man of twenty-six when his daughter, Phylis, was born. It was the height of the fabled era of George M. Cohan and the Ziegfeld Follies, and Isley had yearned to be a Broadway star himself.

"The Broadway man has a better idea of life and things in general than any other class of man in the world. He sees more, meets more, and absorbs more in a day than the average individual will in a month," stated George M. Cohan.

From the perspective of a sophisticated urbanite like Cohan, that might have been true, but in areas of the country like Tulsa, becoming an actor was hardly regarded as an admirable or laudable goal; with few exceptions, actors, actresses, and "the profession" itself were looked down on as sinful, silly, and downright tawdry, if not worse.

Phylis's pretty mother, twenty-four-year-old Flora Mae Suber, was nicknamed "Dolly." Phylis "got her looks from her mother," says Anita Colby, who knew both parents in later years. She remembers Phil Isley as "small in stature" and that as an adult his imaginative daughter would sometimes wonder if indeed some tall, romantic stranger had actually been her father.

Dolly was more grounded than Philip in her desires. When she met Isley she'd been employed in offices that booked tent shows (touring summer stock companies that performed plays in the entertainment-deprived hinterlands of middle America). Phil and Dolly's keen shared interest in theater and the world of show business forged a strong common bond between them. Their romance and marriage promised a relationship offering not only love and companionship, but success in show business, albeit on a small scale. Philip had no intention of giving up the acting profession, and Dolly always encouraged and supported his interests.

The couple was enterprising and ambitious, shrewd enough to capitalize on the tent show genre themselves. They formed their own company, the Isley Stock Company, in which Isley and his wife often played the leads. If, on occasion, the roles they portrayed weren't suited to them, the material was hastily rewritten so that they were.

Mr. Isley's specialty was the heavy in *East Lynne* (*The Old Homestead* was another favorite piece), and in between acts he gave his famous stereopticon (slide show) lecture, "The Evils of New York's Chinatown," although he'd never set eyes on the place.

The company toured the south central states in the summers and was strictly a small-time operation, peopled by veteran actors who were paid about $25 a week. They were looked down on by the luckier souls who'd succeeded in "legitimate" theater.

It wasn't an easy life. The company traveled by truck, on rudimentary roads, from community to community. When they arrived, their tent was raised. Admission was ten cents (front-row seats were twenty cents), and sometimes an old silent film was included as part of the price of "an Isley production." Philip liked to vary the company repertoire—one season he might present a drama, the next a comedy.

Sleeping accommodations sometimes consisted of run-down rooms in small-town hotels or a crude pallet in the back of one of the trucks. To supplement the family income, Philip also managed a movie theater in Tulsa.

Isley was well liked, regarded by many people as "bluff, hearty, and outspoken." Others described him as "a bustling human landmark." Charles ("Charlie") Rawson, one of Phil Isley's friends, has recalled the Isleys "as good-looking, personable, and smart people. Everyone—most everyone—liked Phil, who was a real 'ham'; he liked to be center stage. Dolly got a kick out of him, I think, but always let him know when he got too carried away."

It was into this atmosphere of actors, costumes, makeup, and traveling that Phylis, an only child, grew up. "I've wanted to be an actress ever since I can remember," she once said.

Unlike so many of her Hollywood peers, she never dreamed of becoming a movie star, never longed to enter a world of glamour and adventure as presented on the movie screen (although movies did have an effect on her). From the beginning, live performing was reality to her.

The toddler learned to walk backstage. She grew up observing firsthand the realities and difficulties of putting on a show. She had a vivid imagination and a keen ability to inhabit her own fantasy world. Because she was the daughter of the owners, the other actors made a fuss over her, complimenting her on her pretty face and lovely smile.

The attention often seemed to embarrass her. She was shy and found it difficult to make friends or trust anyone easily. This wasn't surprising, considering the clashing egos that characterized the backstage environment, where saying or doing the wrong thing could result in a vicious tongue-lashing or put-down. Little Phylis blocked this all out by retreating deeply into her own private world.

She was an extraordinarily beautiful child (her childhood pictures are reminiscent of Elizabeth Taylor's), with saucer-size dark eyes and luxuriant dark hair. Beautifully groomed in expensive little dresses, sometimes wearing an accent of fine, delicate gold jewelry, little Phylis was a charmer.

There was no lack of love toward her on her parents' part, although both were preoccupied with running the business. Phylis was Daddy's little girl, a role she never rebelled against—on the contrary, she always seemed comfortable with it.

Phil and Dolly took pains to see that Phylis was properly looked after and protected from the seamier side of theater life. Perhaps to capture and hold her parents' attention, Phylis, by age six, had begun "playacting," reciting Shakespeare and "The Shooting of Dan McGrew" with equal abandon. Her life's goal was clearly formed: to be a great stage actress. Her parents were too familiar with show business and its hardships to encourage her, but little Phylis was determined to enter the arena.

The Isleys moved to Oklahoma City in September 1925. Phylis was enrolled in the Edgemere Public School and made her acting debut as a peppermint candy stick in a school play. School was mundane stuff, however, to a kid who had greasepaint in her blood. Her schoolmates eagerly awaited summers so they could attend camp, swim, play games, and socialize. Phylis, however, couldn't wait until it was time to hit the road with the tent shows.

When she was nine years old, a trip to New York City with Mommy and Daddy provided her with her first glimpse of the Great White Way. One look at the marquees blazing with lights, the plush velvet-and-gilt palaces within, and great artists like monologist Ruth Draper winning standing ovations from cheering audiences, and the child was hooked. Theater had totally captured the girl's imagination and interest.

"Someday *my* name will be in lights," Phylis is supposed to have told her mother.

Back home, her parents appointed Phylis ticket taker for the Isley Company, and she also sold candy to the customers. At ten years old, always an obedient and well-mannered girl, she had no difficulty adapting to her new "job" and performed it well. But Dolly Isley later recalled, "Phylis always had a strong will of her own."

An event that was a traumatic disaster for millions of Americans offered Phil Isley the financial opportunity he'd been waiting for. On October 29, 1929, the stock market crash wiped out businesses from coast to coast; suddenly anyone with cash was in the catbird seat.

Isley had an idea. As a movie theater manager he'd seen the profits to be made from "flicks." Many owners of small movie theaters in middle America, the Southwest in particular, found themselves victims of the Wall Street debacle and without cash to buy sound equipment essential to allow their theaters to remain in the one industry that *was* booming. (Silent films, like the stock market, were yesterday's boom; talkies were revolutionizing the industry.)

Over the next couple of years Isley purchased a number of theaters, which eventually made him one of the prominent exhibitors in the Oklahoma-Texas area. He was strictly minor league compared with the huge, prestigious theater chains owned by Loew's Inc., Paramount Publix, and others—but he was a solid success nevertheless. There were breadlines all over the country. Poverty had assumed a dark national profile once deemed unthinkable in the USA. But there was plenty of money in the Isley family, more than enough to insure a comfortable lifestyle, including a good education for Phylis.

By the age of twelve Phylis was an avid filmgoer, spending long afternoons at one of her father's theaters. Her imagination was piqued not by the glamour girls—although she liked Joan Crawford—but by the *real* actresses like radiant Janet Gaynor and saucer-eyed, dark-haired Sylvia Sidney.

Phylis resembled Sidney physically, and people remarked on it. The girl was entranced by the throaty timbre of the actress's voice and worked on making her own (she tended to speak in "breathy, fast little gushes") sound more like it. Sidney's poignant waiflike quality on screen—"her kind of lost-child wistfulness"—was a quality that would predominate in many of Phylis's adult performances.

Phylis was moved to tears by such Sidney vehicles as *Street Scene* and *An American Tragedy*. (Ms. Sidney summed up both her own acting style and her approach to the business in very unwistful fashion when she noted wryly, "Paramount paid me by the tear." It was the kind of detached, bemused observation that "Jennifer Jones" would never be capable of.)

Phylis had no wild crushes on any male film actors. Loretta Young had had a girlhood yen for Ronald Colman, while both Ava Gardner and Marilyn Monroe adored and fantasized about Clark Gable. But Phylis Isley was not particularly enamored of any of them. Nor did she seem entranced by any of her male classmates. With her faraway gaze and ever-active imagination, she was, it would seem, in love with love, immersed in thoughts of romance but obsessed with the glow of the footlights and dreams of great performances.

School did not enthrall her. "To be honest, I was never a great student," she admitted years later. "Probably because first, last, and always I thought of acting and acting only."

After graduating from Edgemere, she was entered in a prepara-
tory school and junior college for girls, Monte Cassino, considered
one of Tulsa's leading educational institutions. It was run by the
Benedictine sisters (a revered religious order in the Roman
Catholic Church, the Benedictines had a distinguished history, having helped preserve the tradition of Christianity in Western Europe
throughout the Middle Ages).

In this lofty and austere environment, which was less intimidating than it sounded, Phylis blossomed. She made two close friends,
Ruth Bowers and Mary Birmingham, and the three girls created
their own sorority, the "Toppers." Although Phylis was fast developing into a beauty, she was taller than many of her classmates and
didn't consider herself beautiful. In self-deprecating fashion she
viewed herself as too tall and too sweet (a friend later noted that
Phylis's eyes, slightly slanted at the ends, and her dark eyebrows,
strong jaw, and high cheekbones, suggested American Indian).

"Social events didn't interest her much," according to Mary
Birmingham, although the Isley family had achieved social status in
Tulsa, and Phylis's photograph sometimes appeared in the society
columns of the local papers. The family was living at 301 East Twen-
tieth Street (they'd lived initially at 1236 South Owasso Avenue), and
Phil Isley's business interests had expanded to include a circus and
Wild West show. The show featured the famous old frontiersman
"Pawnee Bill." Bill "adopted" Phylis as his protegée and was often
photographed with her at the show and at rodeos. But the "Wild
West" milieu never appealed to the girl.

She spent a summer at Camp Cimarronncita in Ute Park, New
Mexico, where she learned to ride horses. She also learned to drive
a car. "I remember when Phylis first started to drive," recalled Sister
Ursula, one of the Monte Cassino nuns. "You don't know how we all
prayed in chapel that she'd arrive all right."

Although Phylis didn't bubble over with personality, her striking
beauty often made her the center of attention when she and her
friends went out socially. Phylis was always personable and sweet,
and many a young man attempted to catch and hold her attention.

"Dates bored her to death," recalled Mary Birmingham. "Whenever she went out with us she took the whole crowd by storm and
was always the most popular, but she just didn't care for anything
but acting." (Phylis, in white cap and gown, diploma in hand, in-

scribed her graduation photograph: "Sweet 16, and truly never been 'kissed.' ")

Nevertheless, Phylis had fun with her friends. There were visits to Wolferman's candy store and hamburger binges at the local hang-outs ("She was always hungry," recalled Ruth Bowers). But Phylis was the girl with ambition. While her peers simply looked forward to getting married, Phylis had loftier plans. She envisioned marriage for herself—perhaps—at age thirty-five, if not later.

She always won the lead in her school plays and impressed both faculty and students with her enthusiasm and energy. Irene Kendle was Phylis's first dramatics teacher, and she took seriously the girl's dream of becoming an actress. "I'd never before had a pupil as interested in learning all there was to know on the subject," Kendle recalled, noting that Phylis was the opposite of the flighty, giggly girls who usually filled the teacher's classes. "Phylis was a serious girl; her mind was set on becoming a professional actress, and she didn't waver from that desire."

Mary Birmingham neatly summed up her friend Phylis: "Still waters run deep."

According to those who knew her, Phylis held none of the negative personality traits that usually defined creative people: she wasn't obnoxious or moody, her manners were impeccable, and she disapproved of profanity. (David Selznick once described her as "of another generation, of crinoline and lace. She was born too late.")

Marie Barrett, Phylis's French teacher, and Irene Kendle were often guests at the Isley home. Whereas some parents might have to beg their child to "please play the piano" or do whatever it was the daughter or son excelled at, no cajoling was necessary with Phylis. On many a quiet afternoon, under the giant oak tree out in the backyard, Phylis recited a monologue or enacted a scene from a play, and she never failed to enchant her audience. "She had a luminous quality," Marie Barrett remembered, "and a lovely voice. She was tall, and that added to her presence."

By the age of seventeen Phylis was so lovely that her dad was eager to have her appear in the movies. "I can arrange it," he said, ready and willing to employ his contacts for her benefit. The studios were only too happy to arrange an occasional screen test and do other favors for theater chain owners who would reciprocate by arranging choice play dates for their product.

The movies were not what Phylis had in mind, however. Broadway was her goal, as it had been her father's. To prepare for it, she wanted to attend Northwestern University in Evanston, Illinois, which boasted the country's leading college drama department.

Neither Ruth Bowers nor Mary Birmingham planned to attend Northwestern (Bowers had chosen the University of Texas), and as graduation from Monte Cassino approached, Phylis was terribly unhappy that she was going to be separated from her friends. Realizing the Toppers would be disbanded, the girls wept and promised each other that they'd always stay in close touch.

Phylis's popularity resulted in her being chosen May Queen. She was embarrassed by the honor and suggested Ruth do it. But it was Phylis who was "crowned," carrying a bouquet of white flowers and wearing a white satin gown, its long flowing train carried by young girls dressed in tulle and organdy. Ruth Bowers was Phylis's lady-in-waiting.

In the autumn of 1936 Phylis enrolled at Northwestern as a drama major, aiming for a bachelor of arts degree. Unfortunately the university, the first in the United States to establish a school of speech and sponsor a children's theater, didn't turn out to be the enriching experience she'd anticipated.

Phylis had expected a program that would enable her to make immediate progress as an actress; what she encountered was a class full of beginners, all of whom had a very long way to go simply to reach her level (her father's tent show had been an invaluable training ground).

Phylis's fellow female students were downright jealous and hostile toward her and gave her the cold shoulder. "The boys always whistled after her at college," noted an observer. "It was that walk. It had ball bearings."

Phylis didn't make friends in other classes; a sensitive girl, she reacted to people instantly, felt instinctively whether they liked her or not. There was no one at Northwestern like Ruth or Mary whom she could confide in.

In this environment she was a loner and kept in touch with friends from home. Once, visiting home, when Ruth Bowers had two more days of vacation than she, Phylis deliberately missed her train back to Northwestern so that they could drive out into the country for a long excursion together.

At Northwestern, courses that were not related to acting were of absolutely no interest to Phylis, and she soon felt she'd made a major mistake and that perhaps she should have let her father send her off to Hollywood. But she remained at the school, determined to meet the challenge.

She'd avoided any romantic entanglements up to this point. When Andy McBroom, a very tall, good-looking drama student with blond hair and a pleasing personality, took an interest in her, they became friends. He was impressed with her sweet personality and her great beauty, and she was grateful to have someone to alleviate her loneliness.

Her family's reaction was guarded. Phylis was thrilled when her father telephoned and informed her that the Isleys were going to New York City for the upcoming Christmas holidays. Phylis would once again experience the sights and sounds of the Great White Way.

Franklin Delano Roosevelt had just won a landslide victory, sweeping into a second term as president of the United States.

The most scandalous love story in modern history had just reached its historic conclusion when King Edward VIII renounced the British crown for the woman he loved, Mrs. Wallis Warfield Simpson, an American divorcée almost forty years old.

The specter of war in Europe was an ominous cloud on the horizon. Phylis Isley was not oblivious of it all, but she remained focused on her own obsession: the theater. And during that winter holiday season of 1936, to be young and have money in New York City was surely as close to heaven as a beautiful teenage girl yearning to be a professional actress could get.

She was not disappointed on revisiting New York. Her beloved Broadway was bursting with exciting, thrilling talent. The first lady of the theater, Katharine Cornell, famed for her portrayal of Elizabeth Barrett in *The Barretts of Wimpole Street,* was appearing in *Wingless Victory.* Phylis saw the play five times and dreamed of meeting Cornell. She didn't attempt a backstage encounter—that kind of pushy gesture was not (and would never become) her style.

Instead, "I wrote [Cornell] . . . and asked if it wouldn't be better for a girl as obsessed as I to come to New York and concentrate on dramatics rather than go on with my studies. It was only because she wrote back advising me to continue my education that I [returned to] Northwestern."

Cornell had also told her, "There's only one way to become an actress, and that's never to give up trying to be one." They were words that spurred Phylis on.

She may have been shy, but not when it came to making decisions. She decided not to continue at Northwestern beyond the first year, reasoning that she'd make much better use of her time and talent by studying at the American Academy of Dramatic Arts in New York, *the* temple of learning for leading actors of the day.

Back in Tulsa, on Easter break from Northwestern, Phylis confided her plans to Ruth Bowers. The girls, like sisters, found the only sad note was the fact that they were on the road to totally separate lives. Neither could predict when (or if) their paths would cross again.

Phil Isley's contacts once again entered the picture. When he realized that Phylis would not be dissuaded from pursuing an acting career (one account states that Dolly and Phil wanted their daughter to become a lawyer), he decided to finance the Mansfield Players, a stock company headed by Richard Mansfield Dickinson, a respected actor and teacher. After meeting Phylis, Dickinson didn't object to hiring her as leading lady for their summer tour.

Phylis secured a spot in the company for her Northwestern friend, Andy McBroom (who later changed his name to David Bruce and landed a movie contract at Universal).

The tour went well. Production values were top drawer, featuring expensive sets, costumes, and lighting. Later accounts, heavily gilding the lily in an attempt to lend poignancy to Phylis's "struggling" years, claimed she'd "helped put up scenery, painted, cleaned up the stage, and worked props."

Phylis gained important experience on this tour. The company repertoire included such varied productions as *The Family Upstairs, This Thing Called Love,* and the classic *Smilin' Through.* The young actress would be on the cutting edge when, in the fall, she auditioned for the American Academy of Dramatic Arts. This, too, was to be a family undertaking.

•   •   •

Philip and Dolly had no intention of permitting their only child to live an uncomfortable, even mildly "disreputable" type of existence in New York. There would be no cheap hotels or cockroach-infested rooms, no waitressing or wondering where the rent or the next meal was coming from while searching for those maddeningly rare and elusive acting jobs.

("Only one in one hundred thousand stands a chance of becoming a star," Esther Blodgett [Janet Gaynor] is told by a casting agent in a scene from David O. Selznick's film *A Star Is Born,* released only the previous spring. "Yes, I know," answers Blodgett, "but maybe I'll be that one.")

The Isleys trekked to New York. Phil and Dolly had only the best intentions regarding their precious child and were wise in the ways of the pitfalls awaiting her. They had the wherewithal to make her adventure at least physically comfortable, and Phylis accepted their help gladly.

They decided on the Barbizon Hotel for Women. It was a practical choice. Located on Lexington Avenue and Sixty-third Street, it wasn't far from the American Academy, which made its home in the Carnegie Hall building at Fifty-seventh Street and Seventh Avenue. Phylis wouldn't have too long a trek through the "dangerous" streets of New York (and this was 1937!); and, equally important, men were forbidden on the Barbizon premises.

The Isleys gave Phylis an allowance to cover all weekly expenses. Her audition for the academy was set for September 10.

She'd selected two scenes to perform: one from Romeo and Juliet, *one from* Wingless Victory. Phylis's physical resemblance to Katharine Cornell—both were tall, regal brunettes—was an asset. Passing this audition meant everything to Phylis, and she was most anxious and nervous anticipating it.

It's fascinating to peruse the official American Academy audition report on Phylis Isley. The comments, written in pencil in a bold hand, have faded with time but remain very much intact in the bright red leather-bound volume also containing reports on hundreds of other theatrical hopefuls of 1937.

The students were rated very specifically by Proportions, Physical Condition, Personality, Stage Presence, General Education, Previous Training, Stage Experience, Voice, Pronunciation, Reading, Spontaneity, Versatility, Characterization, Distinction, Pantomime, Dramatic Instinct, Temperament, Intelligence, Recitation, and Imagination. At the bottom of the last page were personal comments by a director of the school.

Phylis's report indicated that she was not wasting her time. Her Proportions and Physical Condition were rated "good," her Personality "attractive," her Stage Presence "fairly good." Surprisingly, she'd totally omitted any reference to her considerable summer stock training, the years with her father's tent show; her Previous Training entry simply states "at Northwestern," an entry repeated under Stage Experience. Obviously eighteen-year-old Phylis was not proud of her "professional" background up to this point.

Her Voice was rated "above average," as was her Pronunciation; her Reading (scenes) was deemed "intelligent," and her Spontaneity-Versatility-Characterization-Distinction-Pantomime quotients were all found "promising."

Dramatic Instinct—"yes, definite." Temperament: "sensitive." Her Intelligence was rated "good," and school director Emil Diestel's personal comments were laudatory: "Fine girl of ability—intelligent and sensitive—should do something worthwhile."

The man who ran the academy was the tough, volatile, mercurial Charles ("Jelly") Jehlinger. Under his very strict direction the school was an efficient (and, for some students, intimidating) operation. The students had access to courses in all they'd need to develop their craft from voice and breathing, to speech, dancing, and improvisation—everything necessary to become a professional.

Phylis found the atmosphere at the academy stimulating (plays and scenes were performed in the cozy little auditorium in the basement), but she missed the companionship she'd shared with friends Mary Birmingham and Ruth Bowers. She met pretty redheaded student Estees Potter, they became friends, and Phylis once again had someone her own age to pal around with.

The girls saw the shows currently lighting up the town: Alfred Lunt and Lynn Fontanne in *Amphitryon 38*, Luther Adler and John Garfield in *Golden Boy*, and John Gielgud in Shakespeare's *Richard II*. Phylis was spellbound by Gielgud's masterly performance (the odds of the Oklahoma teenager one day starring with both Gielgud and John Garfield were around the same as winning the Irish sweepstakes).

Her goals were aimed high and did not, as yet, include movies. The trade papers were beginning to fill with tales of young producer David O. Selznick's nationwide search for an unknown actress to portray Scarlett O'Hara. It was the acting plum of the decade, but somehow the Selznick talent scouts had missed the bevy of newcomers at the American Academy. Phylis Isley was one of the few young beauties who didn't audition for the part.

Her classes at the academy began late in the fall of 1937, and Phylis was soon wrapped up in her studies. When Christmas break rolled around, she had the opportunity to return home to Tulsa for a visit; atypically, the eighteen-year-old was annoyed at the interruption in the curriculum.

Her parents understood her passion. Phil and Dolly spoke with their daughter regularly on the telephone, the conversations always including words of caution to their only child to be careful, all by herself, in the big city.

Classes resumed on January 2. There were aspiring young actors on the scene, including nineteen-year-old Robert Walker. Six feet tall and, at 140 pounds, painfully thin, he had wavy reddish hair, intense, twinkling blue eyes (he wore glasses), and a dazzling smile.

He'd spotted Phylis early on, and seen her play scenes in class. He was enchanted by everything about her. From the moment he'd introduced himself, there was a chemistry between them that neither Walker nor Phylis could deny or ignore. In ensuing weeks neither attempted to deflect or diffuse the growing intensity of their feelings.

"I'd love to work with you," Walker had told her, and both knew his intentions were "honorable." There was a poignant charm and an emotional neediness and vulnerability about Walker that touched Phylis's heart. It's unlikely the couple would have believed what the future held in store.

Chapter 2

The description "problem child" might have been invented for Robert Hudson Walker, the script for *Rebel Without a Cause* written with him in mind.

Born in Salt Lake City, Utah, on October 13, 1918, the healthy seven-pound infant was the fourth child of thirty-five-year-old Horace Walker and thirty-two-year-old Zella McQuarrie Walker. Horace, a respected newspaperman, was city editor of Salt Lake City's top paper, the *Deseret News*. Horace and Zella were Mormons (alcohol of any kind, at any time, strictly prohibited). They were not demonstrative or doting parents, and they'd been hoping for a baby girl. There were already three boys in the brood: Wayne, twelve; Walter, ten; and Richard (Dickie), eight.

The Walkers lived in a comfortable private home on F Street, but from the time he could walk, baby Robert seemed intent on only one goal: escape. To his mother's consternation, he managed to do so on many occasions. A friendly neighbor would always bring him back, and a stern scolding would inevitably follow, sometimes even a spanking with a hairbrush. However, "Spare the rod, spoil the child" was not a precept that produced the desired effect on little Robert Walker.

From earliest memory, "the baby" in the brood felt an inner emptiness, a feeling of never having his emotional needs met. He felt unloved, and his desperate need to be loved, waiting for that one magical person to make his world right, was the inevitably un-healthy basis for all the close relationships he'd experience during his lifetime.

As in virtually all large families, the youngest always had to fight for attention. Bob frightened Zella; she wasn't accustomed to a child she couldn't control.

"From childhood I found myself up against mental walls," he later recalled. "The maladjustments of that age grew and branched out all over the place. I was always trying to make an escape from life."

At age ten Bob announced: "I'm going to start smoking." His fa-ther anticipated the obvious, and when Bob became nauseated by the tobacco, he quickly abandoned the pursuit.

"The theater" soon entered the boy's life. He'd exhibited an in-terest in it when, with friends, he wrote and produced plays in the backyard and garage of his home. "We had fun doing it," recalled pal Mabel Anson, "and Bob seemed to have the *most* fun." When, not quite twelve, Bob auditioned for a role in a school operetta, to everyone's surprise he was awarded the lead. (At that time eleven-year-old Phylis Isley was taking tickets and selling candy for her par-ents' tent show.)

However, playacting was no panacea for the boy's discontent, and there was further angst in store for the Walkers. Their youngest child was an emotional time bomb waiting to explode. "I was an aggressive little character," admitted the adult Bob, "but what nobody knew but me was that my 'badness' was only a cover-up for a basic lack of self-confidence, that I really was more afraid than frightening."

Neither Horace nor Zella felt remotely equipped to handle their problem child, so they turned to Zella's sister, Hortense, for advice. Hortense had long ago set her sights on an adventurous life. She'd married and divorced a millionaire, Frank Odlum, and become one of the leading female business executives in New York (from 1934 through 1938 she ran Bonwit Teller, one of the city's outstanding de-partment stores). She lived in a swank New York apartment and had a sumptuous summer place out in Logan Canyon, and her lifestyle was one of glamour and sophistication. To the Walker boys, how-ever, she was simply "Aunt Tenny," and the entire Walker brood of-ten stayed with her in the Logan Canyon home.

Tenny's advice regarding nephew Bobby was in keeping with the latest fad in her social set: When a behavioral problem arose, see a psychiatrist.

Zella was not enthusiastic. Psychiatrists were for crazy people, not for God-fearing Mormons! Besides, how could the family afford a psychiatrist?

Tenny said she would shoulder the expense. Zella's desperation outweighed her fear, and she went along with the suggestion. Hortense arranged for an appointment for her nephew with a leading child psychiatrist at the University of Utah.

The youngster, an instinctive and consummate actor even as a juvenile, gave one of his most convincing performances in the doctor's office. The physician advised the parents that Bob had nothing serious wrong with him; he was simply a child in a hurry to grow up. The doctor told the Walkers to allow Bob "breathing room" and to let nature take its course.

In high school Bob continued to land himself in trouble. Aunt Hortense, consulted once again, suggested military school for her nephew; that solution would combine the best of both worlds for Bobby—an education plus stern discipline.

With Tenny's financial aid, and through her social connections, Bob was enrolled in the respected Davis San Diego Army and Navy Academy. Bob was pleased with at least two aspects of the situation—it was a ticket out of Salt Lake City, and in sunny California he'd be free of parental pressure and supervision.

Not long after his arrival at the academy, Bob celebrated his fourteenth birthday. His relationship with his "Brother Rats" (the nickname for military freshmen) began amiably enough, but the honeymoon was soon over, and once again Bob was engaged in "hostilities."

"He broke rules, talked back, missed classes, neglected his books, exasperated his professors with his bored indifference . . . reports going back to home were grim," related one account.

A talent for playing the drums rescued young Walker from expulsion. William (Bill) Atkinson, the man in charge of the music department, was impressed and asked Walker to take over the lead drum in the school band.

Virginia Atkinson, Bill's wife, was the academy's drama teacher, the only woman on the faculty. It was Mrs. Atkinson who saw the potential Bob Walker possessed as an actor, and she gently coaxed him into auditioning for a small role in a play she was working on for her Masque and Wig Club.

Meeting Mrs. Atkinson was to prove a turning point in Bob Walker's life. In January 1935, in the annual competition between high school drama departments, Cadet Walker was named "Best Actor in San Diego County" for his role in the play *The Other Side.* But it was a confused rather than joyful time for Bob, who didn't regard the hosannas heaped on him as approval of *him;* to his way of thinking, the applause was an acknowledgment that he was a great pretender. After all, he hadn't written the character he'd played, he'd simply performed it. Nor did he view "make-believe" as a profession he wanted to pursue.

His expertise as an actor and a musician did not spill over into his studies; his grades were mostly D's and F's.

Bob was lonely at the academy. Like Phylis Isley, he didn't make friends easily, and many classmates viewed him as "stuck-up." From his vantage point there weren't any boys he could relate to or trust, except for Creighton Horton, his empathetic, sympathetic roommate throughout 1935 and 1936.

In fact, Bob wanted to *be* like Creighton, who was extremely handsome, a good student, and clearly focused on a life's goal: medicine.

Virginia Atkinson continued to coach Walker and build up his confidence. The boy triumphed again in the next high school drama competition (he tied for "Best Actor" of 1936). Important people were beginning to take notice, and the highly regarded Pasadena Playhouse offered him a scholarship.

But Bob's poor scholastic record prevented him from graduating with his class; he'd have to repeat his senior year. He was mortified and became deeply depressed. When he informed the Pasadena Playhouse he would have to turn down their scholarship, they replied that the offer would remain open for the next year. Walker was grateful and relieved; he'd lost time, but nothing else.

He attended academy graduation day, somehow retaining his self-control as his classmates went through the ceremony. Saying good-bye to Creighton Horton almost broke Walker's heart, and Bob later voiced cynical thoughts on the wisdom of allowing himself to get close to anyone again—what was the point? It seemed certain that something beyond his control would cause the relationship to end.

• • •

He returned home to Utah on summer break and returned to military school in the fall. For the 1937 school drama department competitions, Virginia Atkinson had selected a timely and controversial play, *I Am a Jew,* which offered Bob a powerful role as a Jewish scientist (a role, it's safe to say, that few Mormons might have felt equipped to tackle).

Walker was up to the challenge, delivered a "stunning" performance, and won his third "Best Actor" accolade. He also became Cadet Captain Walker.

At the urging of his aunt Tenny and Virginia Atkinson, Bob reluctantly declined the scholarship offered by the Pasadena Playhouse and enrolled at the American Academy of Dramatic Arts. Walker would not be alone in New York—his brothers Walter and Dick were enrolled at Columbia University, and Tenny had rented a Beekman Place apartment for them.

Several of Tenny's friends' daughters were students at the American Academy, and Tenny offered to pay all of Bob's bills. She also assured Zella and Horace that she'd make sure Bob didn't get into any trouble, which he was likely to do, without "personal" supervision, in California.

Bob traveled to New York, where all he had to do was audition and be accepted by the academy. If he was turned down, however, all bets were off.

The big audition day was October 18, 1937 (Walker would turn nineteen on October 13). He chose a scene from *It Pays to Advertise,* a comedy, and *Allison's Lad,* a one-act play about a boy in prison.

Walker's official audition report, like Phylis Isley's, demonstrated that he wasn't wasting his time. He was rated "a good type"; like Phylis, his Voice was rated "fairly good," and his Reading was described as "very intelligent." He was "promising" in all departments, with a "definite dramatic instinct." His Temperament, like Phylis's, was described as "sensitive," and Walker was, over all, judged "a fine boy of ability—good juvenile type—should develop fairly well."

Chapter

3

O*ther students observed the chemistry at*
work between the beautiful brunette from Tulsa and the baby-faced
young man from Salt Lake City. "They were falling in love," recalls
classmate Don Keefer, and the couple spent hours together, working
on scenes, discussing acting, and simply enjoying quiet moments.

"We were both in love with acting, and we were mutually attracted," recalled Walker. "We played love scenes together from two
to four, and then we discovered that we weren't acting."

Don Keefer, today a character actor and back then a hopeful student like Phylis and Bob, vividly recalls the twosome: "You recognized
Phylis, she stood out among the group because she was so beautiful.
The word around was that Bob was one of the most talented of the
men, although he wasn't the most prepossessing looking."

Keefer also observes, "Phylis always seemed more mature than
many of us, even though she was only eighteen. I remember one day
sitting with Phylis and Bob and other students in the Green Room,
the alcove where we all waited and socialized between classes. A girl
from my class was looking around at this group of kids and she said
to me, 'Just think, some of these people are going to be famous.' I remember she was looking straight at Phylis."

The attraction between Phylis and Bob was growing stronger
each day. "I thought it was their ambition, intellect, and talent that

formed the bond between them," says Don Keefer. "Phylis was not a 'silly' girl. She knew exactly what she wanted."

That Keefer would mention mutual ambition as one of the attractions between them underscores a major stumbling block lurking in their future. For the present, Bob and Phylis became, to quote Don Keefer, "inseparable."

The negative aspects of Bob's personality sometimes emerged. He was jealous of handsome young men who made a play for Phylis or whom, he feared, *she* might take an interest in.

He felt inferior to fellow students who had money to spend, a group that included most of the class. As Don Keefer points out, it was the height of the Depression and it was very expensive going to the academy.

"The tuition was five hundred dollars," Keefer recalls, "a *lot* of money." (A legal secretary in New York, for example, working for three lawyers, earned $9 a week.) "The five hundred didn't include living expenses. In those days the academy was a kind of substitute for finishing school for girls of a certain 'class,' and *those* girls certainly didn't take it seriously.

"But Phylis, Bob, myself, and others *not* of that 'chi-chi' bunch took it very, *very* seriously. I was aware, however, that Phylis came from affluence."

Phylis wasn't put off by Bob's moodiness and his personality quirks. She accepted him and wasn't judgmental or demanding. Sharing inexpensive pleasures with Walker was fine with her, since he was sensitive about his inability to entertain her in grand style.

"Don't forget, New York was really glamorous back then," states Don Keefer. "It wasn't unusual to see men in tuxedos and women in glittering gowns out on the streets in the evenings. There were so many nightclubs, formal parties, elegant goings-on uptown *and* downtown!"

For Phylis and Bob, a hamburger and glass of milk was a favorite meal. A romantic cruise on the Staten Island Ferry cost only five cents. Visits to Broadway plays were, of course, on the lovebirds' agenda. *Two* orchestra seats to any leading attraction were only a dollar twenty, including tax, and a trip to the movies at Radio City Music Hall or the Roxy was about fifty cents.

The Isleys were hardly thrilled to learn that Phylis was suddenly romantically involved. She'd just turned nineteen, and her life and career were ahead of her. Philip and Dolly were smart enough, however, not to say or do anything to alienate their daughter. They assumed pragmatically that Phylis would eventually lose interest in the young man, who wasn't a desirable "catch" in their eyes.

Phylis, however, was happy. It was Walker who found himself confronting intense mixed emotions. Could he provide her with a good home, support her in a suitable style? He was all at once exhilarated, terrified, and confused.

A serious event was looming for each of them: they'd have to audition again for the academy faculty, including head honcho "Jelly" Jehlinger.

Don Keefer explains, "At the academy, there were three quarters—fall, winter, and spring. At the end of each of those terms, everyone had to perform in examination plays. You were assigned a lead role, a character role, and a general sort of role.

"The academy staff judged you, and determined whether you would be invited back for the senior year. Perhaps a third of the students would make it (the total student body was around two hundred). It was nerve-racking for those of us who wanted to come back."

Keefer and Phylis appeared together in an act of Noel Coward's *Hay Fever.* "It's a very funny play, very English," notes Keefer. "I was cast as Simon, the son. Phylis played my mother. Actually, I was three years older than Phylis, but she was wonderful in that mature part, and in a comedy. Already she had a wonderful technique and presence, you couldn't miss it. I look back and think how good she was, such a young girl playing that part. I was impressed at the time, and I'm more impressed now, remembering it."

For her lead role, Phylis chose to do a scene from *The Barretts of Wimpole Street.* She was very well suited to play Elizabeth Barrett, but Walker was hardly perfect casting for Robert Browning. They worked hard on perfecting their presentation. Fellow classmates who saw them rehearse were most impressed with the results.

Walker hadn't any doubts that Phylis would impress the panel, and she did. It was a convincing, mature performance for a girl of nineteen.

However, "Jelly" Jehlinger sliced up Walker's performance with a vengeance, criticizing everything he'd done. Like Lee Strasberg in later years, Jehlinger went straight for the jugular, and the young man was devastated. Phylis was shocked.

It turned out that Jehlinger had actually recognized Walker's abilities, and both Bob and Phylis were invited back for the following year. But Walker was mortified and hurt by the personal attack and wanted no future dealings with Jehlinger. A thick skin was not among the young man's defense mechanisms.

Meanwhile Phil Isley had arranged for Phylis to perform in summer stock. Walker was not happy with this latest development and considered it to be just another way for Isley to separate Phylis from Bob. Phylis tried to reassure him, but Bob was jealous and insecure. He was afraid he'd never see her again, that once she'd departed for Tulsa, she'd fall in love with someone else. He grew morose, lost his appetite, and couldn't sleep.

Phylis, of course, had long since made up her mind about Bob. As far as she was concerned, her divine young man had nothing to worry about.

Desperate to get a job in order to earn money quickly so he'd have the finances to ask Phylis to marry him before she changed her mind, Bob was willing to work as a waiter. He tried unsuccessfully for a job at Walgreen's Drugstore on Broadway—not being hired was hardly the end of the world—but when a promising role in a legitimate play fell through, the emotional fallout was heavy. Walker was so dejected that he turned his back on New York, especially on the American Academy. In Walker's view, the school was a total waste of time. He declared that he was going to join the crew of a banana boat, the SS *Pastore*, owned by the United Fruit Company.

His brothers were aghast. They asked him how long he would be gone. He replied that he wasn't sure—a few months, perhaps years.

How, they wondered, would Phylis react to this explosive new development? Walker said that he felt he was doing her a favor. After all, what would she want with someone like him?

Phylis, meanwhile, had no idea of Bob's plans.

Walker sailed on the SS *Pastore*. He wrote Phylis many letters, and she was astonished and concerned by his bizarre behavior. She'd lived her whole life around actors and knew how erratic they could often be, but Bob's actions mystified and troubled her.

At summer's end Bob finally returned to New York, thoroughly disillusioned by life on a banana boat. He'd decided once again to pursue a career as an actor. But the American Academy was definitely off his agenda and he dreaded relating the news to Phylis.

Bob anxiously awaited Phylis's arrival from Tulsa. A bustling Penn Station was the scene of their reunion. When he revealed his decision to quit the academy, he was ready for the worst. But he'd underestimated the depth of her feelings for him. Her reply, in effect: if Bob wasn't going back, neither was she. "We'll just make the rounds together and see what happens."

Phylis and Bob's friends at the academy, including Don Keefer and Ray Colcord and his fiancée (later his wife), Marthanne, a couple, like Phylis and Bob, who'd met and fallen in love at the academy, had no inkling of what was going on. "We never knew why they didn't come back," recalls Keefer, adding, "We knew that they certainly were asked back."

Her parents were concerned and worried by her sudden change in plans. Phylis turning into what would today be termed "a hippie" (the term back then was "bohemian") terrified the Isleys. They were only too happy to bankroll Phylis (and, indirectly, Bob) as "the kids" sought their fortunes as actors.

In retrospect Phylis didn't remotely regard memories of her days at the academy as "golden." Jehlinger's cruel verbal assault on Bob, and the resulting changes it wrought in her own life, were neither forgiven nor forgotten. Almost a half century later, making a contribution to the Kirk Douglas Scholarship Fund at the academy (Douglas attended the school shortly after Phylis and Bob), she made it clear, in a very succinct note, that her gift came out of friendship for the Douglases and not from any sense of alma mater. She did *not,* she stated, consider herself an alumna.

Phylis and Bob made the rounds in New York. Agents and casting directors were unresponsive. Life in the "real" world was incredibly tough. New York wasn't Tulsa, Salt Lake City, or San Diego. It was possible (although, for these two people, not probable) there'd be no rewards, a thought that had certainly occurred to them.

"I asked Phyl what we'd do if neither of us found any work," Walker said, "and she smiled and said that wasn't going to be the case. She said that I would be very successful."

Their period of struggle, in retrospect, might seem short, but living through it was like a terrible toothache—constantly on one's mind no matter what one did for distraction.

It was the autumn of 1938. In New York's Greenwich Village was Paul Gilmore's Cherry Lane Theater. It was a somewhat dilapidated setup in a building that appeared so fragile and run-down, with a backstage area so infested with rodents, that it was amazing it hadn't been condemned.

But the Cherry Lane had what was known as "great charm," along with a certain well-publicized cachet. Gilmore's reputation as a producer-manager was that of a very perceptive man who recognized important young talent.

That autumn Phil and Dolly Isley trekked east. They hadn't met Walker yet, and Philip's desire to see his daughter on a real stage in New York was a lure he could no longer resist. It was ironic that both Phil and Dolly, veterans of crude summer stock tours two decades earlier, were so terribly disheartened on seeing the conditions at the Cherry Lane.

They felt anger and disapproval but did their best to appear unemotional and unconcerned. They hadn't raised their daughter to perform in a firetrap in a dingy part of town. They were determined to get her out of there and away from Walker. In their eyes Bob was not worthy of Phylis; he was a nobody with no future.

Phylis, however, was deeply in love and had no intention of leaving either Walker or New York.

Phil Isley's resolve matched his daughter's (hadn't she inherited that trait from him?), so he came up with a plan—he'd make Phylis an offer she couldn't refuse and nip this whole affair in the bud.

He offered Phylis her own radio show back in Tulsa, a program along the lines of the currently popular Lux Radio Theater, which presented actors in radio versions of plays and films. Isley had a high-level contact at the Mutual station KOME. The executive in charge had once hired Phylis and liked her work (one must assume he also liked the advertising revenues Isley theaters pumped into the station).

The Phylis Isley Radio Theater was to be a thirty-minute show on Sunday afternoons. Phylis's salary was $25 per week (around $450 in today's economy).

However, Phil had underestimated his daughter's commitment to Walker. She informed her father that while she'd love to accept his offer, she couldn't take it unless Bob was hired as costar and paid the same salary ("Bob has so much more talent than I have," she said on many occasions).

Having Phylis back home, even with Bob Walker in tow, was better than thinking of her in the rattrap down in Greenwich Village. Phil Isley arranged everything.

If Phylis or Bob had perhaps anticipated Walker moving into the guest bedroom of the Isley home, with one and all living as one happy family, they were wrong. Walker had to rent a room in a downtown boardinghouse. Most of his time, however, was spent with Phylis, and if Phil and Dolly wanted to spend more time with their daughter, they'd have to include Bob.

Bob finally won over the Isleys with his charm and the special talent that had brought him recognition in military school—his acting. When they saw Walker emote on *The Phylis Isley Show,* they recognized the boy's great ability and perceived him differently. Perhaps Phylis knew what she was doing after all.

Phil Isley saw to it that the show received plenty of publicity. He arranged for Phylis and Bob to make appearances at Pawnee Bill's Oklahoma ranch, where newspaper photographers were always on hand.

Phylis was happy that her family had finally accepted Bob. But why, Mom and Dad wanted to know, did she have to get married so soon? She was so young! What was the rush?

Phylis, a girl who'd scoffed at the thought of tying the knot before the age of thirty-five, had made up her mind. Becoming a wife was obviously a role that she looked forward to playing. Bob was besotted with her. She brought out in him all the qualities that had been dormant and neglected throughout his life. With Phylis he felt loved and was always comfortable in her presence.

Walker brought out the qualities in Phylis that had had no opportunity to flourish in her insulated world. She had always been the be-all and end-all of her universe, an only child pursuing a career in which the focus was essentially and necessarily a selfish one.

Bob also brought out her maternal instincts, and he needed and depended on her totally for emotional sustenance. At times it seemed he *was* a little boy. Yet there was that unpredictable, wild streak in him that could be quite attractive and appealing. It was very flattering for Phylis to be with a person who wanted to be with her *all* the time.

On January 2, 1939, almost a year to the day that they'd first met, they were married. Phylis claimed that taking their vows on the anniversary of their initial meeting had been a romantically inspired decision. Even her best friend, Ruth Bowers King, hadn't been informed very far in advance.

Fewer than a dozen people were on hand at Christ's King Church when Phylis and Bob said their quiet I-dos. Phylis's two-piece red velvet suit ("My lucky outfit") set off her coloring to perfection. Bob wore a new dark brown suit for the happy occasion.

Her dad had purchased a fabulous wedding gift for the newlyweds—a shiny new Packard convertible. They intended to drive it to Ogden for a visit to Bob's parents.

Phil Isley urged the couple to continue on from Ogden to California. Isley had friends in Hollywood, and he'd always thought Phylis had the looks and the talent to make it in the movies.

"You make the decision, Phyl," said Walker.

Phylis liked the idea of going to California, and her decision pleased her father. She further reasoned that if things didn't work out on the West Coast, the newlyweds would simply travel somewhere else.

Chapter

4

*T*he happy couple drove to Ogden. Walker's parents were impressed with their beautiful and well-bred new daughter-in-law and proudly introduced their new family member around town.

After a brief stay, the newlyweds drove on to Hollywood and moved into a boardinghouse. "Aunt Daisy's," on La Brea Avenue just north of Sunset Boulevard, was clean, comfortable, and conveniently located to all the studios.

Phylis carried a list of people her dad had told her to contact. He'd given her letters of recommendation, and both Walkers felt their prospects were promising. Phylis's dark good looks were exactly in the right contemporary groove. Brunettes Gene Tierney, Linda Darnell, Loretta Young, Joan Bennett, and Paulette Goddard were currently hot in the marketplace. Phylis also resembled twenty-six-year-old Hedy Lamarr, *the* dark-haired beauty of the day.

Bob was a commercial type, too, projecting a lanky, innocent, boy-next-door quality similar to James Stewart's. But he was definitely a harder sell than Phylis.

There couldn't have been a more auspicious moment for Phylis or Bob to have arrived on the Hollywood scene. In terms of production activity, quality of product, and interest in newcomers, 1939 was a banner year.

The couple was excited after they'd arranged appointments at Paramount—Phylis recalled it was Sylvia Sidney's old studio! Screen tests were scheduled, but it was immediately apparent that neither young actor had the faintest idea how to "package" or present themselves. The theater-oriented couple prepared two unlikely scenes for their tests—a highly sophisticated one from the comedy *Tovarich* (the worldly Charles Boyer and Claudette Colbert had played the leads in the Warner Brothers film version) and a deadly serious scene from Ibsen's *Ghosts* (in which Phylis and Bob played mother and son).

The studio was not impressed by the tests, although Paramount teetered on the fence for weeks about signing Phylis. Bob just missed out on snagging a role in the studio's *Henry Aldrich,* a film based on the hit radio series. But the final decision on the duo was thumbs down.

This did not deter Phylis. She was a practical person, and when the nest egg she and her husband had accumulated in Tulsa—a few hundred dollars—began to run precariously low, she phoned another contact on her father's list, an executive at Republic Pictures (only Monogram was a notch lower on Hollywood's status scale).

Her interview at Republic went well. MGM had Gable, Garbo, "and more stars than there are in heaven" under contract; RKO boasted of Astaire, Rogers, and Katharine Hepburn; Warner Brothers was home to Bette Davis and James Cagney; and Paramount held contracts on Cecil B. De Mille, Gary Cooper, and Claudette Colbert; but Republic's lone superstar was Gene Autry, the reigning king of the cowboys. A lesser light under contract was thirty-two-year-old John Wayne. Phylis was regarded as yet another pretty young thing the western hero fights for. Bob was passed over altogether, considered out of place on the range.

Phylis was offered a standard deal and signed a six-month contract on June 25, 1939, for $75 a week. She was immediately cast as "the girl" in a Three Mesquiteers programmer, *New Frontier,* starring John Wayne. The Three Mesquiteers was a successful Republic serial that was about to lose its hero: Wayne, whose starring role in John Ford's *Stagecoach,* due to be released before the end of the year, would rocket him to stardom.

New Frontier was Wayne's last appearance in the series. These westerns were filmed outdoors, on a ranch. Shooting schedules were lightning fast: a picture began production on a Monday, and the film would be "wrapped" by Friday (makeup and wardrobe tests alone on any of Phylis's future films took longer than that).

The director, George Sherman, was five feet tall, a dynamic little man who always carried around his bound film script and saw to it that no one ever wasted time. "He never went over budget and by the end of his life had about four hundred films to his credit," states Cleo Ronson Sherman, his widow.

Phylis towered over George Sherman (John Wayne called him "the biggest little man I know"), but Wayne, at six feet four, towered over Phylis, and although he adored brunettes, his association with the beauteous Phylis was strictly platonic.

Director Sherman recognized that Phylis was not a run-of-the-mill Hollywood starlet. "She impressed me—she was very young," recalled Sherman. "It was her first movie, and we had to work fast. I believe we shot the picture in a week. She was observant. She knew when to ask a question and when not to. I worked with another new-comer, years later, who reminded me of Phylis—Joanne Woodward."

In its review of the picture, *Variety* took note of Phylis, but the critic stated that the role "didn't give her a good chance."

Phylis's next Republic assignment was a fifteen-part serial, *Dick Tracy's G-Men.* She portrayed Tracy's faithful gal Friday, had very little to do (her scenes were completed in one week), and was the only female in the cast.

The Walkers moved from Aunt Daisy's to their own place, a tiny "dream cottage" in Laurel Canyon. The rent was $35 per month. Of-ten the couple took long drives along the Pacific coast, discussing their dreams for the future.

Walker landed a couple of bits in movies, including one in Wal-ter Wanger's United Artists production *Winter Carnival,* which starred redheaded Ann Sheridan, a Texas-born girl around Jen-nifer's age. Sheridan, on loan-out from Warner Brothers, was the fastest-rising young star on her home lot.

Walker also had bits in two Lana Turner pictures at MGM, *These Glamour Girls* and *Dancing Co-Ed.* Lana, two years younger than Jen-nifer and a girl with virtually no acting experience at all, had been in the business only three years and was already on the verge of star-dom.

However, "You've got more to offer than any of them, Phyl," Walker told his wife.

Phylis Walker was not one to tread water when she could swim toward a destination. After two months at Republic she wanted out—it was a road to nowhere (the Dick Tracy epic wasn't even reviewed by the local press). To the studio's amazement, she asked for her release. They *liked* her—she was scheduled for more films, including one that teamed her with handsome young cowboy star Roy Rogers. Her request to cancel her contract was denied.

Phylis phoned her father, imploring him to use his influence. Republic pictures regularly played in Isley theaters. Phil made the necessary calls, explaining that his daughter wasn't going to MGM or Paramount, she was leaving Hollywood altogether, anxious to seek theater work back east.

Republic complied.

Phylis and Bob financed their trip back east by selling the beautiful Packard, and the wedding gift brought a nifty $1,200, more than enough to keep the couple fed and clothed in New York for several months, *if* they lived thriftily.

In Manhattan they rented an apartment in Greenwich Village, a $10-a-month walk-up on Tenth Street. Kitchen and living room were "combined," and there was no heat. Robert Walker was not without a sense of humor about their situation. "With all the luxury Phylis had been accustomed to, when we wanted to take a bath, we had to climb a little ladder to the large kitchen sink! Anything to avoid using the dreary bathroom we shared with all the other tenants."

Bad as the living conditions were, Phylis and Bob were ready to take New York by storm and get their stage careers launched. They had new photographs taken and distributed them, along with updated résumés, to leading casting offices all over town. Again they failed to land professional acting jobs.

In the late summer Phylis began feeling nauseated and dizzy in the mornings. A visit to the doctor revealed the cause: she was pregnant. The news had a dramatic effect on Walker. He was suddenly motivated to make sweeping changes in their lives and was eager to pursue a "civilian" job and abandon the theater altogether.

Phylis wouldn't hear of it and assured him *something* would come through if he kept making the rounds.

Determined to take no chances with Phylis's health, they decided to forsake the Village apartment. Winter would be rough in New York, and the apartment was drafty and had leaks.

They finally found a modest but comfortable dwelling out in Long Beach, Long Island, made the move and were barely unpacked when Phylis began having contractions. She had to be rushed to Jamaica Hospital in Queens. The baby, Robert Jr., arrived at five A.M. on April 15, 1940. He was an easy birth (Phylis was in labor for only thirty minutes). The infant was the image of his dad, and his arrival signaled a wonderful change of luck for Robert Sr.

Walker found work as a radio actor. While performing a brief, onetime role in a popular NBC soap opera, *Yesterday's Children,* Walker came to the attention of an important agent, Audrey Wood.

Virtually overnight Walker was hired for other top radio shows—*David Harum, John's Other Wife, Stella Dallas*—and the money began rolling in.

Phylis, meanwhile, modeled millinery for the John Robert Powers Agency. Model Candy Jones recalled her as "very shy, sweet, nervous—not a tough character, as many of the girls were. I had the feeling she hadn't been a graduate of the school of hard knocks."

Most of the time Phylis remained home with her baby. She didn't enjoy housework or cooking, but she did enjoy working closely with Bob on his radio scripts.

"She was wonderful with scripts," recalled Walker. "She had good instincts about what worked, what could be improved. She had creative and practical ideas."

"Bob became very successful in radio," recalls Don Keefer. "He had enormous enthusiasm, very 'up' all the time, very hyper, and extremely likable. He was at me to get into radio and took out his notebook and gave me the names of people I should see, told me how to audition, what to audition with, and to use his name—he was wonderful.

"In those days theater work was so sparse, there was no television, and the only way you could possibly make a living as an actor was on radio. Radio work *supported* actors, enabled them to do Broadway."

Soon the Walkers' small Long Beach domicile was no longer suitable for the family, and they moved to a three-bedroom house at 151 Brompton Road in Nassau County.

Phylis was eagerly planning to resume the rounds of casting agents. However, only three months after she'd given birth to Robert Jr., she was shocked to discover she was pregnant again. It was July 1940. The baby was due in March, when she'd turn twenty-two. By the time her second baby was born, Phylis would have been out of circulation as an actress for almost two years.

She considered abandoning her dream of an acting career. Her husband tried desperately to lift her spirits—such a sacrifice wasn't necessary, he explained; once she was ready, his contacts in the business would work for her. After all, now that he was doing so well, they could afford to hire the best help to take care of both babies.

Phylis accepted his scenario. Her parents were elated about their baby grandson, their grandchild on the way, and Bob Walker's success. The Isleys too assured their daughter that it wasn't too late to achieve her dream; Phil told her that he knew she'd have a wonderful career if she wanted one. She still had her youth, beauty, and talent, plus a family, and she'd had the children early, so she wouldn't have to worry about having them later.

On March 13, 1941, Michael Walker was born. A housekeeper joined the household shortly afterward, and Phylis, within a few weeks, was able to join her husband in Manhattan several times a week, to catch up on the new plays and what was happening in the business.

One of the plays the couple saw, Rose Franken's *Claudia*, totally captured Phylis's imagination and ignited her ambition. The play's tour-de-force title role, performed with great skill and charm by the luminous newcomer Dorothy McGuire, was that of a young, naive bride who learns that her mother has a terminal illness. The knowledge has a stunning effect on her, transforming her from a flighty girl into a mature, fully-faceted woman. The play was enjoying a long run at the Booth Theatre, and Phylis saw it many times. She focused in like a laser on the possibility of playing the role.

The property had been bought for films by David O. Selznick. The thirty-nine-year-old Selznick, seemingly at the height of his success and prestige, was not locked in to the notion of Dorothy McGuire portraying Claudia on screen. Rather, he was like the customer who insists on seeing every object in a store before deciding on a purchase; as he'd done with Scarlett O'Hara, he wanted to explore every possibility of discovering an incredible actress who'd be the perfect Claudia for the movies, just as McGuire was perfect for the role on stage.

Pursuing the screen role never even occurred to Phylis. Creating the character on stage was her obsession. The play's producer, John Golden, was preparing to cast a Chicago production. Phylis was desperate to play the part, although her husband had mixed feelings. He didn't want Phylis far off in Chicago. On the other hand, he saw how much it meant to her. He spoke to Audrey Wood and asked her to make some necessary telephone calls on Phylis's behalf.

On seeing Phylis and watching her play a scene, the casting agents arranged for her to meet directly with the author of *Claudia*, Rose Franken, who had cast approval.

Another exciting young actress was in the running: Phyllis Thaxter. "The first time I met Jennifer—she wasn't Jennifer yet, she was Phylis—was at Rose Franken's farm in Lyme, Connecticut," recalls Ms. Thaxter (formerly Mrs. James Aubrey, today Mrs. Gilbert Lea). "I had been at the Franken farm for about a week before Phylis came up. Like me, she was studying the part, and we were both going to audition. Only one of us was going to be picked to do the play in Chicago. In those days they tested actors in New York, then sent them up to play the roles in Chicago and then go on national tour.

"At Rose's farm, Phylis and I roomed together, and I learned all about her. We talked about everything, life in general . . . we liked each other very much." Ms. Thaxter's father had been a Supreme Court justice, her mother an actress, and the two young women were very simpatico, comfortable confiding in one another.

"She mentioned she'd done a western, and told me at length about her husband, whom she adored, and their two sons. I remember how truly surprised I was that she was married and had two boys. I couldn't believe it because we were *both* so young, only twenty." (Phylis Walker was actually twenty-two).

The actresses returned to New York. Dorothy McGuire had agreed to give up a matinee performance so one of the two aspiring Claudias could go on. For years a tale has persisted that it was Phylis Isley, but it was Phyllis Thaxter.

Both Phyllises had rehearsed with the company in the morning. Thaxter, however, had impressive mentors: the Lunts. She'd worked with Alfred Lunt and Lynn Fontanne for two years, and Fontanne attended the morning rehearsal and indicated to John Golden, who was seated with her, that Thaxter would be her choice.

"Mr. Golden picked me for the Chicago company," recalls Ms. Thaxter, adding with genuine modesty, "But only because I was Lynn Fontanne's protegée. . . ."

(When the *Claudia* company, starring Phyllis Thaxter, later played Tulsa, the actress was visited backstage by Dolly and Phil Isley. "They couldn't have been nicer—they were full of news about

Phylis, what she was doing—they were very proud of her. I remember Mr. Isley telling me that he, too was in 'the business'—they were both very nice, simple people. I remember thinking, Yes, Phylis was obviously their daughter.")

"David Selznick had quite a staff in New York. They were aware of all the important new talent," recalls Don Keefer. They were definitely aware of Phylis Isley. "An agent, Chamberlain Brown, ran a talent showcase in town, at one of the midtown hotels, on Friday afternoons. Actors performed scenes, and agents and producers' representatives were in the audience and looked them over. I remember Phylis and Bob did a scene from *Our Town,* and that's where one of Selznick's people spotted her. It was a springboard for Phylis."

Actually, Katharine ("Kay") Brown, David Selznick's renowned New York rep and the person who'd first called his attention to *Gone With the Wind* when it was only in galley form (as well as Daphne du Maurier's *Rebecca*), knew that Rose Franken was enthusiastic about both Phyllis Thaxter and Phylis Walker for *Claudia.* Certainly Selznick must see *both* girls, she insisted, since either might be right for the film.

Thaxter and Walker were scheduled to meet Selznick. The producer's office was located in Manhattan, at 630 Fifth Avenue, and the actresses were notified he was going to be in New York in mid-July.

"I suppose he wanted to take a look at everybody," Phyllis Thaxter says, laughing.

It was a blistering hot New York summer. Phylis Walker's apprehension matched it in intensity. On July 15 she arrived promptly for her early afternoon appointment, dressed in white, wearing a Scarlett O'Hara–like straw hat and looking cool and beautiful. Selznick noticed her in the reception room (he'd remember her "big eyes," but the next day the harried executive wasn't certain *which* Phylis had caught his fancy—Thaxter or Walker).

Phylis had observed Selznick. She noted that he was tall, over six feet, and husky. He had curly brown hair (writer Gene Fowler affectionately called him "Chinchilla Head") and wore thick eyeglasses (he was nearsighted), and his quick smile was ingratiating. He smoked incessantly.

Selznick had worked out a "system" to save himself, and actors, undue emotionalism and embarrassing scenes. The player would read first for Ms. Brown. If Selznick, in another room, liked what he heard, he'd appear. If not, it would be Ms. Brown's task to offer a "Thank you, dear, we'll let you know."

Phylis hadn't put herself in the proper frame of mind and wasn't sufficiently relaxed to do her best. The opportunity meant too much to her; it was *too* important. Her nerves took charge. "They let me read the part, and I was very bad," she recalled, "and I started to cry." The next thing she knew, however, she was reading the scene for Selznick himself.

Other accounts claim that the actress, very upset, hadn't read for Selznick and had virtually fled the office in tears. "Where the hell did she go?" Selznick wanted to know when he entered the room.

Phylis, according to this version of the story, was inconsolable when she arrived home. When the phone rang, and Kay Brown's secretary told her to return to the office the next afternoon, she dismissed the request as merely good manners on Ms. Brown's part. Obviously Kay Brown was a highly intelligent, well-bred woman and was simply going to let Phylis know politely, in person, that they weren't interested, but she should "keep up the good work." It was an old story. Almost everybody Phylis knew had been through it many times.

The next day, when Phylis didn't show up for the appointment, Selznick wanted to know where she was. A hurried telephone call reached her just as she was stepping out of the shower. With her hair still damp, she got dressed swiftly, summoned a cab, and sped into Manhattan. She instructed the cabdriver to "please keep your windows open!" as she frantically brushed her hair so that it would dry.

This account of Phylis meeting Selznick concludes with the actress arriving just after Phyllis Thaxter had left Selznick's office. Walker was led into the tastefully furnished inner sanctum. On seeing her, the star maker was immediately interested. "In a Tradition of Quality" was his company's credo, and here was a girl who personified it.

Events did occur swiftly and in A Star Is Born *fashion. The facts are that* Phylis, that week, read a scene from *Claudia* for Kay Brown. The executive was impressed and notified Selznick, who okayed a screen test. The next week Brown herself codirected Phylis's test. Several days later a letter of agreement was ready for the actress's signature. But there was a stumbling block. Phylis's agent was asking for a starting salary of $200 a week ($10,000 a year was big money—lower-level corporate executives didn't earn that much). At the end of the multiyear agreement, Phylis's weekly salary would be over $3,000 per week.

Selznick was furious. He recalled how he'd been the laughing-stock of all his friends when he'd paid newcomer Vivien Leigh an even greater starting salary in return for handing her a once-in-a-lifetime role. He wasn't going to repeat that mistake.

Or was he? As any obsessive collector knows, the value placed on a collectible is determined strictly by how desperately a collector wants to acquire it. Phylis was hardly "a collectible"—or was she? She was definitely a potential commodity in the Hollywood market-place, and Selznick had already begun thinking of stars under con-tract to him as a key source of future revenue.

Within a day Selznick had agreed to the "outrageous" terms on acquiring Phylis Isley. She signed the letter of agreement the last week in July 1941, less than two weeks after meeting the producer. From her point of view the starting salary was great, but there were no guarantees the agreement would last beyond the initial six-month option period. New York and Hollywood were full of con-tractees whose options were never picked up.

Certainly Phylis Walker had absolutely no inkling (nor did any-one else in the show business community, with the sole exception of Selznick's wife, Irene) that the thirty-nine-year-old producer's best days were behind him. He'd planted the seeds of his downfall long before he'd ever met Phylis Isley.

Irene Selznick later described Phylis, in the beginning, as "a sweet, eager girl." But for weeks (which to her seemed like months) Phylis had ab-solutely nothing to do. Raring to get started, she was told a full-scale screen test for *Claudia* was on the agenda "soon," but no specifics were forthcoming. *The Keys of the Kingdom* was another potential property Selznick had in mind for her. However, "Hurry up and wait," the classic dilemma facing every actor, was the order of the day.

Bob's career was accelerating beautifully, and he was offered his own series on CBS, *Maudie's Diary,* which included star billing and a whopping salary of $400 a week. But there was a hitch—the show would be broadcast from New York. If Phylis had to go to Hollywood, they'd be separated. Walker considered leaving the series and looking for work in California, so he and his wife could remain together.

Phylis didn't want him to throw away his successful New York career, and she explained to him that no movie ever took more than a couple of months to complete, at which point she would rejoin Bob in New York.

Walker didn't agree. In any case, if David Selznick would simply let them know what his plans were for Phylis, then the Walkers could adjust their lives and plan accordingly.

In early August Phylis was notified to prepare for a trip to California. She flew to Los Angeles on August 11. Her babies and a despondent Bob saw her off at the bucolic La Guardia Airport in Queens, New York. The couple, in tears, embraced many times and declared their love for each other. Phylis held and kissed her children and joked to Bob that there was nothing to cry about—she wasn't exactly going off to war!

On arrival in Los Angeles, Phylis astonished members of Selznick's staff, who'd expected a sophisticated, self-assured young woman. This young beauty trembled with anxiety; she was a veritable bundle of nerves.

On being driven up to the Selznick studios, Phylis was understandably impressed. Located in Culver City, not far from Metro-Goldwyn-Mayer (Phil Isley owned a movie theater, the Miralta, in Culver City), the main building resembled a rambling white-pillared colonial-style mansion of the Old South (the edifice was world famous as the Selznick-International logo). Wisteria and magnolia "dripped all over the place," to quote one visitor, and behind the dignified facade were the sprawling soundstages and workshops that turned David Selznick's dreams into celluloid reality.

She met with Selznick in his office, and he tried to put her at ease. They chatted informally, with Selznick at his most charming and on his most businesslike behavior. Phylis filled him in on her background, including her husband and two children. She completely bypassed any reference to her Republic Pictures adventure.

That was something she'd just as soon Selznick knew nothing about—a quickie western and a serial were not exactly the right credits for a girl longing to play Claudia. She glowed with enthusiasm discussing Rose Franken's play and was not at a loss for words in explaining how deeply she felt about the character of Claudia.

Meanwhile Selznick vice president John Houseman, along with Broadway's notable producer/director Alfred ("Delly") de Liagre, was about to produce a four-week season of summer stock at the Lobero Theater, in Santa Barbara, as a showcase for Selznick's contract players. David's motivation in launching this endeavor: twenty-six-year-old contractee Ingrid Bergman wanted to play the title role in *Anna Christie,* and that was to be the company's premier vehicle. Houseman had also selected the play *Lottie Dundass,* to feature Geraldine Fitzgerald, and *The Devil's Disciple,* to star Janet Gaynor and Cedric Hardwicke.

William Saroyan had written a one-act play, *Hello, Out There,* which Houseman liked. Selznick saw that it offered a role (that of a girl who attempts to help a man in jail escape a lynch mob) that, with rewriting, might suit Phylis Walker. He was anxious to see how a live audience reacted to her.

Phylis, along with actor Henry Bratsburg (he later changed his name to Harry Morgan), read the play for Selznick in his office. Selznick wanted to hear more, and subsequently Phylis, alone, was introduced to a rather terrifying aspect of the Selznick persona: late night business meetings at the office. This was a development that neither the Isley tent shows, the Monte Cassino School, Northwestern University, the American Academy of Dramatic Arts, nor Robert Walker had prepared her for. Selznick secretary Frances Inglis has recalled that she often heard sounds of skirmishing coming from within the office, followed by "[Phylis] running around the desk," followed by the actress, face flushed, hurriedly exiting the premises, dashing to her car, and racing off.

"All producers behave that way," the young newcomer was informed. Nonetheless Phylis pleaded with studio acquaintances not to leave her alone with David.

Business was business, and Selznick was candid. He told Phylis that he wouldn't want to give her "a big opportunity, and make [you] a star," thereby risking the guarantee he'd have by casting an established star, only to encounter problems about her family being three thousand miles away.

Phylis told Selznick that wouldn't happen. She explained that if she moved to California, her husband was ready and willing to make the move with the children "and to settle here permanently."

Selznick was highly curious about Robert Walker and asked Kay Brown to interview him and advise him if Walker should be signed: "Wouldn't it be wonderful if he turned out to be a good bet himself?" Selznick enthused. For whatever reason, this interview never took place.

Walker's radio work kept him very busy in New York, and one day, while Phylis was away, Bob ran into Don Keefer at the NBC studios in Rockefeller Center. "It was just after Phylis had gone to Hollywood," recalls Keefer, "and Walker said, 'Phyl had to go out there, and my contract is here, and boy, I'm lonely.' I could see that he was; the poor guy was so desperate for companionship, he wanted *me* to stay with him!"

Phylis's trip to California marked the first time she'd been separated from Bob since their marriage. Walker spoke to her on the phone every night, "but it was hardly the same as having her home," he later said.

Phylis worked diligently on Hello, Out There. *John Houseman was impressed* with her performance in the one-acter, and subsequently audiences and critics were, too. Houseman was surprised when, after the scintillating opening night performance, Phylis declined to appear at a press conference with the other actors. She begged off with what Houseman regarded as the excuse that she had to call home. In fact, she was telling the truth; also, she secretly feared that someone in the press might remember her from the John Wayne programmer or the Dick Tracy serial that she'd appeared in just a couple of years earlier.

Reviewing the play, *The Hollywood Reporter* critic described the newcomer as "a natural for pictures." It appeared Selznick had guessed right yet again, but he cautiously felt "the girl" had a long way to go, and he wouldn't be rushed into launching Phylis in anything but the perfect vehicle.

Houseman, a highly sophisticated man (many described him as jaded), later observed that Selznick was obviously intrigued by Phylis, and he thought a romance had already begun. However, it would have been inopportune, to say the least, for Selznick, this early, to have attempted to get serious with her. Phylis was constantly declaring to Selznick how talented her husband was and obviously wanted the mogul to take an interest in Walker, too,

Selznick continued to refer to Phylis, in correspondence to his staff, merely as "the girl," reflecting a totally impersonal attitude toward her. This may simply have been prudent and deliberate camouflage, under the circumstances. Certainly Phylis's unavailability on a personal level would have only intensified the nascent obsessive feelings Selznick felt for her.

"We both made a test for Claudia, and I think Phylis went first," recalls Phyllis Thaxter. "We were both so frightened. I liked Selznick—but I wasn't particularly interested in a Hollywood career."

Phylis Walker definitely was. She'd signed her fully executed contract with David O. Selznick Productions on August 31. She made another screen test on September 5. The results were not what Selznick had hoped for. The cameraman, George Barnes, disagreed. "She was beautiful and had a very fresh, sweet quality," he later recalled. "I was tired that day and could have done a better job. Also, the girl was incredibly nervous."

As with Ingrid Bergman, Selznick strove with Phylis to emphasize lack of artifice in all departments, and in the test he felt her hair and makeup had been too contrived. Her wardrobe was right—a simple blouse and cardigan sweater worn over a pleated skirt. Self-conscious about her height, she'd worn flat-heeled shoes.

Selznick's criticisms were hardly a boost to her self-confidence, and future screen tests were in order. Knowing how Phylis yearned to play Claudia, and bolstered by Kay Brown's enthusiasm for her, Selznick agreed she'd probably be right for the part. However, there was a major obstacle, one that even David Selznick could not sweep aside: *Claudia* author Franken expressed negative feelings about Phylis portraying the role.

Selznick passionately defended his discovery and pointed out to

Franken how he'd intentionally kept the actress out of any other project. He stated that everyone who'd seen Phylis, "yourself excepted, has gone overboard about the girl." He lobbied desperately to convince Franken to change her mind, predicting that Phylis would "overnight be a star." He was aware that she wasn't perfect, but "I've seen her perform, I have seen her before audiences—and I know the excitement that she causes in audiences."

He pointed out how everyone at his studio had been "knocked . . . for a loop" by her screen test and stated accurately that the qualities that spelled "star" on screen were often quite different from those that worked on stage.

Franken preferred Dorothy McGuire, but McGuire's availability was still in question, therefore a final decision would have to wait (at this point Selznick envisioned Cary Grant as the leading man).

In late September an emotionally exhausted Phylis finally returned east to join her husband, who had a surprise waiting for her—a brand new house on Long Island. In her absence, on weekends, he'd taken drives out to the Island (babies in tow) and fallen in love with a beautiful home, set on four acres, in the golden suburb of Sands Point. Walker felt it would be healthy for Bobby and Michael to live there, and healthy for him, too, since radio contracts would keep him in town at least another year.

Most of all, he felt it would be a haven for Phylis, a great place to unwind and relax.

A subtle change had taken place in Phylis's demeanor. Selznick himself had noticed and commented on it: he was fearful "the girl" was getting spoiled. "Already she has lost some of that eager, blushing quality that made her so enchanting when we first saw her. I am terrified that by the time we get *Claudia* in work she will be wrong for it, because the bloom will be off the peach."

Meantime, "the peach" settled comfortably in the new Sands Point home and once again enjoyed the role of wife and mother. She involved herself in Bob's career, working on scripts with him. They bought a recording machine, a bulky valise-sized new model that utilized wax disks (these were pretape days).

The couple enjoyed recording and playing back Bob's radio broadcasts and worked on improvements in his delivery. They recorded Phylis's voice, too, and spent a good deal of time working on her delivery as well.

They bought a new car, a Buick, and took leisurely drives around Long Island. They took relaxing walks on the beach, played tennis, and went to the matches at Forest Hills, strolling afterward, hand in hand, through the lush landscaped vistas of Forest Hills Gardens.

Selznick regularly telephoned Phylis to keep her informed and her spirits up.

"Any word on *Claudia?*" she'd want to know.

"No, no final word yet," he'd reply, advising her not to be so impatient. The producer's constant references to the fact that Phylis's debut on screen, if not in *Claudia,* would be in something important and very special, had planted seeds of fear in her mind. However "special" the vehicle, she knew—and Selznick didn't—that it *wouldn't* be her debut. Republic Pictures, unfortunately, could take credit for that—and probably would.

This "secret" weighed on her mind, more each day, until finally she made a decision. She'd have to tell Selznick the truth. She had no choice, since it would be an unspeakable disaster if the facts came out after he'd made a huge investment in her.

Selznick arrived in New York in early October, on one of his frequent business trips. At that time Phylis made additional tests for *Claudia.* There were, however, other crucial matters on the producer's mind. The Selznick film empire had recently undergone monumental change, and Selznick-International was in the final phases of being liquidated for tax purposes.

It's often been told, with benefit of hindsight, how Selznick became the loser in this transaction, which initiated what would thereafter be known as the capital gains deal. By selling to Jock Whitney his interest in *Gone With the Wind* (because Whitney didn't want to sell *his* share to Selznick), Selznick gave up all future participation in the incredible profits to come from rerelease of the spectacle in later years.

The liquidation of Selznick-International directly affected Phylis. In splitting up the assets, the company packaged and sold *Claudia* to 20th Century–Fox, in a deal that included Dorothy McGuire as star (Selznick by then had signed her to a contract).

Phylis was unaware of all of this. All she knew was that for her own peace of mind, she'd have to tell Selznick about the Republic contract and wait for the roof to cave in.

It didn't. The mogul wasn't particularly concerned about what Phylis had told him, and she loved him for that. He knew that studio publicity departments had for years successfully kept far more insidious skeletons out of the press, so suppressing this information would be a piece of cake.

But he did fear that Republic might still have a contractual hold on Phylis without her realizing it. To Phylis's—and Selznick's—relief, it turned out that Phil Isley had indeed secured for his daughter a valid release from the contract.

It was a stunning blow to Phylis when she learned from Selznick that she'd lost *Claudia.* What parts *did* he have in mind for her? she demanded to know. There was the role of Nora in *The Keys of the Kingdom,* he told her, and asked her to have patience, to have faith that all would work out. After all, he had access to *all* studios, and one of them was bound to have the right property. It was the approach he'd taken with Ingrid Bergman, and Bergman's career was falling into place magnificently.

But Phylis, like Ingrid, wanted to work. Perhaps now, she said, was the time to try for something on Broadway. Selznick advised against it, explaining that such a commitment could tie her up for over a year. He knew there was already theatrical interest in Phylis (as well as from another studio, Warner Brothers), thanks to his own interest in her, and he told his staff he hoped she wasn't being made aware of it. "I wish she would stay away from producers and agents and everything in connection with the theater until she comes [back] to the coast," he said.

What was she supposed to do with her time? she wanted to know. The studio had scheduled an agenda: acting lessons with Sanford Meisner, a leading teacher based in New York whose students included the most renowned talents on both coasts. There'd be classes in diction and movement, even classes in literature and fine arts, at Columbia University.

Apparently, as far as David Selznick was concerned, Phylis had a lot of work to do on herself, but the prospect seemed to appeal to her.

Chapter
5

*I*t was obvious and inevitable that the
United States was going to be drawn into the horrific war engulfing
Europe. The draft was already in progress, but Phylis was relieved
that Bob couldn't be called—he was rated 4-F because of his terrible
eyesight.

On Sunday, December 7, 1941, Walker arrived at the CBS radio
studios in Manhattan, at 485 Madison Avenue, to perform in a
broadcast. It was abruptly canceled. All stations carried reports on a
sneak attack early that morning on Pearl Harbor, a naval base in the
Pacific that most Americans had never heard of. The United States
and Japan were at war.

One man who was most anxious to join the U.S. Armed Forces
was David Selznick. To the mogul's intense dismay, he was unable to
garner a suitable commission. He was aware that he had a reputation as a hard-driving, "egotistical," "monomaniacal" perfectionist,
not exactly attributes the government was searching for (at least not
as far as Selznick was concerned; Zanuck, Warner, and the others
were hardly mild-mannered, order-obeying yes-men). Resigned, he
decided that since the U.S. government wasn't complying with his
fervent entreaties to enlist him, he would continue to devote his awesome energies to the world of films.

"Where the hell's that new name for Phylis Isley?" he wanted to know. It was January 8, 1942, and Selznick had decided on "Jennifer," a favorite name. He wanted a quick, memorable second name, and reminded his staff that he thought "the best synthetic name in pictures," recently, was Veronica Lake's.

He'd checked with Phylis on his plans first (as he had with Ingrid Bergman, who'd decided to keep her real name). "Any objections to our finding a new name for you?" he'd asked. "Yours is awfully similar to Phyllis Thaxter's, she's doing *Claudia* on stage . . . and may soon be in pictures."

Phylis had no objections. So in late January 1942, an official announcement was made: "Jennifer Jones" was launched as David O. Selznick's latest discovery. It's amusing how many tall tales arose on how Jennifer got her name. "My mother must have been reading an old English novel," she was quoted as saying. It was reported that "she took her name from the nursery rhyme 'We'll go to see Miss Jenny O. Jones, Miss Jenny O. Jones'. . . ."

"Perhaps," wrote one bemused reporter, "it was merely that a good name had come into Selznick's head for a young actress—Jennifer Jones—and he had to find somebody who looked like Jennifer Jones."

Another story was that Selznick had rechristened Phylis "because he'd always wanted a daughter named Jennifer." An acerbic critic who disliked the name would later write: " 'Jennifer Jones' sounds like something Selznick found in the poems of A. A. Milne."

Of such stuff and nonsense were screen legends born.

The spring and summer were a very frustrating time for Jennifer, worry and doubt her constant companions. Were the lessons producing results? Were the experts pleased with her progress? She didn't keep her complaints to herself and talked freely to Bob about whatever bothered her. (In later years an actress under contract to Selznick observed that Jennifer was "a whiner," a person not averse to lamenting over anything and everything; perhaps, the actress conjectured, that was why Jennifer didn't have too many women friends. Certain men, on the other hand, listened sympathetically and attentively to the woes of a beautiful woman.)

Walker commiserated with his wife on the hard time she was having with the day-to-day uncertainty regarding her career. There was little he could do but listen understandingly and assure her that the situation would resolve itself.

"Jennifer Jones" (she liked the name; in later years she bristled when acquaintances from the old days called her Phylis) turned twenty-three in March. Michael was a year old; Robert Jr. turned two on April 15.

Jennifer was upset to learn that Kay Brown was leaving the Selznick company. She'd had a wonderful camaraderie with Brown, liked and trusted her (and the feeling was mutual).

Jennifer's option was due for renewal in late July. So far she'd been paid almost $10,000 for doing virtually nothing. She was anxious, willing, and able to work, but Selznick hadn't permitted it. If her option was picked up, she'd receive a raise for doing more of the same—waiting.

The option was renewed. Selznick arrived in New York for business meetings in August. Irene Selznick, as she often did, remained in California. Selznick was not a man to resist an impulse. He phoned Jennifer and invited her to dinner so they could talk about her future.

Accounts of this dinner date relate that the young actress wore a light summer dress, her dark shoulder-length hair perfectly framing her blushing, madonnalike face. On this occasion Selznick was no more threatening than "a giant teddy bear" (a description once offered by Anita Colby).

At dinner Jennifer was relaxed and charming, and the talkative Selznick seemed entranced. Obviously this lovely, soft-spoken twenty-three-year-old creature (David had turned forty in May) was as far removed from the prototypical Hollywood "broad" as a snowball from a slab of granite.

Jennifer could not, by now, have failed to confront in her own mind the fact of David's fast-growing and very personal interest in her. Her feelings were with her own family. She was young enough to be Selznick's daughter. The feeling that she came away with, after this evening, was that she could trust him. (Jennifer had no way of knowing that Selznick was momentarily infatuated with another actress, twenty-one-year-old Fox contract player Nancy Kelly.)

Meanwhile, Walker was pleased and relieved that "Phyl" (he never called her Jennifer in private) finally seemed relaxed about her situation. After all, he was the hyper one in the family, and one highstrung partner in a marriage was enough. They could relax now and enjoy the many distractions their financial success afforded them.

Chapter
6

he call came in October. Selznick had arranged for Jennifer to make a test, at 20th Century–Fox, for the title role in *The Song of Bernadette.* She was nervous and excited on learning the news.

Selznick immediately requested an extension of their contract for an additional year, so that the past year, during which Jennifer had been idle, wouldn't be deducted from their agreement. The new document was drafted, as was his custom, in the form of a letter from Jennifer ("the Artist") to David O. Selznick Productions ("the Producer").

Lest Jennifer miss the point, the language bluntly spelled out all that Selznick had done and was doing for her: "In consideration of the advice and counsel that you have given me [Jennifer] in directing my development and career as an actress, and of the expenditures you have made and will continue to make for my schooling and my training as an actress . . . and further in consideration of the efforts, time, and money you are expending in endeavoring to secure for me a test for the role of 'Bernadette' in 'The Song of Bernadette' . . . and in consideration of your agreement to pay my expenses to California, for the making of that test, my expenses while there, and my expenses for return to New York, I hereby grant you the following alternative options on my services. . . ."

Selznick's options: He could employ Jennifer for two or three pictures (his choice) over a one-year period (at a salary of $4,000 per week during production); or he could employ her for a guaranteed forty weeks at $2,250 per week, with the number of pictures during that period unspecified.

Jennifer's head must have reeled at the figures, but money was not her concern. Preparation for the test preoccupied her thoughts, along with the ever-present realization that she'd already suffered one major disappointment—losing the role of Claudia—and wasn't foolish enough to regard Bernadette as anything close to a sure thing.

With her Catholic upbringing, Jennifer was familiar with the legend of Bernadette Soubirous, the teenage girl from Lourdes, France, who in 1858 saw a vision of the Virgin Mary in a village grotto. Her claim caused enormous controversy, polarizing residents of the town. Was Bernadette a saint or a charlatan? Regarded by believers as a saint, she was finally canonized by the Catholic Church in 1933. Twentieth's film of the epic tale was to be based on Franz Werfel's recent best-selling novel.

Jennifer's friend, Ruth Bowers King, had sent Jennifer a copy of the book when it was published in 1941, remarking that if ever a movie was made of it, Bernadette would be a wonderful role for Jennifer to play.

Without Selznick (or someone like him) working for her, Jennifer would never have had an inside track on the opportunity that loomed up now. It was the kind of star-making vehicle that surfaced perhaps twice in a decade, and the competition for such plums was ferocious. "Jennifer's just not a 'fighter,' " explains Joan Fontaine. "And I don't think she believed in herself."

"There have always been fewer 'great' roles for women than for men," notes Charlton Heston. "The person who's looking out for an actress's interests often makes all the difference."

Selznick was furiously maneuvering for Jennifer behind the scenes. It was always unlikely that one studio would award another studio's contract player an opportunity to become a star, since the "home" studio always benefited most from the result. Selznick thought this way himself, and even if Jennifer was 20th's choice, there'd be a great deal of bargaining before all parties were satisfied.

Fortunately for Jennifer, Fox production chief Darryl F. Zanuck was momentarily off the studio premises (he was a lieutenant colonel in the army). If Zanuck had been on the lot, many felt Loretta Young would have been asked to return to her alma mater to play the role (an ultradevout Roman Catholic, the radiant Loretta regarded the camera as her friend because she felt it photographed her "spirituality." Six years older than Jennifer, and a star for over a decade, Young was hardly the new face the project ostensibly called for).

Jennifer's competition included many of Fox's current young contract players: the very accomplished Anne Baxter; Zanuck's personal protegée, twenty-one-year-old Linda Darnell; and the spectacular Gene Tierney. There were also almost two thousand applicants bombarding the studio from all over the country for the opportunity to test for the part.

Selznick's brother-in-law, William Goetz, was currently in charge of production at Fox. Their father-in-law, L. B. Mayer, had been directly responsible for obtaining the job for Goetz ("Bill Goetz wouldn't know a good script from a roll of toilet paper," Zanuck once quipped).

There was no guarantee that brother-in-law Goetz would prove a reliable ally to Selznick, although he'd certainly be easier to deal with than Zanuck. On such quirks of fate were careers successfully launched or aborted.

Robert Walker wished his apprehensive wife all the luck in the world when Jennifer embarked on the five-day journey, by luxury train, to California. The couple had discussed their future and made key decisions. Bob would relocate to the West Coast as soon as his current commitments expired toward the end of the year. The climate in California would be great for the kids, and one of Walker's agents, Marcella Knapp, assured him there'd be plenty of opportunities for him out there.

Jennifer immersed herself in the Werfel novel on the train journey. Arriving in Los Angeles on a balmy October day, she found Selznick studio representative George Glass waiting for her with a limousine, in which she was driven to a lovely home that had been rented for her in Beverly Hills, close to the Fox studio. She'd have plenty of privacy and time to prepare.

Studios took care of everything for their players, from arranging living accommodations to transportation and entertainment. They were also on hand to exert influence, when necessary, to quash life's daily problems, from annoying trifles like speeding and parking tickets (Jean Howard Feldman, wife of agent Charles Feldman—both close Selznick pals—once bragged how she hadn't even had to take a driver's test to get a license) to far more serious intrusions that might distract an actor from delivering those two crucial commodities—a shining persona and a great performance.

Jennifer's introduction to the seductive gilded-cage lifestyle had begun.

She was acutely aware that Selznick had successfully masterminded Ingrid Bergman's career in exactly the same way that he was setting out to establish her own. Ingrid, who'd arrived in the United States in 1939, was six years older than Jennifer. The two women shared common ground: Selznick was their Svengali; both women were hard workers and enamored of acting; the *work* appealed to them, the rest was secondary.

Henry King was to be the director of *Song of Bernadette.* A tall, attractive man in his fifties, with piercing blue eyes ("A couple of actresses I knew who had worked with Henry said that when he looked at you with those pale blue eyes your knees melted," recalled Gregory Peck), he was able to date his career back to silent pictures (he'd directed over fifty of them). He was the younger brother of Shakespearean actor Thomas J. King and the uncle of Charles King, famous radio and film star of the 1920s.

Thomas J. King's namesake, young Tom King, today a man with over three decades of experience in the broadcasting industry (the last few years with Peter Jennings at ABC News), was another of Henry's nephews. "My uncle got me into the business and at that time I was under contract to Twentieth, but I wasn't that interested in an acting career," he recalls. Tom King led a *very* active social life in Hollywood over the next decade, one that would crisscross with Robert Walker's and, indirectly but importantly, with Jennifer's.

"My uncle Henry was a 'tough guy,' like John Ford and John Huston," states Tom King. "He chewed on a cigar and didn't appreciate or take any nonsense from anyone."

Henry King was known as a "man's director." He'd guided Tyrone Power to top screen stardom in six blockbuster films, most recently *A Yank in the R.A.F.* and *The Black Swan.* King was highly respected on the 20th lot ("He was Zanuck's boy," says Tom King), and Selznick thought him the right director for Jennifer.

"My uncle liked Jennifer," says Tom King, "because she was cooperative. And she was a good actress. When an actor was good, he left you alone."

The choice of cameraman was another crucial element in creating a star. For Jennifer's test, Selznick lobbied and secured the services of Leon Shamroy, one of the best in the business. While technically Selznick had nothing to do with Jennifer's test or the movie itself, he met privately with Shamroy and carefully outlined how he felt Jennifer must be photographed. "Dave Selznick knew exactly what he wanted, and he was usually right, but, Christ, his demands! He could drive you crazy, if you let him," recalled Shamroy. (David had been equally fanatical on how Ingrid Bergman was photographed. He'd gone to great expense to rephotograph many of Bergman's scenes in *Intermezzo,* her first American film and Selznick's own production.)

It remained to be seen which actress projected the "radiant innocence" necessary to create the part of Bernadette. The usual Hollywood qualifications—surface beauty and glamour—were in this instance worthless, indeed detrimental. What *was* essential was an inner glow, a spiritual aura, a purity and sweetness—attributes that couldn't be faked. Like "class," one either projected them or didn't. Soft-focus lenses to the contrary, the camera wouldn't lie.

Neither Jennifer nor Selznick could have slept well on reading Hedda Hopper's prognostication, on November 2, that while Jennifer had the inside track on the role, thirty-nine other girls were scheduled immediately to face the cameras, including a nineteen-year-old newcomer, Beatrice Pearson, who'd been understudy for the actress currently playing Claudia on Broadway.

"When they've counted all the noses," Hedda stated authoritatively, "it's my hunch that the one who'll be starred in *Bernadette* will be Teresa Wright, who was born for the part." Wright, a brilliant young actress under contract to Sam Goldwyn, had just completed a starring role for Alfred Hitchcock in the about-to-be-released *Shadow of a Doubt.*

For the *Bernadette* test, Henry King filmed two scenes. The first would determine how the actress moved—on camera many beautiful women and men were simply ungraceful and ungainly; and the second would portray the actress's reaction on seeing "the Vision." (As George Cukor noted, "Being photogenic is a question of . . . how the face moves. The smile must illuminate, the mouth must look graceful, the eyes must 'light up.' ") For this scene a stick was held above the camera, and the actress was instructed to gaze at it and imagine that she was a fourteen-year-old peasant girl beholding a vision of the Blessed Virgin.

Jennifer's test went well. "I asked my editor to add Jennifer's scene to the reel with the others, so we could project them all together," recalled Henry King. "When we saw them all, I noticed one outstanding thing. All of the others looked—Jennifer actually *saw*."

Selznick launched immediately into part two of his campaign to have the studio sign her for the part before behind-the-scenes interference by outside parties, namely powerful agents lobbying for other actresses and studio executives pushing their own "discoveries," muddied the waters.

Henry King told producer Bill Perlberg, after screening Jennifer's test, "I think you'd better choose this girl. If you go on testing other actresses, you'll end up confused and you'll settle for some star. That would be a mistake. This girl *is* Bernadette."

The deal began to take shape. Money was not the problem—Selznick was hardly angling for a financial killing. He was told that if he sold Fox half of Jennifer's contract, as he'd done with Dorothy McGuire, Jennifer would get the role. That, he replied, was out of the question; a multiple-picture deal was feasible.

The studio demanded six pictures over the next four years. Selznick vetoed the proposal. The art of the deal (selling his share of *Gone With the Wind* to Jock Whitney notwithstanding) was a talent Selznick possessed.

An agreement for five pictures over five years was reportedly negotiated, with both parties aware that the prospect of Jennifer Jones appearing in five pictures for 20th Century–Fox was most unlikely. In any case, Fox management had to approve.

Jennifer sat home and waited. She was lonely. She idled away the hours by reading, talking on the phone to her husband (she liked to talk on the phone for hours), and occasionally taking drives. There were no friends like Ruth Bowers or Mary Birmingham to talk to, no dinner parties to attend for fun and relaxation. Selznick and his wife had welcomed Ingrid Bergman into their home and inner circle, but this was not the case with Jennifer. David obviously had had something else in mind for her from the beginning.

Selznick spoke with the actress frequently on the telephone and continued to lead his own life, oblivious of the fact that his loyal wife, Irene, busy raising their two sons and running the household, was coping with her own feelings of loneliness and lack of day-to-day purpose.

David and Irene were still very much man and wife, and they were still sleeping together. The couple's preoccupation with appearances, and Irene's strong character and steadfast sense of responsibility, had kept their family functioning smoothly for the past several years. Irene had always been a strong counterbalance to Selznick's often neurotic and wildly emotional behavior. She loved him and was the anchor that kept their relationship from flailing out of control.

Jennifer and Irene were similar in some ways—both women tended to be conservative and had to be drawn out for their opinions and thoughts. For each woman, Selznick was the catalyst.

Jennifer was understandably flattered at the attention the producer lavished on her. With Selznick guiding her, she saw how she could achieve all that she'd longed to accomplish since she was a little girl. David had the power, the talents, and the wherewithal to make her dreams come true. The fabulous plans he outlined for her sounded like tales spun by Scheherazade.

Chapter
7

"*Take what you want from life—and* pay for it," states an old proverb. For most of his life David Selznick took what he wanted. He was loath, however, to suffer the pain or pay the heavy price of his excesses. "He knew himself very well," declares Anita Colby.

"If you knew how to handle David, you could function well," Alfred Hitchcock recalled. "The idea was to listen to everything he had to say, then quietly discard what didn't suit you. I often wondered if the important women in his life didn't pursue this tactic in dealing with him."

By lusting after Jennifer, Selznick was jeopardizing a relationship at home that few men in his position would have risked upsetting. However, those who knew him best realized that David had always been "a mass of contradictions": a high-spirited optimist subject to fits of depression and melancholy, "a son of a bitch," and "a great guy."

Selznick had once considered abandoning the world of movies to become a book publisher (he was offering to compile books on Hollywood and its history as far back as the early 1930s). But his personality was far better suited to the cutthroat world of Hollywood make-believe. He had a sense of humor about himself, and by the time Jennifer met him, he was in many ways still a boy who'd never grown up.

Robert Walker was a man who'd never known love as a child, who'd reached out to Jennifer to fill that gaping void. Unconditional love, however, was a concept David Selznick had experienced early on, and he was used to that depth of commitment from those who loved him.

David's father was film pioneer Lewis J. Selznick. "I never said 'no' to a child of mine," Selznick's father liked to brag.

"Until David got married, his father put him to bed every night, regardless of the hour," recalled Irene Selznick.

"From an apple tree you get apples," as the old saying goes. Lewis Selznick, a Russian Jew, was a self-made man. Born on May 2, 1870, he was one of eighteen children. He married Florence Sachs, an Orthodox Jew, when she was seventeen years old. Selznick was a burningly ambitious young man, successful in the jewelry business before he assailed the world of movies. Over the years he presented his wife with a fabulous collection of jewels (just as David later gifted Irene and then Jennifer with spectacular baubles). These diamond, emerald, and sapphire parures were a source of great pride and joy to Florence Selznick.

But Lewis was equally generous with his mistress, actress Clara Kimball Young (the first star—thanks to Selznick and to the great dismay of his peers—to have her own independent production company). Lewis had a notorious reputation as a womanizer, and his sons followed avidly in his footsteps.

David Selznick (as an adult he added the "O." himself) was born on May 10, 1902, the third of three sons. David's bond with middle brother Myron (four years his senior) was intense. Myron was his mother's favorite, David was the apple of his father's eye, and from the beginning the emotional foundation was in place for both David and Myron to overcome all obstacles and conquer the world.

The eldest Selznick brother—Howard, the "secret" brother— lacked the fierce ambition and drive of his father and siblings. He had musical talent and a minor brain disorder. Howard married and had children, and his brothers and parents supported the whole brood, but because of his "condition," Howard was the outsider; he wasn't encouraged in his musical abilities and never enjoyed an intimate relationship with the rest of the family.

Lewis taught Myron and David every nuance of the treacherous film business, virtually weaning the boys on wheeling and dealing from the time they learned to talk. Lewis was single-minded: the boys *must* become successful, and he instilled in them, to a fanatical degree, the ethic of the workaholic.

David's formal education was barely more than minimal. He attended the Hamilton Institute for Boys, graduated high school, and briefly attended Columbia University, where he quickly dropped out. Myron, too, had dropped out of Columbia to go to work for his father. He rose from shipping clerk to production manager in record time.

By the age of twenty-one Myron was in charge of production for his father's Select Pictures (seventeen-year-old David was vice president) and earning over $1,000 a week (David's salary was not far behind). David edited the house organ for Selznick enterprises and named it *The Brain Exchange.* He was also in charge of the company's newsreel and short subjects departments, and it was David who introduced the innovative concept of "segments" ("What's New in Fashions," "On the Medical Front," and so on) to the newsreel.

Myron became cynical at a young age regarding the opposite sex. David, on the other hand, was "wildly romantic." A voracious reader, he adored the classics (although contemporary writer F. Scott Fitzgerald was his unlikely role model). David's friend, writer Ben Hecht, later offered a sharp-edged observation: "Unfortunately, David, you did all your reading before you were seventeen."

The dark side of David emerged with the passage of years—a David who, to quote Loretta Young, could behave like "a pig."

"Oh, my God, yes!" exclaims Joan Fontaine. "David *chased* me." A typical encounter: "I had a suite at the Hampshire House in New York," recalls Fontaine. "I had a wonderful lady friend staying with me, a gorgeous woman with five children. I knew I'd be safe there.

"One night, we were going to the theater with David. When he arrived, I went into the bathroom to powder my nose—my friend went into her bathroom in the suite to powder her nose. David rushed into my bathroom, got me up against the steamy radiator, and started to paw at me, and I had to make some unfortunate hip movements to get off the hot radiator!

"I got away from him, but he was a violent man. It was a game, I'm sure, they all did it, Zanuck did it—I wonder whether it was the thing to do. It was a power play, it was 'You're my chattel, you're my property, you're under contract.' "

• • •

In his twenties, David fell in love with actress Jean Arthur. She was in the market for a manager-husband, a man who could guide her career. The young David fit the bill, and he was fascinated with her.

Once David had met Irene Gladys Mayer, however, his life changed course. It wasn't love at first sight, but rather a case of "opposites attract." But it was a true love match. She was nineteen, he was twenty-four. Irene was a challenge to him (just as Jennifer later was). Her personality was the exact opposite of David's (just as Jennifer's was). Reared in New England, Irene was self-effacing in the extreme, cautious, practical, economical, and inhibited. L.B. and Margaret Shamberg Mayer had been careful to raise their two daughters in strict Jewish fashion. But to David, Irene was refreshing, *not* the kind of girl he was accustomed to pursuing (just as Jennifer was not the kind of actress he usually encountered).

Irene was radiant and lovely, with dark eyes and dark hair, the coloring combination David adored. Her energy level matched his, and both were in love with movies and the fantastic impact the industry and its creators were having on people all over the world. Irene was keenly intelligent—and a virgin. David attempted the usual forward passes and was sternly rebuffed. Unflustered, he informed her politely, "There's no harm in trying."

The relationship took root and flourished. David became a liberating force in Irene's life and her knight in shining armor. A vibrant new world opened up for her, and with David's encouragement she wasn't afraid to explore it.

Selznick was Irene's Svengali, but with an important twist: he didn't *tell* her what to do, he stimulated her thought processes. She had the intelligence, the ability, and the steely resolve to take it from there. He came to regard her as his most trusted confidante and most valuable critic. She wasn't afraid to tell him the truth, he respected her opinion, and they made a formidable team.

During their three-year courtship, Irene fell madly in love with David and offered him the unconditional love that he was accustomed to and which he took for granted. They were wed on April 29, 1930.

In Hollywood terms the wedding was a social event second only to sister Edie's lavish marriage to Bill Goetz a few months earlier. (Edie had advised her sister against marrying David: "Your children will be too Jewish looking," she'd told her.)

At the time of his marriage, David had risen to the number two position at Paramount. He resigned to become head of production at RKO. His view about making movies was that a film was like an oil painting. While various materials were necessary to create the work of art, the finished product was the work of the painter (in other words, the producer). It was a perspective that was, to say the least, light-years ahead of its time.

Selznick's accomplishments at RKO included the signing of a Broadway musical star about whom other executives at the studio were dubious: Fred Astaire. And Selznick discovered a new star, Katharine Hepburn. The young Hepburn was fascinated by David but was quickly disillusioned. She'd asked for changes in her contract. Selznick agreed. But when the contract was returned to her for signature, "Nothing had been changed," she recalled. The document was subsequently rewritten completely by Hepburn's agent, Leland Hayward, and Hepburn never forgot the incident—she felt Selznick had been dishonest (in later years, however, she and Irene became best friends).

Among the outstanding films Selznick supported during his RKO reign was *King Kong*, a risky, expensive, but innovative tale that went on to stand the test of time and to influence succeeding generations of filmmakers. *What Price Hollywood?*, *Animal Kingdom*, *A Bill of Divorcement*, *Morning Glory*, and *Little Women*, were other Selznick-supervised oeuvres.

Ambitious actresses on and off the lot pursued young David both to further their own careers and, on occasion, out of sheer physical attraction. He was "lavish with affection and niggardly with love," according to one account, and Irene was fortunate that Selznick's crackerjack executive secretary, Marcella Bennett Rabwin, "snipped off infatuations by failing to transmit messages from actresses to David."

Selznick's professional fortunes soared. But the death of his father, on January 25, 1933, at the age of sixty-two, brought the young man's euphoric outlook on life to a shattering halt. Lewis's demise was a trauma that shook the young Selznick to the depths of his soul.

Inconsolable and vulnerable, Selznick plunged into deeper despair after accepting an incredible $4,000-a-week offer to work for MGM, which had been his father's deathbed wish. But David felt he'd sold out, that in a moment of weakness he'd put a price on his reputation and independence. He lobbied desperately for a release from the contract, but father-in-law L. B. Mayer refused, and Irene's life with David became a hell on earth.

A clue as to how intimidating L. B. Mayer could be has been provided by British director Michael Powell: "To be alone with Louis B. Mayer in his office, which curiously enough was quite small, was like being in a pen with a raging bull." And Powell described Irene as "a chip off the old block."

The unhappy young Selznick bit the bullet and went on to produce some of the greatest movies in Metro's glittering history—*Dinner at Eight, Dancing Lady, Viva Villa!, Manhattan Melodrama, David Copperfield, A Tale of Two Cities,* and *Anna Karenina.* He survived the biting scorn ("the son-in-law also rises") of his jealous peers and had the last laugh on those who'd demeaned him for joining his father-in-law's company in the first place.

In 1935 his MGM contract finally expired (Jennifer was then sixteen years old and about to graduate from convent school). Thirty-three-year-old David Selznick went on to realize his lifelong dream: to establish his own company, an amazing accomplishment in a town run tightly by so very few tough, ruthless men who didn't take kindly to competition.

Selznick's financial backing came primarily from megamillionaire Jock Whitney; from Whitney's sister, Joan; Sonny Whitney and his two sisters; John Hertz; Arthur and Robert Lehman; and Myron Selznick, who'd achieved revenge on his father's enemies by becoming the industry's first superagent/"packager" (the prototype for later powerhouses like Lew Wasserman and, today, Michael Ovitz). Dr. A. H. Giannini, founder and president of the Bank of America, and attorney Lloyd Wright were also involved in forming and financing Selznick-International.

Additional funds came secretly from MGM's "boy genius," Irving Thalberg (who was three years older than Selznick) and his wife, actress Norma Shearer (the Thalbergs and the Selznicks were great friends). Total capitalization for Selznick-International was around $3.2 million. David invested no cash.

With Irene by his side, David raced breathlessly toward his destiny. Selznick-International quickly became the stuff dreams were made of, as David inspired those who worked for him to crash through boundaries that had previously defined their artistic capabilities. "What choice did one have?" observed close associate William Cameron Menzies. "It was either deliver or you were out!"

The secretaries worked as hard as the executives. Frances Inglis and Virginia Olds were the equivalent of human recording machines, as Selznick churned out thoughts and ideas, nonstop, for the lengthy memos that would one day become famous.

One evening, the story goes, a Selznick stenographer was preparing to leave the office. "Where are you going?" Selznick asked. The girl replied that she was meeting her husband for dinner. "Nobody in this office has a dinner engagement," he declared.

When one hardworking secretary supposedly suffered a nervous breakdown, Selznick couldn't understand why. But he magnanimously offered to send her off to the Menninger Clinic.

Screenwriter John Lee Mahin observed that Selznick's initials stood for "Death On Sleep" (David never seemed to sleep). When the producer approached writer Nunnally Johnson to work on a project for Selznick-International, Johnson replied: "I should certainly like to work for you, David, although my understanding of it is that an assignment from you consists of three months of work and three months of recuperation."

Selznick set almost impossibly high standards for his productions. He took pride in the fact that his films resonated with his ideals. *Little Lord Fauntleroy, The Garden of Allah, A Star Is Born, Nothing Sacred, The Prisoner of Zenda, The Young in Heart,* and *Tom Sawyer* all reflected the Selznick standard of quality up through 1938.

Irene Selznick had painstakingly adapted both herself and their household to David's eccentricities and the superhuman demands of his all-consuming career. Husband and wife were both driven people, with Irene content to reflect David's desires and ambitions in order to help him achieve his goals. Irene confided in her friend Sara Mankiewicz: "What is more important in my life than to please David?"

"David . . . was a big man of enormous energies and appetites, with a great capacity for work and life," recalled John Huston. "There was something childlike about David. [He was like] a spoiled child. He liked giving commands, telling others what to do and how to do it. The thing is, he knew! . . ."

Michael Powell noted that David Selznick "was a big man in every sense. He thought big, he talked big, he was big, but he wasn't quite as big as he thought. No one could be that. . . ."

At the same time, Powell found Selznick to be "sensitive and unsure of himself" and claimed that he saw through Selznick's pretensions right away "and liked him for them. He was so eager to go one better than everybody over everything. He was so eager to understand things that were not to be understood, only appreciated. Art made no impression on him, only size. He saw himself as a common man, and"—referring to David's perspective as a producer—"if he didn't understand something over which perhaps the director had been slaving for weeks, or perhaps months, out it would go."

Powell also noted: "Socially, he was such a disaster that one could hardly believe it was true. But he was very likable. . . ."

Irene was kept as busy as David's production manager at the studio. Precision, patience, and discipline were traits she'd had to develop and nourish in herself in order to keep their private lives running smoothly. She hired and fired all household help (there were two shifts of cooks, a maid, a personal maid, a nurse and a relief nurse for the two Selznick sons, a chauffeur, and a gardener). There was an ever-changing parade of employees because of the erratic hours and demands of the man of the house, and even Irene's inner resources were strained to the limit after several years.

Irene had learned early on—as Jennifer would have to learn—that Selznick's home-front modus operandi was, to quote those who worked at the Selznick home, "a nightmare." One had to expect the unexpected. Selznick was disorganized, perpetually late for meals, parties, and all else, and often brought home important guests for dinner unannounced. His bathroom habits—number of towels used, time spent in the tub (where he often fell asleep out of sheer exhaustion), et al.—would have suited a Russian czar.

Gladys Luckie, in later years the presiding factotum in the Liberace household, was very much in demand in Hollywood households of the thirties and forties. Luckie recalls, "No one wanted to work for the Selznicks. You never knew when he would want dinner, or if he would bring ten people home and expect immediate service for all. He behaved as though the dining room were a private room in a restaurant!"

But Irene loved David. *He* was her full-time job, and she made it possible for him to indulge his penchant for having everything his way.

She was a consummate and clever hostess. Her good taste and gift for people mixing were reflected in their wonderful and highly regarded parties. Invitations to "David and Irene's" were among the most coveted in town, and their weekly Sunday parties—tennis, followed by dinner for perhaps twenty-five or thirty, then a movie—became a ritual. ("Those occasions were the best Hollywood had to offer," recalled John Huston.)

Press and photographers were never invited to these exclusive gatherings (Jennifer would have been most comfortable with that aspect), and the guest list comprised only those people the Selznicks liked and considered fun—people who, needless to say, usually happened to be either rich, famous, exceptionally talented, and/or highly influential.

David was appreciative and proud of Irene's expertise as a homemaker and conveniently oblivious of the never-ending planning and preparation that constantly went into it. He felt that he was doing his adoring wife a favor by letting her prove to him how right he'd been all along regarding her abilities to do anything she set her mind to. (Little did either of them suspect that Irene's abilities would one day result in an independent career for her as a theatrical producer, a career that would rival David's on the big screen.)

With Irene's unfailing support, David's faith in his boundless luck intensified. The couple's life was so structured that, in retrospect, she was amazed that she'd made it through the years without suffering a breakdown. Her self-imposed rules and regulations were stringent. Away from the house, she always left word where she could be reached "as though she were a doctor on call," her friend Liz Whitney once said. But it was no joke to Irene. She wanted David to be able to get in touch with her on a moment's notice.

She realized that away from the studio, on his own, David was quite helpless. He carried no cash, no keys, and no telephone numbers (although he knew two by heart—the studio and home). But he could reel off the screen credits of virtually any movie he'd ever seen (and some he hadn't), which, Irene was the first to agree, was far more important in his line of work than knowing how to navigate the roads of Los Angeles.

Irene on occasion found it necessary to lay down the law. It was a matter of opinion as to who was the dominant partner. According to friends, each felt dominated by the other. To Hedda Hopper the answer was clear: "Irene Mayer . . . had a brain like a man, plus sound business sense. . . . She was also bossy like her father, and David rebelled against it. He would come home tired from slaving at a studio, which he did as a habit then, but she'd say, 'Take those old clothes off, get into a tub, and dress. We have guests arriving in fifteen minutes.'

"David would grow so mad he'd toss his clothes onto the floor and stomp on them. Then [she'd say], 'David, pick those things up and put them away properly.'

"Louis B. Mayer used to tell me about those scenes," said Hedda. " 'If I were married to Irene, I'd hit her,' he said. 'I love her, but I see all her faults.' "

By 1939, two years before Jennifer came on the scene, David's career had reached a phenomenal peak. In addition to *Gone With the Wind,* he had produced *Rebecca, Intermezzo,* and *Made for Each Other* and had launched and established the careers of Ingrid Bergman, Joan Fontaine, and Alfred Hitchcock.

When Hitchcock was under great pressure on a project, he'd reply: "It's only a movie." To David Selznick, immersed in transferring *Gone With the Wind,* his masterwork, to the screen, life *outside* of the movie became the fantasy. The film, and its million and one elements all merging in his brain, became his reality.

The ordeal of filming *Gone With the Wind* spilled over into his personal life like a vat of boiling oil. Irene was the shock absorber for the doubts, tensions, and fears David dared not reveal to anyone else. The Selznick sons were tucked deep into the background of their father's life during this volatile period. Selznick needed doses of Benzedrine merely to socialize, to enjoy the parties he insisted on attending to relieve the tension "and have some fun!" He constantly had stomach cramps, however, sometimes doubling over from the pain.

The long-suffering, always-in-control Irene wasn't ever able to sit through *Gone With the Wind* without becoming hysterical and having to leave the theater. The film had extracted too high a price from her life; its success had meant *too* much to her, to her husband, and to their future together.

The coup de grâce came after the movie's triumphant premiere in Atlanta on December 15, 1939. The film was expected to sweep the Academy Awards. But on the evening of the awards—February 29, 1940—disaster struck. The jubilant stars of the picture had gathered at the Selznick home prior to leaving for the ceremonies at Grauman's Chinese Theater. The time came to depart, and the glamorous throng proceeded outside. Limousines were gathered and waiting in the driveway. David entered a limo with Clark Gable; his wife, Carole Lombard; and Vivien Leigh and her paramour, Laurence Olivier. The group drove off.

Irene was left standing in the driveway. Alone. She was flabbergasted and emotionally shell-shocked after David didn't return for her.

"It was a total nightmare for David at the academy dinner that night," recalled Selznick publicity chief Russell Birdwell, a glib Texan who'd once been a crime reporter for Hearst's *Los Angeles Examiner.* "Irene wouldn't talk to David, or even sit with him, and even Jock Whitney couldn't convince her to do so!"

Many years later, Irene, in her memoirs, claimed that she eventually forgave David. But she never forgot the private humiliation, which was deeply and sadly revealing of David's state of mind.

The producer of Gone With the Wind *reveled only briefly in his cinematic* accomplishment. But in private his personal demons were tormenting him.

Over the next few months Selznick became depressed and, at one point, alarmed—he thought he was losing his mind. He consulted a leading psychiatrist and was diagnosed as having suffered a nervous breakdown.

Dr. May Romm, the leading "shrink" in Los Angeles in those days, took over the case, and Selznick made fast progress ("Anyone who sees a psychiatrist should have his head examined," quipped his friend Sam Goldwyn). But when Selznick began treating Dr. Romm as though she were a studio employee, to his astonishment she "fired" him (he returned to her later on; meanwhile Irene became a devoted, longtime patient).

Selznick's production of *Rebecca,* directed by Hitchcock and starring Joan Fontaine and Laurence Olivier, won the Oscar as Best Picture the following year, but Selznick was burned out. His focus had shifted from making pictures to making deals, optioning properties, and loaning out actors under contract to him for large sums while paying the players themselves only their much smaller weekly salaries. Irene disapproved strongly.

Late in 1941 an eager United Artists, headed by Mary Pickford and Charlie Chaplin, offered David a partnership, and a whopping cash advance, to develop properties for them. Selznick accepted but produced no immediate films over the next couple of years; instead he continued to cut deals, with other studios, for his players and properties.

As far as Irene was concerned, the most meaningful bond linking her to David was their children. (The Selznick boys and later, to a far greater extent, Jennifer's boys, were the innocent victims of their parents' continual combat with the demons of ambition and success.)

David Selznick was hardly an ideal father. He was thirty years old when his first son, Jeffrey, was born in 1932. David didn't celebrate the birth as the launching of a glorious new chapter in his family life but instead bemoaned the fact that thirty marked the end of his own youth and feared that Jeffrey's arrival would alter the status quo! (One can only speculate on what David must have felt like when he hit forty, the year Jennifer assumed importance in his life.)

Daniel, born in 1936, found a somewhat mellower father. But while the family was a tightly knit group, the responsibility for raising the boys was strictly Irene's. She was no slouch in the parenting department, but problems in the boys' behavior soon developed. David Selznick was the kind of well-meaning parent who, if his child expressed an interest in figure skating, would give the boy a film of an Olympic gold medal–winning performance and expect a similar result in short order from Junior. Consequently Junior swiftly abandoned any pursuit of figure skating.

Irene reacted swiftly, consulting a children's psychiatrist. David wasn't thrilled with this development, and exploded with rage with the diagnosis presented to him—that David considered himself in competition with eldest son, Jeffrey, and the boy was reacting to his father's subconscious hostility toward him!

When Irene became pregnant again, it was obvious her husband didn't want another baby. Dutifully she had an abortion.

To the world at large, even to most of their peers, the Selznicks were more or less living the American dream. There were, in fact, two razor-sharp guillotines continually suspended over their heads, two secrets, addictions that enthralled David (and that Jennifer would have to contend with).

The "manageable" secret was that Selznick's incredible natural energy, a vital element in his ability to function at the pace he'd set for himself, was further enhanced by Benzedrine, a new wonder drug whose side effects were not even close to being evaluated. The medication had been prescribed by the family physician, Sam Hirschfeld, who felt that Selznick's bouts with exhaustion simply required a controlled dose of the amphetamine. Needless to say, with Selznick's penchant for doing everything on a grand scale, the dosage he took went far beyond what the doctor had prescribed (and eventually took a very heavy toll on his health).

Secret number two was the fact that the Selznicks had no money. David's gambling habit was out of control, and his debts ate up all available cash and placed the producer in a constant state of deep debt. At one point he owed over $1 million (equivalent, today, to well over $13 million).

Irene and David quarreled bitterly over his gambling. He'd lie to her, convincing her he was going to quit. Arguments would explode anew when the next debt came due.

After one marathon poker game, Selznick lost more than $100,000 to mogul Joseph Schenck. "David, I'm not going to play with you anymore," Schenck said. "You don't know what you're doing."

Irving Berlin was present on an occasion when David lost tens of thousands of dollars playing roulette. "David, if your father was alive, he would have been proud of you!" quipped Berlin.

But David was regarded as a "pigeon" by the town's professional gamblers, and they kept track of his whereabouts so they could rustle up a high-stakes game on a moment's notice. There were also business repercussions concerning Selznick's gambling. It was no secret to the town's leading money men, and life insurance companies were reticent about granting Selznick large policies.

For Irene, David's gambling was the almost insurmountable obstacle in their marriage. The introduction of Jennifer into David's life presented an altogether different kind of problem for her to cope with.

• • •

Other minefields awaited those who chose to intertwine their personal lives with David Selznick's. The people whose lifestyles and family relationships the producer strove mightily to emulate—Jock Whitney and William S. Paley, in particular—presented Irene (and subsequently Jennifer) with virtually unmatchable role models and goals.

Jock Whitney was *old* money, a leading member of America's WASP aristocracy. His father, financier Payne Whitney, had accumulated the third largest private fortune in the United States. On Whitney's death in 1927, Jock and his sister, Joan, each inherited half of the estate, and Jock, against the advice of family, friends, and his bankers, had proceeded to indulge the adventurous aspects of his personality.

Whitney was fascinated with the movie business, with the excitement and gamble it represented, and his instincts for the industry brought him instant rapport with David Selznick (they'd been introduced by mutual friend Merian C. Cooper, Selznick's trusted associate at RKO). David and Jock were almost the same age (Selznick was two years older). Both were physically big, outgoing men. Each recognized the other's talents and abilities and also shared an appreciation of beautiful women.

David was in awe of Whitney's background, his Groton-Yale-Oxford education, and of Jock's spectacularly beautiful and faultlessly fashionable wife, Liz. David insisted that Irene (and subsequently Jennifer) function on that level, always outfitted in the finest couturier clothes and the highest-quality jewels and, of course organizing and hostessing the chic-est parties. Irene accommodated David beautifully, although those priorities, she said, were low on her list.

Jock Whitney happened to be an expert polo player, and he bred and raised horses, pastimes at which David Selznick was way out of his element. But Whitney's interest in the Museum of Modern Art was an area that David became part of—it was Selznick who introduced films and filmmaking, as an "art," into the vocabulary of the museum.

Millionaire William S. Paley, the other fellow overachiever most highly regarded by David, was a young pioneer in the burgeoning radio industry. He and David, although both Jewish, had highest regard and respect for everything WASP. (Ben Hecht once approached Selznick to lend his name to a Jewish cause. Selznick demurred. "I'm an American, not a Jew," he replied. Hecht proposed a wager—he'd query mutual pals, like Sam Goldwyn, on Selznick's ethnicity. Selznick's cooperation would depend on the replies. Never one to turn down a bet, David agreed—and lost. He lent his name to Hecht's cause.)

David and Paley were the same age and became best friends. Paley's beauteous wife, Dorothy, like Liz Whitney, was one of the nation's best-dressed women, a trend- and style setter for the era's jet set (known then as "café society").

However, appearances were painfully deceiving regarding David's lofty role models. Neither the Paley nor the Whitney marriage was remotely "ideal." William Paley, behind his socially correct facade, was a notorious womanizer. And Irene Selznick had observed how Liz Whitney, in private, often mocked her revered husband.

Perhaps Irene didn't know the half of it. According to a former leading New York nightclub entrepreneur, in later years Whitney (by then remarried to Betsy Cushing Roosevelt) regularly engaged the services of a dominatrix who'd taunt him, "discipline" him, and lead him around like a puppy dog.

For Irene Selznick, by the early 1940s the excitement and lure of Hollywood's fast lane had lost its appeal—the rat race had become boring, repetitive, unfulfilling. She and David had done all that. Both were yearning for something new and meaningful in their lives—and they were searching in separate spheres. For many years David's ambition had held him together. Reaching the very top had created a whole new set of problems for him.

Irene, utilizing an alias to protect her "true" identity, found escape in social work (at one point she became a juvenile probation officer), which she pursued in total anonymity.

David's fast-growing obsession with Jennifer was his escape. He didn't for a moment doubt that he'd continue to enjoy the best of both possible worlds.

Part II

Part II

Chapter 8

*S*elznick *had decided Jennifer's husband*
and family would be an enormous detriment if she was cast as
Bernadette. How could a newcomer portray a saintly teenage virgin
while having a husband and two sons off screen? Image was everything in Hollywood, and here was a massive public relations
dilemma that would really test David's mettle. (The rules of the
game have changed, but the guiding principle of star building remains the same: "[Hollywood] is a place where no one's past is relevant, and all that matters is the present," noted writer/moviemaker
Martin Kaplan a half century later.)

The challenge undoubtedly appealed to David—it was also an
opportunity to demonstrate to Jennifer how clever he was.

A new restriction was placed on the actress: "Do not discuss or
divulge any details of your personal life to the press," she was told.
The effort to keep Jennifer far away from the fourth estate didn't
trouble her in the least. ("Why must I talk about myself? Why must I
play the game?" she said years later. "When they make actors or actresses they should give them that other ingredient—the one that
enables them to cope with publicity. They left that out of me.")

Selznick was accustomed to manipulating all aspects of his actors'
lives. This often proved no easy task. Joan Fontaine was fiercely independent, as was Vivien Leigh, who had her mentor, producer/direc-

tor Alexander Korda, to advise and protect her. Dealing with Ingrid Bergman's austere husband, Peter Lindstrom, had proven troublesome for Selznick, too. Selznick had pulled strings to get Lindstrom, a medical student, into the University of Rochester and thereby away from Hollywood and out of Selznick's hair. But Lindstrom remained steadfastly involved in "managing" Ingrid's career.

Just how difficult Bob Walker would be remained to be seen. Jennifer assured Selznick that Bob would continue his lucrative radio career out on the West Coast. However, the producer realized that radio alone would leave Walker lots of free time, time he might use to become involved in Jennifer's career.

The actress was understandably eager for Bob and their kids to join her in California. Without them she had no personal life. Selznick didn't want her to become depressed, he didn't want anything to affect her "focus." The mogul pulled strings to line up a movie deal, at a studio other than his own, for Robert Walker. Other studios' top leading men were being drafted into the armed services or were enlisting. Opportunities for actors on the home front were suddenly wide open.

MGM, where Selznick had the strongest contacts, was interested in Walker. Walker's agent, Marcella Knapp, didn't even have to phone Metro, they phoned her! Was Walker available to come in for a reading and, if they liked him, to do a test? They'd film it in New York.

MGM was preparing a war film, *Bataan,* to star Robert Taylor. The cast required a full roster of "types," including a boy next door, a bully, and a Latin (twenty-five-year-old Desi Arnaz would land that part). This was an opportunity for Metro to launch a group of new players en masse, so to speak, with Taylor to spearhead the box office take.

Bataan was a remake of a 1934 John Ford film, *The Lost Patrol.* For the new version the characters' nationalities were changed. Englishmen became Americans, Arabs were transformed into Japanese. "For one role [an American character], we were looking for someone young, vulnerable, naive," recalled Dore Schary.

Walker was leery. Things were going nicely for him in radio—why rock the boat? He had no confidence in how he photographed, lowly Republic Pictures hadn't even signed him to a contract, and there had been a total lack of response to him elsewhere after his MGM "bits."

Marcella Knapp pointed out that he had nothing to lose by reading for MGM's New York representatives. The MGM headquarters at 1540 Broadway was smack in midtown Manhattan, a short walk from Radio City. Knapp cautioned Walker not to discuss with MGM the fact that he'd appeared in any films (the ploy Jennifer herself had used by not mentioning her film credits to Selznick).

Metro's casting people were impressed with Walker, without benefit of backstage prompting from Selznick. Billy Grady, the New York casting director, recalled that "Bob Walker was a natural. The talent was there, plus the skill to utilize it. There were rough edges, and of course he was inexperienced, but the goods were there."

The talented actor would obviously have landed in the movies in any event. He tested for MGM, and the test played well to studio executives on the West Coast.

Tay Garnett was assigned to direct *Bataan.* Garnett was a highly experienced pro who'd worked with many of the greats, including Gable and Harlow. Of Walker's test he said, "The boy was very appealing. You believed him, and that's what good acting is all about." The studio offered Walker a seven-year contract.

Jennifer was thrilled. Walker asked her if she'd heard anything definite on *Bernadette,* and she responded glumly that she hadn't. She'd volunteered to test with actors in the running for other key roles, which had pleased director Henry King, who would now have an opportunity to become more familiar with how she worked. Plus it was an opportunity for the actress to accumulate experience in front of a camera.

Bob couldn't join Jennifer on the coast before December, but he hoped to be there before Christmas. *Bataan* was set to begin in January, and Walker had a thought: "How about if I send Henrietta [the housekeeper] out with the babies so you'll be able to spend Thanksgiving with them?"

Jennifer loved the idea—a return to life with a semblance of normalcy to it. She said she'd immediately begin looking for a new house to accommodate the whole family.

Selznick was pleased that Walker had signed with MGM. He only had one special request. In publicizing Bob Walker, please delete all mention of his marriage to Jennifer and avoid any mention of their two sons.

Selznick explained his dilemma vis-à-vis Jennifer's Bernadette image. Howard Strickling, the head of MGM publicity, acquiesced to Selznick's request, pointing out to his buddy that such a "secret" could hardly be kept for long. And one had to question how wise it was, in the long run, to begin a career on a note of deception. Selznick's attitude, however, was like Scarlett O'Hara's: he'd think about that tomorrow.

Meanwhile, Bobby Jr. and Michael, and housekeeper Henrietta, arrived on the West Coast. Jennifer was beside herself with joy at seeing them, and they spent a happy Thanksgiving together. Jennifer received a phone call from Selznick during holiday dinner. David, dining with his own family, had "sneaked off for a few seconds" to call her and wish her a happy holiday. David also had news for her: "We'll have a definite decision from Twentieth in a few days."

She'd heard that report, or some version thereof, many times before.

Selznick began a final assault on Fox. On December 3 he phoned *Bernadette* producer William Perlberg "to ask him what the devil was going on about Jennifer." Perlberg replied that he'd "made up his mind and so had Henry King and, he believed also, Bill Goetz," noted Selznick. However, David was also told that the men had promised a screen test to Anne Baxter, "and they felt they were obligated to do this before finally saying yes." The test was imminent. Selznick "urged [Perlberg] to speed up, pointing out that we had kept our girl idle for a long time and that we were keeping her in Hollywood."

The telephone call from Selznick was a heart stopper: "The part is yours."

An exultant, and jubilant Jennifer immediately phoned her husband in New York to share the incredible news. Walker, on hearing it, was in shock. On December 9, on the entertainment pages of newspapers throughout the country, the big news was that David O. Selznick's newest discovery, Jennifer Jones, had landed "the most coveted film role of the year."

Details regarding the scope of the 20th Century–Fox production were reminiscent of Selznick's own *Gone With the Wind*—an inordinately long shooting schedule of over four months (most "A" films never went longer than twelve weeks, if that long); a $2 million budget (very high for a black-and-white film) and a projected length of almost three hours (the script, by George Seaton, was 320 pages). The release date for the epic was to be a year hence, Christmas 1943.

Now "all" that neophyte Jennifer had to do was create the character of Bernadette and sustain it for sixteen grueling weeks. An incredible supporting cast was assembled, including Gladys Cooper as an overbearing and jealous nun, Charles Bickford as village priest, Anne Revere as Bernadette's mother, Vincent Price as village prosecutor, and Lee J. Cobb as village doctor. William Eythe, Fox's newest handsome young leading man, would also be in the cast.

Robert Walker arrived in Hollywood a week before Christmas, and the family celebrated a festive holiday, complete with tree, trimmings, and gifts.

For this family, 1943 began with the kind of idyllic promise usually found only in romance novels. On January 2 Jennifer and Bob celebrated two intimate milestones: it was five years since they'd met and four since they'd married.

Walker reported to MGM to begin *Bataan*, rewritten as the story of the members of a rearguard suicide mission in Asia, protecting the American retreat down a peninsula. On arriving at the studio, Walker found none of the publicity fanfare that had heralded Jennifer's entrance into the filmmaking world. The actor didn't even have a parking space on the Metro lot (a privilege reserved for top executives and stars).

He was duly impressed with the size, scope, and complexity of the studio setup. The elaborate jungle set for *Bataan* was a marvel of ingenuity, and the number of people it took to make the dream factory function was mind-boggling to the wide-eyed boy from the Midwest.

Walker met with director Garnett and the other actors, including star Robert Taylor. "Bob [Walker] was a talented, sensitive, fey guy who combined the comic abilities of Jack Lemmon and Bob Montgomery, plus a heart-grabbing, little-boy-lost appeal," recalled Garnett. He was familiar with the radio work Bob and Jennifer had done and predicted top careers for both of them.

Everyone on the *Bataan* set was nervous on the first day of shooting, even Robert Taylor. "Relax, kid," Taylor, a midwesterner, told

Walker. "All they can do is give us our walking papers, and then our nervous stomachs can all celebrate." Garnett's only major direction to Walker was to "play the part younger." Walker was twenty-four; his *Bataan* character was in his late teens. (Coincidentally, Jennifer would be tackling a character years younger than her actual age.)

Walker made the adjustment with ease. As the film progressed and Walker became friendly with Garnett, he confided to the director that it seemed peculiar to him that Selznick didn't want him and Jennifer to be seen together "or linked together." He said it was as though "we're clandestine lovers instead of a family."

Walker added that Jennifer had even been "forbidden" to visit his set. Garnett commiserated with the young man and pointed out that a lot of people in Hollywood considered David Selznick a hard guy to understand. "Selznick was feared as well as respected," reflected Garnett in later years. "Power was the name of the game, and Selznick had it."

Garnett related an amusing incident that provides insight into Bob and Jennifer's relationship in those days. During *Bataan,* the director introduced Walker to twenty-one-year-old Judy Garland, who was working on a picture on a neighboring soundstage.

"As I introduced them in Judy's dressing room, Bob's gaze was frankly idolatrous.

"Judy, a prime sophisticate even at that age, caught the whole bit and was amused. She went into her act, saying in Mae West tones, 'I've been hearing a lot about you, honey. Drop around some evening and we'll have a few belts, and get *real* well acquainted.' "

Bob's embarrassment was intense. He backed out of the dressing room, almost tripping over his own feet. "I'm sorry I met her," he told Garnett.

Why? the director wanted to know.

"I've adored her since the first time I saw *The Wizard of Oz*," explained Walker.

"And?" Garnett asked.

"You saw how she acted," replied Walker, "and she's got to know I'm married to Jennifer Jones."

In the highest echelons of MGM, Walker was considered a young man with a big future. After viewing rushes on *Bataan,* they saw a new star. Others on the lot, from Judy Garland to publicist Dore Freeman, were aware of the studio's enthusiasm for the newcomer. "The world was opening up to him," said fellow contract player Barry Nelson.

Following completion of *Bataan,* Walker was cast immediately in a small role in *Madame Curie.* This deluxe "A"-budget epic, based on a true story, starred the studio's biggest and most prestigious dramatic star, Greer Garson (Garson was portraying the celebrated scientist who discovered radium) and Walter Pidgeon. Garson and Pidgeon were currently the biggest team in pictures.

Bob had the role of a young Frenchman and found it ironic that both he and Jennifer, quintessential midwesterners, were portraying French characters in period pictures.

Curie was not a pleasant experience for Walker. Garson and Pidgeon, unlike Robert Taylor, who'd been helpful and unpretentious, were aloof and made absolutely no effort to make the newcomer feel at home. Director Mervyn LeRoy was totally concentrated on keeping the two stars mollified, and Walker enjoyed none of the camaraderie with LeRoy that he'd experienced with Tay Garnett.

A bright-eyed seventeen-year-old actress, June Lockhart, whose father, Gene, was one of the screen's leading character actors, had a small role in the film and recalls Walker as a very pleasant man. Garson balked when the teenage Lockhart had a key scene at the very end of the picture in which her close-ups would have dominated the sequence. At Garson's insistence the scene was dropped. It wasn't lost on Walker that life at the top, judging by this experience, wasn't what it was pictured to be in the movie magazines.

Walker had completed *Bataan* and was working on *Madame Curie* before Jennifer had even begun *Bernadette.* In retrospect the film activity Walker was involved in at this time has been credited to Selznick's Machiavellian maneuvers to keep Walker occupied so that he and Jennifer would effectively be separated, enabling Selznick to ingratiate himself into Jennifer's personal life.

This view is ludicrous. Even David Selznick wasn't powerful enough to dictate what a studio such as MGM, peopled with tough executives like Ben Thau and Eddie Mannix (Mayer's "henchmen," who virtually lived at the studio), should do with its players. Walker had everything it took to become a successful actor, and his new employers had every intention, in their own best interests, of keeping him busy as possible.

Jennifer was no longer biding her time at home. She took a

training course at Los Angeles County Hospital and became a qualified nurses' aide. "Jennifer Jones" might be on the verge of becoming a very special, lofty, and remote icon of the screen, but Phylis Isley (the name she used at the hospital) remained in touch with reality in a more basic way. The odors alone in a hospital ward, and duties such as taking blood samples, produced a sobering effect.

If anything could effectively keep things in perspective for Jennifer, it was working in a hospital.

Chapter
9

*T*he *Walkers definitely needed a larger* home, but Jennifer hadn't found one she liked. Henry King alerted her to an available prospect: Tyrone Power's beautiful house in Bel Air (which was expensive—the Walkers could lease it for just under three hundred dollars a month).

The house was a modern Georgian structure, designed by noted architect Paul Williams. It had been beautifully but comfortably decorated by Power's sophisticated wife, French actress Annabella. A special feature of the house was its staircase at the back, enabling occupants to go directly from any of the bedrooms to the backyard swimming pool.

A staff came with the domicile, including a gardener and a cook, which would boost the Walkers' expenses an additional couple of hundred dollars per month. But the couple could afford it—Jennifer and Bob were each earning tidy salaries.

Jennifer splurged on a new car, a Mercury, although gas was rationed. Walker, to Jennifer's dismay, bought a motorcycle. She argued that it was dangerous, but Walker laughed, pointing out that Clark Gable was a motorcycle enthusiast and nothing had happened to him!

As the March start date of *Bernadette* approached, the press's interest in Jennifer intensified. "Let's get a look at Jennifer Jones.

Where is she from? What's she like? What's going on in her private life?" the columnists demanded to know, particularly the big three, Louella, Hedda, and Sheilah Graham.

Selznick was ready for them. With Jennifer he was repeating the pattern he'd followed with Vivien Leigh on *Gone With the Wind,* a strict news blackout. Twentieth went along with this approach and kept the wraps on Jennifer Jones. No photos were released to the press, and no interviews were to be granted until the movie was completed and ready for release. This would maintain an ongoing element of anticipation and excitement, culminating in a huge curiosity factor when the picture—and the star—were ready to be seen.

As far as Jennifer (for whom privacy was sacred) was concerned, this modus operandi was a godsend. From David Selznick's point of view, this could be turned into an advantage—after all, such an attitude hadn't hurt Garbo. The publicity focus, when it was time, was to be strictly on Jennifer's talent and ability, not on glamour or glitz. It was an approach that was years ahead of its time.

Hedda Hopper, a former actress, and Sheilah Graham, a one-time showgirl, were particularly interested in the lowdown on new girls in town. Both women had failed in their own theatrical quests and weren't noted for their largesse in praising young girls who were about to succeed.

Louella was the best reporter of the trio, but all three missed the boat on the story behind Jennifer Jones. Louella didn't question initial information given out on Jennifer and actually went to press with the fact that she was "an available young miss." The columnist was subsequently embarrassed by her faux pas and never forgot the deception. Thereafter she relentlessly kept after Jennifer and Selznick for information on Jennifer's private life and gave both a taste of what might be in store when she subsequently printed: "Jennifer Jones is a strange, restrained, shy girl, with little of the small talk and frivolous comments on life that characterize the average young woman of her years."

Nonetheless Selznick succeeded in keeping the lid on Jennifer's "real" story, and his scheming almost worked. It remained for a simple, straightforward reporter from Utah—a woman who had about as much clout in Hollywood as a gas station attendant—to unwittingly upset Selznick's apple cart, win the media game, and break the "hot" story of the day.

Alice Pardoe West had no idea that the story she was seeking was "top secret." Ms. West was simply interested in doing a piece on hometown boy Robert Walker. To get through to him, she dutifully went through channels. Late in February 1943 she requested an interview with Walker from MGM's publicity department. From Metro's point of view this was potentially good exposure for their new contract player—after all, they had nothing to gain by keeping Robert Walker a secret while Jennifer Jones, whom they owned no part of, went on to great heights. They informed Walker of the request, and Bob, knowing Mrs. West personally, didn't see how he could say no.

Walker was secretly pleased that Alice West had turned up. The cat was about to be let out of the bag at last (some friends suspected that Walker himself, or a member of his family, had actually contacted West to do the story).

MGM publicity chief Howard Strickling followed the policy that it was better to offer limited cooperation in exchange for a positive story than to extend no cooperation and receive negative publicity. Walker agreed to the interview. When he told Jennifer of his intentions, she was aghast. She knew how Selznick would react and wasn't too thrilled herself.

"Get me Harry Brand!" roared Selznick on learning of the situation. Brand was head of publicity at Fox, which had as much to lose from "exposing" Jennifer as he did. The men conferred and agreed that Jennifer should stay completely out of it, away from Alice West, and let West have her story with Walker. The piece would appear in the Utah paper, and that would be the end of it. Who in Hollywood read anyone except Hedda, Louella, *Daily Variety,* and *The Hollywood Reporter?*

West's interview with Walker went well. Walker spoke glowingly about his marriage and of his and Jennifer's burgeoning careers, and he avoided controversy by omitting the fact that as far as tinseltown was concerned, their marriage was a secret.

Afterward Mrs. West had a reasonable request: "I'd like to interview Jennifer, too, Bob." To her surprise, she was told by the actor that she'd have to contact either the Selznick studio or 20th Century–Fox.

For Jennifer, turning down Mrs. West's request presented no problem. But that wasn't the point, of course; behind the scenes the issue had mushroomed out of all proportion. David Selznick was livid over this intrusion into his carefully structured plan.

A compromise was finally reached. Jennifer would agree to the interview if the questions were limited strictly to *The Song of Bernadette* and avoided her personal life.

Mrs. West dutifully adhered to the conditions. When, to illustrate her story, she requested photographs of the couple together, the studios drew the line and refused.

A resourceful woman, Ms. West subsequently ran individual head shots of Walker and Jennifer, one alongside the other, a simple solution to her dilemma.

West's story turned out to be a publicist's dream, an upbeat and positive piece that raised no uncomfortable questions. "Which one will reach stardom first?" concluded the article. "Or will they come in neck and neck? In this most unusual story of real life, Bob and Jennifer are playing the original roles."

Despite the apprehension, there were no negative repercussions for either Jennifer or Bob after the story appeared. Jennifer was portrayed as a very devoted wife and mother. However, in private, the cumulative impact of living a "secret" life, being a "perfect" wife, a "perfect" mother, a "perfect" actress, was taking its toll.

As the start date for *Bernadette* approached, Jennifer was assailed by fears of failure. What if she were no good? Others in a similar predicament usually turned to the bottle, the popular route of escape in those days. Jennifer, however, was apparently equipped with sufficient inner strength and determination to deal with it soberly. She had both Walker *and* Selznick, at this point, to reassure her and bolster her confidence. In his attempts to calm her, Walker explained that "acting for the cameras is almost foolproof, Phyl, you're protected. If you make a mistake, forget a line, they start again. It's not like the theater. In a movie, you have all day to get one scene right."

Selznick, of course, was already bombarding producer William Perlberg and director Henry King with detailed, seemingly endless suggestions on how Jennifer should be photographed, costumed, and directed. But these men (and, on other films, others like them) were pros. They didn't appreciate Selznick's interference. Perlberg and King felt they were providing the mogul with a star "on a silver platter" and demanded that he simply "leave us the hell alone."

David shared his thoughts with Jennifer on most matters pertaining to her; therefore she was, like it or not (and one presumes she liked it), a partner in his awesome creative input. Theirs was a budding symbiotic relationship, with Jennifer the living, breathing end product of Selznick's dynamic creative urges.

Walker didn't approve of Selznick's approach. He wondered how any actor could absorb so much information and still concentrate on delivering a performance. But there was little he could do to alter the situation. Unlike the great Selznick, he knew nothing of the technical side of filmmaking. Compared with Selznick, with his vast knowledge, experience, and clout, Walker felt pathetically inadequate. He was understandably jealous over Selznick's deepening involvement in his wife's life.

Irene Selznick suspected something was up. "She would call me to chat, girl talk—and I would be trying to get to the studio, and she was obviously having breakfast in bed because I could hear the toast being crunched," recalls Joan Fontaine. Irene was fishing for information; Joan had none to offer.

*J*ennifer celebrated her twenty-fourth birthday on March 2. She was touched and moved by David's thoughtful personal gift—a magnificent leather-bound copy of *The Song of Bernadette,* autographed by the author, Franz Werfel. Selznick had obtained this prize at no small cost and effort, and Werfel would be coming to the coast to meet and be photographed with "Bernadette" in person.

The film began shooting on March 9. Jennifer was getting the full star treatment, including her own beautifully appointed dressing room. On "opening day" the premises overflowed with lavish floral tributes from Selznick, Goetz, and others.

But the moment of truth had arrived: a monumental acting job lay before her. The twenty-four-year-old woman with two young children was setting out to portray an innocent, asthmatic teenager (fourteen at the start of the picture) in nineteenth-century France, a girl who sees a vision of the Virgin Mary and affects the lives of generations of Catholics.

The brilliant cast of supporting actors were all stage-trained pros. Vincent Price recalls, however, that "there was a great deal of time taken with Jennifer. There were weeks when we'd never even get a call, because we were told Henry King was working with her. He'd rehearse with her for hours and hours on end; often they'd go down to the well (on the outdoor set) and talk about the part. I think Jennifer, like Lee Cobb, was a bit of a Method actor, or interested in being one."

Price concedes that Jennifer faced a herculean task in creating a believable Bernadette. "To play that kind of part, I think it's very necessary that an actress really devote her entire time to it. You just don't go out and get drunk the night before!

"Jennifer got along with all of us," he recalls, "but she was very protected by Henry King. We all used to discuss Jennifer practically as a miracle, because anyone who comes in to play such a part in her first movie, you're apt to think of it as a miracle, it's what everybody would like to happen to them!"

Jennifer agreed. "Who am I to be getting a break like this?" she said. "It doesn't happen in fifty years. There's no reason at all that it should happen to me. . . ."

Less than a week into filming, *The New York Times* ran a story on Jennifer and Bob, "Babes in Hollywood," describing them as "the luckiest young couple in Hollywood." (The story incorrectly noted that Selznick had first spotted Jennifer in a Chicago production of *Claudia.*)

"We all used to sit around and ask what Jennifer was like," recalls Vincent Price. "All of us had scenes with her, but none of us ever got to *really* know her. It was due to Henry, he was so protective of her, and it made her a little mysterious to us."

Price and the others had no way of knowing that Selznick had cautioned Jennifer about becoming too friendly with other actors in the cast. "They'll want to offer you advice on everything, and you'll only become confused."

Price offers a concise perspective on director Henry King: "He was a terrible old ham—he'd begun his career as an actor, and was one of those directors who, if you did anything in the way he'd illustrated it, you'd have been thrown off the screen! But somehow he made his point—everything that he overdid you underdid instinctively, and *you* were right—somehow or other you came out 'in the middle' and you were right."

King's nephew Tom recalls that the only argument that arose between Jennifer and Henry King had to do with the "twig" scene, a key scene in which Bernadette, at the behest of the Virgin, must furiously dig in the earth with her hands, rub the soil into her arms and face, and actually eat sticks and twigs. A well, filled with healing waters, springs from that spot in the ground. Tom King remembers, "My uncle didn't want Jennifer to actually eat the twigs, he only wanted her to indicate she was doing so. She wanted to actually *do* it, literally, since Bernadette had been told to do so by her Lady. Jennifer and my uncle discussed it, rather heatedly. My uncle listened to her arguments. They talked at length and, in the end, did it her way."

Throughout production King paid attention to Jennifer's input. "Some people thought Bernadette was dull, almost a victim of fate," Jennifer said, "but I thought she was always a girl of terrific power, of force within herself. I hope I can always play people with force."

"Jennifer is a rare kind of actress," said Henry King. "Nobody could have injected Bernadette into her. Bernadette had to come out of her. She's like a sensitive musical instrument, which, with very careful manipulation, will produce wonderful effects."

Tom King recalls that not everyone on the lot was impressed by Jennifer. "Some people thought she was, well, weird," he says. "That was the word they used—'weird.' "

Jennifer, unlike her husband, couldn't simply unwind and return home to spend a carefree evening with the family. Once the director yelled, "Cut!" she didn't leave her character on the soundstage. She was totally drained, emotionally and physically, at the end of a shooting day. If Walker expected her to sail cheerfully into the house, drink a cocktail, and share the day's events with him, he quickly had to abandon the notion.

"Jennifer wasn't a selfish person," stated Adela Rogers St. Johns, "but she *was* totally self-involved. I never met a successful actress— or actor—who wasn't."

Selznick's admonitions aside, the actor Jennifer became friendly with in the *Bernadette* cast (and they remained friendly for years afterward) was fifty-four-year-old Charles Bickford. Bickford was not a talkative man ("That's how he remained married to the same woman for over twenty years," Hedda Hopper observed).

"I could see how Bickford was the one Jennifer cottoned to," says Vincent Price. "Charles was a very silent man, a very 'inside' kind of fella. I worked with him later on television and liked him enormously." Price focuses on the reason Jennifer was drawn to Bickford: "He was a *very* good listener."

• • •

Robert Walker realized that Jennifer's picture wouldn't go on forever, but the sixteen-week shooting schedule seemed like forever. At home she followed a strict regimen and required ten hours' sleep to function at peak capacity.

Bob coped, not always the most pleasant person to be around when bothered by something. The "problem child" lurked perilously close to the surface at all times.

He was completing his role in *Madame Curie* while *Bernadette* was still in progress. Early mornings it wasn't unusual to see the couple en route to their respective studios, Jennifer driving her Mercury, Bob keeping pace on his motorcycle.

In late April Hedda Hopper finally succeeded in securing an interview with "the mysterious Jennifer." The meeting took place at the actress's home, which Hopper had trouble locating. The columnist arrived in a testy mood ("I've screamed at women for less") but was disarmed by Jennifer's attitude: "She's completely devoid of affectation," noted Hopper. She also stated accurately that "from the age of six Jennifer knew exactly what she wanted to do with her life" and offered the pointed observation that while Jennifer gave one the impression of complete helplessness, "forget it . . . she knows where she is going."

Vincent Price remembers that it was during production on <u>Bernadette</u> *that* Jennifer and Walker's marriage came undone. While other reports claim that the break came months later, Price is definite on the time. "Jennifer was undergoing not the most pleasant separation from Robert Walker," he states, having observed that "whatever happened between them happened during *Bernadette,* because when it happened, the situation was highly frowned on by the high-and-mighty studio."

Price also notes, "Jennifer weathered it terribly well. She was a very determined lady." Price is specific about his recollection because Jennifer's dilemma coincided with a similar crisis he faced at that time—he was himself about to file for a divorce (his wife, Edith Barrow, was in the cast of *Bernadette*).

"Executives of the studio came to me and said, 'You can't get a divorce!' I said, 'Why?' They said it had to do with the nature of *The Song of Bernadette,* and I said, 'That has nothing to do with the Song of Vincent Price.' I wasn't about to change my life for a movie."

One can imagine how "they" viewed Jennifer's situation. The success of *The Song of Bernadette* relied entirely on Jennifer's integrity off the screen as well as on. On the set there were at least moments of comic relief. "The Catholic Church was really running the picture," says Vincent Price, "as you can imagine! There were countless priests and nuns on the set all the time, plus hundreds of extras dressed as priests and nuns. You never knew [who] anybody [was], you never knew if you were patting the right ass or not in the morning!

"At one point, the clerics were having a big pow-wow with studio executives as to whether the Virgin should be seen on screen or not. There was a man calling the shots named Father Devlin, who was sort of the official adviser to the motion picture industry and the Catholic Church. . . . There was this very *big* question as to whether it should be a 'private' vision. All the actors thought so, because we all discussed it the minute we'd heard it. We thought that Bernadette should be the only one who sees it because she *was* the only one who saw it! I think that dilemma was one of the things that held up the picture.

"Anyway, it was very funny, because when they finally decided that the Virgin should be seen, the only way to do it was that terrible device of showing this fuzzy creature up in the corner of the screen, and, to portray Her, they picked Linda Darnell, who was pregnant!"

Price recalls that this sort of comic relief "kept you from going mad, because the film was taken *very* seriously. Franz Werfel was living in California at the time, and *Song of Bernadette* was his heartfelt thank-you to the Virgin for his escape from Germany. . . .'"

MGM executives were highly pleased with Robert Walker's work in Bataan. The picture had previewed successfully, and audiences lauded "the new actor, Robert Walker" as "sensational."

One afternoon Walker was called into a meeting with studio manager Eddie Mannix and offered both a leading role in a new picture and a new contract, complete with a four-figure salary. Walker was dumbfounded. Eddie Mannix claimed, "This script will make you a star."

The project was *See Here, Private Hargrove,* based on the best-selling book by Marion Hargrove. It was a timely, humorous account of one young man's experiences at basic training camp. The story was a welcome relief from the continuing tales of horror that were part and parcel of the daily war news.

Bob couldn't wait to tell Jennifer. There is a vivid account of how he dashed over to the 20th Century–Fox lot, where the extent of Jennifer's total isolation from the outside world suddenly hit home. He attempted to see her ("Tell her it's her husband," he announced to the guards at the gate), but he wasn't permitted to enter.

A series of phone calls produced no further results. "Sorry," reiterated the guards. It was doubtful that any message had ever reached Jennifer. There were simply strict orders "not to disturb Ms. Jones for *any* reason."

Reports claimed that on this very day, when Bob had arrived on his motorcycle, David Selznick had pulled up behind him in his chauffeured limousine and was passed through the gates immediately. A dramatic tableau, ripe with prophecy, if true. The implication was clear: Selznick was on his way to see Jennifer, and that evening, continued the account, Jennifer returned home *very* late.

Other sources, however, asserted that, to the contrary, Jennifer herself often had problems getting through to Selznick. The producer was immersed in his own complex business concerns during these hectic days.

Certainly Walker was bitterly disappointed when Jennifer's reaction to his own wonderful news was not remotely what he'd anticipated. He reasoned that her exhaustion from work, and inability to switch emotional gears and step out of character, had prevented her from responding accordingly. It didn't dawn on him to suspect any additional explanation for Jennifer's increasingly distant behavior.

On *See Here, Private Hargrove,* Walker had his own dressing room–trailer, just as Jennifer did at Fox. There were no problems on the set because of Walker.

Meanwhile Walker became good friends with cast member Keenan Wynn, whom he'd known from the New York days when both were appearing on radio.

"Bob was a delightful guy. [He was] very talented, and we had a strong chemistry on screen as well as off," said Wynn. "The way we played our characters in *Hargrove* reflected this. As to Bob's private life, if there was trouble between him and Phylis, he wasn't talking about it. I certainly wasn't aware of it. I'd known them both very casually back in New York. I became friendly with them in California, and she seemed to be both loving and caring with him."

On Sunday evenings the Walkers did their bit at the famous Hollywood Canteen. The organization, funded by the studios and leading industry personnel, was located at 1450 Cahuenga Boulevard, just south of Sunset. It had opened its doors in October 1942 and was Hollywood's way of entertaining tens of thousands of servicemen. Bette Davis, a founder of the canteen, was its president.

With Davis, Marlene Dietrich, Ginger Rogers, Lana Turner, Joan Crawford, Judy Garland, Linda Darnell, Hedy Lamarr, Deanna Durbin, Dinah Shore, and other show business luminaries staffing the canteen, serving drinks, working in the kitchen, and dancing and chatting with the soldiers, Jennifer was simply a beautiful face with no name.

"Who's that?" GIs wanted to know. Jennifer hadn't yet been seen on screen or featured in the movie magazines.

David Selznick was busy preparing for his return to movie production—his first venture since *Gone With the Wind* and *Rebecca*, three years earlier.

While Jennifer toiled away on *Bernadette*, plans for "David's *new* one," *Since You Went Away*, took shape and were finalized. Selznick's "return" would of course be with a film of epic proportions; it was expected of him, and he expected it of himself. It would also be based on material that was meaningful—that was expected of him, too.

The property was based on a timely novel by Margaret Buell Wilder, in which the leading character writes poignant letters to her husband, fighting in the war overseas. Selznick paid $30,000 for the rights ("It's a modern-day *Little Women*"), and Mrs. Wilder was brought out to the studio to try to adapt her novel into a script. But Selznick himself wrote the final script, using, for publicity purposes, the pseudonym "Jeffrey Daniel," his sons' names. On screen the credit would read Screenplay written by the Producer. The script contained a pantheon of prototypical characters: all-American mother Ann Hilton, her two all-American daughters, Jan and Brig, and, before Selznick was through, a handsome serviceman on the home front, an irascible boarder, a good-natured black servant, a clergyman, a young GI about to be shipped overseas, and a selfish, well-to-do society matron.

The role of the older daughter ("Jan" became "Jane") was a perfect transitional one for Jennifer. It would ease her from an impossible-to-maintain image of saint to an accessible one as girl next door. From there, as David saw it, she could portray anything.

He envisioned an all-star cast for *Since You Went Away*. He'd already signed fifteen-year-old Shirley Temple to a long-term contract, shrewdly anticipating her huge box office value as war-weary Americans looked fondly back to the child, now growing up, who'd pulled them through the Depression. Shirley would portray Jennifer's kid sister, Brig.

Selznick had hired beautiful cover girl Anita Colby as an executive for his new company. (Colby was the prototype for the cool, adventurous siren, played by Grace Kelly, in Alfred Hitchcock's memorable 1954 thriller *Rear Window*.) A former top fashion model, known in the trade as "the Face," Colby had briefly been an actress. Most recently she'd appeared as herself on screen and been a consultant on the big-budget Rita Hayworth vehicle *Cover Girl*. But Colby possessed too many artistic and business abilities to squander her time in front of a camera and had an extensive knowledge of the newspaper world (her father was top cartoonist Bud Counihan). Selznick recognized her value as an ambassador of glamour and goodwill in publicizing Selznick's stars and pictures throughout the country.

Colby functioned as adviser to David's contract stars. Their "image" was her responsibility, including supervision of how they dressed, how they wore their hair, how they were photographed for publicity purposes—even how they looked on screen.

"They groomed us, you see, and when I say grooming, I don't mean we had lessons," explains Joan Fontaine. She reveals a fascinating fact. "David really hired Anita Colby because Jennifer was so insecure about clothes," says Fontaine. "Anita became the adviser to Jennifer about clothes. And since David had put Anita on the studio payroll, he tried to get her to do my clothes as well. I said, 'That's ridiculous. I'm dressed by Hattie Carnegie, and thanks, but no thanks!'

"But even *with* Anita," states Fontaine, "Jennifer remained so undecided!"

"Jennifer needed help," Anita Colby states. "She was very honest, and the prettiest little thing you ever saw. She seemed so young, with her chubby cheeks, and yet she wasn't all that young when I came along (I was all of five years older). But she *seemed* so young and naive. I think that was part of her charm. She was interested in everything, always questioning, 'Why this? Why that?' She was a very special girl." The women soon became (and would remain) close friends.

Hiring Colby proved a wise investment on Selznick's part. Her evaluation of Selznick's other stars was fascinating: "Bergman is so beautiful, you must play it down; you cannot overpower her with clothes." "Keep Shirley looking sweet sixteen with soft hair, pigtails, and girlish pinafores." "Give McGuire that sweater-and-skirt feeling."

Jennifer was "a more complex challenge," said Colby. "Her clothes need the dressmaker, rather than the tailored look. I'd rather have them pretty than terribly chic. If you don't have the kind of dame who can give a fourteen-dollar dress a hundred-dollar look, you have to do something drastic about it."

While Jennifer preferred simple, severe dresses, Colby advised a soft, feminine look, "bouffant rather than sleek." To bolster Jennifer's confidence, Colby suggested Jennifer buy clothes on her own. "After a few months of coaching," said an observer, Colby "had to send back only one out of every four dresses."

Colby's advice to Jennifer went beyond fashion. She taught the actress how to deal with her shyness and how to handle an on-slaught of effusive compliments, which usually rendered Jennifer speechless. "Listen, darling," Colby finally told her, "just raise your eyebrows the next time that happens and say, 'Well, how have *you* been?' "

David's preoccupation with Jennifer became more apparent every day. But while Selznick was selling her a bill of goods on the depth of his feelings, he left plenty of room in his life, apparently, for other diversions. Colby had advised Shirley Temple to "be careful if I found him in stocking feet.

"I was gathering the impression that casual sex could be a condition of employment," recalled Temple. Colby had also alerted Shirley that there was a remote-control door-locking device under the edge of David's desk.

Bernadette finally wrapped in late July. "I've never seen an actress so ex-hausted," said Henry King. "She'd given it everything she had, day after day, month after month, and it had taken a lot out of her. But she'd been a real pro, no explosions of temperament."

"It's the longest picture *I* was ever on," noted Vincent Price. "A dozen years later I was in De Mille's *The Ten Commandments,* and we made *that* in a shorter time! Doing a religious picture is a *boring* thing because everybody is on their best behavior—hoping for the keys to the kingdom, I guess."

For Jennifer, the keys to top Hollywood stardom were finally, it seemed, in her grasp.

"*Jennifer's Up There; So's Bob,*" declared a *Milwaukee Journal* story on "the lovebirds." Sidney Skolsky informed readers of his widely syndicated column that Jennifer was scared at the prospect of seeing herself on screen and didn't watch rushes (film of the previous day's scenes). "I prefer to see the completed movie," declared the neophyte.

Jennifer was delighted to learn that her idol, Katharine Cornell, had contacted Selznick to let him know that she wanted to play the mother in *Since You Went Away*.

"Nobody who goes to the movies knows who Katharine Cornell is," Selznick explained patiently as Jennifer's hopes were dashed. He went through the motions of a dialogue with Cornell but had his sights set on someone everyone knew, someone who'd never played a mother on screen. *That* would be box office. Claudette Colbert, a close friend of Irene and David's (other than Carole Lombard, Claudette was the only non–cast member of *Gone With the Wind* to attend the Atlanta premiere with the Selznicks), was his choice.

A former Oscar winner (for *It Happened One Night* in 1934), and the highest-paid freelancing actress in town, Claudette wasn't pleased to be approached to play a mother (although she was close to forty, the characters she'd portrayed to date had a common thread: they were all "ageless"). But the extraordinary fee, a reported quarter of a million dollars, was an inducement she couldn't refuse, not to mention the prestige of starring in David Selznick's "comeback" production, which she knew would be first-class in every department.

Claudette's brother, Charles Wendling, was her agent, and the deal was closed.

Colbert would play Jennifer's mother. And who, Hollywood wondered, would play Jennifer's love interest, the gentle, vulnerable, sweet young man who goes off to war and never comes back? Only a novelist might have invented this real-life twist in the saga of Jennifer Jones: Selznick wanted Robert Walker.

Was this, in retrospect, some sadistic joke on Selznick's part? Some thought so. Others had different explanations. Walker was not only perfect casting, he was a hot young rising star; *Bataan,* released in June, was a big hit, and Walker had garnered tremendous reviews. Even New York–based columnist Walter Winchell had showered him with praise and predicted a huge career for the actor.

It certainly made box office sense to try to get Walker for *Since You Went Away.* Another credible reason for casting him in the picture was that Jennifer herself had suggested him. Or it was possible that Selznick felt he'd looked like a fool, *not* having signed Walker to a contract when he'd signed Jennifer? This would give him the opportunity to camouflage that error in judgment. Furthermore, costarring Walker with Jennifer would put an end to rumors that his interest in Jennifer was more than professional.

The most cynical speculation on the casting coup centered strictly on Selznick's ego. What better opportunity for him to illustrate firsthand to Jennifer *and* Walker just how powerful he truly was. . . .

Walker, however, was not simply Selznick's for the asking. MGM turned down his request at first, then reconsidered and negotiated an exchange. Selznick could have Walker in return for Ingrid Bergman for *Gaslight.*

Selznick acquiesced—and chuckled because he knew they were doing *him* a big favor. The *Gaslight* project, an "A" venture to be produced by Arthur Hornblow and directed by George Cukor, would greatly enhance Bergman's value, possibly even win her an Oscar (a promise David had made to her long ago). Selznick volunteered to comment on the *Gaslight* script and subsequently offered suggestions on the film's direction and editing (many of his ideas were used).

Robert Walker was thrilled that he and Jennifer would be work-ing together. Their "separation" apparently had been temporarily repaired, at least as far as Bob was concerned. He waited patiently for his wife to regain her pre-*Bernadette* personality. But her enthusi-asm at the prospect of working with him seemed strangely diffused. The theory that Selznick and, indirectly, Jennifer were both "setting Walker up for a lethal blow" has been proffered by Tay Garnett and others.

Selznick was perhaps capable of this; however, "Jennifer was *not* a guileful person," declares Joan Fontaine, an opinion reiterated by Anita Colby and others who knew the actress well. Passive aggres-sion was Jennifer's style, but her basic feelings about Robert Walker were obvious. "I know she was crazy about him," states actor Michael Parks, a confidant and costar of Jennifer's in later years.

Just *when* that vivid emotional moment occurred when Jennifer realized the totality of Selznick's commitment to her and the depth of his feelings as a man, not merely as a producer or career man-ager, is something she will undoubtedly never reveal.

But surely, according to all reports, her reaction to Selznick's overwhelming interest left her, if not bewitched, certainly bothered and bewildered.

An ever more complex scenario was unfolding for Jennifer Jones. Twentieth Century–Fox informed Selznick that a publicity schedule was being prepared for Jennifer to coincide with *The Song of Bernadette's* pro-jected December release in time to qualify for the Academy Awards.

Selznick approved the plans. Since he was now "teaming" Jen-nifer and Bob in *Since You Went Away,* it was suddenly permissible for the Walkers to enter the publicity arena as man and wife. The cou-ple was told it was okay to pose with their kids and to extol the val-ues and virtues of marriage. Indeed, they were to be marketed as "Mr. and Mrs. Cinderella," with publicists selling Jennifer and Bob as the young Hollywood couple living and loving the American dream. Photo sessions were set up with top publications, including the *Ladies' Home Journal.*

While Ronald Reagan and Jane Wyman were at that moment on many magazine covers as the quintessential American serviceman and his working wife on the home front (although in truth Reagan never left U.S. shores), Jennifer Jones and Robert Walker were the All-American couple at home, successfully pursuing individual acting careers while raising a family.

How fortunate, the publicity observed, that audiences would have the opportunity to see Jennifer and Bob together on screen in David O. Selznick's forthcoming production of *Since You Went Away*.

"Beware the publicity you plant," Walter Winchell once warned a press agent. "It can splatter back in your face like pigeon shit."

The other principals had been signed for Since You Went Away, including Joseph Cotten (under contract to Selznick), Lionel Barrymore, Monty Woolley, Agnes Moorehead, and Hattie McDaniel. The director was John Cromwell, a Selznick veteran. The fifty-six-year-old, four-times-married Cromwell was a distinguished, pipe-smoking theater-trained craftsman whose laid-back personality meshed perfectly with Selznick's up-front bombast. He'd directed *Little Lord Fauntleroy, The Prisoner of Zenda,* and *Made for Each Other* for Selznick, as well as *Algiers,* the film that made Hedy Lamarr a star in America, and the memorable *Of Human Bondage,* starring Bette Davis.

Cromwell had his work cut out for him on *Since You Went Away*. To launch the project there was a gala "A"-list party welcoming Selznick back to the fold of active filmmakers. The event took place on the soundstage where the Hilton family "home" had been constructed.

The launch party was cleverly described as a "housewarming."

The entire Selznick stable of stars was on hand. Broad smiles lit everyone's faces as the producer posed for photographers with Jennifer and Robert Walker, Shirley Temple, Joan Fontaine, Ingrid Bergman, and Joseph Cotten. New Selznick contractee Rhonda Fleming, a voluptuous, gorgeous redhead, was also present. She'd met Jennifer one day in the Selznick hairdressing department, and recalls: "She was bent way over, brushing her long brown hair—I learned this was a ritual of hers—and I couldn't see her face! When she finally stood up, we said hello. She was pleasant, but not very talkative."

Publicist Mitchel Rawson and photographer Marty Crail made certain that every photo opportunity was covered. Selznick, a ciga-

rette dangling constantly from his mouth, spent the evening min-
gling. Jennifer and Walker came over to say good night and left
holding hands. Selznick was visibly angry as he watched the couple
walk off.

For those who envied the incredible luck that seemed to have sailed Jennifer's
way—*two* great roles back to back, with the Selznick picture certain
to be a success—the truth was that she was unhappy with the new assignment.

"I'm too old for the part, and too big and gawky. I'm all wrong
for 'Jane,' I'll never be believable." She had a point—again she was
cast as a teenager, an "average" one this time, even harder to play.

Shirley Temple (whose breasts had to be taped down so she
wouldn't appear too "mature") *was* a teenager, and she and Jennifer
were slated to have important scenes together. Jennifer feared the
contrast would be too great, and she didn't look forward to wearing
"young" clothes throughout the picture and having to concentrate
herself into an even younger state of mind for over twenty grueling
weeks.

Walker tried to soothe her, even assured her that the great
Selznick must know what he was doing, but at this point everything
seemed to bother her. The old "Phyl" emerged only occasionally,
when spending time with kids, but such moments of contentment
and tranquillity were rare.

Walker lost patience with her on one occasion and shouted at
her, which sent her sobbing to their bedroom.

For Jennifer it was a no-win situation. If she abandoned
Selznick, she'd spend the rest of her life regretting the missed opportunity. If she left Walker, he was young, he'd recover, she'd always
love him, and they'd always have the kids to link them together. Bob
said he wanted her to be happy, that he loved her; she wondered
why he couldn't see that she couldn't be happy with things continuing as they were. . . .

If Walker had exhibited some strength of character, and not
been so weak and unresourceful in the face of a vital crisis, perhaps
things would have turned out differently.

• • • •

<u>*Since You Went Away*</u> *began production on September 8. Since there had* been a production hiatus on *See Here, Private Hargrove* due to script rewrites, Walker was needed back at MGM for retakes. Tay Garnett, called in to replace Wesley Ruggles, was to complete direction of the film.

"It became apparent that something was seriously wrong with Bob," recalled Garnett. "He seemed to be falling apart. His color was pasty, his eyes were bloodshot, and he couldn't remember his lines.

"Taking him aside, I asked, 'What's wrong, Bob?' Fighting tears, he blurted, 'Jennifer has left me.' "

Walker began drinking heavily. The "problem child" burst forth with a vengeance, fueled by self-pity and Scotch.

"One noon he came into the small bar just outside the MGM gate, belted a few—quite a few—then walked carefully to the cashier, check in hand," recalled Garnett. A cigarette machine, with a mirror, stood next to the cashier's counter. As Walker pocketed his change, "he caught sight of his reflected face. Suddenly, he drove his clenched fist through the mirror, scattering shards of glass in every direction, breaking several knuckles and severing an artery.

"He was carried to the studio hospital," said Garnett. The doctor attended the wounds "and gave him some fatherly advice," recalled Garnett. "Bob heeded it. Briefly."

The official news, in October, of the separation of Jennifer Jones and Robert Walker did not receive prominent play in the press (quite the opposite: "Jennifer Jones has Everything," proclaimed an October 3 article in the *Portland Journal Sun*). The powerful Selznick, Fox, and MGM publicity executives combined forces, and while they were not able totally to suppress the news, they certainly managed to have it relegated to the back pages of local newspapers. It was "an amicable separation," and Jennifer was quoted: "It won't make any difference in our acting in *Since You Went Away*. Bob and I are both troupers."

While Walker was reeling around the Metro lot doing retakes on *Hargrove,* Jennifer was briefly back on the Fox lot finishing up bits and pieces for *Bernadette*. Her opportunities for reflection, thanks to Selznick, were virtually nonexistent. For example, waiting for her in her dressing room one morning was a full-length sable coat. Her dream merchant wasn't missing a bet.

How Jennifer and Walker would spend the next months working together, in the intimate and insulated atmosphere peculiar to the world of making a movie, was anybody's guess. If, by leaving Walker, Jennifer had anticipated that Selznick would recast the role of Bill, therefore making her life far less anxiety-ridden, she was wrong.

The last thing Robert Walker wanted was to be replaced; he had prayed that Selznick wouldn't recast. Working with Jennifer over the next few weeks, he was certain, would help him win her back somehow.

Selznick had many other problems to contend with on this picture. He was relentless in his demands on everyone, including long-time production manager Ray Klune, hospitalized with pneumonia. While Klune was fighting for his life, Selznick angrily expressed his displeasure over production details. Klune later told Selznick off, and after production was completed, to Selznick's astonishment and dismay, he quit.

Irene Selznick, in retrospect, described her husband as "more compulsive than ever" during production on this film, yet his usual confidence and enthusiasm were lacking. Director Cromwell said, "He seemed to get more hysterical during this picture than I heard he had during *Gone With the Wind*."

There were many annoyances. One of them was adhering to Claudette Colbert's insistence on being photographed so that only the "good" side of her face (the left) was to the camera. ("The only time I insisted," swore the actress in later years, "was in a love scene in a big close-up. But why not have your good side showing?")

Colbert's contract also guaranteed her three days off per month during the onset of her menstrual cycle, days that Selznick would have liked her to be available for filming and which ended up, over the course of the shooting schedule, costing $5,000 per month!

Selznick pointed out to Colbert's brother, her agent, that Jennifer had no days off for this purpose, a fact that hardly inspired Claudette to part with her own hard-won perquisites.

"I think David was careful and respectful of Claudette, not only because he respected her self-sufficient professionalism, but because she was the indispensable centerpiece of the whole thing and he didn't dare rub her the wrong way," said director John Cromwell. (In fact, the indefatigable Selznick had pursued Claudette in his inner sanctum, subsequently offering profuse and abject apologies.)

Claudette was at times almost like a surrogate mother to Jennifer. But with this all-star cast, clashing egos were inevitable. Monty Woolley, famous for portraying the unforgettable Sheridan Whiteside in *The Man Who Came to Dinner,* told his friend Cole Porter that the atmosphere on the set of *Since You Went Away* was so highly charged that no one dared light a cigarette for fear the whole soundstage would go up in flames.

Selznick put his foot down. "There's room for only one prima donna on this lot—me," he informed one and all.

As production progressed, a flu epidemic spread through the company, and production had to shut down for two weeks. Veteran cameraman George Barnes, the man who'd photographed Jennifer's first screen test, was suddenly fired. Others on the set saw how increasingly preoccupied Selznick was with everything pertaining to the beautiful young brunette.

The sound man was chewed out for suggesting that Jennifer raise her voice ("throw it") during filming. Selznick was livid. He felt that Jennifer had "learned the technique [during *Bernadette*] of talking in natural tones." Selznick noted angrily that if the sound department was back in the Dark Ages and couldn't accommodate Jennifer's contemporary method of speaking dialogue, "let's throw them [the sound mixers] out rather than let them ruin the performances of our players . . ."

Selznick felt that this was the reason Jennifer's work on camera wasn't on a par with her scene readings off stage. She simply wasn't relaxed while having to concentrate on the volume of her voice. She had let Selznick know this was the problem, but she had also implored him not to be quoted to the technicians involved. In strong terms Selznick informed the director and production manager of the situation, pointing out that Jennifer was "fanatically considerate—to her own harm—of everyone, and is panic-stricken to talk about anything in connection with the picture lest she should seem to be criticizing anybody."

Off screen Jennifer "hated to have her picture taken," recalls Anita Colby. "She'd been photographed so badly in the past that she just didn't want to do any more. It was difficult to get her to hold still, but photographing her off set was essential for publicity. I hired a good photographer, one who'd photographed me at RKO. I brought him over to the studio, and then Jennifer wasn't difficult."

Shirley Temple, a much tougher and shrewder young person off screen than any of her fans could possibly have imagined, wasn't at all pleased with the interest Selznick exhibited in "beautiful, blushing" Jennifer Jones. "Perhaps I was mildly envious," Temple admitted years later, noting in her memoirs that Jennifer's "absorption of Selznick's time and attention inevitably crimped my chance to gain equally intense professional supervision. Both Jennifer and I could have been seen as competitors for future ingenue roles with him. He obviously had chosen."

Walker had moved out of their home and was living in an apartment-hotel. He pulled himself together sufficiently to function on the set. Common sense, and concerned friends like Keenan Wynn (who'd been cast in *Since You Went Away*), had advised him not to say or do anything that would upset or embarrass Jennifer, pointing out how that tactic would simply drive her even further away. But it wasn't, in all fairness to Walker, a "tactic" on his part; the man couldn't help himself (a foible that many beautiful women subsequently found appealing and, in a couple of cases, irresistible).

John Cromwell was an old hand at dealing both with fragile personalities and tough producers. But even he was surprised at all the dynamics at play on this production. The director created, as best he could, a favorable climate on the set so that Jennifer and Walker could perform their scenes together. Both actors were able to make the characters come to life even under extreme stress. Once a scene between them was completed, however, Jennifer, to Walker's dismay, retreated hastily to her dressing room.

"Time and again during filming the undercurrent tensions in her personal life erupted in sudden, enigmatic behavior," recalled Shirley Temple. "On one occasion we two sisters were being filmed in bed, carrying on a sentimental dialogue about Walker. She wriggled under the sheets, a slight twisting and rolling of her hips. Suggestive movements really had no relationship to her specific lines, so at first I read this as simple scene stealing, ingenious at that. When the scene finished, however, she leaped from bed, burst into unrehearsed, copious sobbing, and fled to her dressing room. No road map was needed to show where events were leading, but she was having one hard time getting there."

The discipline Walker had been forcing himself to exercise finally collapsed. One evening after work he suffered a serious motorcycle accident and was rushed to the hospital. When asked who should be notified, at first he replied his wife; then he reconsidered and told doctors to contact either John Cromwell or David Selznick's executive secretary.

Selznick's chief concern was not Walker's health (accident or no, there was never a question of casting another actor), but the disrupted shooting schedule. Selznick was writing the script himself, and Walker's absence meant a sudden shift in shooting plans. A frenzied David, working with playwright F. Hugh Herbert, worked day and night to compensate for this emergency. Selznick, as he'd done so often in the past, relied on Benzedrine to keep his energies at a peak.

Keenan Wynn observed a dramatic change for the worse in Robert Walker's personality. But as *Since You Went Away* sailed the stormy seas of production, neither Jennifer nor Walker was in a position to alter their situation.

Observers noted that Selznick was always on the set during the couple's intimate scenes. He seemed to be enjoying the spectacle. Walker perhaps would have won both self-respect and the admiration of his peers if, under these circumstances, he'd simply walked out. Selznick would have had no choice but to retreat. However, Walker was afraid of him.

John Cromwell noted that Jennifer was "as unhappy as I've ever seen a girl to be. She was not only uncomfortable in the part. She was also uncomfortable playing the very poignant love scenes with her about-to-be ex-husband, and on two occasions her emotional upsets caused her to flee the set in tears. Selznick had to come to her dressing room [and calm her down] before she could continue."

A reporter asked Walker, "How can you stand to make love like that to your wife when you've just separated?" There was a long pause. "Why, that's got nothing to do with me and Phyl," he said wryly. "You see, it's acting."

In Cromwell's opinion, *"Jennifer was half repelled, half attracted"* to Selznick. He felt that David's power, and not his money, was the aphrodisiac. "I guess it got to her. Jennifer was on edge all through the picture.

She was worried about her role and Selznick and her boys and her guilt about Walker and just about everything. . . .

"And David's neurotic courtship of Jennifer kept her in a state of mild hysteria. With all that was going on behind the camera, it's a wonder she got through it at all. Claudette and I had a time calming her down."

Joseph Cotten has confirmed that "the set tended to be a hectic one. David sending in changes, Jennifer in a highly nervous state, especially in her scenes with Bob Walker. . . .

"Claudette and John Cromwell held it all together beautifully, though. I always felt Claudette, underneath her gaiety and charm and warmth, was an extremely tough woman. She knew how to roll with the punches." (Frank Capra's admiring description of Colbert was along the same lines: "Tough dame, that lovely frog.")

Joseph Cotten has recalled how in the film Jennifer was supposed to have a schoolgirl crush on him. "The poor girl had to gaze adoringly at me nonstop. One day we were shooting a large party scene. Jennifer was overdressed and trying to look grown-up. They were photographing from the ceiling down, a complicated and enormous shot. The director, the cameraman, and David were way up high, shooting the scene. I looked at Jennifer. She'd shifted her adoring look from me to David, and he was just gazing down at her. 'Have you ever seen such an ugly man in your life?' I said very seriously to Jennifer.

"She wheeled around at me, white with fury, and said, 'Mr. Cotten, I don't agree with you at all.' Then she turned around and dashed off the set."

Cotten (who became a close friend of both Jennifer and David) describes her as "painfully shy. Compared with her, Garbo would seem a screaming extrovert. I can't imagine how it ever occurred to her to become an actress."

Cotten notes that Jennifer was always "eerily sensitive to her environment . . . [and as a friend] uncompromisingly loyal." He noted that with Jennifer, over the years, there was "little chitchat on the set. She reads her book; I work my puzzle." Their serious conversations took place on the telephone.

• • •

The endless stream of new script pages kept the cast on edge.

Shirley Temple has explained how, after long private conferences Selznick had with Jennifer, the producer "usually emerged . . . to create new scenes around Jones." This was a development that did not thrill the rest of the actors. Temple also noted, "Every role except Jones's diminished."

Jennifer was not exactly buoyed by this professional development. "I detected little evidence that she was as exuberant as she deserved to be," observed Temple, "with expanded opportunity raining down on her each new day. To the contrary, she always seemed to be suffering acutely, and her love scenes with Walker continued painful to witness."

Selznick had written a beautiful love scene for Bill and Jane: they're walking along in a field, and a sudden thunderstorm forces them to take refuge in a barn, where their intense feelings for each other are finally expressed. (Selznick was infuriated at the unnecessary time John Cromwell took to set up the establishing shot. If indeed David had derived masochistic pleasure early on out of seeing Jones and Walker working together, the mounting production costs had shifted his emphasis. He was now interested in getting the film finished.)

Walker played their love-scene-in-a-haystack to the hilt. If ever Jennifer was to know how he felt, this was his opportunity to show her. The scene was blocked, rehearsed, and shot, and the marriage of make-believe and reality built to a high pitch. Walker took pains to look his very best. He was clear-eyed, clear-skinned, and carefully groomed in an army private's uniform. There was no slurring of his words, and a definite, easy but intense chemistry existed between him and Jennifer. The intimate dialogue struck close to home:

"I never thought anyone would care about me—anybody like you," he tells her.

"I'll be thinking about you all the time," she tells him, gazing into his eyes. "I love your face—it's the cutest face I've ever seen—and you're such a baby!"

Their passionate kiss, judging from the eloquent melting expression in Jennifer's eyes, was not faked. "Would you be sorry if I were killed?" he asks.

"Of course!" she replies, horror-struck at the thought. She couldn't turn off her emotions and became hysterical.

Shirley Temple was present. "Selznick was on the set and led her off alone to his office," she recalled. "Shooting stopped, and everyone lounged around drinking coffee. Walker had disappeared, literally as well as figuratively."

In another version of the incident, Jennifer wasn't able to complete even a single take of the scene before she lost control and fled to her dressing room in tears. In this scenario Walker told Cromwell quietly, "I'll be ready for another take whenever Jennifer is."

On the sidelines, Selznick quickly dashed over to Jennifer's trailer. The door was locked, and he demanded that she let him in. He disappeared inside and, apparently, calmed her down, since she reappeared on the set to complete the scene. Jennifer and Bob went in opposite directions when Cromwell was satisfied and called out a final, "Cut and print."

Shirley Temple has noted, "Thereafter, Jones was regularly called to Selznick for long conferences, leaving the rest of us to hang around the set, waiting."

The producer spent many late evenings at the studio. According to an account related by Selznick secretary Lois Hamby to author David Thomson, Irene Selznick would phone, inquiring about her husband. Hamby would reply that the boss was "in the projection room." Irene scoffed at the response, and Ms. Hamby didn't blame her. "He was in [the office]," Hamby recalled, "on the couch with Jennifer."

Certainly Jennifer was in the office, behind closed doors—how Ms. Hamby (or anyone else) could be so absolutely certain of what was going on is another matter.

Production continued. The "look" of the film was perfect. Two of the film's big production sequences included Robert Walker. An elaborate local neighborhood dance takes place in what's supposed to be an airplane hangar. William Pereira had created a spectacular cavernous setting. The lighting effects were flawless, and intimate action was beautifully combined with large-scale production values.

Selznick devised a memorable and highly dramatic sequence in which Bill and Jane say a final, dramatic good-bye. The setting is a train station (the one that'd been used in *Gone With the Wind*), lit almost surreally to foretell the bleak future awaiting the sweethearts.

Selznick had decided that Walker's character was going to die over-seas. After this moment, the lovers would never see each other again.

Jennifer runs alongside Walker's departing train, shouting to him, "Good-bye, darling, I love you. Good-bye, darling. . . ." She's left standing alone on the isolated train platform, a tragic, solitary figure representing tens of thousands of young women on the home front—and, unknown to the public, also representing herself.

To the consternation of director Cromwell, Selznick brought in another director for this sequence (he'd done this to Cromwell once before, bringing in George Cukor to direct a romantic scene between Ronald Colman and Madeleine Carroll in *Prisoner of Zenda*). It was Jennifer's biggest dramatic moment in the film, and Selznick was taking no chances—it had to be absolutely perfect.

Many takes were required to get the scene right photographically as well as dramatically, but the effort was worth it. The final results, underscored by Max Steiner's haunting musical score, were stunning. It was one of the most poignant and memorable scenes in the picture, one of the best in any Selznick picture.

Selznick had no compunctions about writing into Jennifer's character specific details from her private life. He decided to add sequences featuring Jennifer as a nurses' aide, including her taking the nurses' oath, in which she very convincingly states: "I will accept no compensation and seek no reward . . ."

Jennifer's former classmates at General Hospital appeared in the scene with her. Selznick authorized his publicity department to release photographs of Jennifer, posed with Red Cross representative to the film industry Jack Beaman, taken at the time that she'd actually graduated as a nurses' aide. And subsequently, in cross-country recruiting drives, Jennifer made personal appearances to plead for more nurses' aides.

Walker, his role in the film completed, spent time with his sons at Jennifer's house. She voiced no objection, as long as she wasn't on the premises.

MGM supposedly wanted to arrange "dates" for Walker, with any and all starlets on the lot, a common practice at all the studios to garner publicity for their players. He wasn't interested. "Phyl might think I'm cheating," he supposedly said. However, insiders were well aware that Walker and Judy Garland were now (albeit briefly) romantically involved.

The Walkers' in-laws could hardly believe everything taking place in their children's lives. According to informed sources, neither Jennifer nor Walker enlightened relatives with details. Phil Isley was reportedly not at all pleased with the Prince Charming who'd charged into his daughter's life (Isley was only nine years older than Selznick). At the same time, no one knew better than Isley that once Jennifer was decided on something, she was intractable. The Isleys hadn't approved of Robert Walker at first, and Jennifer had promptly married him. Now, however, they were very fond of him; after all, he was the father of their grandchildren.

Madame Curie was released in November and became a huge success. Walker was hardly the star, but he was singled out and received favorable notice in many important reviews.

MGM had assembled a final cut of *See Here, Private Hargrove,* and the picture was previewed with sensational results. The exciting news caused barely a ripple in Walker's demeanor, but it enabled Selznick to comfort Jennifer: "He'll be fine. He's going to be a big star, don't worry about him!" That Selznick was actually jealous over Walker's success was an opinion that many in the industry voiced in private.

The *Ladies' Home Journal* had scheduled its "Meet Two Rising Stars" feature on Jennifer and Bob for its January issue, on sale in December. But another PR emergency now arose. The *Journal,* on learning of Jennifer and Bob's separation, had no intention of going to press with an article that made the magazine appear ridiculous. The piece was hastily rewritten, informing the nation that this was one "perfect marriage" that was unraveling. The news, however, was handled adroitly, explaining the couple would very likely get back together.

"Top secret" plans were being formulated for the next step of the Jennifer-Walker saga: the divorce. Timing was crucial. There was no doubt, except perhaps in Jennifer's mind, that she would be nominated for an Oscar for *Bernadette.* Obviously no legal steps jeopardizing her image could be taken before that, decreed Selznick.

Robert Walker was slated to begin *Meet Me in St. Louis* with Judy Garland, but the studio recast the role with Tom Drake. Walker, to his dismay, was cast in another war movie, *Thirty Seconds Over Tokyo.*

The formula on how to use him was working well. Once again he'd be a key member in an MGM ensemble, this time headed by Spencer Tracy.

If Walker felt it odd that this casting news was delivered to him personally by bespectacled studio chief Louis B. Mayer, he soon learned the mogul's motive. Mayer inquired about the status of the Walker-Jones relationship.

"We're separated," Walker replied.

"Do you want a divorce?" inquired Mayer.

"No. But if Jennifer does, I won't stand in her way . . . ."

To Walker's astonishment, Mayer went on to explain that his son-in-law, William Goetz, had already spoken to Jennifer, who'd promised not to rock any boats. Goetz was fearful that Bob might do something rash and that a scandal might explode before the opening of *The Song of Bernadette*.

Walker, too caught up in the highly charged emotions of the moment to voice his real feelings and tell Mayer who the real villain in this story was, said instead that he'd never do anything to hurt Jennifer, and of course he had no intention of discussing the matter in interviews.

Since You Went Away was in its fourth month of production. Jennifer's relationship with Selznick was far from trouble free.

"I saw her socially with David. She always looked perfectly beautiful but rather frightened," recalls Joan Fontaine. "She impressed me as insecure and frightened."

The opening of *The Song of Bernadette* at the Carthay Circle Theater in Los Angeles should have been a triumphant and joyful moment in Jennifer's life. Instead she wasn't on hand to appreciate it—Selznick had thrown a wrench into the proceedings.

Producer William Perlberg had invited Jennifer to join him and his wife as their guest for the festivities. After all, Selznick could hardly escort Jennifer Jones without her husband!

"Absolutely not," ruled Selznick. Jennifer was not a 20th Century–Fox star, he exclaimed, she was a Selznick star, and no other studio was going to take credit for the success of Jennifer Jones. Jennifer was the one who suffered in this game of egomania. She solved the dilemma by remaining home. It was almost a relief, she was fearful of a crowd's reaction to her on screen and spared herself the ordeal. She also deprived herself of a magical experience ("She was so lovely in the picture," recalled Joan Fontaine).

Many top celebrities attended the exciting premiere on December 27, including Mary Pickford and Buddy Rogers, Hedy Lamarr, and Irene Dunne, one of the industry's most popular and enduring stars. Dunne received a huge ovation from the crowd. To the delight of gathered fans, twenty-seven-year-old singing star Dinah Shore and handsome 20th Century–Fox leading man George Montgomery made their first public appearance together since their marriage.

Advance word on *Bernadette* had been exceptional. The publisher of *The Hollywood Reporter,* W. R. "Billy" Wilkerson (the man who'd "discovered" Lana Turner at a drugstore soda fountain), personally extolled the quality and impact of the film in a page one editorial: "Now that this industry has reached a perfection that affords a *Song of Bernadette, anything* is possible for it to accomplish. No concern is too deep, no sky is too high, for it to reach out and select great thoughts to contribute to the thinking—and betterment—of this world."

Fox was behind the picture 110 percent and launched its striking Oscar campaign. A deluxe full-color, three-page ad proclaimed it "The Story of a Masterpiece" and was run in all the trade papers. Artist Norman Rockwell had been commissioned to paint a portrait of the radiant Jennifer as Bernadette; his was the key artwork used in the ad and also to advertise and promote the picture nationally.

The Catholic clergy was delighted with the film. "The Catholic churches throughout the nation . . . [have] appealed to their congregations to go see *The Song of Bernadette,*" noted trade stories, and some industry reporters offered the opinion that the film seemed directed "almost exclusively to members of the Catholic faith."

Jennifer did not attend the New York premiere, either. Selznick's view was that the aura of mystery that surrounded the actress simply enhanced her value commercially. Let other actresses be accessible for publicity; Jennifer Jones was above that—*talent* was her stock in trade.

Jennifer's reviews for the picture were glowing: "Through Jennifer Jones, a new actress who plays the difficult role of Bernadette, [the film] achieves a rare quality of sweetness that lifts it above its common faults," wrote Bosley Crowther in *The New York Times*.

"It is an inspirationally sensitive and arresting performance that sets [Jennifer] solid as a screen personality," observed *Variety*.

Newsweek stated that "the outstanding feature of an elaborate production is the fine acting of a hand-picked cast. . . . But isolated from the rest—less by the trying demands of the titular role than by the luminous spirituality and simplicity she brings to Bernadette—is the cinematic Cinderella who," the magazine observed perceptively, "has been cautiously publicized as Jennifer Jones."

Kate Cameron of the New York *Daily News* gave the picture her highest rating, four stars. She wrote of Jennifer, "She not only reaches stardom, but she must be counted a phenomenon, and I doubt if she will ever equal or come close to the perfection of her first performance."

The New Yorker cautiously praised the actress: "I won't say that Jennifer Jones, the young discovery who plays Bernadette, is the greatest find of the decade . . . but she is unquestionably appealing and makes no noticeable mistakes." The critic voiced a qualm: "I will say . . . that she has been given one of the worst screen names in the business."

James Agee wrote in *Time* magazine that "newcomer Jennifer Jones makes one of the most impressive screen debuts in years," and he observed acutely: "It remains to be seen whether or not Cinemactress Jones can do in other roles [the] things she achieves as this little peasant saint. If she can, Hollywood should watch and guard [her] as sedulously as the Church watched over Bernadette."

Selznick was ecstatic. He had created a star and was determined that nothing would stand in her way.

Jennifer and Bob's fifth wedding anniversary arrived on January 2, 1944. Walker celebrated alone with his thoughts and a bottle.

Jennifer was occupied with trying to get her life in order and to decide if she should file for divorce in California or move to Reno for six weeks and obtain a Nevada divorce. She was asking no alimony or child support; Walker would have access to their children whenever he liked. The actress wanted desperately to avoid any further hostility, acrimony, or heartbreak—even David Selznick was powerless to arrange that. Discretion, however, was certainly the order of the day. A bare minimum of unavoidable publicity on the divorce was the goal, and Selznick could, to an extent, control the flow of information.

In contrast, Jennifer's contemporaries were making banner headlines with their romantic lives, with twenty-two-year-old Lana Turner and twenty-five-year-old Rita Hayworth leading the pack with a flamboyant lifestyle that was as foreign to Jennifer as posing for cheesecake photos. Lana had already jettisoned husband number two, with whom she reconciled when she discovered she was pregnant. Rita made headlines when her first husband sued her for nonpayment of alimony due him. Jennifer wanted no part of that kind of attention, then or later.

She received a very special request to attend an out-of-town premiere of *The Song of Bernadette,* and she couldn't turn it down. It was a request even Selznick dared not nullify. Jennifer's dad had a big blast in mind and was looking forward to a gala Tulsa opening of the film at two of his theaters, the Ritz and the Orpheum. Jennifer would be on hand to celebrate both a splendid film and a triumphant homecoming.

In December Isley had paid a visit to his daughter in Los Angeles. He wanted his only child to be happy and had attempted to effect a reconciliation between Jennifer and Bob. But he soon realized that Jennifer's course was irreversible, and Isley accepted the inevitable.

Jennifer's faith in Selznick and his Nostradamus-like predictions about her career took on a fabulous glow in February, when the Academy Award nominations were announced. She was a Best Actress nominee, along with Greer Garson, Joan Fontaine, Ingrid Bergman, and Jean Arthur. Not in her wildest dreams, a year earlier, had Jennifer imagined being part of such a prestigious lineup.

"Even if Jennifer doesn't win, the nomination is a great honor," wrote an impressed Louella Parsons. But Jennifer wanted to win, and it augured well for her chances when she won her first award, the first Golden Globe Award ever presented by the Hollywood Foreign Press Association. It was a new accolade, however, and people hadn't heard of it, but they certainly had heard of two other prestigious prizes that came her way: the National Board of Review's Best Acting award, and the Outstanding Achievement Award from *Look* magazine.

Jennifer had become friendly with young actress Evelyn Keyes, who'd played one of Scarlett O'Hara's sisters in *Gone With the Wind*. Keyes was having an affair with a highly sophisticated "older" man (he was in his late forties), director Charles Vidor. The couple's marriage was imminent, and Evelyn asked Jennifer to be her matron of honor at the wedding. The bride and groom's relationship mirrored Jennifer and David's on at least one level: everyone knew Vidor was obviously obsessed with Keyes.

The Tulsa premiere of The Song of Bernadette was scheduled for February 25, scarcely a week before the Academy Awards in Los Angeles. Jennifer agreed to participate in a full schedule of promotional events in Tulsa, and the happiest executive in Hollywood, on hearing the news, was none other than William Goetz. "Jesus, it's about fucking time," he remarked to fellow executive William Koenig. "She hasn't done a goddamn thing to publicize this movie."

Jennifer's itinerary, prepared for her by her father's staff (working closely with Fox), was thorough, including a press conference–reception at the town's leading hotel, the Mayo. An ironclad condition was relayed to reporters in advance: no questions about Robert Walker.

Local leaders would be on hand, as well as Jennifer's old schoolmates and teachers. Jennifer's time in Tulsa was to be limited; she was keyed up about the Oscars, and there were additional scenes still to be filmed in Hollywood for the never-ending *Since You Went Away*.

Her sons accompanied her to Tulsa. The family traveled by train, first to Kansas City, where they were met by Jennifer's father, along with her close school chum Ruth Bowers King, a Fox publicist, and a hand-picked reporter from the *Tulsa Tribune*, Roger V. Devlin. There was a three-hour layover before boarding the connecting train to Tulsa, during which Jennifer and the boys relaxed in a downtown luxury hotel suite.

Devlin's comments on Jennifer, in this controlled environment, were predictably laudatory. He described the hometown girl as "the girl next door," and Jennifer confessed trepidation about the upcoming festivities: "I'm just a little frightened . . . I can't help being a little scared."

It was an ironic attitude for a girl who'd been raised performing for live audiences, but she wasn't portraying a character in this real-life adventure; she was "playing" herself, a task most actors find far more intimidating than the most difficult role.

Waiting for Jennifer at the Tulsa train station were her mother, Mayor C. H. Veale, Mrs. Veale, a police escort, and thousands of cheering Tulsans, including many of her former classmates. The Chamber of Commerce had arranged the event, and Jennifer was incredulous and embarrassed at the tumultuous reception.

"I'm so glad to be here, I could almost die!" she exclaimed.

Huge "Welcome, Jennifer Jones" banners were strung across Main Street. Giant posters of Norman Rockwell's painting of Jennifer as Bernadette were prominently displayed. Two huge posters were mounted over the marquee of the Ritz Theater.

Lavish floral tributes from local friends and Hollywood well-wishers like William Perlberg and William Goetz were waiting for Jennifer in her hotel suite. The largest arrangement, of course, was from David Selznick.

She wore the black taffeta dress she planned on wearing to the Oscars to the 6:30 P.M. reception and dinner. That evening another childhood dream came true: Jennifer saw her name blazing in lights over Fourth and Main Streets, Tulsa's "Little Times Square."

At the Ritz Theater she appeared on the flower-bedecked stage before the picture began, and the crowd was moved by her remarks: "Oh, I wanted to come back so much. I love Oklahoma flowers much more than Hollywood's anytime . . . ." She returned to her seat, followed by a wave of thunderous applause.

The next day a radiant Jennifer, Selznick's sable coat draped casually over her arm, visited her Monte Cassino alma mater. The beaming nuns greeted her effusively. Photographs were taken. Later she attended a Chamber of Commerce luncheon and actually seemed to enjoy it. More photographs were taken. She remembered Colby's advice: "Always look people directly in the eye."

Publicity man Bob Underwood recalls, "Jennifer was one of the most cooperative stars I ever worked with. She did exactly what we asked her to do, but seemed *very* relieved when an event was over."

Exhausted, Jennifer and the boys spent a "quiet" weekend with her parents before rushing back to Hollywood to attend the Academy Award ceremonies.

Jennifer didn't respond well to all the hometown hoopla and the total lack of privacy, since she never did anything like it again. The experience was an ordeal for her, physically and mentally draining in the extreme. ("Everyone who meets you wants a little piece of you," explained Marilyn Monroe, one of the individuals who thrived—indeed came to life—in the publicity spotlight.)

"Doing publicity is exhausting, but so is sewing bugle beads on chiffon. In both cases the results are well worth it," noted the late Carole Lombard, one of Selznick's favorite stars, a woman who had a great talent and ability for generating and sustaining publicity. For Lombard, it was fun. Vivien Leigh enjoyed the attention and sparkled brilliantly in the media spotlight. Bette Davis, too, appreciated and exploited the value of her studio's publicity department. Joan Fontaine had a definite knack for PR, and Ingrid Bergman managed to cope with it. But stars like Katharine Hepburn and Garbo avoided it, and after the Tulsa junket Jennifer obviously decided that she could and would live very well without it.

Tulsa's reaction to *The Song of Bernadette* was all that Fox had hoped for, and business was sensational. Jennifer's performance was lauded as "inspired" and "incredible." Phil Isley had accomplished the impossible: in all local coverage, there wasn't a single mention of Jennifer's marriage to Robert Walker.

As <u>*Song of Bernadette*</u> *premiered in* *Tulsa,* <u>*See Here, Private Hargrove*</u> *went* into national release. It was a smash, but Robert Walker wasn't enjoying the experience.

Walker's attitude about his work began to sour, and he expressed his displeasure over his role in *Thirty Seconds over Tokyo*. The film was a showcase for newcomer Van Johnson, just as *Bataan* had been the launching pad for Walker. "What's Walker complaining about?" angry studio executives wanted to know. "He's got more lines of dialogue in the picture than Spencer Tracy."

Van Johnson has recalled that Walker wasn't difficult during production—just lost in a world of his own.

However, there was a bright spot: Phyllis Thaxter had a featured role in the picture. Bob liked her immensely, and for the same reasons Jennifer had—she was sweet, intelligent, and a good listener. She reminded him of Jennifer.

Thaxter's screen test for *Claudia* had been "sort of floating around at the Selznick studio," she recalls, and producer Sam Zimbalist saw the test and had signed Thaxter for *Thirty Seconds over Tokyo.* Myron Selznick was now her agent.

Thaxter and Walker "went out a few times," she recalls. "He was a very sweet person," says Thaxter, who also recalled the topic of conversation always came back to Jennifer. "He adored her. He talked about her all the time."

Thaxter's and Jennifer's paths crossed briefly a bit later on. "Jennifer and Anita Colby were on the same train as I. I was on my way to Chicago to meet my first husband's [James Aubrey's] family. Jennifer, Anita, and I sat together and had lunch." The women enjoyed each other's company—but, needless to say, the topic of Robert Walker did not come up.

Chapter

12

*W*alker did not attend the Academy Awards ceremonies on March 2. He remained home, once again, with his dark thoughts and bottles of Scotch. He needn't have been alone, according to Keenan Wynn. "You couldn't talk to Bob when he drank and his mind was focused on Jennifer."

Walker's personal demons and his obsessive love for Jennifer was wreaking havoc on him personally and, eventually, professionally. Selznick's behavior, too, over the next few years would prove to be equally unhealthy.

But on stage of Grauman's Chinese that enchanted March 2 evening, Jennifer's thoughts were on neither Walker nor Selznick. She trembled visibly on accepting her Oscar, clutching it to her bosom. Her voice quivered as she whispered her thank-yous into the microphone. Backstage she burst into tears and rested her head on Jack Benny's shoulder.

How did it feel to win an Oscar? "I'd been trying for so long and with such poor luck to get started on a career, and then all of a sudden—wham! I had success in my hands. I guess I felt like a starving person sitting down unexpectedly to a sumptuous banquet with no warning. That was me when I walked on that stage and accepted the little statue. It was weeks before the full significance of what had happened dawned on me." She said she hoped she'd be better prepared the next time, *if* there was a next time. "Perhaps," she said, "I'll even be able to make a speech."

She felt guilty Ingrid Bergman hadn't won and apologized to her friend. "You should have won," she told Ingrid.

"No, Jennifer, your Bernadette was better than my Maria," Ingrid replied. At the dinner afterward (there was no official academy soiree this year, out of deference to the war), Selznick sat between Jennifer and Ingrid but gazed adoringly at Jennifer, his feelings emblazoned on his face for the world to see. Jennifer frequently reached forward to caress her Oscar, which stood alongside her soup plate. Bergman was smiling. She'd lost but seemed perfectly content. "Don't worry," David assured her, "You're going to win one, too."

(Selznick was obviously a man who could concentrate on several things simultaneously. At the exact moment Jennifer had won her Oscar, Selznick, seated beside Shirley Temple, had turned to the teenager and said: "I'm picking up your option.")

Jennifer was excited and joyful as filmdom's elite practically waited in line to offer their congratulations and express their admiration and fervent hopes of working with her in the future.

Only four Oscars had gone to *The Song of Bernadette*. It seemed Fox's "prestige" campaign to win votes for the film had backfired. By opening the movie as a high-priced, reserved-seat attraction, many of the industry's "extra" players—all of whom voted in those years—hadn't been able to afford to see it.

In any event, Jennifer Jones was the Best Actress of the year. And on Oscar night, "You want someone to share all of that excitement with, someone to express all of your innermost feelings to," explained Tom Lewis, husband of subsequent Oscar winner Loretta Young, recalling how, when Loretta won (in 1947, for *The Farmer's Daughter*), "she was so keyed up that we stayed up all night, just talking."

Jennifer didn't have that luxury. Walker was out of the picture. David Selznick had a wife waiting for him at home. And Jennifer's two sons were fast asleep when she arrived home. So the Best Actress of the year was forced to return to a dark and quiet house, with no one to keep her company but Oscar.

The next day Jennifer initiated divorce proceedings against Walker. Press agents had done a masterful job in muddying the waters of her private life. In late March, when *See Here, Private Hargrove* opened in New York, a major article appeared in the *New York Herald-Tribune* portraying Jennifer and Bob as a happy couple.

Three weeks after Jennifer won her Oscar, David Selznick was struck by a numbing personal tragedy, one that hit him as hard as his beloved father's death a decade earlier. On March 23, Myron Selznick, age forty-five, died suddenly after suffering a heart attack. An alcoholic, he'd been in terrible physical condition for years, but no one had remotely expected him to die.

There'd been resentment and anger, as well as love, between the two brothers, but their blood ties and deep feelings for each other had surpassed all other considerations. They were each other's best and most trusted friends in a town where trust was virtually a nonexistent commodity.

Jennifer, of course, was not present for the funeral at Temple Israel. David had to be supported by friends as he stumbled down the aisle. William Powell read the eulogy, which quoted Florence Selznick's description of her beloved son: "He was a little boy who never grew up. . . ."

David never totally recovered from the loss. There was little that Jennifer, Irene, or anyone else could say or do in ensuing weeks to heal the wound. "When Myron died, it left a terrible hole," Irene said.

While David lived like a millionaire, it was Myron who'd accumulated the millions. Myron's wealth—his monthly income at the time of his death was $20,000—was estimated at $10 million. That included the Myron Selznick Building on Wilshire Boulevard, plus a resort he'd financed at Running Springs in the San Bernardino Mountains.

Myron's wife, the former actress Marjorie Daw, and their daughter, Joan, were the beneficiaries of the huge estate. It included an annuity worth even more millions—the 6 percent share in *Gone With the Wind* that Myron had refused to sell to either Jock Whitney or MGM.

David's legatees wouldn't ever realize a cent from the epic film, which wouldn't have existed without his efforts.

Selznick's character changed and his business judgment seemed affected by the tragedy. Perhaps out of feelings of guilt at his brother's death, David assumed, in his business dealings, the most abrasive flesh-peddling tactics in an agent's repertoire.

He also made his first major blunder regarding Jennifer's career. In April, 20th Century–Fox offered Jennifer the starring role in *Laura,* a sophisticated mystery thriller based on the best-selling novel by Vera Caspary. The role offered Jones the opportunity to portray an ambitious, soft-spoken, intelligent young woman who attracts men—and murder.

Laura was an obvious winner, the kind of potentially perfect script (Selznick and Jennifer saw an early draft) that an expert like David Selznick usually didn't fail to recognize and pounce on. So why did Selznick turn it down? Had the fact that Laura is the object of an older man's obsession hit too close to home? Jennifer later claimed *she* hadn't wanted to do the picture. "I thought Gene Tierney was great in it," she said, "but I'm still glad I didn't play in it as was originally intended. I really wouldn't have been good. There was, for me, nothing I could get my teeth into in the part."

After Selznick turned *Laura* down, Fox promptly responded with a lawsuit for $613,000 (and tried to get Rita Hayworth for the role). Negotiations began for a compromise. Jennifer would do some other picture for Fox, later on.

Selznick had had elaborate plans for another epic production, *Tales of Passion and Romance.* He envisioned it as a three-part film, to be directed by Alfred Hitchcock, Alexander Korda, and William Dieterle. He intended to star his entire roster of luminaries—Jennifer, Ingrid Bergman, Vivien Leigh (in the Korda-directed segment), Joan Fontaine, Shirley Temple, and Joseph Cotten.

The film never got off the ground. Myron's death, and other projects in which Selznick was already involved, made it impossible for him personally to launch another venture. He'd bought Robert Nathan's best-selling novel, *Portrait of Jennie,* as a vehicle for Shirley Temple and was well into preproduction on *The House of Dr. Edwardes* (later renamed *Spellbound*), slated to be directed by Alfred Hitchcock. Selznick's personal encounters with psychotherapy had prompted his interest in buying this psychological thriller.

Selznick debated casting Jennifer in *Spellbound* opposite Gregory Peck, not yet a star but obviously a sure bet to become one in the near future.

"I didn't want Jennifer for it because David would have been on the set every second," said Hitchcock. But he said nothing to the producer and bided his time. "I liked Jennifer. I always suspected there was a sexy blond personality lurking beneath that cool brunette exterior," he said. "That's what intrigued David, too, in my opinion. I would have liked to work with her, but the right property never presented itself."

Selznick decided the role of the female psychiatrist was better suited to Ingrid Bergman.

Jennifer got to play the role of Esther Blodgett in *A Star Is Born*—on radio, with Walter Pidgeon as Norman Maine. She'd been unhappy with the adaptation, which concentrated on the Maine character. Selznick responded to Jennifer's entreaties and rectified the situation.

Gene Tierney was one of Hollywood's most successful and adept young hostesses. Her friend Vincent Price was a guest, one evening, at one of her well-attended parties. He recalls that at this soiree, "a young woman, looking almost like a floozy, with very fancy, frizzed hair and lots of makeup and rouge, came up and said, 'Hello, how are you, Dutour?' " (That was the name of the character Price had played in *Song of Bernadette*). "It was Jennifer," recalls Price, "and I didn't even recognize her!

"She was trying to change her image. It was perfectly understandable. When, on your first picture, you win the Academy Award playing a saint, you'd want to get away from that because there aren't many other good parts in that category!

"While everyone was sort of shocked at how Jennifer looked, we all understood it. She was a lady very determined to be a star. She realized she couldn't go on playing little waifs. The day of Janet Gaynor had passed, [and] she knew that."

It's interesting that Price, who'd known Gene Tierney since she was seventeen years old, believes that Jennifer would not have made a good *Laura* (Price had a featured role in that film, too). "Gene was so *right*," he says. "I don't think Jennifer had any sophistication at all—to me, she didn't have that quality Gene had, which was being 'born to the cloth,' as it were.

"Gene was very 'social.' She'd come from a classy family in Greenwich, Connecticut, or one of those places. The family had lost all its money in the crash, but she was a 'classy' dame. Jennifer is a very straight and honest lady, but I don't think she's got *that* kind of class."

• • • •

Heavy negative publicity surrounding Jennifer's pending divorce from Walker began to accumulate and impact on her image. In the forefront of the disillusioned was feature writer Adela Rogers St. Johns. St. Johns observed that Jennifer's troubles began "when someone said of Jennifer Jones, 'She *is* Bernadette.' " The writer went on to describe Jennifer's break with Robert Walker as "a tragedy more dramatic than any other I have known in my many years of telling tales of the movie world and its people."

(Other tinseltown scribes echoed this same theme: "Not since the breakup of Mary Pickford and Douglas Fairbanks in 1929 had a Hollywood divorce caused so much unhappiness," was the tenor of many editorials. Of course, this was a ludicrous comparison. Pickford and Fairbanks had been beloved superstars for many years. Their parting shocked the world and had assumed almost mythic proportions. Jennifer and Bob were virtual newcomers, and the fact that reporters would make a comparison with Mary and Doug Fairbanks indicated the popularity Jones and Walker had achieved seemingly overnight.)

Adela neatly summed up Jennifer's dilemma and the public's problem in accepting the actress's "real life" behavior: "The girl who is Bernadette in that exquisite and unforgettable *Song* has stated that she is going to Reno to get a divorce from her young husband, Robert Walker, whom by now you have seen as Private Hargrove. . . . No Hollywood star ever before crashed through a dream we had built around her quite so violently, so suddenly, so heartbreakingly."

She recalled how in World War I it had been the Little Flower, St. Therese, who had become the friend of all soldiers—and for this war, claimed Mrs. St. Johns, it was Bernadette. "I am not a Catholic myself, but I believe that the Little Flower and Bernadette belong to all hearts of goodwill everywhere. . . .

"So when I read in the papers that Bernadette was going to Reno to get a divorce, I stopped and rubbed my eyes."

To make matters even worse, St. Johns pointed out that Bernadette was divorcing Private Hargrove, "that clean-cut, typical American doughboy; he was the Infantry that we're depending upon to mop up this war in the end. No, he wasn't; he was Bob Walker."

Adela painted a vivid picture: "Bernadette standing in a tawdry divorce court in Reno saying, 'My husband and I are incompatible. . . . ' "

The writer's loyalty to the film industry was not forgotten. Mrs. St. Johns wanted to be fair: "*She* [Jennifer] didn't see the Lady at Lourdes. . . . She's just a human being, with her own troubles and problems and suffering. . . .

"Something very bitter and terrible must have happened to split them up now. I think we may be sure that both she and her young husband were torn to pieces as they stood at that crossroad. . . .

"In the thirty years I've written Hollywood history I've never known a case just like this. . . . You may feel that Jennifer Jones should have waited and endured before she tagged the words *Reno* and *divorce* onto *The Song of Bernadette*, [for those words] seemed to say none of it was true. Maybe there hadn't been any miracles at Lourdes at all, maybe it was all just a motion picture."

Knowing full well the intimate details of Jennifer's breakup, St. Johns nonetheless avoided even a hint of a revelation as to what was going on behind the scenes: "What the real truth is, we don't purport to know." However, she informed Jennifer (and at the same time St. Johns's millions of readers) that "you have been innocently involved in wounding more people than you can possibly guess by this decision to part—not to mention the two small people whose presence in the world is due solely to you and your husband, your sons, Bobby and Michael. . . ."

Mrs. St. Johns ended on a note of forgiveness: "I went to see *The Song of Bernadette* again. The one thing I know now is that Bernadette is truly there. . . . We can forgive [Jennifer]. . . . She's very young, and everybody makes mistakes . . . nothing can touch Bernadette. . . . Perhaps she came back to play herself inside the cloak of one Jennifer Jones, to perform before our unknowing eyes another miracle."

Jennifer was devastated and deeply hurt by the onslaught of Hollywood reporters who tried to "tear my personal life apart." She agonized over the situation and said she couldn't understand why people wanted to pry every emotion out of her and give them to a curious public to try on for color and size. She refused to discuss her private life, dismissing all queries by stating: "Things just happen, and there's nothing that can be done about it. And that's all."

In publicity on Jennifer originating from the Selznick studio, the actress continued to be presented as a dedicated professional and a devoted mother, extolling the virtues of her two sons and her about-to-be ex-husband.

Mentions of David Selznick were limited to "the important and necessary role" he was portraying in her career. She was quoted as expressing her unreserved faith in his plans for her and reiterated: "I want to work. Work all the time."

With Anita Colby's guidance, Jennifer went on a no-holds-barred shopping spree. But it was not nearly as satisfying a substitute for a juicy role. Although she'd just completed around 130 shooting days on *Since You Went Away,* she was restless to start another film. But she acknowledged that David Selznick "will wait until he has just the right role for me," and she added: "I hope I have a good picture soon."

A gala preview of Since You Went Away was scheduled for May, with the formal premiere scheduled for Los Angeles' Carthay Circle Theater in June. Important details, including final editing of certain sequences of the picture, remained to be finalized. Although still reeling emotionally from the death of his brother, Selznick knew there were business decisions that could no longer be delayed. Urged on by Ben Hecht and other friends not to abandon the picture because of his grief, he buried himself in the workload.

He worked through the nights, helped by his never-ending supply of Benzedrine tablets. When, toward daybreak, he'd finally pass out, he was put in his car and deposited home by his driver. In the morning he'd be revived by the butler, James Farr, and the cycle would begin all over again.

Jennifer had discreetly resumed her nurses' aide activities, working six A.M.–to-noon shifts at the hospital.

The industry was eagerly waiting to get a look at *Since You Went Away.* The film's prologue neatly summed up the movie's timely plot: "This is a story of the Unconquerable Fortress: the American Home . . . 1943." One of the key ad lines for the film declared: "*Since*

You Went Away—the four most important words since *Gone With the Wind.*"

At around $2.78 million it was the most expensive—and longest—picture made since *Gone With the Wind.* United Artists, the film's distributor, joined forces with the Selznick studio to launch the picture in appropriate fashion. An invitation-only preview was scheduled for May 9, with an exclusive private party afterward to be hosted by the Selznicks at the Scandia restaurant on Sunset Boulevard.

The town's "A" list turned out in force for the screening. The stars of the picture, with one exception, were all on hand: impeccably groomed, elegantly gowned and jeweled Claudette Colbert with her husband, Dr. Joel Pressman; Shirley Temple; Joseph Cotten and his wife, Lenore; Ingrid Bergman, escorted by publicist Joe Steele; Joan Fontaine; Dorothy McGuire; Gregory Peck and his wife, Greta; Anita Colby; and, of course, Jennifer. Irene Selznick was front and center, along with sister Edie and husband Bill Goetz. The absent star on this occasion was Robert Walker. He hadn't been invited, according to friends; others stated that he simply couldn't bring himself to attend.

The applause after the final scene of the movie signaled a success; to the veteran Selznick ear, however, there was a missing dimension to the response. Anita Colby remembers, "People sat on their hands. There was incredible jealousy of David. People were reluctant to give him full credit."

Jennifer had certainly sustained the admiration and respect of her peers, although some criticized her performance as overly "intense." (Irene Selznick was among those who disliked Jennifer's performance—in fact, she disliked everything about her. The "sweet and eager" girl was too sweet, too eager, and obviously too tenacious. It was truly ironic that Irene, as her husband's silent partner in the recently formed David O. Selznick Productions, was co-owner of Jennifer's contract.)

After the screening, the usual accolades surrounded the producer and his entourage as the glittering group made its way to Scandia and afterward to the Trocadero. "Jennifer looked spectacular in a high-necked white lace evening gown," recalled Henry Willson. "Lana [Turner] was there, looking very daring. Her long blond hair was cascading down her back, she wore a black strapless evening gown cut down to *there* [and] long black gloves. [Compared to her] Jennifer looked like a madonna. . . . Both were *so* gorgeous, and all the men were tripping over themselves to get a look at both of them."

At the restaurant, the Selznick table was naturally the focus of attention, but there was tension in the air. Selznick was fast slipping into a foul mood, disappointed by the way the movie had played. *Since You Went Away* hadn't delivered the kind of all-out excitement of *Gone With the Wind* or *Rebecca*. He was angry, perplexed, and his mood grew darker as he drank the night away. At one point, to everyone's embarrassment, he verbally insulted Joan Fontaine.

"Do you think we should leave?" Ingrid Bergman whispered to Joe Steele. The publicist vetoed the suggestion.

Jennifer sat wide-eyed and at a loss, observing David's unaccountably rude behavior. Irene, of course, had shared many Jekyll-and-Hyde evenings with David. Her patience had just about run out, although she didn't confront the fact for a while longer.

Jennifer, for what may have been one of the first times, surely observed that her Prince Charming had quite a neurotic streak that would have to be dealt with—perhaps very soon. At least he'd been comfortable enough to make a fool of himself in her presence.

Selznick's arrogance extended to his attitudes regarding Jennifer and Irene. At one point he told his sister-in-law, Edie Goetz, that he had every intention of having his cake and eating it, too. Edie recognized Selznick's dilemma. (Like brother-in-law David, Edie was an incurable romantic. In later years she fell in love with Tyrone Power, who encouraged her "crush." He turned it into a profitable movie deal involving none other than Bill Goetz.)

Undoubtedly Edie was angered by her sister's inability (or unwillingness) to destroy the relationship with Jennifer. Edie, who believed in taking the bull by its horns and twisting, was a startling contrast to Irene, who employed a more laid-back and nonconfrontational modus operandi. If Bill Goetz, and not David Selznick, had relentlessly pursued Jennifer, one assumes the actress would have had to react quite differently—Edie would have forced an early confrontation.

Joan Fontaine neatly sums up Edie Goetz: "There are princesses, you know?" In later years Edie claimed that Bill Goetz had produced films that Selznick had produced. Joan Fontaine recalls, "She was very loyal to Bill, and Bill was a funny man, had lots of humor. I'll never forget the shock that we first felt when, in their home, under the painting by Monet, as we sat to see a film, the painting lifted up and there was the movie screen! It was the first setup of that kind, and Danny Kaye made a wonderful remark. Kaye said, 'You know what Bill should do? He should show his paintings and hang his films!'"

Jennifer, photographed by Philippe Halsman, appeared on the cover of the July 24, 1944, issue of Life magazine (a Life cover was the most sought-after exposure an actor could achieve). "Jennifer Jones, a quiet twenty-four-year-old movie newcomer, last March startled Hollywood by winning the Academy Award for her performance in The Song of Bernadette," observed the publication. "In her second major movie, *Since You Went Away,* she gives another warm and sensitive performance. She is especially good in scenes with her real-life husband, Robert Walker, from whom she is separated."

Since You Went Away premiered that month at the Capitol Theatre in New York City. The movie went on to rack up tremendous grosses throughout the country.

"Jennifer Jones is surpassingly sweet as a well-bred American daughter in the first bloom of womanhood and love," wrote Bosley Crowther in *The New York Times*.

James Agee, in *Time* magazine, applauded Selznick for having led Jennifer "out of the cloister" and making her an all-American girl. "She rewards him with a nervous, carefully studied, and somewhat overly intense performance. . . . What makes *Since You Went Away* surefire is in part its homely subject matter, which has never before been so earnestly tackled in a film, in part its all-star acting, [and] most of all David Selznick's extremely astute screenplay and production. . . . Though idealized, the Selznick characterizations are authentic to a degree seldom achieved in Hollywood. . . ."

The film produced an unexpected bonus for Selznick: twenty-two-year-old Robert Mosely, an exceptionally handsome blond who had been spotted by Selznick talent executive Henry Willson (Mosely was serving in the Coast Guard) and signed to a low-figure seven-year contract. Renamed Guy Madison, the former telephone lineman was cast as a sailor in *Since You Went Away* and now became an overnight "teenage" idol, a valuable property with substantial loan-out value.

While *Since You Went Away* was a smash ("Selznick's Latest!" was how many theaters chose to label their marquees), it wasn't *Gone With the Wind,* either at the box office or with the critics (the film brought in over $4.3 million in domestic rentals, a huge figure but less than half the total at that point for *Gone With the Wind*). Selznick felt deeply let down. The movie, however, had easily succeeded in placing Jennifer far beyond the "one-shot sensation" category. She was a top star after only two pictures.

As was the case with Ingrid Bergman, studios sent Selznick scripts they felt that Jennifer would be suitable for. He dismissed most of them, but one, from RKO, had intriguing possibilities. It was a western, *Duel in the Sun,* with an innovative twist: the leading lady was a half-breed Indian girl, a sexpot who wreaks havoc on the lives of the two brothers who love her. There was additional controversy—a rape scene in which the girl enjoys the violence *and* the lovemaking.

Written by Niven Busch, the script for *Duel* was based on his novel, which had been published that year. Critics lambasted the work, criticizing its "unreal characters" and "historical inaccuracies." But the material intrigued Selznick, who'd known Busch for years (he'd been a screenwriter at Warner Brothers, 20th Century–Fox, Goldwyn, Paramount, and Universal and was currently working on a screenplay for MGM entitled *The Postman Always Rings Twice*).

Busch had intended the film of *Duel in the Sun* as a vehicle for his wife, Teresa Wright, the superlative young actress who'd been typecast in "sweet" roles. But when Wright became pregnant, she dropped out of the project. The studio then wanted to cast reigning sex symbol Hedy Lamarr, but Hedy was pregnant, too ("I had nothing to do with that," joked Busch).

In *Duel in the Sun,* Selznick saw a radical and exciting image-changing story idea for Jennifer. But he was miffed that Jones hadn't been RKO's first choice and informed them that it wasn't an important enough project "to warrant lending Ms. Jones."

He kept the door open, however, with other hurdles for the studio to jump over before he'd agree to lend Jennifer. The casting of one of the brothers, "the sexy one," was in Selznick's view all wrong (John Wayne, a favorite actor of Niven Busch's, was set for that role). And Selznick wasn't comfortable with RKO's choice of Busch as the film's producer.

He was blunt: he didn't believe that Jennifer, now an Academy Award winner, "should be placed in the hands of a fledgling producer," and went on to affirm that Jennifer's career was his to create and protect "exactly as I have that of my other stars, and I should be very disappointed if she is not a very great star for the next ten or fifteen years."

RKO finally abandoned the project. Selznick bought it, and it joined the many other properties he owned that were in various stages of development. He envisioned building a vast movie production complex, "Selznick City," that he would rent out to other independent producers. He proudly told Irene that the Selznick company, at this point, was worth at least $6 million. Irene, all too familiar with David's profligate ways, was understandably skeptical at the assessment.

Incredibly, Robert Walker continued to hold out hope that Jennifer would change her mind and return to him. He was incapable of accepting her final decision and foolishly refused to take steps to climb out of his emotional pit.

He found a new friend and confidant, thirty-three-year-old James ("Jim") Henaghan. The men had met one night in the fashionable LaRue's restaurant on Sunset Strip, where Henaghan was looking for news items. Henaghan (or "Big Jim," as his young wife, teenage Gwen Verdon, called him) wrote a column for *The Hollywood Reporter.*

"I really think the two men's relationship was based on the fact that Jim Henaghan was also a drinker, a *terrible* drinker, a *Lost Weekend* drinker," states Gwen Verdon. "He was much older than Robert Walker. He was good friends with Errol Flynn and John Barrymore and Gene Fowler. I remember one time Big Jim called me from Kansas City, and he had no recollection of getting there, so I think that Jim recognized that Robert Walker was that kind of drinker, and he would always try to 'save' Robert Walker."

Verdon's celebrated dance career hadn't yet begun. "I had this baby child!" she explains, and she also had her hands full contending full-time with Henaghan's drinking and wildly unpredictable behavior. It was a pattern Walker had already fallen into by the time he and Henaghan became pals.

Verdon hadn't known Walker before the breakup with Jennifer, but based on her own experiences with Bob, her sympathies are strongly with Jennifer.

In Verdon's opinion, which offers a startling new slant on the Jennifer–Robert Walker relationship, Walker's drinking was perhaps even responsible for the final split-up.

Verdon's recollections of Walker's often bizarre behavior are vivid: "There was nothing to hold [Jennifer] back [in her career] except possibly having to deal with Robert Walker [and his self-destructive behavior], and I adored him.

"It was not just feeling sorry for him—when he was sober he was so sweet and funny and gentle and very bright . . . but I think long before his breakup with Jennifer, I'm sure he had a drinking problem.

"Maybe [his drinking] had never flourished (if 'flourish' is the right word) until Jennifer became successful, which would have been a threat to him. I know something had to touch it off. Very possibly it was [not David Selznick, but] her success."

Verdon's theory has been echoed by Dore Schary: "Walker's career had flowered at the same time as that of his wife's, [but then] Jennifer's career passed his with her sure stardom in *Song of Bernadette,* [and] his marriage broke up. . . ."

Verdon explains further: "While two kids are struggling to become good, they have a common interest, but if one makes it and the other doesn't, after about two years, boy, the one that didn't make it is eating on a lot of hostility, no matter *how* much the other one tries."

To further illuminate her point, Verdon relates an amusing anecdote: "After Jessica Tandy got her Oscar [as Best Actress of 1989 for *Driving Miss Daisy*], Hume Cronyn turned to her and said, 'You think this is gonna split us up?' So obviously there's some truth to it; there's got to be."

A Gallup poll commissioned by Selznick confirmed that Jennifer was the fastest-rising young female star in films.

And Robert Walker represented to the public, as Adela Rogers

St. Johns had observed so pointedly, the quintessential young American GI. MGM lost no time in cashing in on the image. Walker's next assignment was another GI Joe, but it was his most prestigious assignment to date—a starring role opposite Judy Garland in *The Clock.*

Judy was poised to reach the very peak of her success with the imminent release of *Meet Me in St. Louis* (in which Bob had almost been her costar). *The Clock,* slated to begin production in mid-August, would provide Garland with the opportunity to display her gifts as a dramatic actress. There would be no musical numbers; to the dismay of the MGM sales force, Judy wouldn't sing a note in *The Clock.*

Garland had a sixth sense about people, an unerring, almost eerie ability to detect their weaknesses and failings. "She could size someone up almost instantaneously," observed her friend, dancer/choreographer (later director) Charles Walters.

From Judy's first meeting with Walker on the lot almost a year earlier, when she'd playfully teased him because he'd seemed so straitlaced, and especially now, after their brief fling, Judy had pegged Walker as "being in even worse shape, psychologically, than I am!" She'd been married and divorced (from composer David Rose), been under the care of psychiatrists, was dependent on chemical substances, and had had many failed romances, including one with brilliant young writer-producer Joseph L. Mankiewicz and a recent one with Vincente Minnelli, director of *Meet Me in St. Louis.* She'd also fallen deeply in love with Tyrone Power and was no stranger to unrequited love.

"In her heart of hearts, what Judy really wanted to be was a great beauty like Lana Turner or Jennifer Jones," said Charles Walters. "When she saw the impact a beautiful woman had on a man's life— Jennifer on Walker [was] a prime example—she longed to have that impact herself.

"She'd even devised her own way of accomplishing it. By using her incredible personality and her acting ability, [she made] men respond to her . . . sometimes they even fell in love with her.

"But she had to *work* at it, you see; to somebody like Jennifer Jones, or Lana or Ava, those things simply *happened.*

"Judy was actually wonderful with people like Robert Walker," recalled Walters. "She knew the hell he was going through, since she'd been there, or somewhere similar, in her relationships. She understood all too well Walker's weakness, his lack of inner strength. But she was very excited about making *The Clock.* It wasn't a musical, and it offered her the opportunity to prove she was a great actress. The film was a chance to let her make her mark doing something different.

"She thought she and Walker would make a terrific match on screen, and succeeded in making him equally enthusiastic."

As far as Jennifer was concerned, she was undoubtedly relieved to know Walker's star was rising and that she wouldn't have to worry about jobs coming his way. She hadn't ruined his career or spoiled his chances. Few actors had brighter professional prospects than Robert Walker.

Walker was always cautious about his behavior when dealing with Jennifer in connection with their children. "He was absolutely crazy about those two kids," recalls Gwen Verdon, "and they were beautiful boys. Michael looked like Jennifer, he was very dark, and Robert junior looked very much like his father. Bob did everything he could to spend as much time as possible with them.

"But he also must have driven Jennifer just crazy because he would sit on the curb opposite her house and just sit there and look at it. . . .

"He flirted with destruction constantly. I was not aware of it then. Everyone just thought, Oh, he's just so brokenhearted. But, I mean, you've just got to have that potential to self-destruct, or you just don't, no matter how bad things are. You just don't, especially with children, you don't act that way."

Jennifer continued with her nurses' aide activities as Walker worked diligently on *The Clock.* Keenan Wynn was in the cast, so Bob had a buddy close by. But the picture ran into major difficulties. Judy was unhappy working with director Fred Zinnemann—there was no chemistry between them.

The front office, unhappy with the rushes, agreed. Each scene seemed to be from a separate movie. The picture was canceled.

Garland prevailed on producer Arthur Freed to save the ship. Vincente Minnelli was called in, and in September 1944 the film began production from scratch (the impressive New York Pennsylvania Station set, constructed at great expense on the back lot, remained in the picture).

This was Minnelli's first nonmusical film, and even he was nervous about it. He decided to make New York City a third major character in the story, but all Manhattan locations would be suggested through clever use of rear-screen projection of film already shot for the movie by a second unit on actual locations in New York.

Walker, with Judy's support and encouragement, remained sober. But his fragile state soon shattered as he observed a close personal relationship develop and flourish between Garland and Vincente Minnelli. The May-December aspect of the pairing raised the specter of his own wife's relationship.

Walker reacted badly to new script changes that favored Judy's character in the movie, and as shooting progressed, Walker plunged off the wagon. Judy and makeup woman (and close friend) Dot Pondell "actually went through west side bars looking for Bob," recalled Vincente Minnelli. "They finally found him and took him to Dotty's to dry him out for the next morning's shooting."

Tom King went along on some of these forays with Judy, and minces no words in describing the "joints" Walker had crept into. "They were awful. Very seedy places with dangerous-looking characters all over the place. Walker was looking for trouble, and he's lucky he wasn't badly roughed up.

"I remember one bar, Planet Earth, on Wilcox. Sailors frequented the place, and it was a real dump. When you entered, it was so dark you couldn't make out faces. Everything was bathed in purple light. It was so dark Judy Garland wasn't even recognized, and her white blouse glowed like a neon sign in that purple light. She found Walker and talked him out of there. We had a limo waiting outside."

MGM producer Sam Marx has recalled that an actress who dated Walker at this time was frightened away when Walker, who knew she had just come out of a bad relationship, proposed driving her, along with himself, off a cliff. The actress was shocked not that Walker was simply thinking of such a thing—but that he really *meant* it.

Walker's appetite faltered, and he became alarmingly thin. The makeup people had to disguise the bags beginning to appear under his eyes and to use eyedrops to eliminate the constant bleariness.

Walker, who was only twenty-six, "on some days looked forty-five," recalled Dot Ponedel.

•   •   •

Jennifer was unaware that Walker was exhibiting suicidal tendencies as he continued to spend as much time as possible with their sons.

Gwen Verdon recalls an incident that occurred when she and "Big Jim," along with their son, went to pick up the Walker boys for an afternoon outing (the three boys played together all the time).

"Bob was at the house," recalls Verdon. "He and Big Jim suddenly said, 'We'll take them alone.' Jennifer never came out of the house, and they left me standing on the street! It was up to me to get home. Drinkers are like that, even when they're sober. I have great sympathy for Jennifer because I know she loved Bob Walker. *That* I know."

Gwen Verdon relates another incident. "There used to be a little bar, I think it was called Edward's, right opposite what is now the Thalberg gate at MGM, and we used to go rescue Bob there, or I'd have to rescue *both* of them [Bob and "Big Jim"], just hoping they would still *be* there when I would get the phone call, 'Come and get them.'

"I was only seventeen. I couldn't deal with people like this. I don't know if Bob Walker had an oxygen tank in the bedroom, but Big Jim did. There was a newspaperman who worked for Louella Parsons, and he was also a drinker. His wife would call and we would go and get [him] and bring him up to the house in Laurel Canyon, and he would get B_{12} shots *and* oxygen, which would straighten him out.

"I didn't want to deal with this. I finally just didn't." (Verdon's marriage to Henaghan ended in 1945.) "In my opinion, and I was younger than Jennifer, I'm *sure* she felt the same way."

Based on her personal experience dealing with Robert Walker, Gwen Verdon states: "Knowing Robert, and as much as I liked him, it must have been absolute agony for Jennifer, never knowing what you were going to find when you came home, never knowing what kind of phone call you would get while you were working. I mean, she could [be tracked down] in traffic while driving on Hollywood Boulevard, because he'd do things like that, you know, so it must have been awful for her."

In Verdon's view, based on her encounters with the Walker boys, Jennifer never bad-mouthed Bob. "I'm sure it was impossible *not* to talk against their father, yet I doubt she ever did," she says.

Verdon points out that while Jennifer "always gets rapped" for her involvement with Selznick, she feels that Selznick was "a father figure to her. I'm sure he was someone Jennifer could depend on," she states.

When one is forced to contend with a person with an addiction as all-consuming as Henaghan's or Walker's, there is only one way, in Gwen Verdon's view, to handle the situation in order to survive. "You just walk away—children and all," she says. "You just walk away. There's nothing, *nothing* you can do."

There was a harrowing encounter among Walker, Judy Garland, and Vincente Minnelli in which Walker displayed the kind of nightmarish behavior Gwen Verdon has described, behavior that neither Jennifer nor anyone else could have tolerated or lived with for very long.

Minnelli and Judy received a telephone call one night from Bob. "He drunkenly informed us he was going to kill himself," recalled Minnelli. "We both got on the phone, alternately talking to him, trying to get him to tell us where he was. He steadfastly refused to say. After much cajoling, he agreed to come over to our house."

Within half an hour Walker arrived. He commanded belligerently, "Give me a drink, and make it snappy."

"I fixed him a drink," recalled Minnelli, "and sat down with him and Judy. . . ."

A Kafka-esque evening ensued. "[Bob] hated the town, he hated the people in it . . . but most of all Bob hated himself," recalled Minnelli, "and then he zeroed in on Judy and me. We heard a lot of ugly things. . . . Judy reacted with superhuman patience. She was loving. She wanted to show that someone cared. . . . The resentments he must have been storing up during filming [of *The Clock*] came spilling out. I chose to endure them.

"Finally, around dawn, the doctor [summoned by Minnelli] arrived. Bob took one look at him, let out a stream of profanity, and the doctor indignantly walked out.

"At about this time, I realized the only solution would be to keep giving him drinks until he passed out.

"I reached Bob's doctor at last, and he came right over. He called the hospital. 'I'll be bringing in Mr. Walker,' he said. 'We'll use the rear entrance and register him under another name. Please make all the arrangements.' The doctor had obviously been through all this before."

• • •

Selznick, all too aware of Jennifer's anxiety over Walker and her desire to begin a new project, gave in to her pleadings and arranged a loan-out deal to Paramount for *Love Letters,* a tale of melodrama, murder, and (like *The Clock*) bittersweet romance. The lead character, Singleton, is an idealistic girl who, as a result of severe emotional shock, becomes a victim of amnesia.

There's a touch of *Cyrano de Bergerac* to the plot—Singleton has fallen in love with a man she believes has been sending her beautiful love letters (actually written by his friend). She marries the man, who turns out to be a scoundrel and a wife beater. Singleton's foster mother (played by Gladys Cooper) kills him, then dies herself. Singleton is then accused of the man's murder.

The script was by Ayn Rand, no less, author of the novel *The Fountainhead.* The producer was the formidable Hal Wallis, former executive producer at Warner Brothers, who'd been Jack Warner's chief executive for years. Wallis had set up independent production at Paramount and was every bit as shrewd and tough-minded as David Selznick.

Wallis had discovered the *Love Letters* property. "I picked up the obscure novel, by a writer named Chris Massie, in paperback at an airport," he said. When a treatment was prepared, "I wanted Jennifer Jones to play the girl. She had the nervousness, the fey quality, the sense of abstraction the role demanded." He sent Selznick the treatment "with some trepidation."

Obtaining Jennifer's services was an ordeal Wallis wasn't looking forward to. "One didn't communicate with Ms. Jones directly," he noted, "only through Selznick. She was shy and withdrawn and wouldn't make a decision without him, and he was extremely protective of her.

"I remembered what I had gone through with him when I had borrowed Ingrid Bergman for *Casablanca.* . . . It was a case of history repeating itself, and I had to go through exactly the same procedure." Finally, after a visit to New York to personally discuss the project with Selznick, the loan-out deal was arranged.

Wallis's insistence that Jennifer had always been his one and only choice wasn't true. An actress already on the Paramount lot, Ann Richards, had originally been cast in the role, but Jennifer's availability revised that decision (Richards was assigned "the best friend" role in the film).

If, in fact, Vivien Leigh had been in America (she was living and working in England but was still technically under contract to Selznick), Wallis would undoubtedly have focused on signing her, since "Scarlett's" services were always in demand and the Singleton character was British.

Jennifer was delighted with the role, which offered her a real challenge. In order to portray an amnesiac, "I had to find out what the reactions of such a person would be to new situations, so I talked with a psychiatrist [May Romm, courtesy of David Selznick]. I found it would be as if you were a child. Having had no experience with the bad part of people, you'd be always happy and honest."

Jennifer would have no idle time for many months; immediately after *Love Letters,* she was scheduled to begin *Duel in the Sun,* which Selznick had been working on for almost a year.

Momentarily, to Jennifer's horror, it seemed the Paramount deal was going to be called off. Production was slated to begin on October 23, cutting it perilously close to the February start date for *Duel.* Jennifer needed some breathing space. After further discussions with Wallis, who guaranteed that *Love Letters* would definitely be completed by January 1, Selznick gave the okay.

Selznick was pleased about the *Love Letters* deal. Hal Wallis had produced Bette Davis's greatest successes at Warners and, of course Ingrid's *Casablanca.* He was looking to establish himself as a leading independent and would be certain, in his own best interests, to surround Jennifer with a top-notch production.

Wallis had hired the director suggested by Selznick, the German-born William Dieterle. In his early fifties, Dieterle was a former actor and stage director. He'd worked with Wallis back at Warner Brothers on some of the studio's biggest hits, including *The Story of Louis Pasteur* and *The Life of Emile Zola.* He'd directed Bette Davis and Paul Muni in *Juarez* (and, earlier, Bette in *Satan Met a Lady,* a flop remade successfully by John Huston as *The Maltese Falcon*). Dieterle had recently directed Marlene Dietrich and Ronald Colman in the lavish MGM musical *Kismet* and had just worked for Selznick directing the Dore Schary project *I'll Be Seeing You,* starring Ginger Rogers, Joseph Cotten, and Shirley Temple. Dieterle spoke with a heavy accent and always wore white gloves. He worked fast and had a strong visual style.

Selznick sent Wallis voluminous memos containing instructions regarding Jennifer's makeup, wardrobe, and how she should be photographed. "I think David sometimes forgot that I was producing the picture," recalled Wallis (although Selznick, as part of the deal for lending Jennifer and Joseph Cotten, got a percentage of the gross). "He wanted to see and approve all of Jennifer's costume sketches and called in photographer Lee Garmes, whom he had personally asked me to use, to discuss the lighting of her face."

The two-month shooting schedule on *Love Letters* was welcomed by Jennifer. Here was a film with a beginning, a middle, and an end, with no major rewriting and a completion date that *had* to be adhered to—something Jennifer hadn't yet experienced (her Dick Tracy serial and Republic western excepted).

During filming, according to Hal Wallis, "Selznick called up daily to see how things were going. It was with great difficulty that I dissuaded him from coming onto the set and interfering with William Dieterle's direction."

Under Dieterle's workmanlike hand the picture experienced no problems. "Jennifer was a creative actress," recalled Dieterle. "She came to work prepared, with her characterization carefully thought out. Her instincts were good, and she never argued if she had confidence in you, if she felt you knew what you were doing.

"She wanted to be directed. I'm sure she always conferred with David over how things were going; he was never shy about telling any of us how things should be done, you know. But Hal Wallis was as strong a character as Selznick, and there wasn't any interference from Selznick on this picture."

Chapter
13

*W*allis *kept his word, and Jennifer*
wrapped *Love Letters* on January 1, 1945. She'd already begun preparing mentally and physically to plunge into *Duel in the Sun*—due to
start filming on February 28—when she found her personal world
suddenly on the verge of imminent catastrophe, possibly collapse.

Irene Selznick had announced to an astonished David that their
marriage was over and declared that she wanted him out of their
house. He was nonplussed. The confrontation, according to Mrs.
Selznick, had shocked David into revealing the fact that he was having an affair with Jennifer.

Irene claimed, somewhat improbably, that prior to that moment
she hadn't known anything about it, which confirmed in her mind
just how far apart she and David had grown. Irene felt she should
have suspected and, in earlier years, would have.

According to Irene, David now made *his* choice: he said he'd
drop Jennifer, and, continued Mrs. Selznick's account, he *did* drop
Jennifer "and wanted my sympathy for the hard time Jennifer was
giving him."

With benefit of both hindsight and many years of analysis and
reflection, Mrs. Selznick logically and unemotionally concluded in
her memoir that poor Jennifer "hadn't caused our situation. If it
hadn't been her, it would have been someone else."

Anita Colby, Jennifer's closest friend and confidante during these years, indicates that perhaps Irene Selznick's version of events was not entirely accurate. One is reminded of the classic Japanese drama *Rashomon*, where a violent event, involving several people, is recounted from each one's point of view, and each view is dramatically different.

Colby certainly puts a fascinating spin on events by recounting the explanation Selznick used to offer in commenting on Irene's actions: "She was the one who lost, you've got to understand that."

Certainly for Selznick, on hearing Irene's pronouncement that she wanted him out, the battle horns had sounded. Just as Robert Walker had been unable to accept Jennifer's rejection of him, Selznick was unable to accept Irene's rejection; his reaction to the situation was every bit as irrational as Walker's had been vis-à-vis Jennifer.

Selznick girded up for no-holds-barred family war, his objective to achieve the impossible no matter what the financial and/or emotional cost to all combatants, Jennifer, Irene, and himself included.

From Jennifer's point of view, the dilemma was a nightmare. She had abandoned one ship for another, suddenly to find the captain of the second vessel advising her that *he* was abandoning *their* ship, the one he'd created especially for her!

But she had made her commitment—she'd even gone so far as to display affection for David in public. Joan Fontaine recalls socializing with the couple. "I once saw him kiss Jennifer—I mean, he *inhaled* her face in his mouth—ugh! David was, in all ways, a *smothering* man."

Furthermore, Fontaine rarely observed any joy in Jennifer's demeanor when with Selznick. "I never heard her make a joke. Charming, pleasant, affable [but] . . . not outgoing at all. Never laughing, never [being spontaneous]—sad, actually."

The month of February 1945 was full of surprises for Jennifer Jones. Once again she was nominated for an Oscar, for her performance in *Since You Went Away*. This time, however, it wasn't for Best Actress, but as Best Supporting Actress. Her competition was twenty-year-old Angela Lansbury (for *Gaslight*, Lansbury's first movie); veteran actresses Aline MacMahon (*Dragon Seed*), Agnes Moorehead (*Mrs.*

Parkington), and the legendary Ethel Barrymore (*None but the Lonely Heart*).

Selznick had allocated a hefty advertising budget and mounted a major campaign to win Oscar nominations for both his picture and his contract people. The performances of Jennifer, Claudette Colbert, and Monty Woolley had been heralded daily, during January 1945, in a series of impressive full-page ads in *Daily Variety* and *The Hollywood Reporter;* so were those of other Selznick contractees Ingrid Bergman (for *Gaslight*), Joseph Cotten (for *I'll Be Seeing You*), and Alfred Hitchcock (for *Lifeboat*).

Louella Parsons described *Since You Went Away* as "another great picture like *Gone With the Wind.*" Selznick distributed to academy members a deluxe, forty-page large-format booklet on the picture, containing favorable quotes from every imaginable source.

But the excessive campaign paid off. *Since You Went Away* was nominated for nine Oscars, including Best Picture, and the competition was truly formidable: *Double Indemnity, Gaslight, Going My Way,* and Darryl F. Zanuck's personally produced epic, *Wilson.*

Claudette Colbert, who employed her own influential independent press agent, Henry Rogers, had garnered a Best Actress nod. Ingrid Bergman in *Gaslight*, Bette Davis in *Mr. Skeffington*, Greer Garson in *Mrs. Parkington,* and Barbara Stanwyck in *Double Indemnity* rounded out the glittering category.

Monty Woolley's performance in *Since You Went Away* had won him a Best Supporting Actor nomination. This group, too, was filled with incomparable talents: Hume Cronyn (*The Seventh Cross*), Barry Fitzgerald (*Going My Way*), Claude Rains (*Mr. Skeffington*), and Clifton Webb (*Laura*).

However, Selznick's script was not in contention, nor was director John Cromwell. Other nominations for *Since You Went Away* were in technical categories (Cinematography, Interior Decoration, Musical Score—by Max Steiner, who composed the score for *Gone With the Wind*—Film Editing and Special Effects).

The excitement generated by Jennifer's nomination was hardly a panacea for the stress in her private life, although the Oscar campaign certainly provided ample distraction for David.

April 1945 would mark David and Irene's fifteenth wedding anniversary. Selznick begged Irene not to throw him out before then and she agreed reluctantly. From Selznick's frantic point of view, he had bought time to somehow convince Irene to change her mind.

What he would try to convince Jennifer to do was anybody's guess.

David reasoned, somewhat irrationally, that he could in effect bribe Irene to continue the marriage. As an anniversary gift he planned to present her with a fabulous diamond bracelet from Harry Winston, although Selznick knew that Irene was the last person in the world to respond to a bribe, however well intentioned.

Irene had lost confidence in David's judgment on all levels. She'd been dumbfounded to learn that he was producing a western, his least favorite type of movie but a surefire money-maker. And on the personal front, although she didn't say so, David's faithless performance as a husband devastated her.

Selznick, however, intended to observe no conventional rules, with either Irene or Jennifer, to get what he wanted.

On March 15, virtually a year to the day that she'd won her Best Actress Oscar, Jennifer was back at Grauman's Chinese Theater for the Academy Awards. According to custom, whether or not she won this evening, as last year's winner she'd be presenting an Oscar to this year's Best Actress.

Wearing her hair in a sophisticated upsweep, and clad in a dressy tailored suit, Jennifer attended the festivities with Ingrid Bergman (who wore the same dress she'd worn last year).

Going My Way won many of the major awards, and Jennifer lost Best Supporting Actress to Ethel Barrymore.

Bob Hope, cohosting the ceremonies with director John Cromwell, finally introduced Jennifer to present Best Actress. Jones received an outstanding ovation from the audience and, trembling, stepped up to the microphone. She read the list of nominees and tore open the envelope, and a smile lit up her face: "Ingrid Bergman, for *Gaslight!*"

There was thunderous applause as Bergman came up on stage to accept the award. Jennifer, handing it to her, said emotionally: "Your artistry has won our vote, and your graciousness has won our hearts."

Bergman was due to begin what would become one of the biggest hits of her career, *The Bells of St. Mary's,* in which she'd portray a nun. Two of tonight's big winners, Bing Crosby (Best Actor) and Barry Fitzgerald (Best Supporting Actor), would be her costars. And Best Director winner Leo McCarey would be their director.

"Tomorrow I go to work in a picture with Bing and Mr. Mc-Carey," said Bergman, "and I'm afraid if I didn't have an Oscar, too, they wouldn't speak to me."

Laughter and applause greeted her remarks. Ingrid and Jennifer waved to the throng and bowed off. Neither woman could have guessed that portraying a nun would have far greater repercussions for Ingrid, regarding her image, than playing a saint had had for Jennifer.

In most photographs taken at the ceremonies, Jennifer looked morose. The problems in her personal life were definitely taking their toll.

The Duel in the Sun company embarked on a costly Arizona location trip. The director, fifty-year-old King Vidor, was one of the giants of the industry. His impressive body of work reflected a strong social conscience, a romantic sensibility, and an exciting visual flair. He'd directed the epic silent film of World War I, *The Big Parade;* as well as *The Crowd* and the first all-black film, *Hallelujah. The Champ* was a Vidor classic of the thirties, along with *Bird of Paradise* (produced under Selznick's regime at RKO), *Cynara,* and *Stella Dallas.*

By the time of *Duel,* however, he hadn't had a hit in several years. But Selznick knew that Vidor had the "epic feel," combined with the ability to tell an intimate story, necessary to make *Duel in the Sun* come to life.

The picture boldly cast both Jennifer and Gregory Peck against type. "Everybody felt Jennifer could never make the transition," recalled Anita Colby. "Even the secretaries and workmen around the studio visited the set the day she tested, never believing she could do it."

Gregory Peck, fresh from a triumph portraying Father Chisholm in *The Keys of the Kingdom,* was in this film playing, in his words, "a rapist, a forger, a killer, a liar, a thoroughly rotten no-good, but with a certain likability. I played a very bad boy, and I played the part for fun."

Jennifer was playing a very "bad" girl, but she was hardly playing the part "for fun."

"It will be quite a sight to see the erstwhile Father Chisholm leering at the onetime Saint Bernadette," observed one columnist, setting the stage for the controversy to come, the brunt of which would be Jennifer's and Selznick's to bear.

Vidor and the principals arrived to begin the picture on March 4. Jennifer rejoined them after the Academy Awards. The large crew consisted of 150 men. There were tons of props, truckloads of equipment, a windmill, a two-story prefabricated ranch house, and two barns. The location was forty miles east of Tucson.

Selznick, with the enthusiasm of a fanatic bringing to life his deepest fantasies, had worked compulsively on the script, and there'd be no self-effacing, sentimental "Jeffrey Daniel" or "By the Producer" script credit this time—the on-screen title card was to read "Script by David O. Selznick, adaptation by Oliver H. P. Garrett." (Garrett was one of many writers who'd worked with Selznick on the script of *Gone With the Wind.*) The men had completely refashioned the original material. The overriding theme of the new script was lust. A melodramatic ending for the story had been conceived by Selznick, "a perfectly magnificent finish that can be played superbly by Ms. Jones," noted the producer.

If other studios were exploring (and exploiting) the dark side of human nature with productions in the genre soon to be known as film noir—*Double Indemnity, Mildred Pierce,* and *The Postman Always Rings Twice,* to name a few—Selznick would be the first to produce a western noir.

One of the settings for the film's sexual action was a swimming hole, known in the story as "the sump." Anita Colby recalls that Alfred Hitchcock liked to refer to *Duel in the Sun* as "Hump in the Sump." Comedians of the day referred to it as "Lust in the Dust."

The censorship problems inherent in the story concerned Selznick but didn't deter him. But during production, to protect himself, he consulted with the Breen Office (formerly the Hays Office), the industry's self-censorship agency, on many occasions. Before the film was ready for release, he made a number of changes suggested by production code chief Joseph I. Breen.

Since the film's script obviously reflected Selznick's state of mind, the mind boggles. If the freedom of expression that exists in movies today had existed then, would Jennifer Jones have starred in the first multimillion-dollar, platinum-edged porn film? As it was, the script abounded with suggestive scenes, calling for Jennifer to display herself accordingly. Anita Colby had to arrange for a special brassiere to accentuate (within the limits of both the production code and the outer limits of Jennifer's sensibilities) the actress's natural assets.

Selznick was even more autocratic and quick-tempered behind the scenes than usual. He was determined to make *Duel in the Sun* both his crowning achievement and a high-water mark in Jennifer's career—"Pearl Chavez" would be the Scarlett O'Hara of the Old West. But the Selznick "luck" was turning sour.

Out on the vast Arizona desert, the huge company was assailed by problems. The one element over which David Selznick exercised no control—the weather—betrayed him. Temperatures on location fell to twenty-five degrees, and there were furious winds of frostbite intensity. (Later, when complimented on how cold and blue she looked in these scenes and how believable her acting was, Jennifer replied: "I *was* cold and blue. It was no feat of acting.")

Conditions often forced the company indoors.

Jennifer's sons, accompanied by their nurse, were on location with her for part of the shoot as was Anita Colby. "Before beginning *Duel*," she says, "Jennifer spent weeks studying how to walk like the Indian girl, until she got it down to perfection. She took dancing lessons to prepare for the dance she'd have to do in the picture, and voice lessons to acquire that low-pitched, sexy voice she used. She worked hours on end every day to perfect every motion, mannerism, and inflection she could possibly need. This was work of a kind that never stopped. Nights, days, weekends, she studied. . . . All this for *one* role, mind you.

"Jennifer was *very* serious about her work, had an enormous capacity for it . . . and was never satisfied with anything she did. In preparing for her roles, she was amazingly thorough."

As far as Jennifer was concerned, one could never be *too* thorough—acting was "like practicing the piano. If you keep on doing all the exercises they tell you to, you eventually develop to the point where you can play the things you want to."

Colby also recognized Jennifer as a publicist's nightmare. "Because she's reluctant to talk about herself and refuses to exaggerate for the sake of good copy, she's the despair of publicity people," noted Colby, whose job was to create and coordinate publicity on the star. But Colby liked her. "One thing about Jennifer that you can say about few women [is that] she's very closemouthed, and you can absolutely trust her with any confidence. She'll never betray it."

Jennifer looked up to Colby. She was the kind of gregarious, funny, chic, socially adept woman that Jennifer, at that time, was not. Colby was a trailblazer in the movie industry, virtually the only woman (other than producer Virginia Van Upp at Columbia Pictures) functioning in an important executive position. She also dated Clark Gable, then forty-four years old, who proposed marriage. She turned him down, though, explaining enigmatically today that "he was a little too rough for me." (According to Gable's friends, after Carole Lombard, Anita Colby and socialite Dolly O'Brien were the two great loves of Gable's life.)

Another woman in Jennifer's position might have found Colby an intimidating role model. "Jennifer knew she hadn't the sophistication; she was like a younger sister to me," explained Colby, who observed how the actress tried "very hard to acquire everything she felt she lacked." Colby would tell Jennifer stories about her "pals," people like Ernest Hemingway and Quentin Reynolds, and Jennifer listened "wide-eyed." And when, in New York with Colby, Jennifer met those people at parties, "she simply hung on every word they said."

Jennifer was "very naive in a way," observed Colby, "and yet in many ways she had wisdom beyond her years."

Colby's thinking cap was on regarding Jennifer's publicity. She devised a coup that created a modus operandi for PR movers and shakers of later generations.

"I took Jennifer on location to be photographed by a former *Life* photographer I'd hired who was working freelance," recalls Colby. "We got out to the location, the photographer was ready to shoot, and I simply told Jennifer, 'Act!' She acted all over the place, and was absolutely ravishing. The pictures were then given to *Life, Look,* and the rest of the major magazines, and they ran the pictures we had taken." Colby had hired the former *Life* man "because he was one of their own, you see, and we couldn't see how they could refuse to use the shots, and they didn't, and it was a little picnic that I had dreamed up! We controlled the whole thing, which was the first time that had ever been done."

On the set of *Duel in the Sun* it required a lot more from King Vidor than simply telling Jennifer to "act" to draw the performance out of her. According to Vidor, Jennifer was tackling a role that was totally the opposite of her real self, and Vidor's observations reveal a great deal of who the real Jennifer was.

Jennifer's character, Pearl Chavez, "was a half-degenerate half-breed, dominated by her physical emotions, and Jennifer wasn't like that at all," stated Vidor, who also recalled: "It was a big struggle for her to play that."

Having directed silent films, Vidor appreciated the fact that Jennifer had "a very expressive face, and it signifies her thoughts." But "in order to get her in the character of the girl . . . we would start the day by talking about the story and the characters and the action coming up. She would fix those luminous, intelligent eyes on my face. I could see her gradually becoming Pearl Chavez. Jennifer would disappear as completely as if she had never existed."

This went on every day, and every day "I had to tell her the story . . . up to the part we were at in the script to get her in the mood."

It was the same way that George Cukor had directed Ingrid Bergman in *Gaslight.* Cukor recalled, "I wanted to try to keep up the intensity between takes, so I'd retell Ingrid the story, the emotional point the scene was leading up to. Finally she looked at me very politely and said, 'I'm not a dumb Swede, you've told me that before.' So I apologized and stopped."

But after a few days Arthur Hornblow, the producer, told Cukor that Ingrid and others in the cast seemed to be acting as though they were underwater. "I knew this was true," recalled Cukor, "so I started talking to Ingrid just the way I'd done before, keeping up the pitch, retelling everything, and after a while she began to like it. It worked."

In Jennifer's case Vidor observed that she was like "a young girl you're telling a fairy story to . . . then she becomes that to the best of her ability." Vidor would "tell her how to feel in these situations, and that's the way she wanted to be directed—she wanted to be told the whole story and the whole character. . . . She's like putty in your hands."

However, "Trying to maintain it through the lunch hour was too much," he recalled. "Conversation with me and others always snapped the string. And when we went back to work we'd have to start telling her the story all over again."

Jennifer herself explained how she tackled a role: "I sort of hypnotize myself. I find myself really living the roles I play. I've read about the East Indian fakirs and mystics who are able to throw themselves into a trance, and I think that my own mental state is something like a trance when I'm acting. If anything else, any outside thought or impulse, disturbs the spell by intruding into my consciousness, I have to break off and start all over again."

That's obviously why Jennifer required solitude between setups, why she didn't hang around the set or fraternize with the crew. Her role monopolized her time and her thoughts. The ability to concentrate intently was—and is—an essential for effective screen acting. "Jennifer has terrific drive and concentration when she's working," says Anita Colby. "Her mind is absolutely one-track."

While working on *Duel* (and all her other pictures), Jennifer had a full-time personal maid to attend to her needs as well as a secretary, a car, and a chauffeur on call at all times. She was an avid believer in exercise (it wasn't unusual to encounter her outside her dressing room on the Selznick lot jumping rope or doing cartwheels), and, following through on her fascination with fakirs and mystics, she was learning to practice yoga. Noted for its physical and mental discipline, yoga offers detailed directions for suppressing bodily activity, including breathing. Mental activity is also suppressed until the individual falls into a state of blissful, serene contemplation. Jennifer said she practiced this system for its physical benefits and to relax (she quickly mastered the feat of standing on her head). She expressed interest in one day traveling to India to meditate.

To paraphrase Orson Welles discussing <u>Citizen Kane</u> (Welles, a pal of Selznick's, would speak the voice-over narration for *Duel in the Sun*), *Duel* was David's ultimately wildly out-of-control electric train set.

Selznick was constantly dissatisfied with everything, from the script to Vidor's direction. He frequently rewrote scenes that had been satisfactorily filmed, insisting Vidor shoot the new versions. In most cases the changes were extremely minor. "Is this the scene where I was sitting on the couch with my hand on the back cushion?" Joseph Cotten asked one day. "In the rewrite, my hand is resting on the side cushion."

The producer was on the set virtually all the time and issued strict orders that nothing be filmed "until I was telephoned to come down on the set, to check the lighting, the setup, and the rehearsal. . . ."

Vidor resented the interference but said he understood it—this was Selznick's movie and Selznick's money.

Although gambling was illegal in Tucson, Selznick informed his chief executive Dan O'Shea, "You can always find a gambling spot in every town." Sure enough, one was located. Along with Gregory Peck and his wife, Greta, and Joseph Cotten and his wife, Lenore, and others from the company—Jennifer elected not to go—the Selznick limousine descended on an old wooden roadhouse on the outskirts of town.

There was a roulette wheel on the premises, and a delighted Selznick was in his element. The squalid condition of the establishment didn't deter him. "It's not exactly the Clover Club, but what's the difference?" he said, laughing.

While Peck and Cotten gambled with dollar bills, lost consistently, then dropped out, David played with ten-dollar bills and began winning big. At one point the house owed him $13,000.

He downed one whiskey after another as his number kept coming up. Selznick's friends were fascinated at first, then became bored and embarrassed at the ill fortune faced by the proprietor of the establishment.

As the hour grew very late, Selznick's luck turned and he began losing. Soon his winnings were gone, and he played using IOUs. At dawn Dan O'Shea implored him to call it quits, and after one more losing turn of the wheel, Selznick was ready to leave.

"What do I owe you?" he asked the manager.

"Thirty thousand," he replied.

"Okay. But first I want to see all the moving parts [of the roulette wheel]."

O'Shea was incredulous. "David, you can't do that!"

Selznick insisted—he'd pay, he said, "But first I want to inspect the mechanism."

The manager complied.

"Okay," Selznick told O'Shea, "pay him."

The *"perfectly magnificent finish"* for <u>Duel in the Sun</u> that Selznick had dreamed up for Jennifer and Peck—in which they literally shoot each other down—was the climactic "duel in the sun." As Lewt lies dying, the mortally wounded Pearl crawls over rocky terrain, dragging herself frantically to his side, to be with him when he—and then she—dies.

Jennifer had refused to wear any padding to protect her limbs, which were often bleeding after a day's work on the seemingly end-less sequence, since Selznick was never satisfied with the results.

British director Michael Powell and his partner, Emeric Press-burger, friends of Alfred Hitchcock's (later to become friends of Jennifer's and David's), were shown the rushes on two completed se-quences, and Selznick asked their opinions.

"He was obviously very proud of the picture, and rightly so," said Powell, recalling Jennifer "crawling up the mountain with a rifle to fight it out with her love. David showed us hundreds of feet showing the poor girl crawling on hands and knees up the most horrible rocky path, dragging a rifle, her hands and knees torn and bleed-ing. David didn't actually smack his lips over the power he had over this beautiful girl, tearing herself to pieces for the sake of her, shall we say, art? He was too interested in our reactions. I ventured the opinion that she had guts. He nodded with pashalike detachment toward the screen, and murmured: 'Yeah . . . she sure took a beat-ing that day.' "

It was Selznick's fifteenth wedding anniversary. The occasion was celebrated with a party at the Selznick mansion on Summit Drive. Irene wore the exquisite half-inch-wide diamond bracelet that David had given her. But if she'd changed her plans about separating from David, she didn't say so. He simply assumed that she'd finally come around, and that things thing would soon return to the way they were.

However, Selznick's suitcases were all packed and waiting for him in the front hall of the Summit Drive abode shortly afterward. "Irene threw me out," he told Sam and Frances Goldwyn when he encountered them that evening at Romanoff's restaurant. The for-lorn genius became the Goldwyns' houseguest and poured his heart out to the sympathetic Frances, who was Irene's close friend. "Every-thing will work out," Frances assured him.

Meanwhile it was business as usual back on the set. The contro-versial and crucial rape sequence was being shot. Both Jennifer and Gregory Peck responded enthusiastically to Vidor's direction (to bring Lewt's character into focus for Peck, Vidor had instructed him to think of Sportin' Life in *Porgy and Bess*).

Jennifer's and Peck's uninhibited acting was bolder than any-thing major stars had yet attempted on film. Even Selznick was aroused—Vidor later swore that he could hear David "panting in the background." But were 1940s audiences ready for such frankness? David was certain they were, since *he* most certainly was.

Michael Powell had asked Selznick about Peck's availability to work in England, and Selznick had replied: "Oh, he's all cut up." Powell didn't understand the phrase until it was explained that "young Peck had been signed to a twenty-picture contract by Selznick, and each segment of him, like slices of a pie, had been traded with other studios and producers, and with leading ladies ravenous for a new leading man. There was a ruthless cold-bloodedness about the operation."

Only Jennifer's contract wasn't "all cut up."

As an industrywide union strike closed down production at all studios on April 18, Selznick invited Dore Schary and Dan O'Shea to attend a very private 9:00 P.M. screening, in his Culver City studios private projection room, of a rough cut of *Duel in the Sun.*

"We saw a rattling good western," recalled Schary. Selznick bombarded them with questions, and both Schary and O'Shea were able to reply honestly to David that they "liked the picture" even though they thought it was "a bit too long" and "did not believe there was anything truly wrong with the film." Other than judicious editing and the addition of an exciting musical score, Schary and O'Shea "both believed it would be a smashing success."

Selznick was angry. "It needs a hell of a lot of work," he replied. "I want to do a new opening, giving the audience Jennifer's early story and her relationship with her father. It needs big scenes . . . a train wreck . . . confrontations . . . action . . ."

Too much could hurt the film, countered Schary. But Selznick's theory about picture making, as Schary and everyone else very well knew, was to "make them big—surprise the audience—tell them all they wanted to know—and more."

The arguments continued. Then, according to Schary, "David plopped down on the couch like a deflated life raft. 'I know that when I die, the obituaries will begin, "David O. Selznick, producer of *Gone With the Wind,* died today," and I'm trying like hell to rewrite them.' "

It was 3:30 A.M. when the meeting broke up.

During the long strike, which stretched to eight weeks, Selznick expanded the *Duel* script, adding longer and more elaborate scenes. He'd signed high-priced character actors like Walter Huston, Otto Kruger, and Harry Carey to portray small roles. As it stood, the costs on *Duel* threatened to make it one of the most expensive movies ever made ($4 million was the projected final figure).

Selznick's libido, his obsession with Jennifer and *Duel* notwithstanding, was in full throttle. Seventeen-year-old Shirley Temple had become engaged to be married, and Selznick was poised to direct an elaborate publicity campaign exploiting the happy occasion. Temple had a meeting with boss Selznick in his office when, she recalled, he "eased his shoes off and rested both feet on his desk." Stocking feet, preamble to a wild pass! He chased her around the office. Temple recalled his threat—"If you hold out, you could get loaned out!"

But Temple was too valuable a property to alienate, and she was too show business savvy to appear too upset. She joked her way out of it, and the "meeting" ended with an exhausted Selznick retreating to his desk and Shirley quickly exiting the office.

Did Jennifer know about such goings-on? Since he'd deceived Irene about Jennifer, it's reasonable to assume his tactics hadn't changed. Even if someone had alerted Jennifer to what transpired in David's inner sanctum, there wasn't much, if anything, she could do about it. As long as his indiscretions remained discreet, there was hardly any recourse but to look the other way. ("Sometimes I feel an evil star hangs over my house," she told a fan magazine reporter.)

Jennifer resumed her nurses' aide activities at a Veterans Hospital in Los Angeles. She and Ingrid Bergman palled around, the two actresses commiserating on the unending personal dilemma they faced: career versus motherhood. Both felt guilty about time they weren't able to spend with their children, yet both continued to work at full throttle.

The actresses watched old movies together in the screening room at the Selznick studio, encouraged by David to do so—one learned by watching the best. Garbo was the women's favorite, and Jennifer was Ingrid's biggest fan. "She can take any part and make it positively shining," observed Jones.

One critic had compared Jones and Bergman and wondered:

"Is Jennifer trying to be another Ingrid?" Jennifer had no illusions about her own abilities and no problem confronting a reality: "I consider myself a character actress already," she said. "You don't have to go through the time glamour girls do, when after your youth is gone, you have to spend years reeducating the public to accept you as an actress."

To Selznick, Jennifer was a great actress and under no circumstances was she a "character actress."

On May 7, 1945, the war finally ended in Europe after over five years of "the bloodiest conflict in history." Germany surrendered unconditionally to the Western Allies and the Soviet Union, with the surrender taking place at a little red schoolhouse in Reims, France, where General Dwight D. Eisenhower made his headquarters. Allied Forces, however, were still battling the Japanese in Asia.

On the home front American audiences were flocking in greater numbers than ever to the latest movies. Robert Walker received plaudits for his performance in *The Clock*. It opened in May and further elevated the actor's stature in the film community, being both a critical and commercial success.

The film was given a special premiere in Ogden, and Walker, of course, appeared in his hometown for the event. He adroitly managed to avoid any comment about his personal life and especially Jennifer. If the studio had hoped this jaunt would lift Walker's spirits, it didn't. In private he continued bitterly to voice his hatred of David Selznick.

Louis B. Mayer had taken a personal interest in Robert Walker. Katharine Hepburn later said that Mayer understood Walker's "torment" and the fact that Walker "had trouble with the drink. This isn't a voluntary thing, and it damn well isn't a thing that people can just stop," commented Hepburn. "You might be able to stop it. I might be able to stop it, but maybe others can't. It isn't always that easy. . . ."

Walker had recently gotten friendly with fellow MGM contractee Peter Lawford. Lawford, twenty-one years old, was six years Walker's junior, but the handsome British-born actor was easily two decades ahead of him in terms of sophistication, and his extraordinary good looks had opened all of Hollywood's golden doors. (A deformed right hand, which he deftly concealed by thrusting it deep into the pocket of his slacks or by holding a jacket, was the only flaw in an otherwise striking physical package.)

Lawford and Walker soon became "best friends," states Lawford's young widow, Patricia. Lawford, like Jim Henaghan, was comfortable navigating Hollywood's fast lane. "The beach, sex, and booze," even then, were Lawford's main interests in life.

Walker had just completed production on *Her Highness and the Bellboy,* in which he starred with Hedy Lamarr, "the most beautiful woman in films," and MGM's latest fast-rising girl next door, June Allyson.

It was the petite "Junie," aware of Walker's melancholy disposition, who worked to keep him from becoming depressed during the tedious grind of filmmaking (they made one other film together, *The Sailor Takes a Wife*).

Bob's friends meanwhile tried to fix him up on dates. "Big Jim" Henaghan set him up with nineteen-year-old actress Diana Lynn, but he scared her off with his explosive temper. A starlet named Shirley O'Hara and a voluptuous young actress named Marie Windsor were others. Ms. Windsor later commented on Walker's moodiness and his drinking, recalling how he once passed out cold, and on the fact that Jim Henaghan "was always with us."

Henaghan himself later laughed at some of the talk he knew was circulating around town—that he and Walker were lovers, since they were never apart. But the only great love the two men shared was booze.

The day that both Jennifer and Walker had been dreading finally arrived. On June 20 an anxious Jennifer (Walker wasn't present) arrived in Los Angeles Superior Court to obtain a divorce. She testified on the nature of Walker's "mental cruelty."

"What did he do that was cruel?" asked Judge Charles E. Haas.

"He was very difficult and very sarcastic."

"You can't get a divorce on that," observed the judge.

"He wanted me to go into radio work, against my wishes and the advice of my manager, and he wanted—"

"That's not cruel," declared the judge, an edge to his voice.

Jennifer wasn't anxious to relay further details.

"Did he stay out all night?" asked Judge Haas.

"Yes," answered Jennifer, her voice trembling. She admitted that before they'd separated, Bob had stayed out "sometimes all night" and had caused her "great nervousness and worry."

"Do you know if he was working?" asked the judge.

"No, I don't know. He didn't tell me."

"Now we're getting somewhere," Judge Haas informed her. "That is grounds for divorce."

The details had been worked out. The couple would share joint custody of the boys, who'd continue to live with Jennifer. There'd be no alimony or property settlement. Walker's salary, according to testimony, was $100,000 a year. "Mr. Walker has been most generous in his care of the children," Jennifer said.

When her testimony was concluded, Jennifer's lawyer swiftly rushed her through a rear door and into a waiting limousine.

Walker didn't waste any time after the divorce. A romance with an ambitious twenty-five-year-old socialite-model-divorcée, Florence Pritchett, seemed to be heading in a serious direction, at least as far as Ms. Pritchett was concerned. She was a writer and fashion consultant, an aspiring Anita Colby, it would seem, and the couple's romance got plenty of publicity. Jennifer certainly read about it, since all the stories mentioned Jennifer's name and played on the same theme: "Has beautiful Florence Pritchett managed to douse the torch Bob Walker has been carrying for ex-wife Jennifer Jones?"

But Jennifer had *Duel in the Sun* to divert her. The industry strike ended on June 24, and filming resumed. Selznick had added a monumental train wreck sequence, where Lewt observes the wreckage and merrily sings "I've Been Workin' on the Railroad."

"At that moment," recalled Gregory Peck, explaining how he played the scene, "I just kind of imitated a cousin of mine who was a bit of a rascal, a black sheep in the family, but likable."

When King Vidor pleaded with Selznick to remove the scene, feeling it destroyed what little sympathy the audience had felt for Peck's character, Selznick refused. "I want to make Lewt the worst son of a bitch that's ever been seen on a motion picture screen, and I believe the train wreck scene will prove my point." The sequence remained.

Selznick had begun to advertise the far-from-completed epic almost daily in the trade papers. He believed he was laying the foundation for the film's acceptance as an even greater accomplishment than *Gone With the Wind.*

Frank Capra was quoted as saying, "*Duel in the Sun* is thrilling. It is as good as or better than *Gone With the Wind.*"

"All I can say is that the heat of *Duel in the Sun* will burn up all memories of *Gone With the Wind,*" was Mervyn LeRoy's contribution.

Billy Wilder, hard at work on his own film, *The Lost Weekend,* took a cue from Selznick and placed his own ad: "*Double Indemnity* is the greatest picture I have ever seen. . . ." The quote was signed "George Oblath." Oblath was the owner of a small Hollywood restaurant. Hollywood laughed, but Selznick was infuriated and threatened to cancel the expensive *Duel* ads if the trades accepted any further material ridiculing his picture.

Costs on the film continued to pile up like logs at the mouth of a stream. To act as a special visual consultant, Selznick had signed Josef von Sternberg, the legendary director of Marlene Dietrich's Paramount films, whose once stellar career was less than active as of late. Von Sternberg later said that none of his work appeared in the picture (in fact over four hundred feet of film was his). The dramatically lit close-ups of Jennifer certainly presented a breathtakingly beautiful image of the actress, and the photography throughout the entire picture was outstanding.

Anita Colby recalls that she'd made a suggestion to von Sternberg. She'd seen the innovative British film *Black Narcissus,* directed by Michael Powell and starring Deborah Kerr, which had made fantastic use of Technicolor. Colby had met the film's producer, J. Arthur Rank, and Rank told her (and Colby told von Sternberg) that the reason the color photography was so stunning was that "it was wartime, we didn't have the electricity to use the amount of artificial light we would have liked to use, so we had to experiment without using the required amount of light."

"The results were so dramatic," recalls Colby, "that we applied that principle to *Duel,* and it really changed the look of the whole movie."

• • •

For David Selznick and King Vidor, the presence of down-on-his-luck von Sternberg notwithstanding, the fragile, fleeting nature of Hollywood fame and fortune really hit home with a wallop when "the Greatest Director of Them All," D. W. Griffith, visited the set of *Duel in the Sun* on July 15. (There was a sequence in *Duel* that was Selznick's "homage" to Griffith, "the gathering of the clans," which involved over one thousand extras.)

In 1915 Griffith's *Birth of a Nation* had been the *Gone With the Wind* of its day, an even bigger and more explosive sensation because there'd been absolutely nothing like it before. In *Nation* Griffith had literally invented the basis for modern moviemaking techniques; now, thirty years later, he was without funds and without employment.

Posing with Selznick for a publicity photograph, Griffith looked dour indeed. The younger producer, for once, wore a serious and thoughtful expression, not the usual bright, toothy smile.

Lillian Gish was Griffith's greatest star discovery, and Selznick had lured her out of screen retirement for a small role in *Duel.* Now in her forties, Gish was portraying the long-suffering wife of cattle baron Lionel Barrymore and the mother of Gregory Peck and Joseph Cotten.

Gish and Barrymore were both working on the day Griffith paid his visit. It wasn't a joyful reunion. The presence of the former master made them nervous, and the veteran stars kept messing up their lines. Griffith understood and said his good-byes.

Jennifer was fascinated by Lillian Gish, the screen's quintessential "waif." "She told me about the silent days in pictures, when you had to depend on pantomime entirely to get over scenes," said Jennifer. "After all, there are just so many things you can do with your face! Lillian told me that she began going to insane asylums to see how people reacted there, and in *The White Sister* she borrowed some of those crazy looks and expressions for the scene where she heard that her lover had died."

Jennifer paid close attention to what Gish had to say. Improving on acting technique, and searching for new ways to plumb the depths of her art, was what Jennifer's life was all about.

• • •

On August 6, 1945, the first atomic bomb was dropped on the Japanese city of Hiroshima. No one had ever heard of an "atom bomb," a devastating new weapon equivalent to twenty-thousand tons of TNT. "By God's mercy we beat the Nazis to the bomb," noted British prime minister Winston Churchill, as President Harry S. Truman extolled the virtues of the introduction of the atomic age.

On August 9 the Japanese city of Nagasaki was obliterated by a second atomic bomb, and six days later, on August 14, Japan surrendered unconditionally. The world was momentarily at peace.

In the interim, on August 10, David Selznick lost his own war with King Vidor, an event that, in Hollywood's corridors of power, received as much attention as V-J Day. Increasingly at odds with Vidor throughout the picture, Selznick had allowed his violent temper to erupt once too often. He accused the veteran director of dragging his feet on a location scene. According to Vidor, the Technicolor cameras hadn't even arrived yet, but Selznick would accept no explanations.

He literally screamed and kicked the ground as he yelled at Vidor in front of the entire company. "I had warned him never to do this," said Vidor, who wore a small megaphone around his neck. "I took it off and just handed it to him, and I said, 'You've been wanting to direct for a long time, I'm sure, here's your chance.' " This time Selznick "had gone just too far," recalled Vidor. He told the producer he could "take the picture and shove it," marched over to his waiting limousine, and drove off.

The company stared in silence as the automobile drove down the long desert road and finally disappeared over a hill.

Everyone turned to look at Selznick. "Well," he said matter-of-factly, "that's all for today." He asked an assistant director to dismiss the company.

Selznick's version of events was, of course, completely different. All points of view would be closely examined by union arbitrators when it came time to settle a "dispute" between Vidor and Selznick over Vidor's proper production and direction credit on the film.

(Michael Powell has offered a fascinating observation on David Selznick: "He never had the guts to direct a picture himself. He shunned the responsibility. He preferred to spend hours and days of his life dictating memos telling other people how to direct films. This made him a rather pathetic figure.")

In any event, Vidor was off the picture. Selznick reacted swiftly, bringing in second-unit directors to complete the remaining scenes. Jennifer felt less anxious when Selznick hired William Dieterle, director of *Love Letters,* to shoot the new beginning of the film, which the producer had written to detail Jennifer's character's background. Dieterle also directed other new Jennifer scenes that Selznick had added to the picture.

But another disaster was waiting in the wings. On Friday, August 24, to David's dismay and anger, Irene Selznick dropped her own bombshell. Selznick's pleas to Irene, back on their anniversary, to delay a final decision on their split-up had been so urgent—so heartfelt and pathetic—that to assuage David's shattered feelings, Irene agreed to withhold public announcement of her plans until August.

Louella Parsons ran the exclusive in the *Los Angeles Examiner*: SELZNICKS, WED 15 YEARS, PART. The story had a galvanizing effect on all concerned.

Jennifer was highly agitated by the news and surely nonplussed at reading David's statement to Louella: "I can't think our separation is final. We have been married so many years, and I consider Irene the most brilliant and beautiful woman I know. We haven't discussed divorce, but maybe the separation will clear the air. It was all my fault. I'm difficult. Irene has taken a lot of my temperament."

There was not a word in the column linking Selznick to Jennifer, simply the innuendo resulting from the mention of Jennifer's name, along with those of his other female stars, buried deep in the piece.

The Selznicks' friends were shocked at the news, according to Louella, although the reporter coyly pointed out that "rumors have been fast and furious the last few years that all was not well." Louella noted that the couple's sons, Jeffrey, thirteen, and Danny, eleven, were with their mother, and Irene was quoted as saying that she and David "haven't been getting along, and under those conditions the only thing to do was separate." Irene added, "Neither of us plans to get a divorce."

Louella offered her own opinion: "I had thought their difficulty, which seemed much more serious a few years ago, had been ironed out." Her source for that observation was very obviously her friend David himself.

When Robert Walker heard the news of the Selznicks' official separation he disappeared for four days, presenting Louella with the opportunity to run yet another juicy exclusive. Walker's vanishing act became the talk of the town, and speculation ran wild. The possibility that the actor had committed suicide was openly discussed.

Jennifer, deep in the protective cocoon of production on *Duel in the Sun,* was not reached by a single reporter for comment.

Love Letters was previewed in Pasadena. "David bought up the entire popcorn concession so that people wouldn't make noise or be distracted while gazing at his adored Jennifer," recalled Hal Wallis. "David, however, sat with a small flashlight, dictating notes to his secretary, to the total distraction of those seated in front of and behind him. He then went home and dictated an eight-page memorandum to me with suggestions for changes, as if I were one of his own employees. I read it with interest, and I believe I even adopted one or two of his ideas. But I suspect I was more influenced by the reaction of the public than by the husband [sic] of the star of my picture." (Jennifer and David *weren't,* at this point, married.)

The film opened throughout the country to mixed reviews, but the public liked the movie and business was big. The ad campaign highlighted the intensely romantic nature of the story. Jennifer's beautiful face was the centerpiece of the artwork, locked in an embrace with Joseph Cotten as her huge dark eyes gazed out soulfully at the camera.

When Robert Walker, finally reappeared at work, he was completely indifferent to an angry studio reprimand and acted as though nothing had happened.

His relationship with Florence Pritchett ended abruptly when she accused him of having an affair with another woman. When Jim Henaghan expressed his concern over his buddy's disappearance, Walker confided, "We both know I'm a little crazy."

Reluctantly he was living up to his MGM contract but complaining loudly all the way. He loathed the completed *What Next, Corporal Hargrove?,* the sequel to his hit film that was inferior to the original in all departments.

Powerful studio executives like Ben Thau and Eddie Mannix viewed Walker as a troublemaker and a problem. They knew the actor would have welcomed termination of his contract. But L. B.

Mayer, who claimed he "understood" Walker (Judy Garland was another of those he "understood"), had no intention of throwing Bob out onto the street.

With Irene Selznick out of the picture, virtually no one was left to "control" the volatile David—*all* barriers were down. ("The only way to stop an elephant on the rampage is to shoot it," observed a bemused Robert Benchley.) David erased thoughts of his personal life by totally submerging himself in *Duel in the Sun* and by heatedly pursuing his other favorite obsession: gambling.

Jean Howard Feldman and her husband, Charles Feldman, were two of Selznick's favorite high-stakes gambling cronies. The glamorous Jean adored playing cards and roulette with the high-spirited Selznick, and every weekend they'd be off to a little-known desert city called Las Vegas. (Gangster Benjamin "Bugsy" Siegel was working hard at launching Vegas as a gambling mecca. Financing for his dream, in addition to his own sources, was coming from two Selznick pals, millionaire actress Marion Davies and Countess Dorothy di Frasso.)

Often there were Vegas poker games that lasted the entire weekend. Said Dore Schary, "Selznick was a careless card and roulette player. It was a ruinous course that cost him millions."

Jennifer was not interested in accompanying David on these high-rolling jaunts. "Sometimes I have to be alone, all alone, and I never know how long these moods will last," she said. "The need for [being alone] is hard for other people to understand, I guess. But I think it's important to understand that some people require more of it than others."

In the fall, still in production on *Duel,* Selznick set in motion unprecedented plans to create public interest in the film. A great believer in audience research (George Gallup was one of his good friends), David had commissioned a special survey to determine the public's awareness of the production. The results were highly disappointing.

With *Gone With the Wind,* Selznick had had to prevent publicity from saturating the media in order to sustain the incredible level of interest that had been created by the novel. The opposite was true of *Duel,* and therefore the producer decided he'd have to spend millions to properly advertise and promote the property in advance.

Paul MacNamara (a former managing editor of *Cosmopolitan* magazine) was Selznick's executive in charge of advertising and publicity. Under his supervision, a lavish full-color double-truck (two-page) ad was prepared to run in the Sunday roto sections of major newspapers throughout the country. It featured paintings of a dark-skinned Jennifer "as 'Pearl Chavez.' Built by the devil . . . to drive men crazy."

Gregory Peck smirked provocatively as " 'Lewt McCanles'—violent as the windswept prairie." Joseph Cotten was the "good" brother, and Lionel Barrymore, Herbert Marshall, Lillian Gish, and Walter Huston rounded out the actors featured as part of the "all-star" cast.

Jennifer had been working for weeks on perfecting the provocative dance she was to perform for the scene in which Pearl seduces Lewt. Jennifer was coached for the performance by Tilly Losch, the highly regarded Viennese-born dancer portraying Jennifer's mother at the start of the picture (Losch had worked for Selznick in *The Garden of Allah* back in 1936).

"If Jennifer had been Rita Hayworth, I could see the point," said Sheilah Graham. "But she wasn't Rita. Selznick, however, saw her as a girl of all talents, whose inadequacies he could camouflage with camera work and editing."

Losch's choreography had Jennifer "very suggestively weaving around a tree," recalled Selznick employee Lydia Schiller, who described the dance as "very revolting."

On seeing the rushes, Selznick asked Schiller for an opinion. The lady was frank and told him she didn't like it at all. Selznick screened the scene for industry censor Joe Breen, who found it "unpleasant" and doubted it would ever be passed by the board.

The negative responses forced Jennifer to learn two new dance routines, and the scene was refilmed. "I have never seen Jennifer so exhausted as she was . . . after five hours of dancing, not even after the terrible beating she took in Arizona," wrote Selznick on October 29.

By the end of November, after nine months in production, *Duel in the Sun* finally wrapped. The cost to date was a staggering $4,475,000, more than *Gone With the Wind* and far from a final figure—there was still a great deal of expensive postproduction work to be done. The interest on the money, borrowed from banks, added daily to the cost.

Jennifer was due to begin *Cluny Brown* (the picture Selznick had committed her to at 20th Century–Fox in exchange for the studio dropping its lawsuit over the actress's failure to report for *Laura*) almost immediately, on December 3.

Over at MGM, Robert Walker had been cast as Jerome Kern in *Till the Clouds Roll By,* a lavish Technicolor musical of Kern's life. Arthur Freed was the producer. It was yet another assignment for which Walker felt poorly cast. However, MGM's powerhouse roster of superstars were slated to perform elaborate numbers in the film, including Judy Garland, Lena Horne, and Frank Sinatra. Freed, for whom Walker had great respect, prevailed on the unhappy Bob to take the part.

After wrapping Duel, Jennifer took a vacation far from both the Arizona desert and Hollywood soundstages. She went on a shopping spree in New York.

Her inaccessibility to reporters and her absence from the Hollywood social scene had exacted a price: she was not voted one of the "Most Popular Stars" in *Modern Screen* magazine's annual readers poll. Ironically, though, Walker was.

Selznick was furious and lambasted his harried PR people, who were damned if they did and damned if they didn't obtain coverage on Jennifer (over the years the Selznick studio changed publicity directors more frequently than any studio in town).

"June Allyson is on that goddamn list!" exploded Selznick.

"[But] look who isn't," the publicists countered. Allyson was an overnight rage, a fluke, they said. In this era of great female stars, no other women had made the top ten.

Louella Parsons wrote a monthly column for *Modern Screen* and planned to host a gala party in her home for the winners of the survey. Selznick was invited and said he'd attend out of respect for Louella (and to keep Jennifer's prestige intact despite the magazine's snub).

Robert Walker said he'd be on hand. The actor arrived early—

Louella observed that he "didn't look very happy"—and stayed only briefly, spared the trauma of encountering his hated nemesis, Selznick, who arrived hours later.

David arrived alone and stayed until the party's bitter end, drinking and spending time with Anita Colby and her escort.

As Christmas loomed up, Jennifer looked forward to spending the holidays with David. But Selznick had made other plans for Christmas Eve and Christmas Day. He'd be back—if only temporarily—with Irene and their sons in the familiar, cozy intimacy of the Summit Drive home.

He'd bought his estranged wife spectacular gifts, including a diamond necklace from Harry Winston and a sable coat from Saks Fifth Avenue. "I don't know how Jennifer put up with this," declared Mrs. Selznick.

In fact, Jennifer was approaching a crisis. Selznick didn't consult her on his actions, and even if he had, she was powerless to prevent them. David's main topic of conversation, when with Jennifer, was usually Jennifer and his plans for her, including doing the remake of his own hit film of a dozen years earlier, *Little Women,* with Jennifer in the role of Jo; *Joan of Arc;* and *Portrait of Jennie,* one of Jennifer's favorite books and no longer on the agenda for Shirley Temple (who later said Selznick had spoken to her about playing the role of Jo in *Little Women*).

Jennifer, in private, wasn't without strong opinions, and she wasn't shy about expressing them. There were heated arguments with David, especially about his choice of scripts. "She'd like a script, David wouldn't," recalls Anita Colby. (In retrospect it would seem the actress proved to be correct more often than her esteemed mentor.) But Selznick believed Jennifer could play any role, and David usually had no trouble in finally convincing her of his choice.

No matter how angry she became at him, or how stressed out, Jennifer clung to their relationship. This latest development in David's private life, however, was a killer. After the formal break with Irene, and without a corresponding offer of "Let's tie the knot, Jennifer," the actress now contemplated a desperate act.

Meanwhile, she went forward with *Cluny Brown,* a comedy and, as such, a challenge and something to deflect her thoughts from her erstwhile Romeo.

Chapter

14

"*The role of Cluny Brown requires* great, deep humor, not just a technical humor, not routine comedy with double takes that the audience knows are coming three steps ahead," noted the great German-born director Ernst Lubitsch. "Jennifer Jones is capable of this rare humor," he said, "and that's why she will play Cluny Brown. I welcome the fact that this will be Miss Jones's first comedy role, for it will provide a fresh performance."

The film was a first-class opportunity for Jennifer to work with another top-rated director (*Cluny Brown* was to be the fifty-three-year-old Lubitsch's last completed film). A short, pudgy man who chewed constantly on a cigar and spoke with a thick German accent, Lubitsch was regarded by his peers as the "inventor" of sophisticated film comedy. His cinema oeuvres included *The Love Parade, One Hour with You, Trouble in Paradise, Design for Living,* and *Bluebeard's Eighth Wife* (whose star, Claudette Colbert, said after working with Lubitsch, "He's a better actor than any of us!").

Jennifer was greatly impressed that Lubitsch had directed Garbo in the memorable *Ninotchka,* as well as Carole Lombard in her final film, *To Be or Not to Be.* Most recently he'd directed Gene Tierney in *Heaven Can Wait.*

In *Cluny Brown* Jennifer portrayed a servant girl with a passion for plumbing, a "wide-eyed, unsullied innocent" whom Jennifer's public would undoubtedly respond to. Her costar was Charles Boyer, at the peak of his matinee idol popularity. Selznick had approved Boyer as leading man because, like Joseph Cotten and Gregory Peck, Boyer was happily married and known not to make passes at his leading ladies.

On December 15 *New York Post* gossip columnist Earl Wilson wrote, in a subtle but succinct manner, that Selznick and Jennifer were in effect living together in a secluded beach house. Although Wilson was careful to point out to readers that "Miss Jennifer Jones" was always chaperoned, one didn't have to ferret too deeply between the lines to reach the intended conclusion.

Jennifer, distraught over her situation with David and obviously greatly embarrassed that it was becoming public knowledge, swallowed an overdose of sleeping pills (it was Anita Colby, trying to reach Jennifer at home one evening, who suspected something was wrong and sprang into action).

Jennifer recovered and went back to work, the press none the wiser. (Wilson, many years later [the early 1970s], looking through the bound volumes of his column in his Broadway office, recalled that he had heard about Jennifer taking the pills but elected not to write anything. He also recalled: "Do you know that hypocrite Selznick threatened to sue my paper over that beach house item?")

Peter Lawford had been loaned to Fox to play a supporting role in *Cluny Brown*. In the evenings, Lawford, Robert Walker, and Jim Henaghan hung out together at Bob's apartment, boozing and listening to records. Lawford never brought up Jennifer's name, and neither did Walker.

Lawford later recalled that working with Jennifer had been a strictly impersonal experience. "Peter told me that he thought Jennifer was manic-depressive," states Patricia Lawford, the actor's young widow, "but that was later on, when Peter saw her wandering up and down the beach at Malibu, just walking up and down, up and down . . ."

Even if Jennifer had been looking for off-camera companionship during production of *Cluny Brown*, she wasn't the type of woman Lawford was attracted to. In those years, according to his wife, Lawford was crazy about Lana Turner and wanted to marry her. However, control over actors' lives was the order of the day in the mogul-ruled Hollywood of the 1940s, and L. B. Mayer saw to it that the Lana-Lawford romance quietly expired. (Producer-director

Howard Hawks had once threatened twenty-year-old newcomer Lauren Bacall with career oblivion if she didn't abort her romance with forty-five-year-old Humphrey Bogart. Bacall ignored Hawks's ultimatum but never forgot the threat he'd presented.)

As Jennifer toiled on *Cluny Brown,* Selznick labored over the elaborate, expensive postproduction work to be done on *Duel.* Even the musical score for *Duel in the Sun* was proving monumentally troublesome for David Selznick. Seven composers tried and failed to create music that reflected David's ideas. Dimitri Tiomkin finally completed the assignment, but not before he'd experienced major confrontations with the mogul.

"Dimmy, don't you understand? In the love scenes with Jennifer I want the music to be real f——g music! I want a really good *schtump!*" Selznick exclaimed.

"David," answered the beleaguered composer, "you f—— the way you want to, and I'll orchestrate it the way *I* want to!"

David meanwhile enjoyed discreet social outings with Jennifer. The couple sometimes dined out at leading Hollywood restaurants, like the Chanticleer on Sunset Strip. There were always others in their party, like talent executive Henry Willson, actor Louis Jourdan and his wife, Quique (Jourdan had been signed to a long-term contract by Selznick), and Anita Colby and her escort.

"I always thought Selznick made Jennifer nervous in public," said Willson. "He was such a perfectionist. Her clothes, her hair, even her attitude concerned him. He was always criticizing how she looked, how she spoke. It would have driven most other women crazy. Carole Lombard would have knocked him over the head with a champagne bottle!"

Selznick had rented and was living in the former Miriam Hopkins estate, located high in Beverly Hills at 1400 Tower Grove Drive (Jennifer was now living in Bel Air, at 635 Perugia Way). One evening he hosted a formal dinner party in Jennifer's honor, at which his mother, Florence, acted as hostess (Florence Selznick posed yet another obstacle for Jennifer—she was very fond of Irene and upset at the course David had chosen for himself).

Hollywood's elite was on hand, including Henry and Frances Fonda, the Joseph Cottens, the Charles Boyers, James Stewart, Ingrid Bergman and her husband, Anita Colby, and leading café society chronicler Elsa Maxwell (who considered herself a friend of Irene's as well as David's and Jennifer's).

The trappings were very grand. Baccarat glassware and antique silver sparkled in the soft light flickering from glittering rock-crystal chandeliers. Cocktails and canapés were served on the patio, where an elaborate buffet supper table was installed. Small tables were set up in the drawing room. Jennifer looked glorious in a glamorous, long-sleeved black lace evening gown, with a deep décolletage. She wore no jewelry ("She didn't need any!" said Pat Boyer).

There was an orchestra. During the evening, witty Broadway writer/director Abe Burrows sang a special song he'd composed about *Bernadette,* which delighted both Jennifer and David. Later, Jennifer danced with Selznick once and several times with Joseph Cotten. Elsa Maxwell noted that "within the last two years, Jennifer has had the reality of her divorce from Robert Walker to mature her." Jones was a paradox to Maxwell, "a wide-eyed girl and a woman to be reckoned with." The rumor was that Jennifer would soon become the second Mrs. Selznick. She grew more relaxed as the evening wore on, enjoying the vintage champagne, the wonderful food, the music, and, of course, the latest gossip. Life was very pleasant at times like these.

Selznick had decided Jennifer's next picture would be the remake of *Little Women.* Preparations were already under way. Selznick also had promising plans for his own future. He'd decided personally to produce only one major film a year, with associate Dore Schary producing other, lower-budgeted films for Selznick's subsidiary company, Vanguard. Selznick had also entered into production deals with producers Mark Hellinger and M. J. Siegel for other pictures to be distributed by Vanguard.

The plans took an unexpected turn when RKO studio president Charles Koerner died. Upon Koerner's death, Schary was approached to take over production at RKO. According to Selznick, Schary begged Selznick to be released from his contract so that he could accept the offer. According to Schary, however, it was Selznick who first learned of RKO's interest in Schary, then went to Schary and urged him to take the deal. Selznick then sold Schary's contract to RKO and alienated his partners at United Artists by selling, along with Schary, several important properties Selznick and Schary had been developing, projects that turned out to be enormous money-makers that UA, understandably, thought should have been brought to them, such as *The Spiral Staircase, The Bachelor and the Bobbysoxer,* and *The Farmer's Daughter.*

UA was headed by Mary Pickford and Charlie Chaplin. Chaplin had never liked or trusted Selznick; they'd been neighbors on Summit Drive, and Chaplin had always suspected that the producer had had a sexual relationship, years earlier, with Chaplin's wife, Paulette Goddard (who'd also been involved with Myron Selznick, her agent). But that was a personal matter, not directly related to the hard business decision the company now contemplated (on the other hand, it hardly contributed to an atmosphere of goodwill at a time of dissension and distrust).

UA took its revenge on David, after the RKO deal, by threatening to refuse to distribute the trouble-plagued *Duel in the Sun.* The picture had had its first preview in February 1946, at the Grand Lake Theater in Oakland, and the results weren't good.

Supposedly Selznick's advertising and publicity genius Paul MacNamara had bluntly told his boss that the picture was "lousy" and the only chance of recouping costs was to open it by saturating the country with simultaneous play dates of the film, in hundreds, perhaps thousands, of theaters rather than in one key theater in each city.

It's arguable that Selznick would have tolerated the continued presence on the payroll of an executive who voiced such a negative and hopeless appraisal of his "greatest" film. In any event, while the innovative release plan intrigued him, Selznick frantically went back to the drawing board to improve the picture and mulled over plans to form his own distribution organization.

Jennifer, however, had something to celebrate. "Darling," exclaimed David one morning over the telephone, "you've been nominated for the Academy Award!"

Jennifer was thrilled. *Love Letters* had paid off. The nomination was for Best Actress, and the competition was awesome—Ingrid Bergman for *The Bells of St. Mary's,* Greer Garson for *The Valley of Decision,* Gene Tierney for *Leave Her to Heaven,* and Joan Crawford for *Mildred Pierce.*

A look at the differing career approaches of the veteran Joan Crawford and Jennifer Jones, both successful actresses, offers a dramatic contrast indeed. While Crawford had contempt for women like Jennifer Jones and Norma Shearer (she considered their success a result of "sleeping with the boss"), she had become a star in the 1920s without a mentor like David Selznick and risen to the very top of her profession anyway (Selznick had produced *Dancing Lady,* one of Crawford's biggest hits at MGM). Crawford married the crown prince of Hollywood, Douglas Fairbanks, Jr., and while over the years her husbands changed, she remained under contract to MGM for almost two decades. She was earning $10,000 a week by the end of her contract and left the studio only when the budgets on her films plunged, reflecting her dwindling box office appeal.

While twenty-four-year-old Jennifer was being treated like a Tiffany jewel during production of *The Song of Bernadette,* thirty-nine-year-old Joan was going mad waiting to reactivate her career. *Mildred Pierce* was Joan's triumphant comeback (at a lower salary and at a smaller studio, Warner Brothers). It was a film about mother love and sacrifice, offering her a role that had as much to do with the "real" Joan as Pearl Chavez did with Jennifer. But Joan was also very adept at marketing herself, and unlike Jennifer and other publicity-shy actresses, she was *always* available for interviews. Under the guidance of PR man Henry Rogers, her reappearance in the Hollywood spotlight resulted in far more publicity than any other actress had received that year.

But both Crawford and Jennifer (and everyone else) expected Ingrid Bergman to win the Oscar. She was the star of three current hit movies—*The Bells of St. Mary's,* on its way to becoming the year's top-grossing film; *Saratoga Trunk,* costarring Gary Cooper; and Alfred Hitchcock's *Spellbound,* in which Gregory Peck was Ingrid's leading man.

Peck had also been nominated by the academy as Best Actor for his role as Father Chisholm in *The Keys of the Kingdom,* further escalating his box office value to Selznick for *Duel in the Sun.*

Jennifer, Ingrid, Gene Tierney, and Greer Garson all attended the ceremonies at Grauman's Chinese Theater on March 7. Bob Hope and James Stewart were masters of ceremonies. Jennifer's *Cluny Brown* costar, Charles Boyer, presented the Best Actress award to Joan Crawford, the only nominee in the category not present (she was home in bed with a terminal case of nerves).

Jennifer had no comment on the victory, but Ingrid was ecstatic. "Oh, I'm so glad! I'm so glad!" she told her *Casablanca* director, Michael Curtiz, who'd also directed Crawford in *Mildred Pierce.*

Crawford's later comment: "I voted for Ingrid Bergman myself."

• • •

Around this time Robert Walker made a powerful friend and ally in the press: none other than Hedda Hopper.

Hedda had a long-standing dislike for both L. B. Mayer (who'd chased her around his desk many times when she was an actress) and the Selznicks. She discovered, after meeting him, that she adored Bob, and, to his surprise, he felt the same way about her. She was the concerned, caring mother figure he'd always lacked.

Thereafter, whenever Hedda wrote about Walker, it was with great sympathy, understanding, and a bias in his favor. In ensuing years, as events would prove, he'd definitely need a friend like Hedda in high places.

Cluny Brown hit theaters in May. It had been filmed, assembled, scored, and distributed in five months, less than half the time that *Duel* had merely been before the cameras (it was still not ready for release). The critics were responsive: "Miss Jones, in a part somewhat of a departure from past appearances, does an excellent piece of work," wrote *Variety.*

The New York Times comments were also glowing: "Her performance is opposite and qualitatively equal to her delineation of St. Bernadette, for which she captured the Academy's statuette."

The Hollywood Reporter was an unqualified rave: "In the title role, Jennifer Jones performs her first comedy in Hollywood, and she does magnificently. Few talents are quite as electric as hers, and the account she delivers is superb acting."

Selznick began plans for his next film with Jennifer, *Little Women.* Diana Lynn and Bambi Lynn (the actresses were not related) were signed for costarring roles. Costumes were designed and created, construction began on sets, and tests were scheduled for makeup and wardrobe. But after a few weeks, the *Little Women* project was aborted. Had Selznick had second thoughts about trying to top himself? His original production of the film had been an outstanding success, a film classic. Was he so greatly disappointed with Jennifer in the rushes that he didn't want to expose her to the kind of criticism certain to come her way in comparison with the ever-popular Katharine Hepburn? Or was it simply that both he and

Jennifer were exhausted from *Duel* and didn't want to take on yet another period picture right away?

Whatever the reason (and even Anita Colby wasn't sure what went wrong), it appeared that Selznick was ready to abruptly change course. Fox wanted Jennifer for *The Snake Pit*. But *Portrait of Jennie*, Selznick decided, would be Jennifer's next picture.

Robert Walker, at this time, had the opportunity to work with thirty-nine-year-old Katharine Hepburn and forty-six-year-old Spencer Tracy in *Sea of Grass* (Walker was cast as Hepburn's illegitimate son). It was a fascinating project that proved no matter how incredible a production's ingredients, if the script wasn't right, if the actors were miscast, and if there was no chemistry between performers and director (in this case Elia Kazan), the results were guaranteed: bad and boring.

Phyllis Thaxter was in the film's cast, and, as before, Walker found her tremendously appealing. But Thaxter was married now (to James Aubrey), and Walker remained on the prowl for companionship and relief from his melancholy.

He completed yet another film following *Sea of Grass*, which Louis B. Mayer had sponsored personally: *The Beginning or the End*, a drama whose story dealt with the hottest topic of the day, the atom bomb.

The studio offered Walker a new three-year contract. The money was too enticing to turn down, and despite all his complaints about how the studio wasn't casting him properly, Walker re-signed. Off camera, outward appearances to the contrary, Walker proceeded, at his own destructive pace, on the course he'd long since chosen for himself.

Jennifer's fragile peace of mind was soon to suffer a fresh blow. Beforehand, however, in early August she was front and center at a spectacular party at Tower Grove Drive hosted by David in honor of newlyweds Evelyn Keyes and John Huston. Selznick had invited one hundred and fifty of his "most intimate friends," including such stars as Jimmy Stewart, Henry Fonda, Joan Crawford, Cary Grant, Orson Welles, and Marlene Dietrich. They dined outdoors in a beautifully lit and decorated setting, and guests lingered until the sun rose over the mountains.

According to Anita Colby, Jennifer *did* know how to laugh and had a sense of humor. "Oh, yes!" exclaims Colby, explaining that while Jennifer "might not be the creator of humor, she appreciated it when it was there—and I always made her laugh at herself, so she wouldn't get too upset about things.

"David usually had a wonderful sense of humor, and when he got angry about something, but knew you were right, he'd say 'Touché—you win.'

"Jennifer and David were fun to be with—you were never bored. Some things they did drove me up the wall, but Jennifer and David were really something!"

"David was such a great host," noted a columnist, "many of his guests were still raving about the party [for Huston and Evelyn] long after the newlywed Hustons had their first serious quarrel."

Robert Walker suffered another serious automobile accident. On the evening of August 20, Walker, drunk, was driving his new Chrysler down Santa Monica Boulevard. He hit a bakery truck, the impact tearing off the right fender of the Chrysler. Walker didn't stop to exchange licenses with the truck driver, who notified police.

Walker was apprehended and, on August 22, in Beverly Hills Justice Court, pleaded guilty to a hit-and-run charge.

The *Los Angeles Times* ran a story before MGM could throw the usual PR smog over the proceedings: WALKER, ACTOR, ADMITS HIT-RUN. The whole town took notice. Walker was worried, not because of the threat of a jail term (an unlikely prospect since a fine and a warning were the usual punishment in such a case), but over how Jennifer might respond and how his visitation rights with his boys would be affected.

There were, it turned out, no repercussions from Jennifer. But the judge in the case, Cecil B. Holland, wasn't as understanding or forgiving. He sentenced an astonished Walker to 180 days, "suspended on conditions," a $500 fine, and $50 damages to be paid to the owner of the bakery truck. He also warned Walker to stop drinking, and instructed him to install a speed governor on his automobile engine. What truly incensed Walker was Judge Holland's admonition to him: "You owe it to your public to straighten yourself out."

Walker was enraged that the judge had presumed to tell him that he owed *anything* to "the public" (a concept stars like Frank

Sinatra and Humphrey Bogart agreed with fervently). He told Jim Henaghan, "When that bastard [Selznick] stole my wife, he didn't give a damn what it would do to me, how it would affect my sons. As long as the public didn't know the story, it didn't matter."

Henaghan might have asked (but didn't) why, if Walker felt that way and was so deeply concerned about his sons, he didn't take the necessary steps to start functioning properly.

Jennifer was a victim of the system, too, but, according to journalist/author Beverly Linet, Henaghan felt differently. "Although Bob's hostility was directed solely toward Selznick, I personally felt that, as they say, 'it takes two to tango.' And in my opinion, Jennifer was a greedy, self-centered bitch."

Chapter
15

*J*ennifer *worked hard to maintain her* emotional equilibrium. She practiced her yoga ("I've known Jennifer to stand on her head before breakfast, as well as before dinner," recalled Anita Colby). And she had turned to psychoanalysis. An analyst was objective and nonjudgmental, someone bound by oath to keep a patient's confidences, someone to point out choices one had. (For a while, after consulting with her on *Love Letters*, Jennifer was a patient of May Romm's.)

Although Anita Colby acknowledges that "Jennifer was a very nervous person," Jennifer didn't think so. "People always apply the word *nervous* to me," she noted. "I don't think it's quite the word for me. Maybe 'temperamental' is. I'm not afraid of the word *temperamental* when it's used to mean moody and reacting to things. When it's used to mean flying off at things, then it's bad. I've not done much of that, but when I have, I've found it hurts me personally. I suppose it's a form of discipline you have to learn, to suppress the angry, explosive moments, but to stay sensitive to the real emotional ones, to laughter and happiness."

Any other actress would have been anxious to begin publicizing the dramatic image-changing role she'd just completed in a picture the size and scope of *Duel in the Sun,* but interviews with Jennifer, for the moment, were out of the question, declared Selznick. Gregory Peck, however, for whom the picture also represented a dramatic image change, would be available.

Peck, at this point in time, with three hit films in release, was today's equivalent of Tom Cruise or Kevin Costner. A select interview schedule was prepared for him. One of the writers assigned to do a story was none other than Walker's former lover Florence Pritchett. If Ms. Pritchett perhaps yearned to print some dirt on her ex-boyfriend's beloved ex-wife, Peck was not the man to provide her with the information.

"Jennifer Jones was one of the main reasons I loved this part," he told her. "I had never worked with her before, but had admired her work on screen. She, in my mind, has discovered the great secret of giving herself both as a person and as an actress. It shows in her face and is a great part of her beauty."

Her beauty didn't prevent David from appreciating a beautiful new face in another town. In the fall Selznick was in New York on business. At a social gathering he was introduced to actress Patricia Neal, then appearing on Broadway in *Another Part of the Forest*. In her memoirs Ms. Neal recalled: "[Selznick] got very drunk, told me how much he loved Jennifer Jones, and then tried to get me into bed."

Selznick, in a furious burst of feverish, round-the-clock, high-pitched activity identical with the incredible pressures he faced rushing to get *Gone With the Wind* ready for release, prepared *Duel in the Sun* for its initial engagement. The opening was slated for December 30, just under the line to qualify for Academy Award consideration.

United Artists, as threatened, informed Selznick that they weren't going to release the picture. Lawyers for both sides sprang into action, launching multimillion-dollar lawsuits and countersuits. ("Pushed out? Hell, I jumped," Selznick told inquiring reporters.)

Meanwhile Selznick scrambled to form his own releasing organization. It would consist primarily of individuals, in key cities, shipping prints of the film directly to theaters via the United States post office.

The Skouras brothers, who controlled the powerful Fox West Coast Theaters chain, met with Selznick and agreed to locally exhibit *Duel in the Sun*. Two major Fox houses, the Egyptian and the Vogue, on Hollywood Boulevard were booked to play the picture in its premiere Los Angeles engagement. Audience polls now indi-

Phylis Lee Isley, twelve years old.
(Gene Andrewski Collection)

Below:
The quintessential
all-American girl.
*(The Museum of Modern
Art/Film Stills Archive)*

Above: Phylis, seventeen, around
the time of her high school graduation. *(The Museum of Modern Art/Film
Stills Archive)*

With John Wayne and visitor
"Pawnee Bill" during filming of
New Frontier (1939). Phylis was
twenty, and it was her first movie;
following *Dick Tracy's G-Men*, a serial, she wanted out of her Republic
contract. *(Gene Andrewski Collection)*

With husband Robert Walker
and their two sons, Michael and
Robert Jr. The marriage was about
to encounter great difficulty.
(Photofest)

Renamed Jennifer Jones,
the twenty-four-year-old actress
portrayed Bernadette Soubirous,
the teenager who became
a saint, in *The Song of Bernadette*
(1943). (Movie Star News)

With Charles Bickford in *The Song
of Bernadette*. The actor became
Jennifer's lifelong friend.
(*The Museum of Modern Art/Film
Stills Archive*)

As Bernadette, the actress was immediately typecast. Events in her
private life presented a startling
contrast to her screen persona.
(*Gene Andrewski Collection*)

David O. Selznick in his lair. There was a remote control switch, under the desk, that locked the office door. *(Photofest)*

Ingrid Bergman, Selznick, Jennifer, and the Best Actress Oscar she had just won for *Bernadette.* Selznick's feelings for Jones are plain to see. *(Photofest)*

Joan Fontaine, an Academy Award winner also under contract to Selznick, manages a smile on the dance floor despite the producer's somewhat overbearing demeanor. *(The Museum of Modern Art/Film Stills Archive)*

With Robert Walker, filming *Since You Went Away* (1944). Unknown to the public, their "ecstatically happy" marriage was on the rocks. Jennifer became hysterical during their love scenes. *(Photofest)*

With Shirley Temple and Claudette Colbert in *Since You Went Away*. Jennifer was nominated for a Best Supporting Actress Oscar. *(Photofest)*

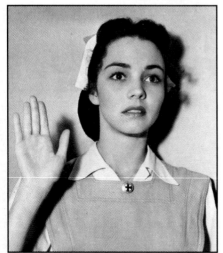

Taking the nurse's oath in *Since You Went Away*. Off camera, Jennifer had become a dedicated nurses' aide. *(Gene Andrewski Collection)*

With twenty-three-year-old Lana Turner, who'd attended the glittering preview of *Since You Went Away*. The press had a field day photographing "the Saint and the Sex Symbol." *(Lou Valentino Collection)*

Robert Walker and Judy Garland in *The Clock* (1945). Walker was on top, but he plunged off the wagon with a vengeance. *(Photofest)*

With Gladys Cooper in *Love Letters* (1945). Jennifer won her third Oscar nomination. *(Photofest)*

With Charles Boyer in *Cluny Brown* (1946). It was producer-director Ernst Lubitsch's last completed film. *(The Museum of Modern Art/Film Stills Archive)*

With Gregory Peck in *Duel in the Sun* (1946). There was high controversy when Selznick cast Jennifer as a sexpot. *(Photofest)*

Director King Vidor, Jennifer, and Peck on the *Duel* set. All had to contend with an out-of-control Selznick. *(Photofest)*

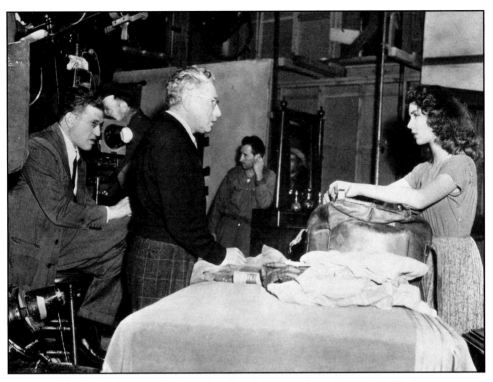

Selznick looks on as the legendary Josef von Sternberg directs Jennifer in a scene from *Duel*. Several directors worked on the troubled picture.
(The Museum of Modern Art/Film Stills Archive)

On the *Duel* set with Anita Colby, who became Jennifer's lifelong friend/confidante/adviser.
(Gene Andrewski Collection)

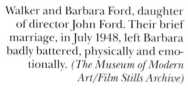

Ava Gardner and Robert Walker in *One Touch of Venus* (1948). Walker was alcoholic and still obsessed with Jennifer; his judgment, work habits, and relationships were in deep turmoil. *(Photofest)*

Walker and Barbara Ford, daughter of director John Ford. Their brief marriage, in July 1948, left Barbara badly battered, physically and emotionally. *(The Museum of Modern Art/Film Stills Archive)*

October 1948. Drunk, disorderly, under arrest. Walker subsequently underwent treatment at the Menninger Clinic. *(Photofest)*

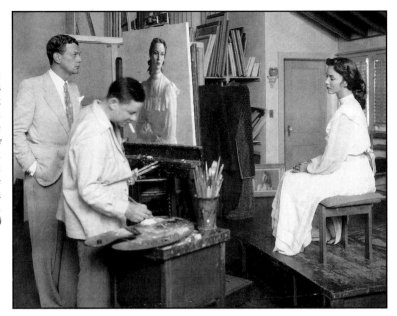

Joseph Cotten looks on as artist Robert Brackman paints the *Portrait of Jennie* that Cotten will "paint" on camera. The 1949 film was a costly disaster. *(Photofest)*

Jennifer welcomes three-year-old Liza Minnelli to the set of *Madame Bovary*, as Papa Vincente, director of the movie, looks on. *(The Museum of Modern Art/Film Stills Archive)*

The ball sequence in *Madame Bovary* (1949). The film was well received by critics. *(The Museum of Modern Art/Film Stills Archive)*

With Selznick and his sons, Danny (left) and an entranced-by-Jennifer Jeffrey, at a gala preview. *(The Museum of Modern Art/Film Stills Archive)*

With John Garfield in John Huston's *We Were Strangers* (1949). *(Photofest)*

Jennifer visits American troops fighting in Korea (1951). She derived great personal satisfaction from such activities, assiduously avoiding any publicity. *(Photofest)*

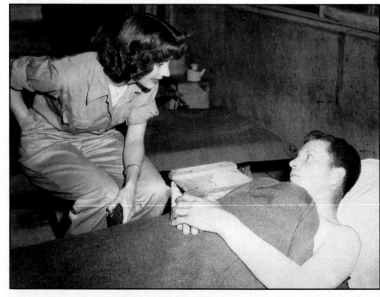

Robert Walker, Jr., and Michael visit their father on the set of his last film, *My Son John* (1951). Walker died under mysterious circumstances shortly afterward. *(The Museum of Modern Art/Film Stills Archive)*

William Wyler directs Jennifer in *Carrie* (1952). *(The Museum of Modern Art/Film Stills Archive)*

With Laurence Oliver in *Carrie*. The film, initially considered unreleasable, had been on the shelf for two years. *(The Museum of Modern Art/Film Stills Archive)*

With Charlton Heston in *Ruby Gentry* (1952). Following *Carrie* and *The Wild Heart*, Jennifer needed a hit badly, and this was it. *(Photofest)*

With Humphrey Bogart in John Huston's *Beat the Devil* (1954). Today a cult favorite, it was a box office flop when initially released. *(Photofest)*

With Vittorio De Sica and Selznick at the start of *Terminal Station* (released in the United States, with new footage, as *Indiscretion of an American Wife* in 1954). *(The Museum of Modern Art/Film Stills Archive)*

With Montgomery Clift in *Indiscretion.* . . . A total dud at the box office. *(Photofest)*

With William Holden in *Love Is a Many Splendored Thing* (1955). The big hit that Jennifer, once again, badly needed. She received her fifth Oscar nomination for the film. *(Photofest)*

With Robert Stack and Biff Elliot in *Good Morning, Miss Dove* (1955). A good character role for the actress. *(Photofest)*

With Gregory Peck in *The Man in the Gray Flannel Suit* (1956). A big grosser, but not a career-enhancing role for Jennifer. *(Photofest)*

With John Gielgud in *The Barretts of Wimpole Street* (1957). She'd always dreamed of playing Elizabeth Barrett Browning. *(Photofest)*

Rock Hudson, Jennifer, Selznick, and John Huston preparing for *A Farewell to Arms* (1957). Huston resigned before production began. The film was to be an overwrought, chaotic endeavor with most of the high drama off camera. *(Photofest)*

With Selznick and their three-year-old daughter, Mary Jennifer, arriving back in the U.S. after overseas production on *Farewell.* *(Photofest)*

A scene from *A Farewell to Arms.* Critics were merciless, box office was respectable, but reputations weren't enhanced. *(Photofest)*

As Nicole in *Tender Is the Night* (1962).
One of Jennifer's greatest career
disappointments. *(Gene Andrewski
Collection)*

With Michael Parks in *The Idol*
(1966). Selznick had died; Jennifer,
highly distraught, fled to England
to make the film. *(Photofest)*

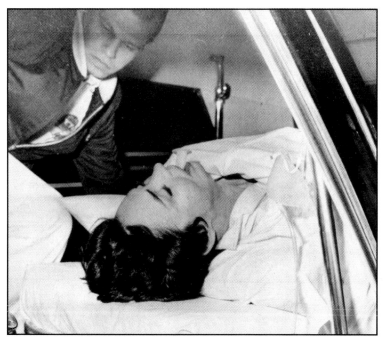

November 1967.
Suicide attempt.
"I cringe when I
admit I've been
suicidal, had
mental problems,"
she later said.
She became a
powerful advocate
for mental health
causes. *(Photofest)*

Back on screen, 1969. A Westmore brother and Sydney Guilaroff prepare fifty-year-old Jennifer for a close-up in the disastrous *Angel, Angel, Down We Go.* *(Gene Andrewski Collection)*

The all-star cast of *The Towering Inferno* (1974). Jennifer, third from right, links arms with O. J. Simpson and Steve McQueen. From left to right: Robert Wagner, Fred Astaire, Richard Chamberlain, Paul Newman, William Holden, Faye Dunaway. Far right: Robert Vaughn. *(Photofest)*

No more "Poor Jennifers" from Hollywood's social set. The actress married billionaire Norton Simon in May 1971. *(AP/Wide World Photos)*

Jennifer today. Los Angeles Airport, September 1994. Pursued by photographers, she ducked into the ladies' room. *(Bob Scott, Celebrity Photo)*

cated there was tremendous public interest in the film. Selznick's costly advertising and publicity campaign had finally paid off. But *Duel* had to go into the national marketplace soon, advised pollsters, before interest began to slide in the opposite direction.

Another obstacle was tossed in *Duel*'s path—the employees at Technicolor went on strike, and it appeared that no print of the film (or any other studio's film) could possibly be processed in time.

Selznick stormed into action and called in favors owed by Herbert Kalmus, president of Technicolor.

Selznick was excited about the completed picture. "I believe we have a really great film," he said. He thought Jennifer was wonderful in it and foresaw blockbuster business and many Academy Awards, acknowledging only two formidable challengers in the major Oscar categories—Samuel Goldwyn's production of *The Best Years of Our Lives,* and Darryl F. Zanuck's production of *The Razor's Edge* (for which Zanuck had wanted to borrow Jennifer).

Selznick's instincts warned him about reaction from New York critics; indeed, he anticipated a negative response, based on previous experiences, and was leery of "a patronizing type of review." But otherwise, his outlook for the film was explosively upbeat.

Jennifer attended the Los Angeles premiere with Selznick. She looked beautiful and aristocratic, the antithesis of the sex symbol she portrayed in the movie. She demurely kept a dark mink stole wrapped tightly around her most of the time.

There was enormous media coverage on the event, but the bubble quickly burst after *Life* magazine's disappointing review of the film appeared. The flagship publication owned by Selznick's dear friend Henry Luce gave the beleaguered producer no quarter in its evaluation of the movie, and Jennifer fared no better in what was described as "the story of Pearl Chavez . . . whose past is as dark as her cocoa-stained skin . . . and who loves everybody, but loves bad Lewt most often. . . ."

The critic went on to note, "When a single movie offers murder, rape, attempted fratricide, train wrecking, fisticuffs, singing, dancing, drunkenness, religion, range wars, prostitution . . . sacred and profane love, all in 135 minutes, the fact that it has neither taste nor art is not likely to deter the unsqueamish."

Daily Variety wrote that the film followed "a motif of sex such as seldom has been pictured on the screen." Columnist Jimmy Fidler had written positively about the movie but felt the heat of industry disapproval. He withdrew his words of praise, claiming a member of his staff had written them!

Selznick's peers were shocked by the picture. David's bombastic advertising campaign had backfired with a vengeance. Billy Wilder's friend and collaborator, Charles Brackett, described *Duel* as "*The Outlaw* in bad taste." (*The Outlaw,* produced by multimillionaire Howard Hughes, was a clumsily made western that had achieved tremendous notoriety because of its blatant exploitation of the extraordinary breasts of twenty-two-year-old starlet Jane Russell.)

Selznick was livid with anger; his movie simply meant too much to him to elicit a tongue-in-cheek retort. He responded archly to Brackett by describing Howard Hughes as a "dilettante" in the movie business, whereas there were "not less than six Academy Award winners associated with the making of *Duel.*" Selznick stated outright that he "resented" any comparisons between *Duel* and the other "enterprise."

While submerged in the quagmire of launching Duel in the Sun, *Selznick had* to confront a business catastrophe: the loss of two vitally important contract people, Ingrid Bergman and Alfred Hitchcock. Selznick felt betrayed. An anxious Ingrid, reluctantly following the advice of her husband, had delayed re-signing with David, and negotiations had dragged on for months.

Dr. Lindstrom was highly resentful that Selznick wouldn't share the huge fees studios paid to "rent" Ingrid, while Ingrid collected "only" her $60,000 yearly salary from Selznick.

Alfred Hitchcock, with Lew Wasserman masterminding his career, had reportedly made secret agreements with Bergman and Cary Grant for future productions. According to some, "Hitch" had no intention of re-signing with Selznick, although negotiations with Hitchcock, too, had gone on for many months. Selznick was simply unwilling to put certain points in writing, and Hitchcock was bitter. "If you knew the compromises I had to make," he complained later, "regarding casting, story points . . ."

Selznick complained bitterly about the situation to his chief executive, Dan O'Shea, pointing out that of all their major contract people, only Jennifer had promptly re-signed.

"Just before I was going off to New York to start rehearsing *Joan of Lorraine,*" recalled Ingrid Bergman (she was to appear on Broadway in the Maxwell Anderson play), "I met David Selznick at a party. He didn't come near me. So while most of the people at his table were dancing and he sat alone, I went over and sat down with him. I said, 'I hate to leave Hollywood knowing you are angry with me. I want you to wish me good luck before I go off to do *Joan.*' So he looked at me and said, 'Good luck.' And the next week he announced in the papers that he was going to do a Joan of Arc film with Jennifer Jones!"

Selznick wasn't kidding, but Jennifer absolutely refused. This was one issue that wasn't negotiable. Under no circumstances, declared Jennifer, would she play Joan of Arc if Ingrid was playing her.

Without David Selznick guiding Bergman—in his view the actress had good instincts but made bad judgments—Bergman's career would nosedive. *Notorious,* the last Selznick package to star Ingrid, was a smash, but flop after flop ensued. With Jennifer the opposite proved true. With Selznick guiding her, there were problems galore on every picture. He was obsessed with Ingrid not as a woman, but as a star; he was obsessed with Jennifer on both levels, and his lack of objectivity was to prove disastrous for both of them.

Jennifer won the prestigious Outstanding Achievement Award from *Look* magazine for *Duel in the Sun* (she'd won it in 1943 for *Song of Bernadette*). But suddenly and unexpectedly, and to her great dismay, she found herself trapped in a raging controversy with the Catholic Church. On January 17, 1947, in *The Tidings,* the leading Catholic journal, Archbishop John J. Cantwell of the archdiocese of Los Angeles wrote that *Duel in the Sun* "tends to throw audience sympathy on the side of sin. . . . Pending classification by the Legion of Decency, Catholic people may not, with a free conscience, attend the motion picture *Duel in the Sun.* . . . It appears to be morally offensive and spiritually depressing."

One can imagine how Jennifer (a Catholic), her family, and her friend Anita Colby (a devout Catholic) felt on learning of this development. "It made our life a hell," recalls Colby.

Selznick was furious. He responded at once, writing the archbishop that he was greatly surprised at the reaction, considering the fact that "we worked very closely with the Production Code Administration" and had abided by all of their suggestions and had received "the Code seal of approval without a question."

William Mooring, film critic for *The Tidings,* replied by stating to readers that although the film had a seal, he, and others, considered it "far worse in the moral sense than *The Outlaw.*" *Duel* was, in his opinion, not only an immoral story, but a dangerous harbinger of what might be forthcoming from the motion picture industry; he stated that any attempts by Selznick to justify the venture on the basis of the fact that it was offering the kind of realism the public now demanded would never "justify the screen representation of lust as if it were love."

He also said, in effect, that the whole venture was in bad taste. To Selznick's horror he zeroed in on Jennifer, saying among other things that "Jennifer Jones is unduly, if not indecently, exposed."

What undoubtedly irked clerics most of all was the fact, as Mooring had stated, that "a character [Walter Huston], acting as a minister of religion, parodies prayer and thus becomes a comical figure."

Selznick was in the position of the thief who wasn't at all sorry that he'd stolen, only that he'd been caught. He dictated an angry reply to the editor of *The Tidings,* all pretense at cordiality abandoned. He vented his wrath at the "calloused and diseased mind" that had "thoroughly attacked" Selznick's reputation, which, the producer pointed out, he'd "scrupulously built up over a period of twenty years."

Most unforgivable, said Selznick, was the "wicked and wanton slur" the critic had cast upon "Miss Jennifer Jones," whom Selznick described as "a distinguished artist" and one, he was quick to point out, who was "a Catholic, who received her education in a convent." He reminded one and all that she'd even been "honored by the Church for her contribution in the role of Bernadette."

With the righteous indignation of an evangelist whose dearest follower has been maligned, Selznick demanded an apology for Jennifer, describing her as a girl who'd devoted "a lifetime of respect and aggressive friendship for the Catholic Church." Selznick felt "there should be some sort of retraction and apology for the sake of the record, for the effect upon Miss Jones's children, and to eliminate the results upon her own Catholic conscience of this outrage."

Selznick's concerns for "her Catholic conscience" was hypocritical in the extreme. At this point the couple had been "living in sin" for quite some time, and by now their relationship was an open secret throughout all Hollywood.

Phil and Dolly Isley, and the sisters at the Monte Cassino school, were predictably nonplussed at this latest development. A statement from Jennifer was released: "I was never Bernadette, nor was I Pearl Chavez. Each was simply a role I as an actress tried to interpret."

Film historian John Griggs has noted, "Presumably Father Chisholm [Peck] was held to a much less strict code of moral conduct." Griggs was commenting wryly on the total absence of criticism of Gregory Peck, who'd just portrayed a priest in *The Keys of the Kingdom.*

Meanwhile *Duel in the Sun* was a turning point insofar as Robert Walker's obsessive hate for David Selznick was concerned. After seeing the film, Walker was stunned. "How could he do that to her?" he exclaimed. Thereafter, in private or in the company of friends, Walker would sometimes, without warning, begin screaming out Selznick's name. Then he'd apologize, embarrassed at his outburst, and change the subject.

Jim Henaghan observed later, "He could find a connection with Jennifer in just about everything. That was part of his sickness."

The controversy surrounding *Duel* didn't hurt the box office; on the contrary, it apparently helped, since the film was an unqualified smash in its Los Angeles engagement (ticket prices had been hiked to a hefty $1.20, the price usually charged for reserved-seat attractions). Round-the-clock showings were quickly scheduled. However, posters of Jennifer in front of the Egyptian Theater brought complaints ("too provocative") and were replaced by other shots of the actress, displaying less cleavage.

Jennifer became the target of an anonymous "hate letter" campaign. *The Hollywood Reporter* subsequently revealed that the Los Angeles district attorney investigated "those 'poison pen' letters that some vicious crackpot has been sending to most of the columnists and reviewers here who have said anything good about Jennifer Jones and her performance in *Duel in the Sun.*"

Selznick hired a former FBI man to find out exactly who was responsible for the "scurrilous attacks." The "culprit," it turned out, was the overzealous press agent of a rival actress. The letters ceased.

Meanwhile Selznick feared the repercussions of a "C" ("condemned") rating at the box office nationwide. The National Legion of Decency rated films either A-1—suitable for all; A-2—not recommended for children; B—morally objectionable in part for all; or C—condemned.

The desperate producer lobbied frantically to get the rating reduced before the film opened throughout the country. With behind-the-scenes aid from influential Catholics in the movie industry (like publisher Martin Quigley), he succeeded in securing a "B" rating for the movie (the rating accorded *The Best Years of Our Lives* and *The Razor's Edge*), but only by very reluctantly making cuts in several scenes, particularly the "rape" scene. Archbishop Cantwell subsequently congratulated Selznick on his self-censorship.

No scenes were totally eliminated from the film, however, and this was later emphasized in advertising for the picture. Anita Colby recalls, "It would have been a much better picture if we'd left in what was taken out. . . . It would have been a *great* picture. . . ."

Jennifer was attempting to structure her private life. She'd moved into an expensive new house at 650 Firth Avenue in the exclusive Brentwood section of Los Angeles, and set about decorating it. It was a beautiful pink stucco home with numerous fireplaces and an ocean view. Gossips said that this was the abode she was preparing for the day when she and David became man and wife, but to those in the know, it appeared the new house was not at all equipped to accommodate David Selznick.

Jennifer instructed her decorator to convert the second story into a separate wing for the children (the boys' bathroom was to feature a mural of two little boys in a boat). A governess had charge of Bobby and Michael, and friends observed that Jennifer had learned "to turn a deaf ear" to her offspring's sometimes raucous behavior. The actress's powers of concentration were so intense that whatever activity she might be involved in, whether memorizing lines or taking a painting lesson, she seemed to be able to block out all distractions.

Portrait of Jennie was scheduled to start production in New York on February 11, 1947, under the direction of William Dieterle. Selznick knew how much Jennifer was looking forward to playing the role and had proceeded with the film despite grave misgivings about the script and preproduction planning that left much to be desired. He feared the project might very well turn out to be a production disaster.

Dramatic fantasy was the most difficult genre to bring off successfully, even with the best of scripts. Jennifer would be portraying a ghost, a girl seen only by the disillusioned young artist (Joseph Cotten) who falls in love with her.

Selznick was deeply troubled, as well, over the state of another script, *The Paradine Case,* on which key commitments had been made. Alfred Hitchcock was set to direct (his last commitment to Selznick), Gregory Peck to star.

Meanwhile, at the studio, expenses were mounting at an alarming rate, and Selznick demanded drastic cost-cutting measures. With *Duel* set to open nationwide in three months (May), with luck the studio coffers would fill up once again. But life with David Selznick during these difficult times was not very pleasant.

Despite the blistering reviews of Duel in the Sun, *fate once again smiled kindly* on Jennifer Jones. Her performance landed her an Oscar nomination as Best Actress—the fourth time in four years.

It was a powerful group of contenders, with Rosalind Russell in *Sister Kenny,* Jane Wyman in *The Yearling,* Olivia De Havilland in *To Each His Own,* and a virtually unknown British actress named Celia Johnson in *Brief Encounter.*

Lillian Gish won a Best Supporting Actress nomination for *Duel,* and this category, too, posed an impressive derby: Ethel Barrymore in *The Spiral Staircase,* Flora Robson in *Saratoga Trunk,* Gale Sondergaard in *Anna and the King of Siam,* and Anne Baxter in *The Razor's Edge.*

Selznick was in a rage when he learned that *Duel* wasn't nominated for Best Picture or in any of the other major categories (the Best Picture nominees were *The Best Years of Our Lives, It's a Wonderful Life, The Razor's Edge, The Yearling,* and *Henry V*).

A new industry trend, one that would directly affect the careers of both Jennifer and Selznick, was already in motion and working against big-budget, star-studded films such as *Duel in the Sun:* the postwar emergence of inexpensively produced but powerfully moving foreign films as major artistic and box office successes. This was the year of Roberto Rossellini's *Open City,* starring Anna Magnani, and Marcel Carne's *Children of Paradise* (the latter described as France's answer to *Gone With the Wind*).

And it was Sam Goldwyn and William Wyler's *The Best Years of*

Our Lives that was in the vanguard of the new American "social conscience" film, representing a new genre of "realism" soon to satu-
rate the marketplace. A blatant sex-and-adventure fantasy like *Duel
in the Sun* was exciting entertainment but hardly, by the standards of
the day, "relevant."

Controversy aside, Jennifer's chances for an Oscar looked good.
Florabel Muir reported that for the first time gamblers were making
book on the Oscar derby. Before *Duel,* Olivia De Havilland had
been in top place, three to one. Then came the premiere of *Duel* in
Los Angeles, "and the next odds sheet showed that a new and sharp
young filly named Jennifer Jones had moved up into first position at
the prohibitive price of six to five."

Selznick insisted that Jennifer agree to an interview with Muir.
The meeting would take place in the private dining room at the
Selznick studio, a coup for Florabel, who noted that off screen Jen-
nifer was no sizzling Pearl Chavez but looked more like "a young so-
ciety debutante just turned loose on Park Avenue from Miss
Spence's school and a postgraduate training at Mme. Balsan's in
Paris."

Muir related that Jennifer was called "Jonesy" around the studio—highly dubious, since Selznick would have disapproved in the
same way he wouldn't have appreciated people calling Garbo
"Garbs."

While Jennifer had no objections to commenting on current
events, she froze when Muir, despite an understanding that she
wouldn't, dared to broach the subject of Robert Walker. Jennifer refused point-blank to discuss her ex-husband. Muir intentionally said
some uncomplimentary things about him, just to see what kind of
response she'd arouse, and noted that Jennifer "instantly flew to his
defense." He was the father of her boys, she said, and noted that
"both of them look like him."

Muir made an interesting observation about Jennifer's former
husband. "I don't believe Robert Walker, whom she loved wildly as a
young girl, ever had a full awareness of her." The journalist commented knowingly on the relationship everyone in town was so
highly curious about: "Dave Selznick is the only man who under-
stands Jennifer with an unerring instinct," she observed, "because
he himself, like her, has lived his life under the whiplash of a driving
urge. . . . David created the Jennifer Jones of today. He breathed life
into her, fanned the flame of talent . . . as surely as the sculptor Pyg-

malion breathed life into his creation, Galatea."

Jennifer, however, was not one to be totally "owned." "Jennifer has an integrity of her own that instinctively resists the obliterating of her ego," was Muir's politely phrased but penetrating comment, which illuminated the "secret" of Jennifer's ability to survive. In the reporter's opinion, Jennifer's future could be summed up in a single word: "Career." Muir observed that the actress was "driven by an inner necessity to go on and on scaling the heights as an actress." She described Jennifer and David as the "fire and flint of Jones and Selznick" and bluntly indicated the extent of the couple's ambitions: "The screen has never had a Bernhardt. . . . If that glory does lie in Jennifer's destiny . . . Selznick will not be far away."

(Selznick had signed Ben Hecht to write a script based on Bernhardt's life, but the project was intended for Ingrid Bergman. With Bergman out of the fold, Selznick tried to lure Garbo out of retirement to play it. Jennifer was never a serious contender.)

"I came back to New York with Jennifer to get her started on Portrait of Jennie," recalls Anita Colby. "I asked my sister, Francine, to take ice-skating lessons with her, since there was a brief skating sequence in the picture, and Jennifer didn't want to take lessons by herself."

Colby arranged everything and then returned to California. "A few days later my sister called and said, 'Jennifer and I fell so many times, we decided you should get Sonja Henie and call the picture *Portrait of Sonja.*" Colby laughs at the recollection. "Francine also told me that people kept coming over to Jennifer at the rink and asking her, 'Aren't you Jennifer Jones?' Jennifer would answer, 'No, *she* is,' and point to Francine!"

Jennifer's old acquaintance from her American Academy days, Don Keefer, answered a *Portrait* call for actors who could ice-skate. "I borrowed Monty Clift's ice skates," recalled Keefer, "and went down to Central Park, where they would be filming, to audition.

"Jennifer—I still called her Phylis—remembered me at once, and was extraordinarily nice—there was nothing phony about her. We talked about some of our old classmates and joked about how it was always the people you didn't want to hear from who kept trying to get in touch with you!"

Associate producer David Hempstead was a wreck trying to line up locations that would please the sour-dispositioned Selznick. "I had no problems with Jennifer, but David was impossible to satisfy," he recalled. Jennifer wasn't blind to the fact that already there were major problems on the film and worked hard to keep herself calm and collected. She'd taken her sons with her to New York and had instructed her interior decorator to send her photographs on the progress made on the Brentwood house.

However, her attempts at keeping a semblance of normalcy were short-lived. Selznick was livid when he saw initial rushes on the film. He disliked everything from the direction to the photography of Jennifer (he felt she looked younger in color) and the locations. As he'd feared, he felt the script simply wasn't working and was nonplussed at mounting costs. To everyone's dismay he pulled the plug and halted production after barely two weeks.

The industry watched and waited. Was *Jennie* to be another expensive write-off? Jennifer's feelings aside, Selznick seriously considered scrapping the picture, but he was in too deep. Banks would hardly continue to finance Selznick pictures if he abandoned costly productions midway.

A new screenwriter, Paul Osborn, was hired, and filming was slated to begin anew.

If an account by Irene Selznick is to be believed, Jennifer's personal relationship with David had reached a breaking point. Irene had moved to New York and was on her way to becoming one of the most successful theatrical producers of the decade. According to Irene, Jennifer, while in New York, wanted desperately to talk with her. Irene was unavailable.

Jennifer lied to Irene's secretary, according to the account by Mrs. Selznick, and said that she was a dear friend of Irene's, using the friend's name. Jennifer waited hours for Irene outside the theater where her play was in rehearsal. On leaving the theater, Irene was cornered.

"I told my driver to take us through Central Park," recalled Mrs. Selznick, who then learned that Jennifer "was distraught about David's unhappiness. He claimed his life was ruined, and Jennifer blamed herself. She was bad for him. His career was over. He didn't love her, he loved me. He didn't want her sons, he wanted his. If only I would take him back, I could restore him. . . ."

She has recalled how Jennifer "grew hysterical and tried to throw herself out of the car. I just managed to pull her back. . . . As I quieted her down, I told her David was bad for himself, and nothing she did or didn't do could change that. It was a dramatic episode, and saddening."

Anita Colby states today that Jennifer is very angry about Irene Selznick's version of events. "There was a meeting," states Colby, strongly implying that nothing quite so melodramatic as jumping out of the limo had taken place.

"David forgave Irene a lot of things," observes Colby. "[And] a few things she did were not nice at all." Colby adds: "Irene Selznick had the last laugh; she [certainly] had the last word."

Irene Selznick's relations with others from her Hollywood days indicated a dramatic change in her personality. When she encountered Joan Fontaine, "she cut me dead several times," recalls Fontaine. "I don't know what I did to her. I ran into her socially. Once she asked, 'Do you ever see David anymore?' Getting rid of him was just a terrible thing. I said, 'No, he's still seeing Jennifer as far as I know.' "

Jennifer lost the Oscar to Olivia De Havilland on March 13. Joan Fontaine presented the Best Actor award that evening (afterward she was snubbed backstage by her sister, Olivia De Havilland, whom Joan wanted to congratulate. Their reported feud became front-page news).

David Selznick flew back east to personally supervise *Portrait*— and to try, once again, to manipulate his personal life to where he wanted it to be. Certain scenes for *Jennie* (scenes not involving Jennifer) were scheduled to be filmed at Boston Harbor (another location trip that would prove disastrous). Selznick took advantage of the opportunity to travel to Boston and confront Irene, there for tryouts of her troubled play, Arthur Laurents's *Heartsong*.

Selznick was happy to offer his estranged wife the benefit of his advice on her play (in which Phyllis Thaxter and Barry Nelson had just replaced Lloyd Bridges and Nancy Coleman in the leads). But, according to Irene, Selznick had really journeyed to Boston to make a frantic plea to salvage their marriage.

Irene's energies were severely depleted from her involvement in *Heartsong*. David refused to defer their discussion. "At least there was no mention of Jennifer," recalled Mrs. Selznick.

• • •

Problems on Portrait of Jennie multiplied. "Jennifer was in an emotional state and often failed to appear," related one account. Once again the actress apparently considered her situation desperate.

According to those on the scene, she now threatened to jump out a hotel window. Selznick, out of town, had apparently argued with her on the phone, but then he swiftly dispatched a production executive to hightail it over to Jennifer's suite. On arriving, the executive decided that Jennifer seemed to be in no imminent danger. The crisis passed, and production continued on the film.

Meanwhile, in May, *Duel* opened throughout the country. "Remember the Day, the Seventh of May" was the ad line devised as a teaser for the picture. "The Picture of a Thousand Memorable Moments" was another key ad line.

The picture was an enormous financial success, playing simultaneously in precedent-shattering multiple-theater engagements. Momentarily it seemed that the incredible angst of creating *Duel in the Sun* had been worth it.

David was delighted to learn that Jennifer was the favorite actress of none other than writer Henry Miller, the man who'd raised the erotic novel to the level of literature. "But he's a dirty old man!" exclaimed Anita Colby.

"Don't talk like that if he's crazy about me!" replied Jennifer, who was "getting annoyed," recalls Colby, amused.

The revenue from *Duel in the Sun* forestalled the financial disaster closing in around the Selznick studio. Only one other film that year, the critically acclaimed *The Best Years of Our Lives,* would earn bigger dollars. No film, however, would receive more vehement critical pans than *Duel in the Sun.* It was the *Heaven's Gate* of its day, a whopping artistic failure, and Selznick was devastated.

Not *all* reviews were bad, though. Bosley Crowther, in *The New York Times,* said the film "has some flashes of brilliance in it" but called it "a spectacularly disappointing job . . . a clutter of clichés worn thin in a hundred previous Westerns. . . . Selznick . . . seems to have been more anxious to emphasize the clash of love and lust than to seek some illumination of a complex of arrogance and greed."

Variety wrote: "Miss Jones . . . proves herself extremely capable in quieter sequences but is overly meller in others. Same is true of Peck. . . ."

Howard Barnes, writing in the *New York Herald-Tribune*, noted that *Duel* was "a more or less conventional horse opera. . . . Jennifer Jones plays . . . with no more conviction than some heavy makeup contributes to the portrayal. She overacts at every turn . . . a top-heavy and trying motion picture."

Perhaps *Time* magazine was most accurate in putting the picture in perspective, describing it as "a knowing blend of oats and aphrodisiac . . . the costliest, most lushly Technicolored, the most lavishly cast, the loudest ballyhooed, and the sexiest horse opera ever made. . . . Mr. Selznick may well be Hollywood's smartest businessman. . . ."

After the relentless and intense efforts Jennifer had poured into portraying Pearl Chavez, reading the reviews was surely torturous. It's impossible for an artist *not* to take bad reviews to heart, especially when each artistic endeavor assumes the importance Jennifer attached to it. "I do not agree with people who think criticism and rejection are good for the development of a strong character," noted actress/author Louise Brooks. She poignantly observed that her own soul was "shrunken and scarred with rejection" and that every knock "robbed you of a little faith in yourself."

It's fascinating that Henry Fonda, near the end of his life, couldn't particularly recall any of the rave notices he'd received throughout his long career but was able to quote verbatim his first bad review.

Jennifer sent her sons back to California in June to spend the summer with their father. For relief from the tension and tedium of *Portrait of Jennie*, Selznick told her to take a couple of weeks off. She embarked on a Bermuda vacation, accompanied by Anita Colby.

Thanks to *Duel*, Jennifer was one of the top female box office stars for the year, along with Ingrid Bergman, Greer Garson, Rita Hayworth, Lana Turner, Gene Tierney, and June Allyson.

Robert Walker made only one feature in 1947, *Song of Love*, a period piece based on the lives of Clara Wieck, Robert Schumann, and Johannes Brahms. Walker was ridiculously cast in this picture, as was its star, Katharine Hepburn. Only European-born Paul Henreid seemed suitable for, and comfortable in, his role. The film was a total artistic and financial failure.

Walker asked MGM for a release from his new contract, but the answer was a resounding no. Like Jennifer, Walker was trapped in a situation he couldn't escape. With Jennifer too much care was being exercised over what roles she played; in Walker's case *no* care was being taken, either in the selection of his vehicles or the use of his abilities.

Walker spent his spare time—and he had lots of it, with no immediate assignments from MGM—indulging his penchant for being difficult.

"He didn't trust women anymore," noted his friend Hedda Hopper, "especially any woman who was an actress. If he dated a 'civilian,' he never took her to any of the well-known Hollywood hangouts." Walker insisted, when cornered by a reporter and pressed to comment on his ex-wife, that he wasn't "carrying a torch for Jennifer Jones."

Walker was not oblivious of new beauties in town, nor was David Selznick. Selznick had signed a beautiful, eighteen-year-old brunette named Ricki Soma (later described as his protégée) to a seven-year contract. A former ballerina, Soma had appeared on a recent *Life* magazine cover, a result of having been spotted by photographer Philippe Halsman.

Selznick was intrigued by the young Soma, and so was Robert Walker. Years later Soma complained about living in Hollywood because she said she'd found it boring, having to attend a lot of parties with "all those old guys [like] Spencer Tracy [and] Humphrey Bogart" (neither of whom had yet hit fifty).

Soma dated Walker for a while, then dropped him for John Huston (at forty-one, another "old guy"). Huston was still married to Evelyn Keyes and had met Ricki at one of Selznick's parties. The couple would eventually marry when Ricki told him she was pregnant. (One of Huston and Ricki's later offspring, Anjelica, far surpassed Mama's professional accomplishments.)

Meanwhile Jim Henaghan dismissed the importance of any new girl in Walker's life. "He was still madly in love with the woman—or, more precisely, the girl—who was his 'Phyl,' even though that girl no longer existed," he said.

• • •

Jennifer wanted to perform in a prestigious new summer stock company that had recently debuted on the West Coast. The Actors Company was the brainchild of Dorothy McGuire and Gregory Peck and was head-quartered out of the Playhouse in wealthy La Jolla, California. The company would revive hit shows and feature movie stars in the lead roles for a limited run. Selznick agreed to allow Jennifer to partic-ipate at some point, "when her schedule permits."

Meanwhile the lives of Jennifer Jones and David and Irene Selznick were racing toward a moment of truth.

In the interim, Selznick's tarnished professional image was momentarily restored with the rerelease of *Gone With the Wind*. While Selznick wouldn't re-alize any desperately needed dollars from the enormous success of the born-again epic, he was firmly reestablished in the eyes of his peers and the public as one of the greatest of all filmmakers.

Miffed that MGM hadn't had the courtesy to consult him and in-clude him on publicizing the rerelease, he issued his own elaborate press release stating that *Duel in the Sun* was following through on the box office legacy established by *Gone With the Wind*. Privately the impact of what he'd given up by selling his share of the picture to Jock Whitney now hit him full force, and he became more fanatical than ever in negotiating any and all future contracts.

David Selznick was exhausted, and that exhaustion was in part responsible for the blunder he now made that irrevocably shattered what was left of his fragile marriage to Irene. The situation could and should have been easily avoided. His son, Daniel, required mi-nor surgery. Irene, on the East Coast for her forthcoming produc-tion of *A Streetcar Named Desire*, flew home to be with her son before and after the operation.

Selznick was not on hand, and the shocked and infuriated Irene, like a tigress protecting her cub, washed her hands once and for all of her "impossible" husband. No excuse that he subsequently offered was acceptable. David's failure to be present on so crucial an occasion triggered Irene's irreversible decision to file immediately for divorce.

(Selznick had also been foolishly instrumental in "leaking" an anonymous item to a gossip columnist claiming that a famous pro-ducer's wife was "standing in the way of her husband's remarriage."

If he had planted this information to mollify Jennifer, and to make her off-stage role easier to play, it backfired accordingly.)

In November Irene Selznick filed for divorce. She had other painful, personal dilemmas to cope with. Her mother, Margaret, was about to file for divorce (after forty-three years of marriage) from the womanizing Louis B. Mayer.

Ironically, as events would prove, Irene's decision to divorce David was an unsettling development for Jennifer. Jennifer apparently wasn't sure now that she wanted a change in the status quo. Jones, twenty-eight, and Selznick, forty-five, had already been together for five years. In David's years with Jennifer, his Pandora's box of neuroses had, if anything, multiplied and intensified. So had Jennifer's. Selznick's undiminished determination to elevate Jennifer to superstardom seemed the strongest link in the emotional chain binding them together, but even that link was wearing thin.

Jennifer and David were worn out from *Portrait of Jennie*. Finally, in November, after eight months and close to $3 million, New York production on the film was wrapped (as far as Selznick was concerned, the picture was far from finished).

Jennifer thought her job was done. The exhausted actress had worked hard and diligently to maintain the integrity of the delicate characterization throughout all the rewrites and production chaos, and she now looked forward to a new and challenging assignment, whatever it might be.

Chapter

16

*R*obert Walker returned home to Ogden
for the first time in two years. He'd just turned twenty-nine on October 13, and Horace wanted his son home for the occasion. Bob
found that nothing had changed; spending time with his parents was
still a depressing experience. Before he left town, he implored them
not to give any interviews about his private life.

Back in Hollywood, Walker read about Irene Selznick's move to
divorce Selznick. He threw no tantrums—he'd already died a thousand deaths anticipating that turn of events. He'd found a new
woman friend, Lee Russell Marshall, recently divorced from actor
Herbert Marshall (who'd played Jennifer's father in *Duel in the Sun*).
This wasn't a wild, passionate romance, but a meeting of two hurt-
ing, unhappy souls who understood each other's heartbreak. The relationship eased Bob's pain and offered him a shoulder to cry on,
but it was not a panacea for his illness.

Jennifer's image was badly in need of polishing. The local press corps actively
disliked her and considered her unavailability a reflection of an ar-
rogant, imperious attitude. In 1947 she received the press's "Sour
Apple" award as Hollywood's least cooperative star. (Elsa Maxwell

noted that a journalist who'd interviewed Jennifer "reports that her discomfiture was acute, that she sat pulling one hair after another out of her head as they talked.")

Whereas today Jennifer's "secret" life with Selznick would be all over the tabloids, in the 1940s Hollywood media judiciously observed the amenities. Selznick's publicists worked hard to portray a friendlier Jennifer by distributing sunny new photo sittings on the star.

Additional scenes for *Portrait* were filmed, and then Selznick rewarded Jennifer: a trip to New York, to be followed by a leisurely tour of Europe. Jennifer would be traveling abroad with her sons, but without David, who'd be working on *Portrait*. And Jennifer would be conveniently out of the country, unavailable to answer the inevitable, prying queries from the press regarding the upcoming Selznick divorce hearing.

Jennifer departed for the East Coast in November. There was another purpose for her trip: it was to be a time of reflection for her, during which she could arrive at some decisions regarding her future with Selznick. Insiders knew that the intensity of their relationship had on occasion resulted in violence (one recalls Joan Fontaine's statement: "[David] was a violent man"). Anita Colby remembered being present once when Selznick struck Jennifer, with Selznick informing Colby it was nothing to worry about, that Jennifer enjoyed it! Others at the studio had seen Jennifer with a "shiner" (a black eye).

They were an unlikely duo, Jennifer and David, yet they seemed unable to live either with each other or without each other.

As the Christmas season approached, with Jennifer away David promptly departed for New York to attend the December 3 Broadway debut of Irene's production of *A Streetcar Named Desire*. He hadn't been invited, and his presence, to say the least, wasn't appreciated. On seeing him, Irene was nonplussed. She felt that David of all people should have realized the pressure she was under and not subjected her to any more. But David seemed incapable of letting go and of believing that his luck had finally run out.

But it had, and he knew now that there was no turning back. His letters to Irene, from this point on, no longer began "Darling." Henceforth the salutation was "Dear Irene."

• • •

David Selznick was more determined than ever to prove that Jennifer Jones was the greatest film actress of all. Back at Culver City he assembled and viewed what had been filmed of *Portrait of Jennie.* It fell so far short of his expectations that he alerted his staff that major new sequences would have to be filmed and a great deal more money spent.

Back in New York the press continued to lavish all-out hosannas on *Streetcar,* heralding the production as "theatrical history." Three huge new stars—Marlon Brando, Tennessee Williams, and, off stage, Irene Selznick—had been born. Selznick's pride in Irene's accomplishments could hardly have pleased Jennifer (or any other woman in Jennifer's position). It was yet another subject over which to quarrel.

While *Streetcar* was the kind of megahit that Hollywood would fall all over itself to acquire, David Selznick was not remotely contemplating the purchase of any expensive new properties; simply staying afloat and completing projects already out of the starting gate was his current goal. When forty-four-year-old producer Mark Hellinger suddenly died on Christmas Day, Selznick's proposed new production organization aborted before its birth.

The Paradine Case, released in January 1948, flopped dismally. It was an enormous write-off for the Selznick studio at a time when the producer could least afford it. He was stunned: the film was his first major financial failure. His judgment was off on other matters as well. He'd turned down distribution rights to *Red River,* saying the Howard Hawks film starring John Wayne and Montgomery Clift was nothing but a "routine western." United Artists acquired it, and it was a major success.

MGM finally came up with a role for Robert Walker. He'd be loaned out to Universal for the film *One Touch of Venus,* the hit Broadway musical by Kurt Weill, S. J. Perelman, and Ogden Nash.

Walker's costar, the actress portraying *Venus,* was fellow MGM contract player Ava Gardner (also on loan-out). Like Jennifer, Ava was a brunette with alabaster skin and high-impact looks (according to second husband Artie Shaw, "The great beauties in town turned to stare at Ava, an unknown, when she entered a room").

Ava was three years younger than Jennifer (in later years the actresses vied for two key roles: Lady Brett in *The Sun Also Rises,* which Jennifer turned down; and *The Barefoot Contessa,* which Jennifer wanted desperately to play). At nineteen Ava had married the country's number one movie star, Mickey Rooney (and to Rooney's astonishment Ava had been a virgin on their wedding night). The marriage lasted seven months, and then, at twenty-four, Ava married Artie Shaw, one of the music world's most famous musicians (her marriage to thirty-four-year-old Shaw, one of Hollywood's leading womanizers, lasted eight months).

Ava, like Jennifer, was intelligent, shy, and had a soft-spoken manner. Unlike Jennifer, she was overtly sensual and often indulged a wildly adventurous streak in her personality that frequently landed her in trouble.

Both women engendered obsessive behavior in men but responded to it in entirely different ways. Jennifer's response was to quietly endure; Ava, on the other hand, wasn't averse to hauling off and striking a man who had upset her by saying or doing the wrong thing (she once knocked Howard Hughes unconscious with a heavy silver candelabra).

However, Ava empathized with Jennifer's dilemma. She understood how a man like David Selznick would be "intoxicated" with Jennifer "and had pursued her as only a determined producer can. When a girl is young and beautiful and an ambitious actress, it's very hard to resist that kind of attention," she noted.

When production began on *One Touch of Venus,* Ava had already become the obsession of handsome actor Howard Duff, a brawny, dark-haired, dark-eyed "hunk" under contract to Universal. Gardner was hardly searching for a new playmate, but Walker, according to one version of events, wasn't satisfied with either the friendly working relationship—or the pleasant social one—that developed between himself and the beauteous actress.

Initially they enjoyed a drink or two after hours, sharing a few laughs and lots of complaints about MGM. Ava was sweet, immensely likable, and charming when she wanted to be, her southern drawl often surfacing despite rigid MGM training to the contrary. Some people have said that Ava simply wanted a drinking companion. But "Ava was not a heavy drinker in those years," noted Adela Rogers St. Johns, who knew Ava and liked her and was no stranger to recognizing people (including herself) who had a problem with alcohol.

Bob's problem with booze was painfully apparent to all who knew him. He was as sad a soul as Ava had ever seen, although when drunk, as Gwen Verdon so vividly recalls, Walker was not so much a charmer as a dangerous character. Danger, however, always appealed to Ava Gardner.

Accounts of Walker and Ava's sexual involvement during the making of *One Touch of Venus*—stories that Ava later denied unequivocally—went so far as to state that Walker's downfall was a direct result of the "cruel" treatment he received at the hands of an uncaring and unconcerned Ava. The tales further state that Walker hadn't realized Ava was involved with Howard Duff, and when he discovered them together in Ava's dressing room he smacked Ava across the face and pasted up a sign on her dressing room door labeling her, in the crudest language, the vilest of women. All accounts, however, including those by Walker's friends and associates, portray Bob Walker as far too sensitive for his own good.

The director of *One Touch of Venus,* William Seiter, worked hard to pull the picture together despite the obstacle of Walker's boozing, the actor's hostility toward Ava, and Ava's inexperience as an actress.

"Sometimes Walker was so drunk we had to print his lines on cards, which we held up out of camera range," recalled the director. "But Ava was no problem. She was eager to be good, and responded well to direction. I thought she was very sympathetic to Walker on the days he seemed out of it."

In later years, on at least one occasion, in private, Ava recalled the "terrible" drinking problem Walker had had and, like Gwen Verdon, expressed sympathy for Jennifer in having to deal with it. Then, sipping champagne, Ava said with emphasis: "They killed him!"

One assumed at the time that she was referring to the "system," the studio moguls and their uncaring outlook regarding *all* actors. Ava's memories of the "old days" and the studio executives were anything but warmly nostalgic. Quite the contrary. Certainly her statement—"They killed him!"—and the definitive, exclamatory way she said it—remained vivid in one's mind.

After wrapping *One Touch of Venus,* Walker proclaimed that he no longer wanted to have anything to do with beautiful women.

But pal Jim Henaghan's little black book had many compartments.

Chapter
17

$\mathcal{H}$enaghan had introduced Robert Walker to the charming and intelligent Barbara Ford. ("I'll regret it till the day I die," Henaghan lamented many years later in Hollywood, at the Beverly Wilshire Hotel, to young friend Pat Gaston Manville, a statuesque blond beauty from Texas who'd married asbestos heir Tommy Manville.)

Barbara Ford's father, director John Ford, was "the best director in Hollywood," declared Darryl Zanuck, and few disputed the description. Ford was an acknowledged poet of the screen, a man whose films radiated incredible sensitivity and strength. He was auteur of such classics as *The Informer, Stagecoach* (which David Selznick had dismissed as noncommercial and refused to produce), *The Grapes of Wrath, How Green Was My Valley,* and *The Oxbow Incident.*

A former actor, Ford was a tough, aggressive, cigar-chewing, hard-drinking ex-marine whose closest buddies were John Wayne and Ward Bond. Described as the leader of Hollywood's "Irish Mafia," Ford, in his early fifties, was a man of rigid personal beliefs, and a strict and protective father. Ford and his wife, Mary, were staunch Catholics who'd been married almost twenty-eight years, an extraordinary achievement in Hollywood.

"Most men were afraid to date Barbara Ford because they were scared shitless of her father," noted Bruce Cabot, an actor who was a member of Ford's inner circle. But while Barbara possessed personality and intelligence, she didn't have that vital requirement carrying maximum weight on the Hollywood scene: physical beauty. She was exactly the kind of woman Bob Walker had said he wanted to meet, one who couldn't possibly attract the kind of men who gravitated automatically toward a Jennifer Jones or an Ava Gardner.

Walker's whirlwind courtship of Barbara swept her off her feet. "He's divorced . . . he's not Catholic," Barbara's parents complained privately. Things moved fast despite their misgivings. Bob and Barbara had met in early June, and by the end of the month they obtained a marriage license. Bob phoned Hedda Hopper with the scoop on the nuptials.

John and Mary Ford were due to celebrate their wedding anniversary on July 3. Bob and Barbara decided they'd marry on that day. The ceremony was scheduled to take place at the Ford home at 6860 Odin Street. Walker then phoned Hedda to alert her to a change in plans—the ceremony would take place not at the Ford home, but at sea, aboard the *Araner,* the Ford yacht anchored off the coast of Catalina island.

Jim Henaghan was nonplussed by the news. "He told me he'd wanted to scream at Bob, 'Don't do it!' " recalls Pat Manville. "It was so many years later, and [Jim] remembered all the details. It obviously still weighed heavily on his conscience."

Henaghan was skeptical of his close pal's intentions and fearful of what lay in store for Barbara Ford. He didn't want to see her hurt, both for her own sake and for Bob's. Ford was a very powerful man in town, a man who reacted violently when provoked.

Henaghan knew what Barbara didn't—that Walker didn't love her. The most terrifying aspect of the situation was that Henaghan suspected that Walker didn't even *like* her! The hastily arranged wedding ceremony took place on July 8 at the Beverly Hills Club. Publicity executive Harry Brand's brother was presiding judge, and Barbara's friend, actress Nancy Guild, was maid of honor. Henaghan, at Walker's request, was best man. Conspicuously absent from the proceedings were John and Mary Ford, who were opposed to the marriage. The press appeared at the door, and the casually dressed Walker and his bride invited them in.

The wedding party enjoyed dinner afterward at a local restaurant, the Tropics, and then the couple spent their wedding night at Bob's apartment (Barbara later denied that the marriage was never consummated).

Jennifer had spent almost three months traveling abroad. Selznick encouraged her to spend, spend, spend, and she did. The couple spoke frequently by phone. To her consternation and embarrassment, even aboard ship he'd have her paged many times a day.

She'd returned to the United States in February 1948, with more scenes to film for *Portrait of Jennie*. The next several months were reasonably tranquil, but one can safely surmise that it was an emotional moment for Jennifer on reading the *Los Angeles Times* on July 9. There, on the front page, was a four-column-wide photograph of her ex-husband and his new bride. Whether she felt a sense of relief or abandonment is not clear, but the news would at least in part explain her reported actions and behavior over the next few weeks.

Meanwhile Barbara Ford experienced the impact of Walker's Jekyll-and-Hyde personality within days after their wedding. He'd abruptly canceled their honeymoon plans, taking his new bride instead to Utah to meet her in-laws. The trip was a disaster.

"Jim [Henaghan] told me that when he'd heard the details, he became sick over the whole situation," recalls Pat Manville, "and I felt so sorry for Jim because it had happened so long ago and the poor devil still felt responsible."

Back in California Barbara concentrated on somehow making the marriage work. She set about decorating the new home she and Bob had moved into. "Then," Barbara recalled, "Jennifer Jones started phoning. Just to hound him, in my opinion. I think she was very evil to Bob."

According to Barbara, Jennifer's calls were about strictly trivial matters, things her household staff could easily have attended to. But Bob, with Barbara in tow, always complied with Jennifer's requests. Jones was never home, recalled Barbara, at least that's what they were told, "and we dropped the packages off with her maid."

Walker's moods would blacken after the humiliation of being treated "like a delivery boy," recalled Barbara. The transformation of his personality was terrifying to the young woman. She strove mightily to turn the tide. "I was insanely in love with him," she said.

But he was insanely in love with someone else, and on August 14 his schizophrenic behavior finally erupted in physical violence. He beat Barbara up so badly that afterward she had difficulty picking up a telephone and calling for help. Walker was on a fast downward spiral, and he was dragging his new bride into his hell with him.

The battered young Barbara Ford tearfully faced the inevitable: her brief marriage to Robert Walker was over. Accompanied by her mother and two friends, Nancy Guild and actress Joanne Dru, Barbara quickly and quietly left town for the privacy and seclusion offered by the Ford yacht.

Through her father's spokespeople she issued a statement to the effect that she and Bob were simply calling it quits; there was no clue of the physical abuse that had taken place.

Walker, as in the past, simply disappeared (as did *One Touch of Venus,* which sailed into and out of theaters that August). Walker secretly retreated back to Ogden, where he remained incommunicado to the outside world.

Mental illness was not a topic people discussed in those days. Bob was simply being the same impossible, willful "problem child" he'd been while growing up.

Jennifer's reaction to the news of Walker's pending divorce was, "No comment."

Jennifer had returned to her "roots" in live theater. With Selznick's grudging approval she was appearing, for the week of August 14, in a revival of *Serena Blandish,* produced by the Actors Company at the La Jolla Playhouse.

"I was not quite ready for the role," Jennifer admitted, "but David gave me permission to do it, believing it would help me with my screen roles."

Audiences were receptive, and she found the response immensely gratifying. Fisher Harris, a local businessman, and his wife, Ruth, were in the audience. "I had never been a fan of Jennifer Jones, but my wife was, so we went. After seeing her in person, I was hooked. I was surprised that she was so spectacular to look at. In most of the parts she'd played on screen, she was so sweet and demure.

"And you only looked at her, no matter who else was on stage. When I saw her in films after that, I always told my wife that the camera didn't do her justice."

Jennifer told a local reporter that "hearing real applause . . . was as great a thrill as winning my Oscar." Her next stop—Broadway. "I definitely plan to make my Broadway debut as soon as I'm free of movie commitments," she said, confident that David would encourage her. *Romeo and Juliet,* no less, was the vehicle she envisioned.

But an engagement on Broadway was not on Jennifer's agenda for the near future. Selznick needed funds desperately, and now, in effect, it was Jennifer's turn to help him. He was going to loan her out.

The brilliant writer-director John Huston had recently completed his Warner Brothers contract and had formed an independent company, Horizon Pictures, with producer S. P. Eagle (soon to become Sam Spiegel). Privately the men referred to their new corporation as "Shit Creek Productions."

Huston was planning, as his first venture for his new company, a property called *Rough Sketch,* a romantic adventure drama set in Cuba that dealt with corruption and an attempt to overthrow the government. Huston and Peter Viertel had collaborated on the script, and freelance star John Garfield was about to sign on as leading man. Jennifer Jones as leading lady convinced the actor to commit to the project.

Selznick regarded John Huston as one of the top talents in the business. The breathtaking *The Treasure of the Sierra Madre* and *Key Largo* were both currently in release and certain to receive many Oscars. A highly original thinker, Huston was a dynamic and resourceful director, and it was a coup for any actor to work with him.

Huston was also a liberal Democrat and an outspoken and opinionated man, and he and Selznick were often at opposite ends of the spectrum politically. Jennifer had remained far removed from the highly controversial and ugly political situation Hollywood was currently confronting. Selznick, for a while, had become involved, but Huston was in the thick of it.

In September 1947 the House Un-American Activities Committee had turned its full attention to Hollywood, and a group of outraged industry members, headed by John Huston, writer Philip Dunne, director William Wyler, and actor Alexander Knox, had formed the Committee for the First Amendment to demonstrate their revulsion at what they considered witch-hunt tactics and in-fringements on constitutional rights.

(Selznick, too, had attempted to form a bipartisan group of lib-eral Republicans and Democrats to combat HUAC's activities, which he felt were unconstitutional. But personality clashes soon led to the dissolution of the Selznick group.)

Top names were involved with the Committee for the First Amendment, including Bogart and Bacall, Paulette Goddard and Burgess Meredith, Katharine Hepburn, Gregory Peck, Danny Kaye, Burt Lancaster, Edward G. Robinson, Charles Boyer, Billy Wilder, and John Garfield. Judy Garland, Lucille Ball, and Frank Sinatra, among others, had made public statements supporting the group.

Huston was in the forefront of those taking positive action (in retrospect the director considered his actions "very naive"). And any picture Huston now made was sure to be subjected to harsh scrutiny by his enemies. Selznick ignored such considerations and had no problems doing business with Huston. Both men appreci-ated each other's great filmmaking abilities. Although Jennifer didn't like either the script or the character she was to portray in *Rough Sketch* (a Cuban patriot named China, pronounced "Chee-na," Valdez), the package offered too many promising elements for Selznick to turn down, not the least of which was the six-figure loan-out fee for Jennifer's services.

Cuba, of course, was to exist mostly on the back lot of Columbia Pictures (a second unit would shoot actual footage in Cuba, for which Huston would personally scout the locations). Jennifer ef-fected a whole new look for the movie. Her long dark hair was cut short for the first time. She'd turned twenty-nine, and the haircut vi-sually proclaimed that she was no longer a girl.

Jennifer and Brooklyn-born John Garfield (née Julius Garfin-kle) were portraying Cubans, but there was no attempt by either ac-tor to use much of an accent. Both stars, in fact, were miscast, but that's not what troubled Huston. "It was one of those pictures that didn't come together," Huston said. "The script wasn't very good. In-stead of having a natural climax, it went cliché. The hero became a cardboard hero."

What was it like to direct Jennifer? "Jennifer Jones looked for di-rection in every move she made," said Huston. "I would say, 'Sit over there, Jennifer.' She would say, 'How?' At first I was confounded, but

I discovered that Jennifer wanted to be told when and how to sit, stand, or walk across a room. She put herself completely in the hands of the director, more than any other actress I've ever worked with. And she was not an automaton. Jennifer took what you gave her and made it distinctly her own."

Huston was a powerful presence. A lanky six feet five, with a mesmerizing voice, he smoked, drank, and called Jennifer "honey." He was a collector of art, houses, animals, and people. He had a sense of humor and could laugh at himself, but "he had a cruel streak," noted daughter Anjelica. Bogart had nicknamed Huston "the Monster."

The director tended to be intentionally rough on his actors, and Jennifer was no exception. For one sequence in the movie he had her wallowing in wet clay for days. Notorious for playing pranks, Huston had planned an elaborate one. As Jennifer was digging furiously in a graveyard, a key scene in the film, she struck a buried coffin with her shovel, as planned. When she hit it, however, the lid suddenly popped open and a greenish, decomposed hand (made of sponge rubber) flew out. Jennifer screamed in horror, and Huston roared with delight.

Jennifer wasn't amused, and she got even on two occasions. For one important close-up that had taken hours to light, she smiled on cue, but she'd painted two of her teeth black. Her second opportunity for revenge took place at the wrap party for the picture. She presented Huston with a live monkey, which wouldn't let Huston out of its sight. Garfield, too, played his own prank by presenting Huston with a pregnant burro. Jennifer didn't appreciate the animal's name—"Jennie."

The crew liked Jennifer and were very protective of her. She knew many of them by name and was quick to smile. However, "painfully shy" was still the description most often applied to Jennifer Jones.

The picture, as well as an emergency appendectomy, had taken its toll on Jennifer's energies; she was exhausted. With Selznick mired in the mammoth job of keeping his studio afloat, Jennifer's private life offered no peaceful haven. Ignoring Selznick's wishes—a radical behavioral departure for her—Jennifer traveled again to Europe in late fall, taking young Bobby and Michael with her.

"I'm never going to take the boys to Europe again. It's just not right," she said later. "Even though I had a tutor for them in Switzerland, they lost too much time from their studies and got too far away from their normal routines." And they were becoming a discipline problem.

According to Jennifer's friends, the true purpose of the trip had been to meet Carl Jung, the world-famous Swiss psychologist and psychiatrist. Jung, seventy-three years old, had developed analytical psychology and the use of free association to study personal problems. Friends said that Jennifer was intrigued by Jung's theories—his explanation of behavior placed more emphasis on vital forces within the individual than on sexual urges, as Freudian Theory asserted.

The Jung Institute had just opened in Zurich, and Jennifer sought advice on the one dilemma plaguing her life: Why was she so reluctant to marry Selznick? Whether or not to marry David was a decision she'd be confronted with very soon. Obviously she preferred her freedom, which the intense—but not legally binding—relationship with David allowed her.

There were no doubts in Louella Parsons's mind as to where Jennifer's relationship with David was headed. "I'm dead certain that Jennifer will be married to the man she loves," she predicted. Jennifer's reply was not as certain—"I don't know, Louella. I honestly don't know. But when I do, I promise I'll tell you."

Louella admitted that if she'd received such an "indefinite" answer to "a question intriguing all of Hollywood" from any other actress, "I might have been thoroughly irritated." An understatement, to be sure, since banishment from Louella's column in those days was a big step on the path to professional suicide.

However, the triumph of romantic love over seemingly impossible odds was Louella Parsons's favorite theme. According to Louella, Jennifer "idolized" David; to Jennifer "he is a god, controlling not only her career, but her life, her laughter, and even her tears."

Louella stated that she knew "the unspoken things" about the Jennifer-David "romance" and went on to compare Jennifer with a lady of the royal court, on the verge of marrying a prince of the realm, who was merely exercising the same level of discretion about her future plans.

• • •

To Jennifer's great disappointment, Jung was ill and unable to see her (accord- ing to Anita Colby, he did see her on a later occasion). Dr. C. A. Meier would become her analyst. Meanwhile Selznick's European representatives quickly made arrangements for the actress and her sons to leave for Paris. The great fashion houses were back in full throttle and eager to provide wealthy American women with their latest creations. ("There's nothing like a no-holds-barred shopping spree in Paris to make a girl's spirits soar," noted none other than Madonna in 1991, visiting the House of Chanel after an arduous concert tour.)

The Selznick empire may have been in great financial difficulty, but no one would have guessed, judging from Jennifer's extravagant lifestyle overseas. David, of course, expected it of her and encouraged her to fulfill her desires for beautiful things; he always wanted her to be the best-dressed, most beautiful woman of all and spoiled her as though she were a princess.

But Selznick's fortunes had ebbed so low that many bills were going unpaid. He was desperate enough to ask Irene for a small cash loan of under $20,000. She gave it to him but wondered sadly what would happen if David hadn't had access to the modest amount he'd requested.

"She gave a loan to David," recalls Anita Colby. "He gave her a valuable painting [a Matisse] as collateral. Do you know that she wouldn't give the painting back?"

Artist Robert Brackman had painted a magnificent portrait of Jennifer, used in *Portrait of Jennie,* which Selznick had acquired for his personal collection (just as an equally enraptured Norton Simon would acquire the painting decades hence). It depicted Jennifer in all her radiant, ethereal glory as Jennie, attired in a high-necked, long-sleeved white lace dress, her long dark hair pulled back softly from her face and gathered at the nape of her neck with a satin bow. The painting was prominently displayed in the formal dining room of David's home.

One evening Jennifer, along with Joseph Cotten and his wife, Lenore, and Daniel O'Shea, Selznick's chief executive, attended an exclusive dinner party Selznick was hosting for longtime friends

Clare and Henry Luce (the Luces had also remained friends with Irene).

In the old days Selznick had always been the first to appreciate a good joke, and as a practical joke O'Shea and Cotten had replaced the painting with a facsimile and drawn a bold, black handlebar mustache on Jennifer's face.

Cotten recalled, "In retrospect it was a foolish prank, but we thought David, who had always enjoyed our practical jokes before, would be highly amused."

The Luces, of course, had been alerted, and it was Clare Luce who innocently complimented David on the "unusual" painting of Jennifer. When Selznick gazed at the portrait, his eyes widened and suddenly he turned beet red.

"He became so enraged that he failed to realize the picture was only a copy," recalled Cotten. The producer's subsequent explosion of anger, and the sour mood that lingered afterward, cast a pall over the rest of the evening.

The "party" ended early, and Jennifer was among the first to leave.

Anita Colby had received an offer she couldn't refuse. "Paramount [wanted me] to come in as executive assistant to Henry Ginsburg, the head of the studio. David was very upset," she recalls. "He wanted me to stay. I said, 'David, I can't.' " Jennifer was even more upset.

Colby, of course, was well aware of Selznick's business problems and tried her best to help out. "When I got to Paramount, I suggested to Ginsburg that Paramount buy *Little Women* [to which David owned the rights] and make a musical out of it."

It was MGM, though, that eventually bought *Little Women*—to be remade not as a musical, but in Technicolor and starring June Allyson, seventeen-year-old Elizabeth Taylor, and teenage Janet Leigh.

Meanwhile, back at Paramount Colby had discovered what a studio could be like without the guidance and, more important, the protection of David O. Selznick. There was more than one person to please, and powerful studio costume designer Edith Head regarded Colby as dangerous competition.

"Edith was *so* upset I was at the studio that she ran around telling everybody tall tales about me," recalls Colby. "She got Betty Hutton so riled up—Betty was the studio's top star, and very loyal to her—that Betty said things [about me] to the press. Apparently no one dared to cross Edith Head!"

And Ingrid Bergman certainly must have regretted "crossing" David O. Selznick. *Joan of Arc,* released in October 1948, was an artistic and financial disaster, an incredible disappointment. Many in the industry believed it would have been a smash had David produced and marketed it. "Let's see now what he's done with Jennifer," was the attitude regarding the much discussed *Portrait of Jennie.*

Robert Walker had quietly reappeared in Hollywood in the fall. He behaved as though he'd been on a vacation and that his marriage to Barbara Ford had never occurred. Jennifer, he learned, was planning to enroll Bobby, eight, and Michael, seven, in the Black Foxe Military Academy. Walker, himself a military school graduate, was said to be delighted. The school, located at Melrose and Wilcox Avenues in Los Angeles, had a first-rate reputation. Many children of the rich and famous were enrolled there. It was an institution that had a well-earned reputation for discipline and was later described by alumnus Samuel Goldwyn, Jr., as "sheer fucking hell."

MGM had no roles for Bob, and there were no requests from other studios to borrow him. The word was out, loud and clear— Robert Walker was trouble, and not a big enough star to warrant putting up with his problems.

Walker became friends with actress Ida Lupino. She was one of the few women he didn't find annoying or abrasive.

"Bob was a darling," Lupino recalled. "So unhappy, but so talented. With the right dramatic part, I felt he could easily establish himself as a top actor."

Walker was delighted to learn of David Selznick's multitudinous business problems. He realized, however, that the producer's relationship with Jennifer wasn't necessarily coming apart as well; gloating over Selznick's misfortunes brought him only fleeting satisfaction.

Selznick wasn't the only mogul in trouble. L. B. Mayer's days at MGM were numbered. Dore Schary was expected to succeed him, and Schary, currently Metro's head of production, was one of

Walker's great admirers. (Schary had been at MGM when the actor made *Bataan.*) The executive felt the studio had wasted the young man's potential. He summoned Bob for a meeting and told him so. Walker trusted Schary and believed him when Schary assured him that he'd find good roles for him.

In an interview in *The Hollywood Reporter,* Walker stated that by no longer having to worry about the parts the studio intended to assign him, "and with the lessons I have learned, I'm sure that I'll be able to run my life on an even keel."

The impact of the level-headed sentiments expressed by Walker was shattered by the actor's subsequent actions. On October 22 Jennifer—along with Selznick, Schary, and everyone else in town—was shocked at brutally candid photographs of Walker featured on the front pages of leading newspapers after his arrest for drunk and disorderly conduct. Bob's face was twisted into an ugly, angry grimace; he was unkempt, his shirttail hanging out of his buttoned suit jacket. He was sitting stiffly on a chair, one hand clenched into a fist, the other tightly grabbing hold of the arm of the chair.

It seemed that Walker and a companion, former MGM contract actress (and the former Mrs. Tommy Dorsey) Patricia Dane, had gone for a drive after a few drinks at a neighborhood bar. Dane had reportedly been at the wheel of Walker's new Cadillac when police stopped the vehicle, and Bob became belligerent with officers L. L. Brown and E. L. Trinkletter. Walker later portrayed himself as having been thoroughly victimized by the cops, but his statement to police was deeply revealing: "Why, I've been drunk for twenty-five years," he said, the words indicating how far back his troubles may have actually begun (and reinforcing Gwen Verdon's educated guess that there'd always been a drinking problem). There is no evidence, though, that he began drinking as a child.

After his arrest, a dazed Walker "pleaded with the detective in charge to telephone his wife, Jennifer Jones, to ask if she would help him get out of jail." When authorities volunteered to telephone Walker's lawyer, Walker once again lost control and had to be restrained. Jennifer, alarmed, rushed back from a vacation in Del Mar and appealed to Bob, for the sake of Michael and Bobby, to pull himself together.

Ironically it was Selznick who interceded with MGM on Walker's behalf; there was a morals' clause in every actor's contract, and this incident qualified as grounds for dismissal. One can imagine

Walker's reaction had he learned that David Selznick had engaged in discussions on his behalf involving the subject of morals!

In exchange for an exclusive interview with Jennifer, David saw to it that Louella Parsons included Jennifer's side of the story. The columnist stretched the limits of credibility when she stated, "Never can it be said in truth that Jennifer came between Irene and David. . . . Long before there was any thought of a romance between Jennifer and David, she and Bob Walker had separated."

Parsons also noted that "Jennifer never talks about Walker." Regarding the actress's feelings about Walker's troubles, Louella described Jennifer as "greatly concerned . . . it is not fair, after their long separation, to blame his front-page antics on her."

Louella believed that Jennifer's feelings for Bob were maternal, whereas her love for David was of the all-consuming "big love of her life" variety. Parsons climbed out on a limb and deflected the gossip that Jennifer's ambition to be a great actress was all that really mattered to her: "I honestly believe that if David asked her to give up her career tomorrow, she would do it."

Parsons was sixty-eight years old, still Hollywood's leading sob sister and a devout romantic. She was a woman who both sympathized and empathized with her friend David for having lost his heart to Jennifer. But Louella, cunning reporter that she was, even with her claws sheathed and on her best behavior managed, between the lines, to relay to her readers the details of where things really stood in the couple's relationship.

The reporter admitted that "it had taken quite a bit of doing to arrange our appointment," since Jennifer's reputation "for dodging interviews" was by now legendary. Getting Jennifer to say anything about her relationship with David was a coup for Louella, and Parsons had exercised considerable clout to prevent cancellation of the interview.

An interview with Louella usually meant sitting down with the reporter and her assistant, Dorothy Manners (if not Manners, ace fan magazine reporter Ruth Waterbury), for tea. Henry Rogers recalled Claudette Colbert's description of being interviewed by Louella: "She takes a couple of good belts and gets sloshed, then Dorothy Manners or Ruth Waterbury sits in and actually does the interview."

Jennifer faced the ordeal. She acknowledged that she knew how she'd been "criticized for not talking to the press and not answering every question they see fit to ask me" and explained that it wasn't because she wanted to be difficult; she realized that reporters were only trying to do their jobs and that an actress, indeed any public figure, "has no right to object to questions . . . but there are many things in my life I'm not free to discuss. They involve other people."

Jennifer was perfectly willing to reply to any questions limited solely to herself, her work, and her plans (she was about to make another tour of Veterans Administration hospitals). "But it is neither fair nor decent to talk about situations involving other people's lives." That, she said, was the reason she'd always fought for privacy, "even though I know I've antagonized many people."

Louella insisted, however, that Jennifer comment on David Selznick, and the actress did, praising his instincts and his brilliant mind. "He's the most wonderful man I have ever known."

That wasn't what Louella had in mind. Did she *love* him? the columnist wanted to know. Jennifer wouldn't make that declaration, so Louella subsequently did: "In the long time they have been in love, it has not always been happy for her. It never is for women who give their hearts to brilliant and erratic men." She didn't stop there: "But I think Jennifer would rather be miserable with David than happy with any other man."

It was an undeniably unsettled time in the lives of Jennifer Jones and David Selznick. Reports bluntly characterized their relationship as "in turmoil" and stated that Jennifer "felt guilt over the crack-up that Bob Walker had been undergoing since their divorce."

Selznick was distracted and tense coping with the never-ending troubles besieging his fast-disintegrating empire. His only hope of staving off financial catastrophe was *Portrait of Jennie,* due for release in Los Angeles in late December to qualify for Academy Award consideration. The film had been in production for over twenty months. Cameraman Joseph August had suffered a heart attack and died as a result of the terrific pressure.

Selznick had decided that the gossamer tale required an epic finale; the public *expected* magnitude and scope from a Selznick production. Additional money was borrowed and allocated to the picture's already hopelessly swollen budget.

Jennifer was soon to begin working again, this time on loan-out to MGM. It was a prospect that didn't appeal to her at all. Among other reasons, she knew many friends of Walker's were employed on the lot. But Selznick had concluded arrangements for her to portray the title role in a film version of Gustave Flaubert's literary masterpiece, *Madame Bovary,* to be directed by Vincente Minnelli.

Jennifer hadn't been Minnelli's or producer Pandro Berman's first choice. Lana Turner, who'd scored a critical as well as box office success the previous year in the highly dramatic *Green Dolphin Street,* had been the front-runner. (Jennifer, at Selznick's urging, had reportedly turned down the starring role opposite Spencer Tracy in MGM's *Cass Timberlane,* which became one of Lana's biggest hits.) But Turner was pregnant, and her condition opened the door for cash-hungry Selznick to engage in high-level maneuverings for Jennifer to play Emma Bovary.

Insiders believed that the primary reason Jennifer hadn't wanted to play the part was that many in Hollywood regarded *Madame Bovary,* although set in the nineteenth century, as a tale that closely paralleled Jennifer's situation. Emma is a woman searching for "the flower beyond the dung hill," a woman who dreams of high romance and impossible love and who dwells on images of things that never existed.

As in Jennifer's life, the character of Emma attended convent schools, where the lonely girl learned "to live within herself." She was a girl with "one kind of dream, another kind of life." In Emma Bovary "there was a terrifying capacity for pursuing the impossible. . . . Experience would always be a prison, freedom would lie just beyond the horizon."

The description offered of Charles, Emma's infatuated young husband (played by Van Heflin), is also telling—"He is not Prince Charming—he is only a man. . . ." And when Charles observes Emma's restlessness, she tells him, "How do I know what I want?" Emma realizes that she's burningly ambitious, and she doesn't dislike herself for it: "I can't help it, it's how I am," she explains.

Those in Hollywood familiar with the charged atmosphere that had enveloped the set of *Since You Went Away* couldn't fail to draw parallels between Jennifer, Selznick, and Walker and the scene in *Madame Bovary* in which the rich and powerful nobleman Rodolphe (Louis Jourdan) makes a blatant pass at Emma, which she tries to rebuff: "My husband is sitting not thirty feet from this window. . . ." Emma begs Rodolphe: "Don't torture me."

"Don't destroy me," he replies.

For all the alleged similarities between Jennifer and Emma, there were sharp differences: From the start, Emma is a bored woman, hungry for diversion, excitement, romance. A man doesn't charge into her life; she is constantly and boldly on the lookout for one. And unlike the doomed Emma, Jennifer certainly saw her "dreams" come true.

The closing narration, after Emma has committed suicide: "She had touched on numerous lives—some despised her; some profited by her; and some she had ruined would never cease to love her."

Scheduled to begin production in mid-December, *Madame Bovary* placed Jennifer in talented hands. Producer Pandro Berman had been Selznick's former assistant at RKO fifteen years earlier. A shrewd and gifted man, he'd risen to become head of production at that studio and knew how to mount, fight for, and market a prestige film.

Director Minnelli's painstaking attention to detail and great sense of visual style were highly respected by Selznick. This would be Minnelli's tenth film. He hadn't directed a film in over a year, after the traumatic experience of making *The Pirate* with his wife, Judy Garland. Their marriage was on shaky ground, and Minnelli was a bundle of nerves. He was also an expert at presenting beautiful people at their most beautiful. Jennifer would be showcased with optimum skill, and to complete the *Bovary* package, Selznick loaned out contract players Louis Jourdan and Christopher Kent (later to achieve renown under his actual name, Alf Kjellin).

"Oh, what an interesting project!" exclaimed Judy Garland, jealous that husband Minnelli wasn't "typecast" by the studio as she was. To Minnelli's chagrin, she complained bitterly about "the formula shit they keep putting me into!"

Studio executives Ben Thau and Eddie Mannix recognized a juicy opportunity: fire Robert Walker at once, which would thereby prevent the possibility that the actor might upset Jennifer while she was working on the lot (not to mention remove the burden of dealing with Walker from their own lives).

Dore Schary had other ideas. "I had a long talk with Bob in which I suggested he go to the Menninger Clinic in Topeka for treatment," recalled Schary. "He responded by yelling that he wasn't crazy, but when reassured that that was not my diagnosis, he listened as I explained that if he had TB, he would be neither ashamed nor reluctant to try to cure himself."

Schary could do nothing but offer an ultimatum. If he went for help, the studio would pick up the hospital bills; if not, his contract would be terminated.

When Jennifer learned that Walker had decided to seek treatment at Menninger's (the Betty Ford Clinic of its day), she was greatly relieved. So, too, was Selznick, who'd often told friends that Walker had been driving them both crazy for years. (Dorothy Parker, tongue firmly in cheek, remarked that perhaps Jennifer and David, and not Robert Walker, should have been sent to Menninger's for observation.)

Jennifer's sons were at the time unaware of their father's upcoming ordeal at Menninger's. They were told, "Dad is going to be away on location for a movie," and had no reason to question or doubt it. Their parents' self-involvement had been a fact of life from day one—whose mother or father wasn't away working on a movie most of the time?

As the December 16 start date for *Madame Bovary* approached, Jennifer was immersed in the myriad details that went into the making of a motion picture.

Robert Ardrey's script had remained as true to the spirit of Flaubert's novel as censors would permit. The Breen Office had insisted many sex scenes be eliminated, pointing out to MGM that "adultery was presented too attractively." To overcome censors' objections, the script had finally been structured to present the author of *Madame Bovary*, Gustave Flaubert (James Mason) in a prologue and epilogue to the story, explaining Emma's tale during the course of his own obscenity trial (on publication in Paris, in 1857, the novel was banned as an "outrage against public morals").

The film was a difficult shoot physically. The elaborate period costumes were constructed of heavy fabrics and required Jennifer to wear tight corsets morning to night while working under hot lights. To relax between setups, she'd have to recline stiffly on a wooden plank to prevent her costume from wrinkling.

Selznick bombarded Minnelli and Pan Berman with suggestions on Jennifer's appearance. He was satisfied with hairdresser Larry Germain (who, under Selznick's personal supervision, created hairpieces for Jennifer to wear in the film). He was pleased with the costume designs of the brilliant Walter Plunkett, who'd created the costumes for *Gone With the Wind* and was everybody's choice for the *Bovary* wardrobe.

However, Selznick was greatly concerned about Jennifer's makeup and feared that an attempt would be made to pluck her heavy eyebrows. He told Minnelli not to worry about the eyebrows, describing them as part of "her unique loveliness," and virtually implored the director to leave Jennifer's eyebrows "strictly alone."

Minnelli's favorite make-up person, Dotty Ponedel, who'd done a masterful makeover job on Judy Garland for *Meet Me in St. Louis,* devised a makeup for Jennifer. Selznick hated it, criticizing the masklike result. It wasn't his last word on the subject. He saw further makeup tests and angrily informed the producer and director that Jennifer's appearance had been changed so drastically "that she looks like a cross between Lynn Bari and Buff Cobb." (These were well-publicized but hardly top-level actresses of the day.)

He was not without a further sense of humor at Jennifer's expense: "Apparently whoever made her up was under the impression that Emma Bovary is a Javanese." His criticisms were very specific: the makeup made her face too pointy; the lip rouge was ludicrous, making her mouth look like Joan Crawford's; and Jennifer's most striking feature, her eyes, were, according to Selznick's evaluation of the makeup, minimized. "I urge that whoever made her up *not* be used, because I cannot tell you how strongly I feel that this makeup is just awful, and precisely what is not indicated, either for Miss Jones or the role."

Needless to say, the makeup person was changed.

Robert Walker was making trouble once again. On December 5 he tried to escape from Menninger's. Doctors had recommended he be committed for at least a year, and with a heavy heart Walker's father had signed the necessary forms. Bob, with Dore Schary's long-distance encouragement, had coped with the hospital regimen for about a month. Now he wanted out.

Always the consummate actor, Walker had talked his doctors into letting him go into town. There he and three newly met "pals" soon landed downtown at police headquarters, charged with being drunk and disorderly.

Police sergeant Russell Purdie, upon discovering that Walker was a Menninger's patient, contacted the clinic. A staff doctor was dispatched to the stationhouse to bring the actor back to the hospital. Before he arrived, Walker had plunged his fist through a glass case. "He was a wild one," recalled Sergeant Purdie, whose shoulder was bruised in an ensuing struggle. Purdie also noted that Walker, afterward, seemed to be "in deep shock," his hands slashed and bleeding. He was taken to a hospital by Menninger's physician Fred M. Tatzlaff. At the hospital Walker had to be physically restrained by Dr. Tatzlaff, as Dr. James Bowden sewed up the actor's wounds (which required over a hundred stitches).

City attorney Frank Eresch, who described Walker as "a very sick man," dropped the drunk and disorderly charges. The actor later had no recollection of anything that had occurred.

Jennifer began Madame Bovary *on December 16, the day Minnelli and Pan* Berman received a twenty-five-page memo from Selznick outlining his thoughts on her character's motivation. Minnelli found Selznick's suggestions "totally impossible to implement."

Coincidentally, that same day Barbara Ford was granted her divorce from Robert Walker on the grounds of "extreme cruelty." In court Barbara cited the physical abuse she'd received and related other unhappy specifics regarding the brief marriage, such as how Walker had called her names and, after a movie premiere, wouldn't let her in his car and drove off alone.

She requested no alimony. Incredibly, she retained no bitter memories of the marriage—quite the contrary. Over the years Walker never apologized or attempted to make amends.

Vincente Minnelli was meticulous in his demands, and Jennifer strove to meet them. Overall he was pleased with her efforts. She did her best work in later scenes, when she was playing not the very young Emma, but the more mature, disillusioned young woman. (It's interesting that in later years Jennifer reflected on how she wished she'd played the role later in her career.) She beautifully underplays the moment when, screamed at by her husband—who does not realize that she has swallowed a lethal dose of arsenic—she replies: "Don't hate me, Charles, don't hate me now. . . ."

There was a disturbing incident during production that sharply reflected Jennifer's state of mind. As filming progressed, she got ever deeper into her character. The day came to film a key scene involving Emma, her very young daughter, and the child's nurse. Emma has returned home after committing adultery; consumed with guilt, she tries to hug and kiss her little girl. The child senses something different about her mother and recoils from her.

"To get the right reaction from the little girl," recalled Minnelli, "she was not permitted to meet Jennifer." When the cameras were ready to roll, Minnelli told Jennifer "to take away the little girl's favorite pair of red shoes." The actress did so, the child was totally surprised, "and we got the required reaction," recalled Minnelli. However, "The little girl . . . hadn't distinguished between the real and the make-believe, and continued turning her back on Jennifer."

It came time to film Jennifer's death scene. "Now Jennifer had to court the little girl," recalled Minnelli. "She had her to lunch in her dressing room and brought her little presents. [When it] came time for rehearsal the little girl still refused to have anything to do with Jennifer. 'She took my red shoes,' she said, glaring accusingly. It was more than Jennifer could bear. She fled the set in tears. I set out in pursuit.

" 'She doesn't like me,' Jennifer cried. 'She thinks I'm terrible. Nobody likes me.' "

It was an astonishing moment. Ignoring the larger implications of Jennifer's hysterical admission, Minnelli tried to calm her. "Jennifer," he said, "we planned it this way. You have to work with her and have a little patience." Jennifer "came around," recalled Minnelli, "but her first instinct had been the slightly neurotic reaction to run and cry"—just as she'd done six years earlier when she'd become upset working with Robert Walker on the set of *Since You Went Away.*

• • •

Portrait of Jennie opened on *December 25, 1948, at the Carthay Circle Theater* (the same theater where *The Song of Bernadette* had premiered) in Los Angeles. The previous day, to Selznick's dismay, a negative *Hollywood Reporter* review of the film had appeared. Jennifer "gives a sensitive, appealing performance," stated the critic, who then went on to note that the picture "never comes to life." *Variety* described Jennifer's talents as "showcased inspiringly," then said that the film's "very spiritual quality, no matter how tastefully done, lacks the earthy warmth needed to spellbind." Press reaction in general was cool, and box office receipts were highly disappointing. The public had accepted her as saint, sinner, and girl next door, but as a demure ghost the chemistry for drawing crowds was apparently negative.

The worst was yet to come. The actress's performance didn't garner an Oscar nomination (nor were there nominations for any of the film's other creative people, other than the special effects department). Selznick withdrew *Portrait* from further distribution and invested more capital to enhance the movie's finale, apparently ignorant of the old maxim "When you're in a hole, quit digging." He was confident that by March, when the picture was scheduled to premiere in New York, he'd have turned *Portrait of Jennie* around.

Incredibly, Selznick was still up to his old tricks. At Christmastime there had been another business meeting with Shirley Temple, now twenty years old. Selznick was in his stocking feet. Shirley attempted to leave, and like a scene from a "B" movie, Selznick locked the door with the remote-control switch under his desk. He chased the actress around the room, but Temple was an agile twenty, and the forty-six-year-old producer began wheezing. He made light of the situation. "It's just the game that oils Hollywood's wheels," he quipped. "Makes them run smoothly."

Shirley once again joked her way out of the situation. "Banter was more effective with Selznick than a knee," she later observed philosophically.

David was involved, long distance, in a "small" project, the brainchild of the brilliant Alexander Korda. They were coproducing *The Third Man*, based on Graham Greene's novel, a contemporary romantic thriller to be filmed by director Carol Reed on locations in Europe. Selznick was providing partial financing, American distribution—and lots of difficulties.

Selznick respected the renowned Korda, a preeminent creative force in the British film industry (to Selznick's dismay, the Hungarian-born Korda, in America, had at one point almost succeeded in taking control of United Artists). Korda was one of the few who matched Selznick in daring, foresight, and a flair for showmanship and standards of production (both men shared another trait—each had formed intense bonds with siblings, in Korda's case his brothers Zoltan and Vincent). Korda, however, surpassed Selznick in the courage department. Korda had directed as well as produced films, with spectacular success. *The Private Life of Henry VIII* was already a classic, and *That Hamilton Woman,* starring Vivien Leigh and Laurence Olivier, was Winston Churchill's favorite movie (Korda also happened to be one of Churchill's favorite people). While Selznick had longed to participate in the war, Korda had done so, as a special operative for the British government. Korda had also "created," and subsequently married, the sultry and ambitious Merle Oberon (the couple ultimately divorced). Korda, unlike Selznick, was a virtuoso in practically any social situation and was the first moviemaker to be awarded a knighthood. Irene Selznick referred to Sir Alex as "the spellbinder."

With the caliber of talents involved, *The Third Man* promised to be something unique and special. Carol Reed and Graham Greene (who'd also written the script) had traveled to the United States for meetings with Selznick at the time when Jennifer was appearing on stage in *Serena Blandish.* To the dismay of the distinguished director and author, Selznick was immersed in Jennifer's play. Script conferences on *The Third Man* took place late at night, when Selznick's mind seemed elsewhere. (*Tess of the D'Urbervilles* was another project under discussion for Jennifer, to be coproduced by Selznick and Korda and directed by Reed.) Selznick subsequently offered detailed advice on the *Third Man* script via lengthy memos and transatlantic telephone calls. He was already aware that Jennifer's future, as well as his own, would unfold overseas.

Chapter
18

*J*anuary 2 *marked the tenth anniversary of* Robert Walker's marriage to Jennifer. As merrymakers ushered in 1949, Walker was undergoing treatment at Menninger's.

"I went into that clinic a beaten guy," he said, "frightened and desperately unhappy, tortured by a sense of guilt and anger, doomed to the living death of an alcoholic." He described himself as "really off my rocker."

In Hollywood Jennifer remained immersed in the awesome task of filming a major movie and creating a believable character. Any stress in her private life was an asset insofar as her characterization of Emma Bovary was concerned. Anxiety and tension were essential emotions throughout the story.

"I thought Jennifer a very professional actress," said Van Heflin. "She was high-strung, but intent on getting things right. She listened very closely to the director and didn't throw her weight around, as some of the other star ladies I'd worked with often did."

Jennifer was nervous about filming the big production sequence for *Madame Bovary,* a formal ball involving hundreds of full-dress extras, during which she was to be waltzed around the ballroom at ever-increasing speed, the crane-mounted camera following her every move.

Composer Miklos Rozsa had composed an exciting "neurotic waltz" for the sequence. Minnelli had carefully choreographed every moment of the action to match the music. It was, in effect, a musical number making a vital story point—Emma's most dazzling moment and a turning point in her fortunes. It was easily the film's most memorable sequence.

Walter Plunkett had designed a breathtaking, low-cut white ball gown for Jennifer to wear. "Jennifer did it justice," said Plunkett. "She wore the gown, it didn't wear her. In that costume, Jennifer reminded me of Vivien as Scarlett. Small waist, exquisite shoulders— really stunningly beautiful, regal and sensuous at the same time."

Jennifer's toiling on the Metro lot coincided with publicity trumpeting the studio's gala twenty-fifth anniversary. A special celebratory luncheon was scheduled to take place on one of the giant soundstages. The studio's stars, by royal command of Messrs. Mayer and Schary, were to be present. MGM newsreel cameras were going to film the proceedings and exhibit the footage as part of the weekly newsreel presented in Loew's theaters throughout the country. The stars were also scheduled to pose for a group photo for *Look* magazine.

"But I'm not an MGM star," Jennifer observed accurately when her presence was requested. But David agreed with the studio. He regarded the publicity as both positive and safe, as there would be no interviews, only pictures.

Jennifer took a break during shooting to attend the luncheon. Long rows of tables, draped in white cloths, were arranged in tiers, banquet style, to accommodate the guests. Jennifer was the only star to show up in costume, an exquisite lace mantilla framing her face. Stress and strain were hardly evident in her appearance that day. She dutifully picked at her meal and sat only a few seats away from Ava Gardner, who'd recently begun her torrid affair with thirty-four-year-old Frank Sinatra.

Ava, laughing and joking, wore a simple tailored suit and absolutely no makeup, and she looked as though she hadn't slept in a week. Judy Garland was on hand, slim, bubbly, and vivacious. (Judy, like Robert Walker, was undergoing intense psychotherapy, soon to include electroshock treatments. She'd attempt suicide and would be fired by the studio within less than a year.)

• • •

As production on <u>Bovary</u> wore on, Jennifer found herself playing a far more demanding and personal role. On the home front she was, like it or not, Selznick's hostess. This was one ongoing performance—or obligation—for which there was no script and for which no director was on hand to orchestrate her every move (although Selznick was not beyond taking over that function).

For a less resolute and determined woman, the situation would have been overwhelming. Selznick was a perfectionist and at first expected as much from Jennifer. In retrospect it's amazing she survived this period without suffering a breakdown.

Jennifer's role as hostess was a challenge neither the actress nor the woman was particularly anxious to meet. She hadn't cultivated the ability to organize big-time social gatherings, a specialized talent that was an art in itself (Jennifer's favorite food in her Walker years was a hamburger and a glass of milk).

The type of entertaining that David and his friends were used to and expected, often on very short notice, required the expertise of a city planner—detailed menu books, special notes on people's favorite dishes, their preferred cocktails, knowing where to buy food and flowers. David liked handwritten place cards with personal messages for each guest.

The comparison between Jennifer and Irene in this area was most unflattering to the actress. But Selznick grudgingly accepted Jennifer's limitations—what choice did he have?

Selznick's staff, of course, saw to the overall mechanics of the parties (and the less formal atmosphere was in fact preferred by some friends). The personal touch, however, the people-mixing aspects of entertaining, required a savoir faire that eluded and possibly didn't even interest Jennifer.

Jennifer was late coming home from the studio one evening. It had been a very long, exhausting day, and it was after eight P.M. She was supposed to be hosting an informal party for David and his friends but was nowhere in sight when the guests arrived.

For an hour the visitors milled about without any refreshments. Selznick was informed that the lady of the house was upstairs, having her hair done. When she finally appeared, half-empty martini glass in hand, Selznick was furious. She apologized and seemed genuinely surprised the maid hadn't served drinks. But her faux pas was compounded, in the eyes of the thirsty throng, by the sight of her own half-consumed cocktail (which, said friends, she'd been sipping "to bolster her courage and her spirits").

Sparks flew, and Jennifer and David argued for the rest of the evening, sounding at times like an angry father and a rebellious daughter.

The Selznick divorce had been finalized in January, but David continued to send Irene expensive gifts. Irene was at a loss as to how to stop him from making such extravagant gestures, which he could ill afford and which were ridiculously inappropriate.

Jennifer was simply at a loss. Quarreling with David, a situation she found emotionally draining in the extreme, seemed the rule now.

David was officially free to wed, but Jennifer continued to maintain total silence on the subject. Pressed by Louella Parsons for details on their plans, Selznick told the reporter that there was a strong possibility he and Jennifer would wed that summer in Europe.

Selznick's sons seemed to like her and she them, and on occasion young Jeffrey even accompanied his father and Jennifer to screenings.

German actress Hildegarde Knef had emigrated to the United States, and Selznick signed her to a contract, reasoning that she'd have box office value abroad. Bartering actors' services to other studios was a game he needed to play more than ever. (When the subject of his lending out his actors for profit was discussed with Jennifer, she would reply, "David never loans out actors under contract to him for pictures he doesn't believe in himself. Money doesn't mean that much to him.")

One evening Knef received a telephone call at home from one of Selznick's secretaries. "Mr. Selznick would like you to be here in half an hour." It was ten P.M., but Knef's husband drove her to the studio and told her he'd wait for her in the parking lot.

When Knef was ushered into Selznick's office, he was seated behind his desk, deep in conversation on the telephone. He remained engrossed in his call, then finally "looked over at me and pointed to an armchair." Details of the encounter remained vivid in Knef's memory. She recalled that "logs burning in the fireplace dispensed intolerable heat; two standard lamps shed discreet light;

through an open door I saw a bathroom with a shower."

Selznick remained on the phone for what seemed an eternity; then a second telephone began ringing. He took the second call and placed yet another to Mexico City.

"I sat there feeling like a fish out of water, exposed, peeled, seen through," remembered Knef. "With each minute I felt more certain that Selznick had summoned me only to say 'Your contract is invalid, work permit refused, option dropped.' "

At midnight Selznick finally hung up the phone. He stood up. "He crossed to a mirror, polishing his glasses, placed them on his nose, stroked his hair, and said to his reflection, 'Tell me about yourself.'

" 'What would you like to know?'

" 'Everything.' " Knef said that she felt "like someone who has been ordered to tell a funny story." Selznick plopped down on a sofa, stretched his legs, and waited for her tale to begin. Knef did her best as Selznick took notes. "Could make a good story," he said.

He went into the bathroom. "I heard the shower gushing, heard gasps and gargling," recalled Knef. "When he returned, his hair was wet and his shirt fresh. 'You're an interesting girl. . . .' " He was standing in front of the frightened actress.

"I thought it wiser to stand up, but the edge of the seat pressed against the backs of my knees, and I plopped down again," she recalled. "This stimulated his sense of humor. 'Do you like me a little?' he asked, pulling me up."

Knef was near panic. "I don't know you very well," she said, sounding to herself like a total fool.

"That could be changed," replied Selznick.

Knef recalled: "I stared at the wide neck, the tight smile, a smile that meant power. 'I don't know any German girls,' he said, and tugged at my jacket. . . .

"The man, smelling of mouthwash and after-shave, was more menacing than the Russians. . . .

" 'I feel sick,' I said, because I felt sick, and ran for the bathroom. I couldn't find the toilet, so I vomited into the basin, looked at myself across the bottles and tubes."

When Knef returned from the bathroom, Selznick was back on the telephone. "As I crossed to the door, he called out, 'Nine o'-clock tomorrow at MGM, they want to test you for a new film. If you get the part, I'll loan you out.' "

• • •

Jennifer turned thirty on March 2. Moviegoers were going to have the opportunity to see her in two films this year, with the New York opening date for *Portrait of Jennie* set for March 29, at the Rivoli Theater. It would be a special benefit premiere for Mrs. William Randolph Hearst's favorite charity, the Milk Fund. Selznick was pulling out all stops to launch the film in spectacular fashion, even using a gimmick called a Cyclorama to augment the hurricane finale of the picture.

He'd attempted unsuccessfully to interest former partner Mary Pickford, still in control of United Artists, into codistributing the film nationally. A United Artists deal, however, wouldn't have made much difference. It was the worst of times for the movie industry. Thousands of movie theaters had already closed all over the country, as television fast became the land's new leisure-time obsession. The lush days were over. Surviving movie houses had begun using giveaway gimmicks to lure customers. In the old days it had been sets of dishes, now it was automobiles!

The Cyclorama paid off for *Portrait of Jennie* in the film's Rivoli engagement, but the equipment was far too costly—and scarce—to install in other theaters in other cities. And without it *Jennie* would, to David's deep dismay, prove to be a dismal box office failure. Nor were many critics ecstatic about either Jennifer or the movie. "There is a grave sincerity about [Jennifer's] portrayal which gives a bit of plausibility to a drama of the spirit," wrote Howard Barnes in the *New York Herald-Tribune.* Jennifer never saw the finished picture, indicating how traumatic an experience it had been for her.

The movie wasn't yet in wide release when, in April, the industry received a shock. The Selznick studio (i.e., its physical equipment) went on the auction block. *The Hollywood Reporter* headline, on April 7, 1949, was a stunner, a chilling reminder to all filmmakers on how vulnerable they'd all become: SELZNICK STUDIOS GOES ON THE BLOCK. TWO-DAY AUCTION SALE OF ALL PRODUCTION EQUIPMENT.

(Irene, to the end a silent partner in David's company, was bought out for under $100,000, quite a bit less than the $5–$6 million Selznick said the company had been worth after the release of *Since You Went Away* only five years earlier.)

Jennifer and Selznick were in New York at the time of the auction. They attended an exclusive costume party celebrating powerful gossip columnist Dorothy Kilgallen's ninth wedding anniversary.

The event took place at Kilgallen's sixteen-room Park Avenue apartment. The theme of the soiree was *Gone With the Wind* (Kilgallen was costumed as Scarlett O'Hara). Jennifer and David arrived after an evening at the theater. They were the only guests who'd been permitted to attend in "ordinary" evening dress, and the waltz from *Gone With the Wind* was played on their entrance. Games of all kinds, including roulette, were set up throughout the apartment. Jennifer tried a "sex appeal machine." Her reading: "Fair."

Despite Selznick's sad financial condition, appearances, even during this critical period, never faltered. Jennifer continued to purchase closets full of the finest designer clothing and accessories and to employ a complete household staff. (To Selznick's surprise, at one point Jennifer offered to sell her belongings, if he needed money. He was touched by the gesture and fearful she might do it! At the same time, Jennifer often forgot where she'd placed expensive jewelry and had misplaced, perhaps intentionally, her Oscar.)

When Jennifer traveled, with or without David, it was still strictly first class all the way. She departed for Europe not long after the New York premiere of *Portrait of Jennie*. The anxiety of the past weeks had taken its toll. By the time her plane landed at Shannon Airport in Ireland, the actress was in a state of collapse and was diagnosed as suffering from fatigue.

On the home front, Selznick continued to maneuver and hustle furiously behind the scenes, liquidating some assets and juggling others, to keep up a flow of income. The results were better than anticipated. He sold outright the contracts of Gregory Peck, Shirley Temple, Joseph Cotten, Louis Jourdan, and Rhonda Fleming for around $1.5 million. Eagle-Lion, a minor company, purchased reissue rights to ten Selznick films, including those he'd made with Jennifer.

Selznick's bank debts, a reported $12 million in all, were corporate and not linked to his personal funds (although his gambling losses were). Of course, when one owes $10,000 to a bank and can't pay, one is in deep trouble. When one owns $10 million and can't pay, the bank is in trouble.

Others in Selznick's position would have simply declared bankruptcy and begun anew. But David's sense of integrity and the ghastly specter of how his father had ended up penniless precluded such a decision. He shuddered at how it would have looked to such dear and respected friends as Jock Whitney and William Paley to see the one and only David O. Selznick not only go down the financial drain, but also renege on his debts. (Paley lent him a considerable sum, interest free, during this period, and Selznick paid him back every cent.)

Rough Sketch, by now retitled *We Were Strangers,* was released in the spring. Because of John Huston's outspoken political views, the film, as some had feared, encountered a nasty attack from *The Hollywood Reporter.* Jennifer, by association, found herself in the center of an ugly controversy. The trade paper described the movie as "blatant propaganda" and "the heaviest dish of Red theory ever served to an audience outside the Soviet." Columbia Pictures czar Harry Cohn was so incensed by the comments that he withdrew his studio's advertising from the *Reporter* (and kept it out for years).

Jennifer remained silent as Huston's brief response to the attack said it all: "Absurd." The writer-director had just won Oscars for his script and direction of *The Treasure of the Sierra Madre,* and interest in his latest venture was at a peak. But influential critics had mixed feelings about the movie. *Time* magazine found the film "murky . . . but above average." *The New York Times* described it as "a passionless action film" and found Jennifer's performance "lacking."

It was Jennifer's second box office dud.

Robert Walker was released from Menninger's on May 15. Six months of successful treatment had ostensibly effected a "cure." He wasn't reluctant to talk about the experience and reveal the lessons he'd learned. "The way I reacted to reality, such as my divorce from Jennifer, reflected my immaturity," he said. The breakup with Jennifer had given him an excuse to drink and feel sorry for himself. "I have nothing to hide now," he said, and he wasn't afraid to let his sons know the truth. He'd decided to hold nothing back from them, since mental illness was just that—an *illness*—and could be treated.

These views were so far ahead of what the public of the day could either understand or accept that MGM publicity director Howard Strickling, who knew where all skeletons were buried in everyone's closets (including L. B. Mayer's), requested that Walker refrain from any more talking.

The actor's doctors recommended periodic return visits to the clinic, and Walker voiced no objections. Dore Schary was told that Walker could return to work, but the executive was cautioned to cast him initially in a nondemanding role.

Please Believe Me was a romantic comedy starring Deborah Kerr that was slated for a late August start. That gave Walker several months to adjust to being a "civilian" and enabled him to ease himself back onto a soundstage. He'd also have a friend close by. Peter Lawford was one of the film's two other leading men (Mark Stevens, whose wife, Annelle, was one of Barbara Ford's close friends, was the other).

Bobby junior and Michael would once again be spending the summer with their dad. Jennifer, assuming she was doing Bob a favor, offered to lend him her house (she would be in Europe). Walker declined and instead rented a house for himself and the boys in Pacific Palisades.

Slim Hawks Hayward (she'd married agent-producer Leland Hayward in June) recalled that she, Leland, and Quique and Louis Jourdan were "the impresarios in charge of getting David Selznick married to Jennifer Jones."

For personal reasons, despite Jennifer's and David's entreaties, Anita Colby chose not to be part of the festivities. To begin with, there was no love lost between Colby and Slim Hawks Hayward. Colby knew far more than most about the real story behind Slim's marriage to director Howard Hawks and her subsequent rise to fame as a symbol of great style and chic.

"Norma Shearer told me how, in the beginning, Slim, then a brash sixteen-year-old, had simply moved in with Hawks, knowing full well that his wife, Athole—Norma's sister—was not well and living upstairs. Athole remained bedridden upstairs virtually the entire time Hawks and Slim had their affair."

The state of Athole's mental health declined precipitously. According to Shearer's account to Colby, Slim couldn't have cared less. Colby also states emphatically, and photographs of the day confirm, that "Slim copied me—my hair, my clothes, my look. And yet she claimed to be this great 'original.'"

Only a couple of months earlier, prior to the Selznick nuptials, Colby had declined an invitation to Rita Hayworth's wedding to

Prince Aly Khan in Vallauris, France. Colby quietly explains today that both Rita's and Jennifer's weddings were—Colby chooses her words extremely carefully—"too Hollywood," she finally says. A devout Catholic, she didn't want her name used in connection with either event (Rita, like Jennifer, was a Catholic, and the Vatican subsequently pronounced Hayworth's controversial civil marriage "illicit" in the eyes of the Church).

According to one account, Colby had even "tried to convince Jennifer that marriage to David would be a mistake, and Jennifer was almost persuaded." But finally David felt he'd look ridiculous if she *didn't* marry him.

The date for Jennifer's marriage to David was finally set: July 13. The plan was to board Selznick's chartered thirty-three-ton English yacht, *Manona,* "in Antibes, sail to Portofino, then drive to Genoa for the marriage," recalled Slim Hawks. But Jennifer was still vacillating. Selznick kept after her with such intensity that on one occasion, on board the yacht, she dove into the water and swam ashore.

One night after dinner, on deck, under the beautiful Mediterranean moon, Jennifer suddenly asked, "David, why are we doing this?"

Slim was astonished. "What are you saying?" she asked Jennifer.

"Well," replied Jennifer, "we're perfectly happy the way we are. I don't know why we're getting married."

Slim Hawks Hayward pointed out to her friend Jennifer, "You're getting married because you've gotten four friends to come out on this rotten boat and sail to Genoa, and by God, you're getting married! We're not going to let you out of it!"

The actress, however, "held her ground," recalled Slim, "and the air was soon rent with the sound of four people shrieking, 'You cannot do this!' "

Slim noted David's reaction. "David said nothing. He only sat there, looking puzzled."

The voyage continued. Very early one morning the boat finally arrived at Portofino and dropped anchor outside the harbor. Paparazzi in motorboats soon surrounded the craft.

"This was no encouragement to Jennifer," recalled Slim, "who decided her safety lay in spending the rest of her life in her stateroom. To get her off that boat and on to dry land was not easy."

It was like a scene from a spy movie, as Jennifer was sneaked off the boat and onto a speedboat belonging to a friend, Prince Pignatelli. The craft could easily outrace all others, and it swiftly set course for Rapallo, where Selznick had rented suites for the entire wedding party.

"During the night, as we traveled by sea, Jennifer's maid, chauffeur, and all her dresses traveled by land," recalled Slim. When they arrived in Portofino, the dresses were hung up "all around her room."

Slim was mystified. "What are they for?" she wanted to know.

Jennifer, "who'd been standing on her head doing her yoga," recalled Slim, "eased herself to the floor. 'I'm going to get married in one of them,' she said.

"One would have been enough," answered Slim.

"Well, I can't make up my mind which one I want to wear, so I brought them all. What are you going to wear?"

Slim explained that it hardly mattered what she wore; it was Jennifer's wedding. Jennifer finally selected a dress. However, "it looked just wrong for the occasion," recalled Slim. "There are moments to keep your mouth shut. This wasn't one of them. 'No, I don't like it,' I told her. 'Take it off! Give it to the maid.' "

When Jennifer was finally dressed, "she looked so young and damp and beautiful. One forgave her everything."

Slim gave Jennifer "something borrowed, something blue," the sapphire ring Leland Hayward had just given her as a wedding present. "Wear my ring, Jenny," she said. "It will bring both of our marriages good luck."

They traveled by car to Genoa and were married in City Hall.

"The service was translated, with a lot of help and lots of laughs," recalled Slim. "There's a phrase in the ceremony that calls for the bride to support her husband if he comes upon hard times. I kept saying, 'Don't agree to that!' We were all having hysterics and behaving very poorly!"

Selznick, however, "took it most seriously," observed Slim. After the ceremony he cabled Irene at her apartment at the Pierre Hotel in New York. The cable contained no message, only David's name. Irene phoned the telegraph company, asking for the rest of the message. She'd received the entire message, she was told.

Then she understood. (On future occasions David would sometimes sign a letter or a telegram, "Bigamist.")

• • •

Jennifer sent no telegrams to Robert Walker, who remained calm on reading of the nuptials. His only comment was, "I wish her all the happiness she deserves," a remark easily interpreted for its obvious implications. But Walker added: "She is first and foremost the mother of my sons."

He referred to Jennifer as "Mrs. Selznick" and refused to be drawn into any rehash of their years together. He made a point of the fact that he was looking forward to being a good father to his sons and making sure they "never suffer the torments I went through."

<u>Madame Bovary</u> *previewed well in Pasadena and Santa Monica, California,* and hopes were high as the film went into release in August. Jennifer and the movie received many positive, and some positively glowing, reviews.

Time magazine found the picture "fascinating" and "Miss Jones, in her best picture to date . . . gives a performance that is hardly ever out of focus, a feat that even the finicky Flaubert could admire."

Box office reaction in the United States was respectable (it grossed over $2 million domestic; $4 million was the magic number in those days). European audiences, however, were more responsive to the film. Jennifer won the Best Foreign Actress Award at the Paris Film Festival and the Film Français Grand Prix des Directeurs de Cinema from theater managers of France and North Africa. Interestingly, foreign audiences also liked her in *Portrait of Jennie*—she won the Spanish Triunfo Award as Best Actress, and *Cinemonde,* the French film publication, voted her the most popular and best foreign actress of the year.

The Selznicks now relocated to Europe (both Jennifer and David would commute frequently to the United States). The idea of a dramatic change of scenery appealed to them both, and Selznick's business prospects overseas were excellent. He'd have access to funds, earned by past films, which he'd been prohibited from transferring out of the countries in which they'd been earned. He also controlled valuable rights to many of his old films, which he intended to release for the first time in foreign territories that had only recently opened up.

The Selznicks were following a road many prominent Hollywood notables were taking (there were tax advantages for Americans living abroad), and they were in the forefront of high-profile Americans rediscovering the soundstages and playgrounds of Europe. Through Elsa Maxwell, Jennifer and David socialized with the crème de la crème of international café society, including the duke and duchess of Windsor. "The Windsors are wonderful people," Elsa told Jennifer, "you mustn't be afraid of them! The duchess adores your work." (The duchess, of course, was a former Baltimore girl.) Phil Isley's little girl, too, had come a long way in the years since she'd posed with Pawnee Bill for publicity photographs on the wide-open plains of Oklahoma. She didn't seem out of her element fraternizing with nobility, since, to paraphrase writer-producer-director Preston Sturges, Jennifer had always been a member in good standing of the aristocracy of beauty.

Jennifer and David were regarded with awe and respect by European filmmakers. Jennifer, too, relished the artistic challenges awaiting her. She was relieved to be away from the pressures of living under the Hollywood microscope. One is reminded of H. L. Mencken's observation on how Hollywood was "full of unhappy people. . . . I don't think that many of them are satisfied. The sort of attention that falls upon a movie personage is irksome and, in most of its aspects, insulting." Sentiments with which Jennifer undoubtedly concurred.

To Jennifer's consternation, an astonishing rumor was gaining credence both home and abroad. Ingrid Bergman, still married to Dr. Lindstrom, was pregnant with Italian director Robert Rossellini's child. Hedda Hopper flew to Italy to confront the star. Ingrid declared she was definitely *not* pregnant ("Do I *look* it?" she asked, laughing), and Hedda seemed satisfied.

Jennifer was relieved that Ingrid wasn't going to have to face a nightmarish scandal, but the persecution in the media that awaited Bergman had only momentarily been averted. After the blockbuster *The Bells of St. Mary's*, Ingrid's "saintly" image had lingered even longer than Jennifer's after *The Song of Bernadette*. While the recent *Joan of Arc* had flopped, the tidal wave of publicity featuring Bergman as St. Joan had gone a long way toward reestablishing that image. Ingrid had even won an Oscar nomination as Best Actress for her static performance as St. Joan.

Another Bergman flop was soon to be released, *Under Capricorn*, directed by Alfred Hitchcock, whose own career was hardly off to a promising post-Selznick start with this Technicolor turkey. (Years later, in New York for promotion and publicity on one of his final films, Hitchcock—after an afternoon of drinking—wasn't particularly warm in his recollections of either David Selznick or Ingrid Bergman. Of Ingrid he said, rather ungallantly: "She'd do it with doorknobs.")

Selznick's coproduction deal with Alexander Korda had begun auspiciously. *The Third Man* was a blockbuster hit throughout Europe and was due for release in the United States (where Selznick controlled its distribution) after the first of the year.

Revenue from the film's soundtrack alone—*The Third Man* theme was played by a single instrument, the zither (to the present day it is possibly the least expensive and most profitable movie soundtrack ever produced)—had already provided Selznick with a small fortune, and the film's box office success would be instrumental in enabling Selznick to reestablish his financial credibility.

Jennifer was due to begin a Selznick/Korda coventure, *Gone to Earth,* to be created by the brilliant team of Michael Powell and Emeric Pressburger. Both men were at their peak—their production of *The Red Shoes,* the highly innovative film about the ballet world, had proven to be an artistic and box office smash all over the world.

Selznick had great expectations regarding what Powell and Pressburger could do for Jennifer. So, of course, did she. But a successful collaboration among Powell, Pressburger, and the Selznicks was not in the cards. *Gone to Earth* was a Gothic tale, based on a Mary Webb novel, in which Jennifer was cast as a wild, superstitious Gypsy girl. The film's supporting cast featured David Farrar, Cyril Cusack, Sybil Thorndike, and Hugh Griffith.

Jennifer had to assume an English accent for the part and was subsequently criticized for it. Michael Powell, however, was delighted with it. "I thought it was fine. My mother was from that area of England, and I was very familiar with that particular accent." And Powell liked Jennifer. "She was very professional, but not coldly professional. She would often chat with the crew, and I sensed that she would have enjoyed talking to them even more, had not Selznick occupied so much of her time."

Both Jennifer and David liked "Mickey" Powell immensely, but David was greatly disappointed at what was turning up on screen, particularly Jennifer's close-ups (in fact, in a recent viewing of Powell's cut of the film, Jennifer's close-ups are ravishing). "I tended to ignore his advice and opinions, which was a mistake," Powell said. The director's close friends, Alfred Hitchcock and Carol Reed, had known how to handle Selznick. On *The Third Man,* recalled Powell, "Carol would phone him up in the middle of the night, and ask his advice on every step of the picture, and then go on entirely his own way."

Finally, after several months, production was completed, or so everyone thought. No other female star in the business had faced production schedules as extended as Jennifer's on her Selznick productions. Her movies with David weren't simply films, they were "like catastrophic events," remarked Michael Powell, "giant cauldrons in which the ingredients were stirred and changed so frequently that the chef lost track of the dish."

By now Jennifer longed to see her sons ("they were *very* much a part of her life," declares Anita Colby) and was distressed over the length of time she'd been separated from them. She made plans to return with David to the States at Christmastime, gather up the boys, and return with them to Europe. She didn't seem overly concerned at interrupting their education or separating them from the friends they'd made at the Black Foxe Academy.

"I have been begging Jennifer to take a rest for a year or more," Selznick wrote to Jack Warner, whose studio was supposed to distribute *Gone to Earth* in the United States, "but she has overruled me because of her desire to keep working. . . ."

Selznick had lined up a big production program for himself in Europe, but not at the expense of being separated from Jennifer. "Neither of us wants any further separations from the other," declared Selznick. "Jennifer will be with me in Europe regardless of whether she does pictures there or not." A bit of wishful thinking, since Selznick was acutely aware that all plans could change if some fantastic opportunity arose for Jennifer, in which case their personal lives would be secondary to her career.

● ● ●

Walker was hardly pleased on learning of Jennifer's plans to take the boys to Europe. Among other concerns, he was afraid the free-spending Selznick would spoil Michael and Bobby. But he seemed to accept the fact that he had little control over the situation.

Walker was involved in yet another automobile accident at this time. The incident occurred after he'd learned of Jennifer's plans, and speculation arose immediately that the two events were somehow connected and that he'd once again attempted to self-destruct.

Absolutely not, according to Walker. The accident was a minor one and not his fault, he said, and he claimed that police reports bore him out. Proof of how minor the accident had been was that he hadn't missed a single day of filming on the new picture in which he'd been cast, *The Skipper Surprised His Wife.* This low-budget comedy costarred Joan Leslie and was hardly indicative of the "important properties" Schary had led Walker to believe were on the agenda for him.

When Walker once again met with the executive, Schary asked him to be patient; he explained that among other projects in development was a major film to be based on the best-selling novel *Raintree County,* by Ross Lockridge. It was a Civil War saga to be produced on the scale of *Gone With the Wind,* and one of the leading roles, Schary said, was earmarked for Walker (Montgomery Clift eventually played the part).

What really concerned Walker at the moment was the block of free time he faced, since the studio had no scripts for him.

Chapter

19

ichael and Bobby would not be uprooted from the United States after all. Instead Jennifer and David would be returning to America for several months at least. Selznick had decided to reshoot much of *Gone to Earth* in Hollywood with a new director (Rouben Mamoulian). In Selznick's view, the film in its present form was unreleasable in the United States; he'd simply fly the British cast to the States to work on new scenes for the picture.

Once home, gossip-hungry friends bombarded the Selznicks with queries about Ingrid Bergman and her relationship with Rossellini. Jennifer, of course, never revealed any details about her friend. To her horror, however, Ingrid's true condition was finally revealed.

Ingrid *was* pregnant, reported Louella Parsons in February 1950, with the baby due in three months. The actress's fans wanted desperately to believe the denials emanating from Ingrid's camp, but Louella stuck by her story, claiming her source was irrefutable. (Many insiders assumed it was William Randolph Hearst, who'd received the news from his Rome bureau chief. To throw people off the track, Louella hinted her source might be Howard Hughes, producer of the forthcoming Rossellini-Bergman film, *Stromboli*. It was

Hearst, however, who stood to profit by the millions of newspapers to be sold as the story unfolded.)

The church groups that had descended with a vengeance on Jennifer for her erotic performance in *Duel in the Sun,* and on Rita Hayworth after she'd begun her romance with Aly Khan, now had a really hot issue to pursue. For the next three months, until Ingrid's baby was due, Hollywood spoke of little else. *Stromboli* was released in the United States and bombed. According to Selznick, it failed not because of the scandal, but because it was a bad picture. Ingrid in a good picture, he claimed, would still be a great success. He was risking public censure by taking such a stand; not many in Hollywood dared to defend the actress at this point, and Jennifer was proud of him.

The world watched and waited. Reverberations from this story, the likes of which had never been experienced by the modern motion picture industry, affected the way public personalities behaved for the next decade and a half. (Naturally, in earlier years stars had become pregnant out of wedlock, but they'd conveniently "disappeared" from public view, had the baby in secret, and conveniently reappeared with a newly "adopted" child.)

After Ingrid gave birth, her box office value dropped to zero in the United States, where she was regarded as a pariah. Jennifer and David kept in close touch with her. Selznick envisioned Bergman's great comeback under his aegis. People wondered if Selznick could have somehow prevented the scandal from erupting had Bergman still been under contract to him. After all, he'd managed to muddy the waters for years concerning his affair with Jennifer, whose dignity had been effectively maintained. But it was a question that would never be answered.

Selznick met with Ingrid and Rossellini in Paris, where the couple, finally married, were on their honeymoon. The mogul gave the impression that he'd signed Rossellini to a contract, but it wasn't true. Ingrid's days as a Selznick star were over.

As 1950 played out, Robert Walker had time on his hands. He palled around, as before, with Peter Lawford.

Lawford and Walker were introduced to a new MGM starlet,

twenty-nine-year-old Nancy Davis, who had recently arrived in Hollywood from New York. Ben Thau took a personal interest in Nancy, and Dore Schary liked her "quality." He thought she projected "class" and predicted a bright future for her at MGM. (Davis's competition at the studio for top roles was so imposing, it was almost ludicrous—Lana Turner, Elizabeth Taylor, Ava Gardner, Janet Leigh, Deborah Kerr, Greer Garson, Barbara Stanwyck, and Katharine Hepburn, among others.)

Apparently Nancy Davis found Robert Walker's vulnerable, little-boy-lost quality immensely appealing, just as Jennifer had. The dark side of the actor's personality must have intrigued and appealed to Nancy, too, since the couple saw a great deal of each other.

Bob liked Nancy. She was a brunette like Jennifer, and Walker's sons liked her. A friend of Peter Lawford's recounted an incident to Lawford's widow, Patricia, which involved Bob Walker and Nancy Davis and revealed their intimate relationship. " 'I remember when three or four of us walked into Bob Walker's house and saw a naked Nancy Davis standing there, looking shocked at being caught like that. She grabbed a towel and ran into the bathroom.' "

In later years this alleged incident became a source of great embarrassment to Nancy Davis. Her relationship with Walker was one she later chose to downplay, if not totally ignore, in recounting her Hollywood days, but her involvement with the troubled actor wasn't merely a fling. "Oh, I think it was more than that," declares Joan Fontaine.

The Walker-Davis romance soon ran its course, and each went on to pursue other interests.

Walker considered returning to Menninger's for one of the periodic visits the medical staff there had suggested. He'd faced recent bouts of depression, and recovery, after all, was an ongoing process.

Studio executives suggested to Walker that he simply continue therapy with a psychiatrist in Beverly Hills. Many in Hollywood were turning to the analyst's couch (more than two hundred of them would soon be concentrated on Bedford and Roxbury Drives, the areas nicknamed Libido Lane and Couch Canyon).

Dr. Frederick Hacker was a top local man, particularly adept at working with actors. L. B. Mayer had urged Judy Garland to consult Hacker, with positive results (or so everyone had thought). Hacker was noted for instilling confidence in his patients. He'd actually accompanied Judy to the studio's screening room, sat with her, and commented on how wonderful she was in *The Pirate* (as production on that troubled film went on and on).

Walker, urged on by Dore Schary, complied. The actor was delighted with his next MGM assignment and encouraged by it. He'd play a villain for the first time, in *Vengeance Valley,* a western to star Burt Lancaster. Location filming was scheduled to take place in Colorado in August, and Walker was gratified to learn he could take his sons along.

An opportunity to do a very important film in the United States presented itself to Jennifer. William Wyler, one of the top directors in the industry, was planning to direct another film for Paramount.

The film would be based on Theodore Dreiser's dark novel *Sister Carrie,* and rights had been owned by Paramount for years. In the early 1930s Sylvia Sidney had been the studio's choice for the title role. Ginger Rogers was the front-runner in the early forties. Now Wyler's initial choice was the immensely popular Jeanne Crain. The twenty-five-year-old actress had recently starred in a string of hit films, including *Pinky,* in which she played a black girl who passes for white.

Crain was under exclusive contract to 20th Century–Fox and ultimately unavailable for loan-out. Wyler thought the available Jennifer an excellent alternate and began negotiating with Selznick for her services. Much has been written about Wyler's reluctance to become involved with Jennifer because of the interference he was sure to encounter from Selznick during production. In fact, Wyler sought out Selznick's advice (and followed it) on casting the leading male role and asked for David's opinions on the script.

It was Selznick who was reluctant to offer his criticisms, aware that his input would be resented by writers Ruth and Augustus Goetz. He didn't want to sabotage the collaborative effort required to deliver a great film. It was to Jennifer's advantage, and essential to her career at this point, to appear in a great film.

Jennifer was both thrilled and fearful at the idea of costarring with Laurence Olivier, already acknowledged as "the greatest actor in the English-speaking world." (The studio's choices had ranged from the town's hottest new leading man, Kirk Douglas, to James Stewart, Gary Cooper, and Cary Grant, who'd been offered the part but turned it down.)

Olivier had recently won Oscars as Best Actor and Director for *Hamlet.* He was Selznick's sole recommendation for the male lead in *Sister Carrie.* (Casting him in his own production of *Rebecca* a decade earlier had paid fabulous dividends. And Wyler, of course, had established Olivier as a movie star in *Wuthering Heights.*)

Olivier signed for *Carrie* because it would be made in Hollywood. Lady Olivier, former Selznick crown jewel Vivien Leigh, now thirty-seven years old, was in a precarious mental state. Leigh's film career had been revived by the rerelease of *Gone With the Wind* and she'd be in Hollywood filming the arduous *A Streetcar Named Desire.* Friends understood why Olivier wanted to be nearby (Irene Selznick had produced the London stage production of *Streetcar,* starring Leigh and directed by Olivier, and she'd told friends that Leigh had "gone mental").

There was perhaps another reason, claimed knowledgeable insiders, that Olivier was anxious to spend time in Hollywood. He wanted to be near superstar Danny Kaye, with whom he was later reported to be having an affair. If this was true, it would certainly shed additional light on the reason for the bedraggled state of Vivien Leigh's emotions. (Selznick had lobbied for Jennifer to portray Blanche in the film of *Streetcar.* Director Elia Kazan found the prospect interesting, but Tennessee Williams—and Irene Selznick—wanted Vivien Leigh. Jennifer wasn't disappointed at losing the role—climbing into the skin of the neurotic, needy, desperate, penniless, aging, guilt-ridden Blanche DuBois was not exactly a joyous prospect.)

Jennifer was obviously heartened at the prospect of her juicy role in *Carrie.* Selznick agreed to his wife taking second billing to Olivier (who had specified that his title, "Lord," not be used in advertising or publicity). In the screen credits Jennifer's name would be followed by the legend "By Arrangement with David O. Selznick." "Perhaps," wrote one wag, "that should be the title of her memoirs."

Jennifer and David had dinner one evening with "Larry" and Vivien. Jennifer was understandably anxious at meeting the legendary Leigh, "David's greatest discovery." She was not disappointed—there was no trace of anxiety, fatigue, or distress in Vivien on this occasion. She was stunningly bejeweled and dressed, her unique smile and cunning wit dazzling to behold. Leigh's sophistication and finesse were genuine; she'd come from wealth and a socially correct background. Jennifer appeared awed by Vivien, who tried to put her at ease by telling humorous stories about mutual friends and pointing out how much she and Jennifer had in common: they'd both gone to convent schools, were both discovered by David, "and now you, too, are leading lady to Larry!"

Jennifer breathlessly reported details of the encounter to Anita Colby, who pointed out to Jennifer that she had obviously witnessed an Oscar-caliber performance.

For *Carrie*, Larry Germain once again styled Jennifer's hair, and Edith Head designed her costumes. But the unusual news for Jennifer during filming of this production had nothing to do with its packaging. Costar Eddie Albert recalls, "Jennifer was pregnant, and I recall Willie had to modify some shots to protect her. We were a 'quiet' group on that picture, there was neither high indignation nor great enthusiasm. We were simply good workmen.

"Jennifer was very shy, but a hard worker. She tried not to overexert herself physically. She was protecting her health, I suppose."

Laurence Olivier wasn't in the best physical shape. "He had a bad leg," recalls Albert, "and it was bothering him a lot. Sometimes he limped. But nobody worked as hard, [or was] as concentrated, I should say, as Larry."

Albert himself had worked hard getting ready for the picture. "I prepared for weeks before the picture began. Even then, Willie found a lot of new things in the role I had overlooked, or which hadn't occurred to me. It was a real job." As to subsequent stories that Selznick showed up on the set, and that there were confrontations between Selznick and Wyler, Albert replies: "I never saw David Selznick on the set at any time, [but] of course, I wasn't in every scene of the picture."

Albert would soon work for William Wyler again, on *Roman Holiday*, which introduced twenty-one-year-old Audrey Hepburn to the screen. Albert reflects that Jennifer and Hepburn "were very much alike. Both were top drawer, they knew their roles, worked hard, and never complained, that I know of." Both Jennifer and Audrey "wanted to be very good actresses," he says. Their businesslike approach, in Albert's view, was one "you don't see around much anymore."

Depending on whom one asks, Selznick was either thrilled at the news of Jennifer's pregnancy or ambivalent about it.

Jennifer foolishly denied a report by Louella Parsons that she'd missed a day of work on *Sister Carrie* to visit her doctor. (Louella was the first to learn about pregnancies because she paid off "spies" in the medical laboratories that processed the rabbit tests.) Jennifer told Louella she'd simply seen David off to Europe that day.

Wyler, on reading Louella's column, tolerated no polite denials from Jennifer and asked her bluntly if she was pregnant. She admitted she was and explained she hadn't told Wyler because she hadn't wanted to lose the role.

Wyler, a family-oriented man, told her that "no picture, not even one of mine, is worth risking your health for." He was all too aware of a dedicated actress's tunnel vision when it came to her work. The most single-minded actress of all, Bette Davis, had been determined to marry him; they'd collaborated (or "battled," to quote Davis) a decade earlier on three of her biggest hits, *Jezebel, The Letter,* and *The Little Foxes.* But Wyler knew his personal happiness relied on a mate who wasn't married to "the business."

He'd wedded a gorgeous young actress, Margaret Tallichet ("Talli"), who'd quickly abandoned her acting career when true love came along (she'd once been under contract to the Selznick studio and had tested for the role of Scarlett). Ms. Tallichet had seen for herself the kind of dedication and drive it required to become a star. One day, on a dark soundstage, waiting endlessly for a director to set up a shot, she'd asked herself: What's so great about this? She remained happily married to Wyler until the day he died, decades later.

Wyler assured Jennifer that careful camera angles would prevent any problems insofar as her appearance was concerned. But he was hardly able to help her regarding the tedious grind of making a big-budget movie. The hot lights and confining period costumes were highly uncomfortable. As was the case with *Madame Bovary,* off set Jennifer couldn't sit down and had to recline stiffly on a slant board. A wardrobe person, hot iron in hand, hovered constantly nearby to tend to the costume. And of course ultratight corsets were required for Edith Head's authentic gowns.

Wyler later said he'd told Jennifer she'd have to wear the period corsetry only in long or medium shots. "But she always had herself strapped in," he recalled. "Just watching her made me uncomfortable. She lost the baby after the picture. How much the strapping of her waist had to do with it I don't know."

Wyler was nonetheless impressed with Jennifer's professionalism. In Wyler, Jennifer had found a perfectionist like herself—the director later described *her* as a perfectionist, "always a little tense on the set and extremely conscientious, yet never quite satisfied with her work."

Once again Jennifer was appearing in a film that could easily be interpreted as a metaphor for her own life. "*Carrie* is *so* Jennifer," observes film historian Joan Perry. "The character is a woman with 'protectors'; she's a catalyst for men's misfortunes, a basically passive person. The filmmakers tried to make Carrie noble in the movie, but as written by Dreiser, she simply wasn't a noble sort, she didn't have the ability to feel what other people felt. She wasn't willing to slave in a factory to keep her virtue.

"She was not an evil person, she just didn't *see* things—things didn't get *through*." These characteristics might easily have been applied to Jennifer.

Author Dreiser saw *Sister Carrie* as a tale of "the blind strivings of the human heart." Carrie's mentor is an older man, George Hurstwood (Laurence Olivier), and parallels can certainly be drawn between Hurstwood and David Selznick; if a screenwriter were to prepare a fictional treatment based on the lives of Jennifer Jones and Selznick, he could use dialogue directly from *Carrie*.

A friend asks Hurstwood, "What is it you want, what are you looking for, George?"

"Everything," he answers.

"That's dangerous," replies his friend. "You've got everything any man could want—children, a fine wife [a social-climbing wife, played by Miriam Hopkins]." But Hurstwood wants to have his cake and eat it, too, and he subsequently deceives friends and family. He's obsessed with Carrie—she embodies his desire to recapture his lost youth.

"I want you more than I've ever wanted anything in my life," he tells her.

"I should have waited until I met you, George, but I didn't, and now I'm not free. . . ."

"I can't live without you," he tells her.

"I don't want you to live without me."

All the men in Carrie's life lie to her. Eddie Albert's character, her first lover in the story, has also lied to her by making her believe he's going to marry her.

Albert confronts Hurstwood (much as Robert Walker would have liked to confront David Selznick). "What right have you got to love her? What can *you* do for her? Lock her up someplace while you sneak around town like you've been doing so your wife won't see?"

Respectability is the keynote for the behavior of all characters. And it's made very clear, strongly but subtly, that Carrie is regarded by outsiders as a whore.

She does love Hurstwood, but once they're together his fortunes turn sour. Hurstwood gets his divorce but pays a harrowing price— the loss of all material possessions. Humiliated, he informs Carrie, "I'm broke."

Carrie becomes pregnant (a plot turn that doesn't occur in the novel). She loses the baby. "It's for the best," says Hurstwood. "We don't want to bring a child into this. . . ."

At its core, the film is the story of the disintegration of Hurstwood because of the choice he's made. "I can't advise you, George," Carrie finally tells him, "but I know one thing. I'm still young, and I'm going to live, somehow. . . ."

Olivier had the maturity to deliver an absolutely stunning, multilayered performance. Jennifer's task was less clear-cut. Despite the eerie parallels to her own situation, she seemed almost out of her depth playing certain scenes. Perhaps Carrie's tragic story was too close for comfort.

Like William Wyler, Robert Walker learned about Jennifer's pregnancy in the press. In earlier years he would have disappeared immediately on a bender of Olympian proportions. But on location in Colorado for *Vengeance Valley,* he absorbed the news without incident. The rushes on the picture indicated he was delivering, in Schary's words, "a hell of a performance," aided no doubt by the presence of Walker's sons and a solid friendship that had developed with Burt Lancaster.

While it was Jennifer whose career needed a fine picture to restore her box office luster, it was Walker to whom the better opportunity now presented itself. Ironically there were echoes of Selznick in this venture, too. Alfred Hitchcock had signed a two-picture deal with Warner Brothers, the first to be a thriller called *Strangers on a Train.*

For the role of the baby-faced sophisticate who's a psychopathic killer, Hitchcock signed Robert Walker. It was Hitchcock's theory that spies never looked like spies and killers didn't look like killers. So what better than to have one of America's premier "boys next door" portray a cold-blooded killer!

Filming was scheduled to begin in the fall. The role was the best acting opportunity Robert Walker had had to date, and he knew it. Warner Brothers had initially balked at paying the price of his loanout from MGM, but Hitchcock, backed by Lew Wasserman, prevailed. (Hitchcock lost on another account, though—he'd wanted William Holden for the role that went to Farley Granger.)

Hitchcock liked Walker personally and paid him the ultimate compliment by inviting him to dinner at the Hitchcock home. (The director was a gourmet, and his guests rarely included actors. An exception was Claudette Colbert; in later years Anthony Perkins joined the elite group.)

If *Madame Bovary* and *Carrie* were metaphors for Jennifer's life, *Strangers on a Train* offered frightening parallels to Walker's. Terrifying violence was lurking constantly beneath his character's surface. He's referred to by his mother as her "lunatic son" and pounds the table like a maniac when Mama (played by Marion Lorne) says something that upsets him. He drinks heavily, passing out frequently.

He commits murder and instigates mayhem, and there are strong homosexual overtones to his behavior. "Go someplace where you can get some kind of treatment," he's told. "You can't keep going on bringing destruction into the lives of those you meet."

The Walker character has no redeeming features; he's a classic "heavy." The unforgettable climax of the picture features a death ride on a carousel. Walker's character remains evil to the end, trying to kick Granger's character to death until Walker himself dies, unrepentant.

Filming was completed by Christmas. Bob could hardly wait for the picture to be assembled and previewed; he felt he'd turned a corner in his career.

• • •

Carrie had finally completed shooting in *November*, after an extended shooting schedule of sixteen weeks. The drawn-out schedule had, in part, been Wyler's attempt to accommodate Jennifer's health. But, as Wyler feared, the shoot had been arduous and had taken its toll.

On December 16 Jennifer experienced frightening physical pains and bleeding; an ambulance was summoned and raced her to Cedars of Lebanon hospital in Los Angeles, where, in her sixth month of pregnancy, she suffered a miscarriage.

Life had certainly provided no dividends for this "golden couple" as 1950 drew to a close. *Gone to Earth,* released in England in its initial Powell-Pressburger version, was an abysmal flop.

Retitled *The Wild Heart* for the U.S. market, even with a new director and new script, the revamped film also previewed poorly. Jack Warner decided not to release it "at the current time." Jennifer was not unaware of the implications. "You're only as good as your last film," she frequently told Anita Colby.

Sister Carrie was being assembled and scored and wouldn't be ready for preview for a while. Selznick, in his heart of hearts, held out no great hopes for its commercial success. Time would tell what the film's future held. David assured Jennifer that the film would be a success, certain to create renewed demand for her services. While it was later reported that Jennifer, at that moment, was not in demand, there were offers, but not for the kinds of films that either Selznick or Jennifer would remotely consider acceptable.

Back to Europe was the couple's solution, one welcomed by a depressed Jennifer. She was exhausted, emotionally and physically, and needed desperately to recoup her energy and her enthusiasm.

"She handled the miscarriage well," recalls Anita Colby, adding that Jennifer always survived the disasters that befell her "because she had the best psychiatrists."

Jennifer planned to spend the Christmas holidays in Europe, with David and her sons.

Chapter

20

*D*uring *the early months of 1951, an* idle Jennifer appeared to be at a low ebb emotionally. David was concerned. Doctors had assured the couple they could have other children, and David reassured Jennifer that her career would reignite once *Sister Carrie* (subsequently retitled *Carrie* because the studio thought the public would think it was the story of a nun) was released.

But Paramount, uncertain how to market *Carrie,* decided not to release the film. That piece of bad news did not exactly have a soothing effect on the listless, nervous thirty-two-year-old star and her restless forty-nine-year-old husband.

Jennifer chose to remain home and embroider, walk on the beach, exercise, practice yoga, and see her psychiatrist. On occasion the Louis Jourdans, the Joseph Cottens, or the Charles Bickfords were guests at the Selznick mansion for dinner. David tried to coax Jennifer into attending parties or accompanying him to industry functions, but she wasn't interested. They argued, but she stood firm.

Selznick remained constantly on the lookout for the perfect vehicle for Jennifer. As far as he was concerned, her full potential was unrealized, and she continued to have faith in his judgment, despite the glaring professional errors he'd made on her behalf in the last few years. Although David could be intimidating, Jennifer firmly stated her views when he suggested a project she didn't like, or vice versa.

"That's part of the reason so many of those pictures they made together bombed," explains Anita Colby. The films were never totally representative of what either Jennifer or David wanted them to be.

Jennifer's intense desire for solitude was interpreted at the time as an indication of a deepening depression; more likely it was an act of self-preservation. Jennifer found comfort in being alone, away from the tumult of the sound stages and the crowds of adoring fans and pushy newspeople. Selznick, however, thrived in a crowd.

He solved their dilemma by socializing solo. "Jennifer's indisposed, but I'll be there!" became David's response to invitations. "Poor David," remarked friends behind his back, but Selznick's behavior, like Jennifer's, was also an act of self-preservation. It was healthy for him to seek out people who amused, interested, and, to an extent, idolized him.

If the Selznicks were growing apart, an event was to occur shortly that would forever bind them together and alter the tenor of their lives.

Meanwhile, on March 5, at the Huntington Park Theater, Warner Brothers previewed *Strangers on a Train.* Audience response was enthusiastic. Although it was early in the year, Walker's performance was so effective that an Oscar nomination was predicted. However, his acting was perhaps *too* real and too close to what people thought he was really like. It wasn't acting, mused friends, he was just playing "himself."

Nonetheless, Walker's career outlook was suddenly in high gear. Burt Lancaster and Gary Cooper and his wife, "Rocky," were among his current friends, and through Peter Lawford Walker met and dated a pretty starlet named Sharlee Hudson.

The relationship between Walker and Sharlee Hudson was soon replaced by one that Walker's friends felt was *the* one—possibly serious enough to lead to marriage. Through Jim Henaghan Bob had met Kay Scott Nearny, a former starlet. The petite, soft-spoken divorcée appeared to be a perfect choice for Bob. Elegant and self-assured, she was sensitive to Bob's ever-changing moods.

According to writer-producer Sam Marx, Nearny was not blind to Walker's problems. "According to Kay . . . Bob was still in need of psychiatric help," recalled Marx.

With Kay, Bob had become as introverted as his ex-wife, preferring to stay home, relaxing and listening to Kay play the piano.

There was new demand for Walker's services. Paramount negotiated with MGM to borrow him for an important film to be directed by Leo McCarey, whose string of hits included *The Awful Truth,* a classic screwball comedy, and the blockbusters *Going My Way* and *The Bells of St. Mary's.*

McCarey wanted Walker for his latest picture, *My Son John.* It was the director's ultrapatriotic, personal statement against the ills he felt had recently infiltrated Hollywood: communists, anti-Catholics, and intellectuals.

Walker, who would be playing another "heavy," this time a communist, joined an impressive cast, led by the first lady of the theater, Helen Hayes, playing Walker's mother. "The film was a personal vendetta by Leo," stated Hayes. Her daughter, Mary, had just died of polio, and Hayes's husband, playwright Charles MacArthur, a close friend of McCarey's, had begged Helen to take the role, her first film in years ("I was pushed into it," recalled Hayes). MacArthur hoped it would snap her out of her depression. Van Heflin, Dean Jagger, and Edmund Gwenn had already been cast in other roles.

Kay Nearny, along with Michael and Bobby, visited Walker during production. Horseback riding was their current passion, and Walker looked forward to a summer vacation with his sons at a dude ranch.

While Bob's life seemed filled with satisfying personal and professional activities, Jennifer had no immediate prospects. No new films were on the horizon, and she took a trip to Hawaii. Selznick continued to wheel and deal to repay his debts in full so that he could line up an exciting film project for his wife.

He was attempting to package *Tender Is the Night* and had discussions with producer Jerry Wald. Selznick envisioned a *Tender* cast headed by Jennifer and Cary Grant. Since he was shopping around a potential package, he also mentioned Vivien Leigh as an alternate female star, but the project never got off the ground.

Selznick's former father-in-law, the mighty Louis B. Mayer, succumbed to the hard times shattering the status quo in the movie business. Mayer was ousted from MGM in a power ploy orchestrated by Loew's chairman, Nicholas Schenck ("Nick Skunk," was how Mayer referred to him). Dore Schary moved into the top spot at MGM, and this seemed a high sign for the future of Robert Walker.

Jennifer chose a familiar path to draw herself out of her ennui. The Korean War had broken out the previous June, when President Harry S. Truman had ordered U.S. forces to fight in aid of Korea. Once again American soldiers were in combat.

Without fanfare or publicity, Jennifer traveled to Japan and Korea in mid-May to visit wounded soldiers in American military hospitals. Dressed in battle fatigues, she posed for pictures with hundreds of servicemen. As always, the expressions on the grinning faces of the GIs reflected the impact of her presence. Jennifer always smiled dutifully for these shots, but often she looked slightly embarrassed and ill at ease.

The American Red Cross subsequently awarded her a citation, and the field commander of United Nations Forces, General James Van Fleet, awarded her a gold medal. "That meant as much to her as an Oscar," declared her proud husband, who viewed Jennifer's dedication as nothing short of miraculous.

During her absence, Jennifer's friend, actress Viveca Lindfors, had experienced an encounter with David after a dinner party (Jennifer had asked Lindfors to stand in for her as hostess). Selznick escorted Lindfors home in his limousine. "The battle began the moment we hit the highway," recalled Lindfors, astonished that the chauffeur seemed oblivious of David's behavior on the backseat. She found Selznick's onslaught "ridiculous and pathetic" and wondered—did Jennifer know?

Meanwhile, the Korean tour had a reviving effect on Jennifer's outlook and she agreed to accompany a jubilant David to the Venice Film Festival in August.

After only a couple of weeks, discontent and panic had set in on the set of My Son John. A good-looking, gregarious, piano-playing Irishman, Leo McCarey was the kind of director who encouraged his actors to improvise on camera. But the actors realized that the results weren't any good, and their esteemed director's daily script rewrites were culminating in artistic chaos.

"Making that movie was an awful experience," recalled Helen Hayes. "I was miserable every day we did it. Leo had thrown out the script. . . ."

For Robert Walker, after having worked with the meticulously organized Alfred Hitchcock, the movie was a nightmare. Production was still in progress when Bobby and Michael arrived to begin their summer vacation. A new employee had joined the Walker home, Emily Buck. Buck's credentials were impressive; among other jobs, she'd been governess for Margaret Sullavan and Leland Hayward's children.

But Mrs. Buck would later be identified by columnist Hedda Hopper as "a nurse," and she didn't mean for the children. By this time Robert Walker required more than an ordinary housekeeper on the premises.

On Saturday, August 15, Leo McCarey met with Bob and told him that his role in *My Son John* was completed, except for bits, pieces, and some "looping" (rerecording lines of dialogue that were muddy on the original soundtrack). Walker was relieved to be finished with the picture.

Chapter
21

On Monday, August 28, Jennifer Jones
and Robert Walker achieved a notoriety that neither, in their wildest
dreams, had ever sought. Their names were splashed across headlines of virtually every major newspaper in the world, their photos
appeared on television and in national magazines, and their names
were blared over radio. Robert Walker's name would now be linked
forever with both Jennifer's and David O. Selznick's.

There are several versions of what occurred and one shocking
new theory regarding who might have been responsible.

The day had begun benignly enough. The Walker boys were
away visiting a friend. Except for the housekeeper, Mrs. Buck,
Walker was alone in the Pacific Palisades house. He arose late and
had breakfast. It wasn't a beach day—the weather was bad. He stuck
close to home, lacking both an itinerary for the day and a friend to
keep him company. Between the hours of two P.M. and six P.M., something happened that triggered an emotional outburst from Walker
that, in one version of the story, caused a frightened Mrs. Buck to
place a frantic call to Walker's psychiatrist, Frederick Hacker.

"His housekeeper, Mrs. Emily Buck, called me about six o'clock
last night," Hacker told the press the following day. "Walker was in a
highly emotional state when I reached him. He kept saying, 'I feel

terrible, Doc. Do something quick.' " According to reports, Mrs. Buck said that she'd told Hacker she couldn't handle Walker, that he was out of control.

One theory relates that prior to leaving for Europe, Jennifer had phoned the house to say good-bye to Michael and Bobby, learned that they were out visiting a friend, and had a conversation with Walker that had upset him. In the past this kind of incident would have been more than enough to launch him into a frenzy, but he was supposedly now "in recovery" and beyond that point. ("He was receiving attention from a psychiatrist in Beverly Hills and appeared to be in control," Dore Schary said.)

The speculation that Jennifer had phoned was no more than that—speculation. There was no proof. But, in view of ensuing events, Jennifer's persona, like a vivid jewel dangling on a chain of suspicion, pervaded all aspects of the tragedy that transpired.

At two P.M., according to reports, Walker had spoken on the phone with his business manager, Charles Trezona. Trezona said he knew his client well enough to state with absolute certainty that nothing had seemed at all wrong with Walker; if something had been peculiar, if Walker had been drinking or upset, he, Trezona, would have sensed it.

Accounts stated that Dr. Hacker had arrived at the house soon after six P.M. When Hacker was later asked if Walker had been drinking, he replied that he didn't know.

The accounts continued. On arriving at the house, Hacker had phoned an associate, Dr. Sidney Silver. "I called Dr. Silver to administer sodium Amytal," he explained. "We had given him this sedative twenty-five to thirty times in the past without ill effect. The dosage was seven and a half grains. Often we had given him as much."

At the time Silver corroborated Hacker's statements. "When Dr. Hacker felt a sedative was indicated, he called me.

"Walker was in a very emotional condition. We gave him an intravenous injection of seven and a half grains of sodium Amytal. Many times before, we had given him a similar treatment, and he always reacted successfully and well, by falling asleep and waking relieved and refreshed.

"In this instance, however, the patient soon showed signs of respiratory failure. We gave artificial respiration, then called the rescue squad.

"Fatal effect of the drug happens now and then, unfortunately. Perhaps once in ten thousand times it acts on the brain's respiratory center. While Walker had neither taken nor been given any drug from the time Dr. Hacker arrived at his home at about six P.M., neither of us knew whether or not he had taken any preparation of any kind prior to that hour."

The coroner's autopsy surgeon, Victor Cefalu, later stated that "it would require a dose of about fifteen grains of sodium Amytal for that drug to become toxic. The normal dose—for sedation—is about three grains. However, seven and a half is not an abnormal amount to administer when the patient is extremely emotional."

What happened to Walker?

Reports at the time did not indicate that Jim Henaghan was on the scene. However, Henaghan claimed there was a cover-up and explained to ex-wife Gwen Verdon what had actually occurred: "Walker was *very* depressed," Verdon says. "They were trying all kinds of drugs for depression at that time. I think [the doctors] felt that his real problem was just depression [and not alcoholism]. When I look back, however, I think that if you're a drinker, you're a drinker. . . .

"That day Bob had taken all of his pills for his depression, and he was drinking, and he became, I guess, just berserk and ran out of the house, and the lady who took care of the two boys called Big Jim.

"Big Jim went [to the house], but before he went [there] he called a doctor. Big Jim found Bob just rolling around and yelling and screaming, sort of wandering and physically floundering because he couldn't walk straight.

"The doctor arrived, and Big Jim always contended that because the empty bottle of pills was there, and the booze, and the fact that Bob had been throwing up . . . the doctor [went ahead] and gave him the wrong shots! Now, Big Jim was there and the doctor knew [he made a mistake] the minute he had done it. I won't mention the doctor's name, but . . ."

When told that the doctors have already been identified, Verdon replies: "Well, I doubt if it's the doctor who was [there]. Now, mind you, they were trying to hold this man down, who was [running around] screaming and screeching. He was *totally* out of control.

"After getting the shot, Bob immediately went into a coma. The doctor [seemed] very surprised, and checked what he'd given him and looked through his bag for [something to counteract] what he had just given him, and he didn't have it."

Henaghan later recalled that as the doctors had frantically begun artificial respiration on Walker, he (Henaghan) phoned both the fire department and Dr. Myron Prinzmetal, the leading internist in Beverly Hills. When Prinzmetal claimed he couldn't drive out to the house, Henaghan raced over to Prinzmetal's house and physically commandeered the doctor back to Pacific Palisades to tend to Walker.

By the time they arrived at ten P.M., it was too late. Walker was dead and Prinzmetal, after conferring with the other two doctors, told him that Walker had been dead for more than an hour.

Henaghan, practically hysterical, told Emily Buck to contact Walker's parents in Ogden. Then he phoned Dore Schary and told him the awful news, imploring him to drive over immediately.

"It was too late to tell Bobby and Michael," recalled Henaghan. "I planned to get to them before they heard the news in the morning from some other source." The guilt that engulfed and practically overwhelmed Henaghan remained with him throughout his life. "I could have stopped them," he said. "But I allowed it. I felt like a murderer."

At the time, Dr. Hacker had seemed to be in a daze and was wandering around outside in the rain without even a coat. And Dr. Silver "was pretty shaken up, too," remembered Henaghan.

Dore Schary later recalled, "One rainy night on my immediate return from a preview the phone rang, and when I answered, a voice shouted, 'Dore, Bob's dead, Bob's dead.' It was Red Henaghan, who, through his tears and screams, told me he was in Bob's house. I hung up, got into my car, and rushed to the Uplifter's Ranch, only a mile away. The door to the house was open. Bob's doctor was standing there with his young assistant. They were both in shock. I pushed by them and went into Bob's bedroom, where Henaghan was sitting in a chair and sobbing. Bob was on the bed. He was wearing moccasins, slacks, a plaid woolen shirt with the left sleeve rolled up. There were bloodstains on his arm and the bed. Bob was dead.

"The doctors [told me what happened]. Henaghan had called because Bob had been drinking and getting violent. They had arrived and got Bob to lie down while they administered a shot of sodium Pentothal. Some doctors choose not to run the risk of using such a drug in treating someone who has been drinking. It is not always a fatal risk, but according to some doctors, it is advisable to have oxygen handy when using the drug because of the danger that the effect of the drug, added to the large amount of alcohol [which Bob had ingested], might cause a respiratory arrest.

"Metro's police chief, Whitey Henry . . . advised me to let them take over . . . and to go home."

There are inaccuracies in Schary's version (the drug administered was actually sodium Amytal, not sodium Pentothal), but also confirmation of a key fact. Schary's statement that "the effect of the drug, added to the large amount of alcohol [which Bob had ingested] might cause a respiratory arrest" confirms what Henaghan had told Gwen Verdon. Neither doctor on the scene at the time admitted that Walker had been drinking.

Years later Walker's pal Hedda Hopper wrote that Bob had been drinking and had fought against receiving the fatal injection, pleading, "Don't give it to me! I've been drinking! It will kill me! Please don't give me that shot!"

In the 1990s Dr. Alex Rogawski, a colleague of Dr. Hacker's, told authors Stephen Farber and Marc Green: "Hacker killed Robert Walker. He actually killed him. But a doctor could get away with it back then. . . ."

Dore Schary's mention of veteran MGM police chief Whitey Henry immediately brings to mind the dirty MGM laundry Henry and others had been responsible for covering up and disposing of over the years. Cover-ups had been a way of life in Hollywood from the earliest days. Studio chiefs wielded immense control over local authorities and would stoop to any means to protect their stars and their own pockets. The most notorious had occurred two decades earlier, when the murder of Jean Harlow's husband, Paul Bern, had been called a suicide to protect the career of the twenty-one-year-old blond bombshell.

Another major cover-up, years later, involved the powerful Eddie Mannix. According to Sam Marx, Mannix had been responsible for the death of actor George Reeves (TV's *Superman*) when Mannix discovered Reeves was having an affair with Toni Mannix, his wife. When the death was alleged a "suicide," Reeves's friends cried "cover-up," to no avail.

· · ·

Another scenario that has never been openly discussed provides a truly shocking possibility insofar as Robert Walker's death is concerned. "Walker might have been done in by either John Ford or, more likely, David Selznick," states Tom King.

One of King's close friends—"Charlie," for the purposes of this account—is a man who to this day confides in King and relies on him for advice on financial investments. "Charlie" was one of Walker's drinking buddies; he liked Walker and often recounted to King how Bob, when under the influence, on more than one occasion had plunged his fist through automobile windshields.

"Charlie" was a strikingly handsome, virile, tough young character actor, a man who knew everyone, "who got into their lives, and has a steel-trap memory," explains Tom King. "Charlie" also palled around with Hollywood's Irish Mafia—James Cagney, Pat O'Brien (who were much older than "Charlie"), and often James Henaghan.

Not long before Walker's death, "Charlie" met Walker and Bob's pal Jimmy McHugh, the songwriter who was one of Louella Parsons's favorite "beaux," at the Blue Parrot nightclub on Sunset Strip. The hour grew late. "Charlie" was invited back to McHugh's place, along with Walker and a couple of gorgeous girls, for a "party."

At McHugh's Walker concentrated all his attention not on the girls, but on "Charlie," who recalls that Bob kept remarking on his ["Charlie's"] muscles and declared that he liked men with "hard muscles." "Charlie" thought it peculiar that neither McHugh nor Walker seemed interested in the girls. (The implication—that Walker may have been bisexual—has been raised by others in a position to know. A man who is today a leading talent broker [back then an actor] tells similar tales about Walker. If true, this aspect of Walker's persona enables one to comprehend with fuller understanding the feelings of constant tension, conflict, and stress that dictated Robert Walker's actions.)

"Charlie," who had experience at police work, related to Tom King the details of his involvement following Walker's death. To begin with, everyone in town knew that John Ford and David Selznick had their own motives for wanting Walker dead. Ford wanted to wipe Walker off the face of the earth after he'd beaten up and humiliated his daughter Barbara. And Ford had proven to at least one reliable source that he was capable of murder.

Tom King states, "Sonny Diskin, who became a director of John

Daly's ABC-TV network news show (I worked closely with Sonny on the Daly show) was John Ford's sergeant in the army during World War Two. Sonny told me how both Ford and John Huston had been assigned to making war documentaries, and when Ford was given an assignment that Huston got to first, Ford flew into a rage and decided he was going to kill Huston. He asked Sonny to locate Huston immediately so that he could 'take care of him.'

"Now Sonny was a very serious person, never prone to exaggeration. When he told me this," recalls King, "I thought he was using a figure of speech—'going to kill him' meaning chew him out or beat him up. But Sonny wasn't smiling when he saw my reaction.

" 'No, Tom,' Sonny said, 'Ford was going to *kill* him. First he planned to use his service revolver, then decided it would be wiser to murder him in the field, where it would look like Huston had been hit with a stray bullet. And, believe me,' Sonny told me, 'Ford was serious about doing it.' So one can imagine how Ford regarded Robert Walker after he'd beaten up Barbara and, worse, broken her heart."

According to "Charlie," the buzz around town at the time of Walker's death was that David Selznick had strong reasons for wanting Walker permanently out of the picture. It was no secret that Selznick thought not only that Walker was a bad influence on the children, and a constant embarrassment to Jennifer, but that he would always be a cross for Jennifer and the children to bear.

Selznick was out to get Walker, continues this theory, so that the children wouldn't be plagued by him for the rest of their lives; in addition, Selznick wanted no negative outside influence on the kids, whether they were his own or not. According to "Charlie," further inside scuttlebutt was that Walker was "a hot potato" and "knew a lot of things." Tom King knew, from all he'd heard over the years, including tales from his uncle, Henry King, that "Selznick could be quite mean, terribly nasty."

Meanwhile, after Walker's death, "Charlie" visited the Walker family in Los Angeles. By that time Selznick had put "a certain man" in touch with the Walkers, to serve as their adviser ("Charlie" met and detested this man).

When "Charlie" was finally alone with Horace and Zella, he told them bluntly that their son may have been "murdered" by a lethal overdose, and his own opinion, after speaking with Jim Henaghan, was that two doctors had been on the scene "because one didn't have the guts to do it alone."

Walker's parents didn't want to believe the story. Horace Walker told "Charlie" that "Selznick had prevailed on him [Horace] not to raise suspicion or scandal, explaining that it would be bad for the family name. Selznick was going to raise the family. He assured the Walkers the family would be well taken care of."

"Charlie" began his own investigation and claims he discovered that the men driving the ambulance weren't hospital employees and that the ambulance wasn't even registered (there are no existing records to confirm this allegation).

"Charlie" also told his tale of alleged murder at leading watering holes all over town. One night he was grabbed by thugs and beaten up. They informed him that they didn't want what he was talking about to get around, and that the consequences would be something far worse than a lawsuit.

After the beating, "Charlie" claims he was injected with something. The next time, he was warned, it would be a lethal injection, as it had been with Walker. "Charlie" was found battered and unconscious in Westwood and was taken to a hospital. He fell into a coma but recovered.

He left town, and his promising career was seriously interrupted. ("Charlie" today is still a working actor.)

Tom King, privy at the time to all the rumors floating around, states unequivocally that "those who knew Selznick and Ford felt that either man was definitely capable of murder."

"Jennifer was so upset when she learned of Walker's death," recalls a reflective and sympathetic Anita Colby. "She was in New York with Selznick, en route to Venice, but turned right around and rushed home."

Part III

Part III

Chapter

22

*T*his was hell, and Jennifer was in it.
She'd loved Walker, and no matter how difficult and crazy he'd been,
she'd never wanted anything to happen to him. Guilt and grief
threatened to overwhelm her.

The day after Walker's death, a trembling Jennifer, accompanied
by an ashen-faced Selznick, flew to Los Angeles (a nine-hour trip in
those days). "There was absolutely no color in her face, she looked
terribly worn and tired," commented an onlooker. The couple
dodged reporters and photographers at the airport. Dark glasses
shielded Jennifer's eyes, and her dark hair, pulled back from her
face, was slightly askew. Her custom-made, tailored two-piece suit
was wrinkled from the long trip. She carried a coat over one arm
and avoided looking at either David or the reporters. A waiting limousine drove her directly to her children.

The press speculated that Jennifer was doomed forever to carry
a suffocating psychological burden: that by leaving Bob, she was responsible for his death. It's not an unreasonable assumption, however, that she saw herself as being blamed unfairly for the tragedy.
After all, if people knew everything, knew how she'd suffered
through Walker's drinking binges and his violent rages, they would
see her as the victim.

Anita Colby was a firsthand observer to Jennifer's pain, as were her parents, her psychiatrist, and her husband. Poor Jennifer and the boys, all thought grimly. Selznick was more determined than ever to spare Jennifer all unnecessary angst.

Bobby junior, on learning of his father's death, "screamed [and] went to pieces," recalls Anita Colby. While Jennifer didn't appear in much better shape, Colby's recollections are that Jennifer coped remarkably well.

In relating details on Walker's death, the press made no mention of the fact that Dore Schary, Jim Henaghan, and Dr. Prinzmetal had been on the scene. Selznick and MGM immediately instigated damage control and succeeded in keeping the lid on any explosive speculation. No murder investigation was ever launched; no allegations on the likelihood or even the possibility of foul play ever reached print.

Behind the scenes all agreed that the sensibilities of Jennifer and her sons must be the overriding consideration; after all, nothing could bring Bob back.

Walker's stunned parents had arrived in Los Angeles only hours before Jennifer and David. For appearances' sake, the MGM publicity department issued statements on Horace and Zella's behalf. Reporters were kept far from the grieving family. Arrangements called for Bob to be buried on Friday, September 1, at Forest Lawn Memorial Park, the "Cemetery of the Stars."

Two days before, Jennifer drove her sons to Bob's Pacific Palisades house, where the grief-stricken boys gathered up their clothing and toys. The house, formerly the scene of good times for father and sons, now seemed hollow and empty to them.

Then, suddenly, plans to bury Bob at Forest Lawn were changed. An MGM press release announced, in Zella Walker's name, that her son would be laid to rest back home in Ogden. Zella was quoted as saying that this was the desire of her grandsons. "We decided the ceremony should be where the boys wanted it to be. We want to do only what is best for our grandsons."

What precipitated this change in plans has remained a mystery (although it was said that Selznick had a hand in the decision, reasoning that considerably less publicity would result). Monday, September 4, was the new burial date. Neither Jennifer, her sons, nor Selznick would be on hand. They left for New York, then proceeded to Europe.

Once there, Jennifer struggled to maintain her emotional equilibrium. Walker's death had intensified her involvement with her children, having triggered the realization that she was all they had. Jennifer decided it was in the boys' best interests to permanently remove them—and herself—from the haunting familiarity of their Los Angeles surroundings.

The best private schools were in Switzerland. Arrangements were made for the boys to withdraw from the Black Foxe Military Academy and begin their schooling abroad in the late fall (Selznick's business affairs would require him abroad).

Hundreds of locals, but none of Walker's Hollywood pals, attended the actor's funeral in Ogden. There were floral tributes from Dore Schary, actor Pat O'Brien and his wife, and Alfred Hitchcock and his wife, Alma. And the largest floral tribute of all was from "Mr. and Mrs. David O. Selznick."

Joan Fontaine recalls how David provided Jennifer with "the most extraordinary Christmas." "I heard that he took over an entire floor at the Plaza Hotel in New York and invited their friends for Christmas dinner.

"One entire wall in the dining room was festooned with spectacular ribbons, with beautifully wrapped presents for Jennifer hanging from each bow. On one was a dress, on another a coat, then the shoes, the gloves, the purse, and the jewelry . . .

"It was all done with enormous showmanship, typical of David, of course. Joe Cotten was there and marveled at the whole thing.

"David also had fresh flowers sent up from the florist every day, flowers were rampant throughout their suite, even in the bathrooms! He blew all his dough, but it was done in great style."

Fontaine offers a blunt assessment: "Jennifer was a bird in a gilded cage. Whether she liked it or not, I don't know. I would hate it myself."

Jennifer seemed to like it. David did everything he could to lift her spirits. He acquiesced to her wish to study drama with Constance Collier. Jennifer longed to appear on Broadway, and the New York–based Collier worked with the actress on the classics. Collier liked Jennifer. "She's an actress capable of playing within her own personality," she said. "I believe she can become a leading lady of the theater in the full sense of the word."

As 1952 began, Jennifer was desperate to return to work, to immerse herself in the self-contained fantasy world of making a movie. Selznick had written John Huston, asking whether any of Huston's future films offered good parts for her. Huston had completed *The African Queen* and was preparing *Moulin Rouge* and *Beat the Devil*. He replied to Selznick that the women's roles in the former did not offer "sufficient scope for Jennifer's talents." *Beat the Devil,* however, held possibilities for her, "although, I'm afraid, not a great deal." Huston was to the point. "I think the picture would be more fortunate in getting her than she would be in getting it. . . .

"Jennifer can play anything she pleases in any picture I make. If she'd like to put on a beard and play Toulouse-Lautrec, I'll gladly [stop] negotiations with Ferrer."

Huston was considering other actresses for the role Jennifer was so "right" for in *Beat the Devil*, including Ingrid Bergman, Jean Simmons, and Lauren Bacall.

Back in Hollywood, Joan Fontaine had the inside track on the lead in *Ruby Gentry*, a melodrama for 20th Century–Fox to be directed by King Vidor. Jules Stein, founder of MCA, was handling Fontaine's career, and she recalls, "They offered me the *Ruby* script first, but I felt I couldn't do it and turned it down. The character was a kind of swamp girl. I felt I was simply not capable of capturing the accent and all."

Selznick had already alerted the proper parties of Jennifer's availability.

The *Ruby Gentry* producers were also casting for a leading man. One of the fast-rising young actors on the scene was Charlton Heston. "David Selznick's studio had offered me a contract a few years earlier," recalls Heston, and the company had pursued him vigorously.

"I had already had contract offers from several studios, which I didn't want. What I required was independence, and David Selznick was not prepared to offer that, either," explains Heston. He signed with Hal Wallis instead (who'd had extraordinary success in advancing the careers of Humphrey Bogart, James Cagney, and Edward G. Robinson).

At the time Heston was in the running for *Ruby Gentry*, Cecil B. De Mille's *The Greatest Show on Earth* was in release and had launched Heston's career. "It was only my second picture. When I was approached by King Vidor and his partner, Joe Bernhard, to do *Ruby*, King had already made his deal with Jennifer." (Heston was aware that Vidor had walked off *Duel in the Sun* six years earlier.)

Heston was also aware that "Selznick regarded the producer on a film as auteur, and the director, in David's exact words, was 'the first violinist.' He lost a couple of good directors that way, including John Huston. In my view, the pictures they walked off suffered for it.

"According to King Vidor," recalls Heston, "David had script approval, approval of the leading man, and 'still' [photograph] approval. In return, David was not allowed to set foot on the *Ruby* set or see any assembled footage." It was indicative of how Selznick was currently regarded in Hollywood. "I suppose each side considered they'd gotten what they'd really needed," says Heston.

Before signing for *Ruby,* Heston read the script and liked it. "Now I had to pass the David test. I went up to the Selznick home on Tower Road to have lunch with him, and there I met Jennifer for the first time. She didn't have lunch with us, she simply came out to say hello.

"She was an absolutely stunning-looking lady. I proceeded to have lunch with David, and he said, 'Yes, I think you'll be very good opposite my wife.' And I did the film. I never saw David again during the shoot, which, there again, was part of King's deal."

Since Heston had been in the service during World War II, he hadn't seen any of Jennifer's films during that period, including *Song of Bernadette* ("Not exactly the type of film the troops were interested in seeing!"). He had seen, and liked, *Duel in the Sun* and *Portrait of Jennie.*

Ruby was a crucial film for both Jennifer and Heston. *Dark City,* the film he'd made for Hal Wallis, had been, in Heston's words, "An interesting film noir, but it hardly made people sit up and say 'Wow!' " While *Greatest Show* was a blockbuster, Heston notes, "It didn't occur to anybody that I had much to do with that. No actor could ever claim credit for a De Mille success. De Mille's name was always first on the marquee. *Ruby* had the potential for me to demonstrate that I could pull my oar in a successful film opposite a prominent leading lady."

Jennifer, too, approached her role most seriously. The character of Ruby was a Carolina mountain girl, and Jennifer briefly went to Southport, North Carolina, to research the people and the territory. She roamed freely throughout the town and drove out to see the countryside firsthand. "I met a lot of people and asked a thousand questions," she said, delighted that "nobody asked me a question. And nobody once asked me, 'Aren't you Jennifer Jones?' "

Jennifer kept Anita Colby informed on her progress. "Jennifer had to learn how to shoot and hunt and handle a gun for the movie. She became very adept, as I recall."

Jennifer turned thirty-three as production began. *Ruby* progressed smoothly (King Vidor, too, needed a solid commercial hit). If Jennifer was depressed over the death of Robert Walker, it wasn't evident to her co-workers. "Jennifer certainly didn't bring her private life on the set," recalls Heston. "My relationship with her throughout the shoot was totally professional, which was important to me." (Future working relationships with Ava Gardner and, to a lesser degree, Sophia Loren, were not quite so pleasant.) "Jennifer showed up on time, knew her lines, and hit her marks. She was also, as far as I could tell, the only actress I've worked with who didn't wear makeup in front of the camera," he says with respect. "You could see her coloring change—you could see her flush or pale during a shot."

Heston, like so many before him, comments on how shy Jennifer was. "I learned one of the reasons David had demanded approval of her still photographs. Jennifer would never look at photographs of herself! I was once going through a contact sheet (proof sheet of the photographs taken by the studio photographer on the set), you'd get one every couple of days, and I would say, 'Jennifer, this is great of you,' and she just didn't want to look at them! I'm not trying to paint her as neurotic, but she just didn't want to see them."

King Vidor recalled that, on this shoot, "whenever Jennifer played a scene with a feeling of insecurity, it showed in some strange tricks she did with her mouth. It was the director's responsibility to make certain that this didn't happen."

Heston vividly recalls "the kind of intensity with which Jennifer worked. She was playing a poor southern girl. I was playing a rich southern son of a bitch. Our scenes together worked very well. We had a good chemistry. I think she was an instinctive actress rather than a trained one, but it worked very well. My memory is that she would do a scene with a random instinct, which was usually very good.

"People think Jennifer [is petite] on screen . . . but she's a fairly tall girl"—Heston, well over six feet, jokes that he's not a particularly reliable judge of height—"and physically strong. We were doing a scene in which I was telling her I wasn't going to marry her, no matter what she thought. We quarreled, and she became furious. She was supposed to hit me. I foolishly said, 'Jennifer, go ahead and hit me, don't worry about it.' She struck me with the back of her hand and nearly knocked me down.

"My head was spinning, and she'd broken a bone in her hand! Next time you see the film, you'll notice that in certain random scenes . . . she's wearing what appear to be three or four Mexican-type silver bracelets. In fact, [she's in] a brace. She continued working and never missed a day. As I recall, she didn't make much of a fuss on the set after it happened and wore the brace for days afterward. I was impressed."

Ironically, the southern accent Joan Fontaine feared she'd be unable to muster for *Ruby* turned out to be unnecessary. "All of us in *Ruby* should have spoken in a Carolina accent," notes Heston, "and none of us did. I haven't figured that out yet. Only the brother, who *was* southern, used a southern accent."

During production of *Ruby Gentry* Jennifer's two unreleased films, *Gone to Earth* (retitled *The Wild Heart*) and *Carrie,* were released virtually back to back.

Jennifer's reviews for *The Wild Heart* weren't bad, and the studio drew on her past hits to try to sell it. "The Fury of *Duel in the Sun* . . . the Grandeur of *Song of Bernadette!*" exclaimed the ads. But the public wasn't buying.

Carrie opened in June. Charlton Heston recalls, "*Carrie* was a hard piece of stew," pointing out how difficult it was to translate Dreiser to the screen. The previous year, however, director George Stevens had proven that it could be done with great success—with *A Place in the Sun* (based on Dreiser's *An American Tragedy*).

Critics didn't like *Carrie,* although *The Hollywood Reporter* was enthusiastic about Jennifer: "[She is] perfect in the title role. Her Carrie is sweet, innocent, and generous, yet possessing a certain inscrutability that somehow leaves the impression that despite the noblest of sincere intentions Carrie always will survive while others fall around her. To achieve this effect is sheer artistry on her part."

Carrie was a box office flop. William Wyler later prognosticated, "It was simply released at the wrong time. Its grimness was a bit ahead of its time."

• • •

When shooting completed on Ruby Gentry, *Selznick implored Vidor and* Bernhard to permit him to become involved in postproduction. It was absolutely vital for Jennifer to have a big success, or her career as a first-rank star was over. Selznick zeroed in strictly on the bottom line—namely, making *Ruby Gentry* into a "money" picture. On those terms, Vidor and Bernhard paid attention. Selznick sought to "cut all the junk out of the picture."

Selznick's services were free of charge, and he even volunteered stock footage out of his own film library, at no cost, to beef up the production values. There was no other actress, other than Jennifer Jones, whose manager-husband was in a position to implement such changes in another producer's picture.

Selznick had a sensational money-saving idea—use only a single instrument to play the musical score for the picture. This had proven to be an incredible coup for *The Third Man* (which had used the zither). Vidor and Bernhard concurred. A single harmonica would be the orchestra for *Ruby Gentry*. It was right for the picture and could conceivably result in a theme that would become a hit song.

Jennifer and David intrigued and fascinated their peers to the extent that during the year, a film that fictionalized the producer's private life went into production at MGM.

Selznick was neither flattered nor amused, and Jennifer was fearful, since a host of Hollywood talents familiar with their behind-the-scenes story collaborated on the project, which had been given the go-ahead by former Selznick executive Dore Schary, with another former Selznick executive, John Houseman, as the producer. Jennifer's former director, Vincente Minnelli, was set to direct. Charles Schnee wrote the script, with the working title *Tribute to a Bad Man*.

An all-star cast was assembled as Selznick consulted his attorneys. Kirk Douglas and Lana Turner were assigned the film's leading roles. Douglas was to portray "Jonathan Shields," the young producer whose burning desire is to restore the name of his father to its rightful place in the movie industry. Jonathan is an unscrupulous, ruthless, driven, talented, charming, loving, and, when necessary, unprincipled man who loves no one more than himself. He loses his fortune, but never his power to fascinate ("He's more than a man, he's an experience," remarks another character).

"Georgia Lorrison," the character to be played by Lana Turner, certainly tapped directly into aspects of Jennifer's saga, particularly the way the actress is molded by Jonathan into the girl of his dreams and the way he deliberately makes her fall in love with him (while womanizing on the side). These similarities were right on target.

In addition, the script vividly depicted Jonathan's emotional let-downs, the devastating melancholy that engulfed him after completing a film and its effect on people in his life (especially Georgia).

"Why are you looking at me that way?" he screams at Georgia in a key scene of the film. He has made her into a top star, but she's shattered to discover his infidelities. "Maybe I *like* to feel cheap once in a while, maybe everybody does. . . ."

If that wasn't a scene that had taken place between Jennifer and David, it was certainly one that could have. At one point Jonathan personally takes over the direction of a multimillion-dollar *Duel in the Sun*–like epic he's producing after clashing one time too many with the veteran director "von Ellstein," who walks off the picture. "Every scene cannot be a dramatic climax in the picture," von Ellstein tells him angrily. "You've always wanted to direct a picture. Well, here's your chance!"

Deftly blending fact and fiction and inspiring guessing games all over town as to who else was being portrayed, *Tribute to a Bad Man*—retitled *The Bad and the Beautiful*—certainly provided cutting insight into what it was like for those having to live with Jonathan Shields/David Selznick.

Virtually every character in the film, on some level, is neurotic and dysfunctional, as well as talented and glamorous, of course. But what Selznick objected to most wasn't how Jonathan or Georgia or their relationship might be perceived, but the negative way Jonathan's father is depicted. "He wasn't a heel—he was *the* heel," Jonathan exclaims at one point.

MGM wasn't dissuaded from producing the picture. It was a film everyone at the studio felt could turn out to be *the* "Hollywood picture" of them all, and the usual on-screen disclaimer ("Any similarity to any persons living or dead is purely coincidental") would, its attorneys advised, keep the studio out of hot water.

Louella Parsons wasn't fooled. She wrote that "it is difficult to believe some of the scenes were not suggested by events in the colorful David O. Selznick's life."

Released in November, *The Bad and the Beautiful* was a big success at the box office and actually enhanced Selznick's legend.

In December David and Jennifer finally had some reason to celebrate. *Ruby Gentry* began its initial engagements and pulled in the public. "The picture will unquestionably attract because of the presence of Jennifer Jones, whose excellence as a film actress cannot be questioned," wrote the *Los Angeles Times*.

Newsweek, however, wasn't won over. "It's all very improbable and sadly conceived as a vehicle for Jennifer Jones, who could easily provide her own locomotion without so much outside and off-side assistance."

Fox went to town advertising and promoting the film as the story of "A Siren Who Wrecked a Whole Town—Man by Man—Sin by Sin," with provocative photos of Jennifer in a very tight sweater, her glossy lips parted in invitation.

To Charlton Heston's surprise, Jennifer didn't hit the publicity trail for *Ruby Gentry*. "She didn't do publicity tours. I learned to do it," says Heston, "and it was in my best interests to do it." It was a simple, sensible approach to an important facet of Heston's (or any other actor's) marketability. It was an approach Jennifer would never adopt.

Chapter

23

"*J*ust keep walking, boys," Jennifer advised her sons anxiously. They'd all been spotted by a photographer at Orly Airport in Paris. The boys were dressed in cashmere overcoats, blazers, slacks, and neckties. Jennifer radiated a cool luxe in a sleek Jacques Fath coat and suit ensemble, a velvet beret poised at a jaunty angle atop her head. A thousand-dollar alligator handbag swung casually from her wrist, and the actress stared straight ahead as she strode forward, steering Michael and Bobby away from the lensmen.

She was now perhaps overly concerned about everything relating to her sons, especially their physical health. The slightest signs of illness precipitated consultations with one or more doctors. And to help Bobby through the awful period following his father's death, Jennifer and David had arranged for the boy to have sessions with none other than Dr. Frederick Hacker!

Jennifer was in Europe to costar in *Beat the Devil,* to be filmed in Italy, when an important project suddenly intervened. Fifty-one-year-old Vittorio De Sica was the prime architect of neorealism in Italian cinema. His classic film *The Bicycle Thief* was an acknowledged masterpiece, and *Umberto D,* a striking epic of life in postwar Italy, was currently in successful release. De Sica collaborator Cesare Zavattini had written a script, *Terminal Station,* a simple story about the end of a romance between an Italian man, a professor, and a married American woman, a housewife on vacation in Italy. The story deals with the couple's last tremulous hours together in a bustling train depot in Rome.

Jennifer wasn't the initial element in the production. De Sica had first approached Montgomery Clift, to star. Clift, a great admirer of De Sica's, signed on eagerly.

It was the dawn of the era of "coproductions," and Selznick stepped in and offered to package and finance *Terminal Station,* supplying Jennifer as the female star (some reports characterized De Sica as having been "forced" to cast Jennifer).

From Selznick's point of view, De Sica and Clift were sure to enhance Jennifer's eminence as a screen personality. Clift was one of the most popular and respected young actors in the business. His films to date were successes most actors could only fantasize about: *The Search, Red River, The Heiress, A Place in the Sun.* Only Marlon Brando was a hotter name on the contemporary movie scene. Agent Lew Wasserman had guided Clift's career to the point where the actor now commanded $250,000 per picture (Clift was slated to begin *From Here to Eternity* after *Terminal Station*).

Jennifer was understandably elated. It honestly didn't matter to her who was to receive top billing in *Terminal Station* (in fact, she would) but it did matter that the platinum-edged package had the potential to vault her to the pinnacle of prestige in her profession.

In the meantime, she loved the feeling of anonymity she enjoyed abroad. To her it was the equivalent of having been given a new life and a new personality. Sometimes, in dark glasses, wearing only a simple skirt and blouse, she could explore the shops and sights of a city whose inhabitants didn't instantly recognize and pursue her. "Anonymity was highly prized by Jennifer," confirms Anita Colby. "Jennifer, with her dark coloring, looked like a native Italian, and while she'd often get wolf-whistled at, it was because the Mediterranean men thought she was a great-looking local girl, not because she was recognized as an American movie star."

Jennifer's relaxation time was brief. Unlike *Ruby Gentry, Terminal Station* would be subject to David's scrutiny on all elements of production before, during, and after filming. Although De Sica retained control of the final cut overseas (with Selznick controlling the American version), all knew the collision of the neorealistic school of filmmaking, epitomized by De Sica, and *cinema fantastique,*

Selznick's domain, could easily result in *cinema catastrophe,* with Jennifer's psyche the ultimate victim.

There was a major technical stumbling block facing the actress—De Sica couldn't speak English. "Art transcends language," agreed one and all as Selznick flung aside all obstacles and reassured Jennifer not to worry about anything, "just concentrate on your performance, darling."

It turned out that De Sica was able to converse with Clift in French but eventually had to resort to directing both Jennifer and Clift in pantomime (an ordeal for the actress, who was accustomed to a lot of direction). Well into production, De Sica's direction reached Jennifer through an interpreter.

Another minefield faced by Jennifer was that both she and Clift were actors with definite ideas on how to create their characters. De Sica rarely featured professional actors in his productions; in his films he liked to use people he spotted on the streets who *looked* right for a part, and he was not accustomed to being questioned or challenged.

One can imagine De Sica's dismay at being confronted with these dilemmas on top of Selznick's hands-on concept of moviemaking.

De Sica grew to regard Selznick's elaborate memos with hostility and suspicion, and at one point he consulted a lawyer to be sure the producer wasn't threatening to sue him. De Sica finally learned to handle David the same way Hitchcock did! Alfred Hitchcock would listen to everything Selznick had to say, then do it his own way.

"I very much liked Jennifer, she was so vulnerable and sensitive," recalled De Sica. "I believe she could have done wonderful things, but Selznick was too much the [overbearing] figure."

As always, Selznick belabored the script. Brilliant novelist Carson McCullers had written a version that, to Clift's horror, was discarded. The producer then hired Paul Gallico, followed by Alberto Moravia, for other versions. Truman Capote, twenty-nine years old, was finally hired to work on the script. Selznick recognized (and promoted) Capote's abilities at once ("David absolutely adored him," recalled Jennifer), and the beguiling and Machiavellian Capote, a friend of Clift's, had no trouble working his way into Jennifer's good graces.

Capote had opinions about and answers for everything and was an amusing confidant who seemed to Jennifer to know more about what women thought and felt than women themselves did. ("Tru should have been born a woman," remarked Capote's pal of later years, Ava Gardner. Capote returned the compliment by characterizing Ava as "muy macho.")

Not even the talents of Truman Capote, however, could keep Jennifer pacified or keep the heavy *Terminal* ship of production afloat. Jennifer and Clift had become disenchanted with the constant script rewrites. De Sica and line producer Wolfgang Reinhardt, a Hollywood veteran, recognized disaster on the horizon but were powerless to effect a change, since Selznick was paying the bills.

On *Ruby Gentry* Jennifer had functioned beautifully and delivered quality results with a script that was adhered to, a director who knew what he wanted, a leading man who presented no difficulties, and a fast and efficient production team.

None of these ingredients were present on this shoot, which was further complicated by Selznick's constant presence on the set. Jennifer felt the strain, and Clift, unlike Heston, Peck, or Cotten, was an actor who presented her with a highly complicated persona to contend with.

The personal chemistry between Jennifer and Clift was evidently more intense than either the actress or her husband could have anticipated. Clift was in many ways reminiscent of Robert Walker—sensitive, moody in the extreme, emotionally vulnerable, and at the same time possessing a "jungle intelligence" that enabled him to manipulate people shrewdly.

Jennifer's eyes betrayed her interest. Truman Capote recalled: "Jennifer got some sort of crush on Monty, and believe it or not she didn't realize that Monty really liked fellows. When she found out she got so upset, she went into the portable dressing room and stuffed a mink jacket down the portable toilet."

"Well, get a plumber!" exclaimed Selznick when alerted to the dilemma.

Clift had been accompanied to Rome by a young male lover named Dino, but the two men were soon at odds, "and there was some kind of competition going on between Monty and Truman. It was the one personal problem that I knew Monty was having," recalled Wolfgang Reinhardt.

While Jennifer was apparently oblivious of these churning homosexual undercurrents, Clift was aware of and sympathetic to Jennifer's problems with Selznick. The harried producer was often up all night, dictating memos and rewriting the script. His suggestions regarding Jennifer's appearance were never-ending. He often reprimanded De Sica because Jennifer wasn't being lit properly (De Sica was a proponent of natural light, which hardly presented women in the kind of glossy perfection Selznick insisted on for Jennifer).

Selznick also complained there weren't enough close-ups of Jennifer, and that her basic costume (a tailored suit), although designed by Christian Dior, wasn't properly flattering.

Problems mounted. The film was being shot from ten P.M. to five A.M. in Rome's bustling new train terminal. Wolfgang Reinhardt recalled: "We were running into the Christmas traffic at the station, and the engine drivers complained that as they drove there were too many floodlights. The station manager told us that he could no longer assure the company security from the crowds of people. The workers got irritable. No day went by without someone having a hysterical fit. The worst happened during the great love scene between Monty and Jennifer. . . ."

The scene took place in a deserted railroad car and was played, in take after take, with growing and uninhibited passion by both Jennifer and Clift.

Reinhardt recalled that the scene "had been rewritten two or three hundred times," and in its playing the actors became "so tense that nobody was allowed on the set except the cameramen and principals. It was just awful! As soon as the actors [finished the scene] Selznick would have it rewritten, translated into Italian so that Zavattini, who couldn't read a word of English, could approve it, and then given to the actors to perform again.

"Finally," recalled Reinhardt, "Jennifer threw off her shoes and stockings and ran out into the street. Selznick ran after her, and she was so hysterical she slapped him. [His glasses] broke and he wandered around unable to see, while we all ran after Jennifer and the technicians pretended not to notice what was happening."

Gossip at the time declared that only Jennifer's religious upbringing prevented the actress from seeking a divorce. ("It wasn't true, Jennifer and David *often* fought, and then he'd apologize and become a sorry little boy. And she'd forgive him," said Anita Colby.)

"Let's face it, what do you do for an encore after you've produced *Gone With the Wind?*" asks Joan Fontaine. "David had outgrown the movie business."

Jennifer, on occasion, was peacemaker when violent clashes erupted between Clift and Selznick (whom, according to author Patricia Bosworth, Clift regarded as "an interfering fuck-face"). Clift observed: "Jennifer is madly in love with David, but she talks openly about his emotional instability to me. She says it's almost as bad as her own. They are both in deep analysis."

Jennifer bought Clift a very expensive gift, a beautiful Gucci briefcase, whose clasp kept falling open. When Clift displayed the gift to friends, he observed: "Jennifer Jones gave this to me. It's beautiful, but it doesn't quite work—how like Jennifer!"

The emotionally weary actress, her Louis Vuitton luggage bulging with extravagant gifts from David, journeyed directly to Ravello, Italy to begin *Beat the Devil*. Selznick wasn't feeling well and returned to the United States to consult his doctors and to begin reediting *Terminal Station* for its American release (an endeavor doomed to repeat the obsessive, disastrous postproduction scenario on *Gone to Earth*).

Even without Selznick in Italy calling the shots, Jennifer was soon facing another problem-filled shoot. "What is my character like? She's not clear in the script, how do I play her?" she asked John Huston.

"Don't worry about it, honey," replied the sly, smiling Huston, annoyed any time an actor complained.

Jennifer's costar, Humphrey Bogart, was also producing the film, and at the age of fifty-four he was riding high. The previous year he'd won the Oscar as Best Actor for *The African Queen*. Huston, too, was a hotter property than ever. The recently released *Moulin Rouge* was a big box office and critical success.

Production on *Beat the Devil* began rolling, but the script by Claud Cockburn based on his novel didn't satisfy Huston. ("It stinks," he said privately, confirming the validity of Jennifer's concerns.) The behind-the-scenes circus began. Huston's spirits remained high, though; he was being paid $175,000 and he enjoyed working again with Bogart and Jennifer and the exceptional cast he'd assembled, including Robert Morley, Peter Lorre, and Gina Lollobrigida.

Selznick was furious, however, when he learned Lollobrigida

had joined the cast. His displeasure had to do not with the actress's abilities, or lack of them, but with the unflattering contrast that might be drawn between the voluptuous Gina and Jennifer. (This was Lollobrigida's first American picture. She didn't speak English and learned her role phonetically.)

The lengths to which Selznick would go to protect Jennifer's interests now reached ludicrous heights. Lollobrigida recalled that Selznick privately asked her to drop out of the movie, offering to pay her entire salary. "He thought I was too beautiful to be in a picture with Jennifer Jones," stated Gina, an ambitious woman who not only remained in the picture, but claimed later that "Truman Capote [subsequently hired to work on the script] ended up writing a lot of scenes for me." (Huston's nickname for Lollobrigida was "Lola Frigidaire.")

If Jennifer, aware of Selznick's attempt to remove the alleged "competition" from the cast, was humiliated, she kept silent and concentrated on portraying her ever-evolving character, "Gwendolynne." The role was a dramatic departure for her. The character was decidedly more "human," rather than a saint or a victim.

Because Lollobrigida was a brunette, however, Jennifer affected a dramatic change in her own appearance by wearing a blond wig for the role.

The new *Devil* script failed to receive approval from the Breen Office because of the adulterous relationship between the characters portrayed by Bogart and Jennifer. Huston hadn't liked the new script anyway, and scriptwriters Tony Veiller and Peter Viertel weren't amenable to revising it. Huston wanted to cancel the picture, but Bogart persuaded him to continue.

Jennifer, in rising alarm, kept Selznick informed. On hearing of Huston's discontent with the script, David suggested to the director that he hire Truman Capote. Capote met with Huston, and the director signed the diminutive author to a $1,500-a-week contract. Capote and Huston collaborated on a new script. (Capote later claimed not only that Huston did not write a word, an allegation angrily denied by Huston, but that he and Huston, sharing quarters, had had an affair!)

Jennifer paid scant attention to such gossip, while her doubts and fears over her role continued to grow. Selznick rejoined his anxious wife in Europe. John Barry Ryan, one of Huston's assistants, recalled, "Things happened that could only have happened on a

John Huston set in winter in an Italian town where there was no heat, no electricity, and nothing to eat or drink except what was shipped in.

"Every night there was a great poker game, with Huston, Bogart, and David Selznick. Jennifer was being pursued by a tall Italian lesbian, who was in turn being pursued by a short, dumpy Italian lesbian. David was trying to fight everyone off, and Truman was encouraging the whole thing."

The pressure on Jennifer of having new script pages to memorize every day was nerve-racking. "I always wanted to know where my character was going," she said, "whether she was going to drop dead or jump in the ocean or be knocked over the head. The beginning, the middle, and the end was the way I was structured, so it sometimes threw me a little bit not to know from day to day what she was going to do or not do."

According to Truman Capote, not only Jennifer, but the rest of the cast were "completely bewildered." He noted that "sometimes even Huston didn't seem to know what was going on."

Jennifer and the other actors began improvising on camera. Director of photography Oswald "Ossie" Morris later described Jennifer as "a bit neurotic" and said the actress finally turned to Selznick and confided all her growing fears about the production to him. Selznick, back in the States, was aghast. Immediately he began deluging Huston with voluminous memos about Jennifer.

Huston and Bogart devised a suitable response for Selznick: they wrote him a long, intentionally confusing cable, which, they presumed, would hold Selznick at bay. The cable's pages were numbered consecutively, with one page number deliberately omitted. Huston, when he subsequently spoke with Selznick, referred constantly to information on the missing (and in fact nonexistent) page. This tactic, according to Huston, "drove [Selznick] right up the wall."

And resulted, of course, in the exact opposite effect for Jennifer that Selznick had desired. Selznick's efforts merely inspired Huston, now anxious himself about the picture, to retaliate by providing Jennifer with a rough time on the set. ("Huston was a sadistic son of a bitch," says a later Huston star, Michael Parks.)

For a *Beat the Devil* scene aboard a yacht, Jennifer was slated to be in the background, exercising atop the ship's mast. Huston decided that he also wanted her to stand on her head (he knew she was adept at yoga). Robert Morley recalled that "he made her climb the rigging, which was rather ridiculous. He bullied her. She came down shaking."

Huston was oblivious. Associate producer Jack Clayton was dispatched to take Jennifer back to shore. "She was in tears," he said. "That was part of John's cruel side." Clayton (later a director himself) managed to convince Jennifer to continue with the shot and brought her back to the boat. "When I told John that I had brought her back, he said, 'Why did you do that, kid? I wouldn't shoot her tonight, anyway.'"

Jennifer's sons, now twelve and thirteen, were enrolled in private schools (Bob, over the next few years, attended more than a dozen schools in Europe and the United States). She considered them well taken care of.

Bob visited his mother on location in Italy and enjoyed meeting the actors, although he recalled that at this point he wasn't interested in becoming one. Brother Michael's goal was to become a geologist, which pleased Jennifer.

Familiar faces visited the *Devil* set, including Ingrid Bergman, Roberto Rossellini, and Orson Welles. "Jennifer was a good listener." recalled Welles. "She'd fasten those enormous eyes on you and pay rapt attention."

The *Beat the Devil* company completed interiors for the film in London. By this point Jennifer had no faith in how the picture had turned out, and Bogart especially was concerned with the results. He commiserated with Jennifer and asked Huston if there was even a chance of the picture making its money back. Huston replied that the project had turned into the exact opposite of what it had been intended to be—not an action adventure, but a broad, satiric comedy, and whether or not the picture made money, predicted Huston, depended on whether or not the jokes were funny!

One can imagine how Jennifer and David viewed the situation. It's certain they weren't laughing.

• • •

"What do I do next?" was *Jennifer's constant concern.*

She'd expressed interest in Sam Spiegel's upcoming production of *On the Waterfront,* with a script by Arthur Miller and Elia Kazan as director. Selznick vetoed Jennifer's idea: hers would be a supporting part (Eva Marie Saint subsequently won the Oscar for it). The script of *East of Eden,* another Elia Kazan project slated as a Brando vehicle (James Dean was eventually cast), intrigued Jennifer. Julie Harris was final choice for leading lady. But Jennifer's instincts about good scripts had once again proven accurate.

"David Selznick [later] wanted me to cast Jennifer in the film of *Picnic,*" recalled Joshua Logan (a top director by the fifties, back in the thirties a dialogue director for Selznick). "I told him the role was cast. 'I know,' he said, 'but Jennifer will do a better job than Kim Novak.' 'Tell [studio head] Harry Cohn,' I said [Novak was Columbia's new young superstar]. That was the end of that."

The movie business had experienced a revolutionary technical development called Cinerama, a spectacular new wide-screen process. Twentieth Century–Fox had invested in the development of its own wide-screen process, CinemaScope, for which the screen image would be twice the size of the standard movie screen (and rectangular in shape, not square). Actors' physical flaws would be megamagnified, to the horror of Jennifer and her contemporaries. "Every actress over twenty-five will be finished!" exclaimed MGM contract player Arlene Dahl. The industry awaited the release of the first CinemaScope production, *The Robe,* set to premiere during the 1953 Christmas season.

Jennifer was thirty-four, and history was repeating itself in her career. With one hit in the marketplace, and two potential bombs in the can, she recognized how crucial it was to have another winner lined up, and Selznick was determined to find it.

An opportunity presented itself from an unlikely source. Selznick's former father-in-law, L. B. Mayer, was planning to return to motion picture production with a big-budget biblical spectacle certain to return Mayer to his former eminence. The mogul's proposed "comeback" vehicle was *Joseph and His Brethren.* Mayer eagerly sought Selznick's professional opinion on the script, along with an exquisitely ironic offer—the starring role of Potiphar's wife, for Jennifer.

With the greatest tact, but pulling no punches, Selznick informed Mayer that the script needed a lot of work. Regarding Jennifer's availability, he said, "Jennifer has . . . read the script, and I would like to have her play it, subject, of course, to other commitments . . . and subject also to my belief that the character can be made more three-dimensional. . . ."

Mayer subsequently abandoned the project.

Selznick aggressively pursued every other opportunity for his wife. Jennifer was champing at the bit to portray Maria Vargas in *The Barefoot Contessa,* Joseph L. Mankiewicz's story of a tragic, beautiful, impoverished Spanish girl. Selznick "importuned [Mankiewicz] . . . almost daily" about hiring Jennifer, recalled David Hanna, Mankiewicz's publicity director. But Mankiewicz was determined to cast Ava Gardner (and paid a then extraordinary $350,000 to MGM for Ava's services).

Terminal Station, to Jennifer and David's relief, opened successfully in Europe (but the reviews weren't good). In the United States, however, Selznick ripped the picture apart in the editing room in a desperate attempt to refashion it into a slick love story. The previous July, *From Here to Eternity* had elevated Montgomery Clift to superstar, and Clift's name alone, reasoned Selznick, would guarantee a respectable number of play dates and insure success for Jennifer's movie in the United States.

Selznick had decided that *Indiscretion of an American Wife* was a strong commercial title for the U.S. market, and he made a deal with Columbia Pictures to distribute the picture.

Early in 1954 Jennifer traveled to New York, where she resided at the luxurious Waldorf Towers. The basic purpose of her visit was to attend the funeral of Truman Capote's mother, Nina, who'd died from an overdose of seconal and alcohol. Capote's aunts were charmed by Jones, who brought homemade cookies to the wake.

What Jennifer really wanted to make was a good picture, and finally the right project seemed to surface at the right moment. She was thrilled with an offer from Paramount to play the starring female role in *The Country Girl,* the film version of the hit Broadway play by Clifford Odets.

Bing Crosby and William Holden were set to portray the two leading men, an alcoholic ex-star and a hotshot young Broadway director, in this taut drama of backstage life. Jennifer would play the alcoholic's long-suffering mate, who resurrects her weak husband's life and career but falls in love with his director.

Crosby was delighted with Jennifer's casting. He considered her a strong actress. The crooner was anxious about portraying an un-likable, selfish character for the first time in his career and feared the responsibility of having to carry the picture "alone."

George Seaton, who'd written the screenplay for *Song of Bernadette* and wrote and directed the classic *Miracle on 34th Street*, was set to direct, with William Perlberg (who'd produced *Song of Bernadette*) producing. As far as Jennifer and Selznick were concerned, here at last was *the* golden opportunity: a great script and contemporary role perfectly suited to Jennifer's talents and a first-rate production team familiar with her capabilities. It was a sure Os-car-caliber venture. "She'll be wonderful in the part," declared Seaton. "I think it will be the most important role of her career."

Then a critical situation arose. Jennifer was pregnant (she was in her third month).

Selznick pleaded with producer Perlberg to proceed with *Country Girl* immediately, before Jennifer's condition became apparent. There were no period costume corsets to imperil her physical condition, and the wardrobe for the role was strictly loose-fitting sweaters and skirts and dowdy dresses.

Perlberg refused to be rushed, and Jennifer, her hopes dashed, had to withdraw from the film, enabling agent Jay Kantor and his boss, Lew Wasserman, to negotiate a coup for rising MCA client Grace Kelly. The twenty-four-year-old actress, over initial objections from Bing Crosby, stepped boldly into the role of Georgie Elgin. Crosby had thought Kelly too young and inexperienced, but Kelly had guts and, coincidentally, was the same age Jennifer had been at the time she'd been cast in *Song of Bernadette*.

"Jennifer took such wonderful care of herself physically, she could have done Country Girl and not endangered the baby. Nowadays they'd work it into the script!" exclaims Anita Colby.

Selznick was truly happy that Jennifer was pregnant, and Jen-nifer was pleased she'd be presenting David with a gift money couldn't buy (and that Irene couldn't give him).

The former Mrs. Selznick, with whom David still kept in discreet but close touch, and still turned to for advice, expressed her con-gratulations. But Selznick revealed to Irene how unhappy he was with the state of his own career. At the age of fifty-two David was taking on the enormous responsibility of raising a new family without any *Gone With the Wind* or Selznick-International to support them.

Jennifer was not aware of the depth of David's dilemma. He'd gone to great lengths to conceal the truth from her, and she continued to inhabit the world he'd created for her. Meanwhile, Selznick was middleman for the sale of film rights to Irene's successful stage production of *Bell, Book and Candle.* Irene was delighted. David intended to buy the property and then resell it to a studio. When he asked Irene if $100,000 was a fair price, she replied that it was wonderful. But she wondered where he'd get the money.

David had bought the lavish Spanish-style home on Tower Grove Drive and he'd renovated it into a showplace. "People judged you by the location and size of your house," recalls Anita Colby. "It was essential for David and Jennifer to have the proper setting or they'd have been out of the game."

Jennifer loved the palatial abode. "It was a magical place," she later recalled. It gave her a satisfying sense of solidity and permanence, as if she'd lived that way all her life and didn't doubt that she'd live like that for the rest of it.

It was the perfect oasis for an expectant mother. The multi-leveled dwelling was both intimate and grand, providing the actress with her own private suite of rooms on a downstairs level. According to legend, silent screen star John Gilbert, initial owner of the property, had added the lower wing as a flamboyant romantic gesture to Greta Garbo, at the height of their tempestuous love affair. "There were legendary stories about Gilbert getting wildly drunk and standing stark naked in the patio off the bar, shouting dramatically to guests approaching from below," recalled Jennifer.

A manmade waterfall cascaded past the bedroom windows (Jennifer would take her beauty naps in this boudoir). Upstairs were the living room, libraries, other bedrooms, formal dining room, and entertaining areas (Jennifer's upstairs bedroom was alongside Selznick's, of course). There was one entire glass wall enclosing the stairway to the second floor and another in a long hallway furnished with banquettes.

Beautiful vistas of trees and flowers abounded. Terraces offered spectacular views of the city, and there were tennis courts and, of course, a magnificent swimming pool. The Brackman portrait of Jennifer from *Portrait of Jennie* was installed above the fireplace in the study, where pictures of Selznick's sons were also on display.

Selznick also constructed a separate cottage on the grounds for the Walker boys. (This was not unusual—Hollywood director John Farrow and his wife, actress Maureen O'Sullivan, for example, had eight children, and Farrow insisted that the children and their nannies occupy a totally separate wing of the house.)

Selznick told Michael and Bobby to come to him if they had any problems or needed money. With a baby on the way, especially after the miscarriage, he didn't want Jennifer to have to worry about anything.

Jennifer was back on the big screen in March 1954 when Beat the Devil *began* its domestic engagements. The good news for Jennifer was that the movie garnered a few rave reviews. The *Saturday Review* described it as "a brilliant parody," and *The New Yorker* found it "hugely entertaining . . . with a kind of bright lunacy." As far as *Time* magazine was concerned, "Jennifer Jones . . . does the best with the best part—she managed to catch the mystic fervor of the truly creative liar." The film was described as a "sort of a screwball classic."

The bad news was that the public wasn't interested. The movie eventually became a cult classic, winning an intensely loyal and devoted band of followers. Years after its release, *Los Angeles Times* critic Charles Champlin met Jennifer and told her that his favorite Jones performance was in *Beat the Devil.* "She smiled thinly," recalled Champlin, "and said, 'When Johnny was persuading me to do it, he said. "Jennifer, they'll remember you longer for *Beat the Devil* than for *The Song of Bernadette.*" I think the SOB was right.' "

Selznick declined an invitation to attend MGM's gala rerelease of Gone With the Wind *in Atlanta in May.* Rhett Butler stayed home, too. Fifty-three-year-old Clark Gable had maintained an intense animosity for both Selznick and MGM because he'd never been cut in on the film's incredible profits. (Selznick would turn down Gable as a leading man for Jennifer a few years hence. ("Too old," he noted, although Gable was only a year older than David.)

Currently David's thoughts were not on the rerelease of *Gone With the Wind,* they were on the release of *Indiscretion of an American Wife.* The film opened in June, and despite Jennifer and Clift to lure the customers, and a provocative ad campaign, the film was the box office disaster all had feared it might be. David tried to shield Jennifer from the enormity of the failure. She knew, however, and felt bad for David. A little more of the gilt began to peel off the golden image she'd had of him. Long ago he'd promised her anything she wanted, but she'd learned there were limits to what even he could accomplish.

The Hollywood Reporter noted that "while at times achieving a high degree of poignancy, the story itself is . . . too frail to sustain consistent interest, although the beautiful, sensitive performances of Miss Jones and Clift go a long way toward making the tale more vital than would seem possible."

Jennifer impressed *The New York Times:* "Miss Jones performs the troubled lady with dignity and sentiment. . . . Though the role is a little unpleasant—a little unladylike and cheap—Miss Jones makes it look as though a female with decent and generous instincts is trying to work herself out of a tough spot. In the course of an hour, she makes a woman of little sympathy look much better."

Good reviews notwithstanding, the picture was a summer turkey. To make matters worse, it was virtually unreleasable on a wide scale.

Interestingly, there was a young actor who liked the picture, and Jennifer in particular. The actor was James Dean, and he later named Jennifer his favorite actress.

While Jennifer tried to relax and await the birth of the baby, due in August, her stature, both as Selznick's "star creation" and his wife, was enhanced accordingly with the latest successful rerelease of *Gone With the Wind.* As a new generation fell in love with the fifteen-year-old Technicolor tale of the Old South, Selznick announced that he was going to return to epic filmmaking with a production of Tolstoy's *War and Peace* starring Jennifer Jones. MGM would finance his comeback venture (the announcement received big play, but in fact negotiations were far from complete).

Jennifer was both excited at the prospect of portraying Natasha and fearful of the hazards of creating a flesh-and-blood version of a beloved fictional character from one of the greatest novels of all time.

David saw the film as an opportunity for Jennifer to create another Scarlett, since *War and Peace* had many parallels to *Gone With the Wind.* Here was an epic story that centered around war (in this case, the 1812 war between Russia and France) and the problems of individuals caught up in that war.

In the past, the Motion Picture Association of America, with whom member producers registered their proposed projects in order to prevent rip-offs by their peers, would have protected Selznick's first-on-record claim to *War and Peace.* But times had changed. A brash forty-seven-year-old Broadway entrepreneur named Mike Todd announced that he was going to produce *War and Peace* in a new screen process, Todd-AO. And from Europe came the announcement that producer Dino De Laurentiis, in partnership with Carlo Ponti, was planning his own version of *War and Peace.* Ponti/De Laurentiis outraced their competitors and swiftly lined up a top star, Audrey Hepburn, a director, King Vidor, and a financial partner and distributor, Paramount (where Hepburn was under contract). The film would be ready to go in a relatively short while.

Selznick was angry and, privately, very depressed over this development. Insiders agreed that in times past David would have "digested both Todd and De Laurentiis for dinner." But impending fatherhood placed the professional setback in a new perspective for the aging mogul, and David was determined to come up with an "even better" vehicle for Jennifer.

Meanwhile, he successfully reissued *Duel in the Sun* before the end of the year.

Jennifer gave birth, on August 12, to a healthy seven-pound eight-ounce daughter. The proud parents named her Mary Jennifer. Selznick wrote to well-wisher Michael Powell, "Both Jennifer and I like to believe that your forecasting concerning a wonderful woman are go-

ing to be borne out," and he extolled his infant daughter's "truly extraordinary beauty and talent and brightness. . . ."

Jennifer's third child was born into an environment befitting a
royal princess, complete with servants, nannies, and a doting father
who reveled in her existence. According to Irene Selznick, the boys
in the family were delighted to welcome a baby sister.

But motherhood was hardly a new experience for Jennifer, and
apparently changing diapers was not on her agenda. Obviously she
vividly recalled how her world has been turned upside down when
her sons (now thirteen and fourteen) had been born. She'd been
forced to abandon her career for two years, and she wasn't about to
plunge into that chasm again (although the new baby, and her
nurse, would always remain close by).

Jennifer intended at this moment to fulfill a lifetime ambition,
an opportunity made possible in part because a most unusual project had been offered to Selznick that did not involve her. For the
time being, it would occupy all his time and energy, enabling her to
make a grab for independence.

Chapter 24

*J*ennifer *exercised and dieted religiously to* regain her figure. A personal maid has recalled an at-home scenario not unlike the moments in *Gone With the Wind* when, after Scarlett O'Hara has recovered from the birth of her daughter, Bonnie, she has herself laced into a tight corset in an effort to regain her tiny waist. Jennifer, apparently in the same state of mind, was quite successful in recovering her svelte form.

She relished the opportunity of escaping from the town where "you're only as good as your last picture." She announced she was heading east to tackle her next venture, a starring role on Broadway.

First, along with the baby and her nurse, Jennifer joined David at a bungalow he'd rented at the Beverly Hills Hotel, where he was working on his new project with writer Ben Hecht. David had accepted the challenge of entering the TV production arena to celebrate "Light's Diamond Jubilee," the seventy-fifth anniversary of Edison's invention of the electric light bulb. All four TV networks (CBS, NBC, ABC, and Dumont) were going simultaneously to telecast a three-hour broadcast commemorating the event, and at Bill Paley's urging Selznick took on the project (which included working directly with President Dwight D. Eisenhower).

Nonetheless David had grave misgivings about Jennifer doing the play *Portrait of a Lady,* pointing out that the script was no good ("an impossible adaptation of a book that was probably impossible to adapt"). But the actress was determined to proceed ("When Jennifer has made up her mind about something, that's *it*," observes Anita Colby).

William Wyler had thought about casting Jennifer in *The Lark,* a play about Joan of Arc by Jean Anouilh, adapted by Lillian Hellman, which Wyler was set to direct on Broadway. Jennifer was perfectly willing to comply with Wyler's request that she audition. Selznick refused to permit it (Julie Harris triumphed in the role).

David and Jennifer quarreled about *Portrait.* "I have no judgment about scripts," Jennifer admitted, "as most actors haven't." David (and everyone else) wondered how Jennifer would handle the psychological blow she'd suffer if the show failed and she received devastating notices.

"I think I know what would happen," she said. "I'd be absolutely shattered. I'd dissolve into tears, and be miserable for days, weeks, maybe months. And then I'd turn right around and do another play! I believe it was Ethel Barrymore who said that in this profession you have to have the hide of an elephant. When I started, I didn't have such a hide. I do now. I can take it."

David, hoping to convince Jennifer to change her mind, assailed her with tales of the fabulous plans he had in store for her, plans inspired by the recent splash yet another past Selznick triumph had created. The ultracostly Warner Brothers remake of David's *A Star Is Born,* an elaborate musical version starring Judy Garland and James Mason, had just been released. Selznick was determined to mount a vehicle for Jennifer that would deliver the same dramatic impact, and he'd held on to valuable foreign rights to *A Star Is Born* to enable him to obtain rights to a property owned by Warners that he had in mind for Jennifer.

She reasoned correctly that it would be years, if ever, before the project would come to light. The actress was understandably frustrated by the two great ones that had gotten away. *The Barefoot Contessa,* also released that fall, was a personal triumph for Ava Gardner; and advance word on *The Country Girl,* due for release before the end of the year, was that Grace Kelly was certain to win an Oscar nomination.

Jennifer was desperate to explore an entirely new venue, to recharge her psyche and her career. "It's not good for a relationship when your husband is your manager," noted Doris Day, married to her manager, Martin Melcher. "The romance goes out the window when you feel you're married to your father."

Henry James has long been one of America's greatest novelists, with The Portrait of a Lady, published in 1881, regarded as one of his best novels (*Washington Square, The Bostonians,* and *The Turn of the Screw* are among James's other widely read books). James wrote about the conflicts, both amusing and serious, between American and European manners and customs. This was the theme of *Portrait of a Lady,* the vehicle in which Jennifer had chosen to make her Broadway debut.

She'd be perfectly cast, portraying an innocent and idealistic American girl abroad who winds up marrying a decadent man. But she began to have second thoughts. The New York–based director of the play, the dark, intensely charismatic José Quintero, flew to Hollywood to talk her into it. Quintero was the current wunderkind of the New York theater, and cofounder and -director of the famed Circle in the Square theater company in Greenwich Village. Quintero had cast an unknown young actress, Geraldine Page, in the leading role in the group's production of Tennessee Williams's *Summer and Smoke,* launching Page as a major stage star.

Jennifer and Quintero were simpatico at once, discussing the venture amid the fairy-tale-like comfort and opulence of the actress's home. There were quiet talks by the pool as Quintero, with his dark eyes, soft voice, and dynamic manner, described for Jennifer the intricacies of her role.

She was enthralled. "When José was talking to you, he looked at you with great intensity, as though you were the only one in his universe," recalled a friend, John Connally.

"Jennifer responded to storytelling," recalled Quintero, "she became like a little girl hearing the Scheherazade tale in *Thousand and One Nights.*" Quintero was greatly impressed by Jennifer's physical beauty.

"The director's the thing," Jennifer noted. "I've always placed heavy emphasis on directors." Although Jennifer and Quintero had never met before, "I was a fan of his. I'd seen his production of *Summer and Smoke,* and I'd followed his work. He said he was a fan of mine, too. How can anyone resist a mutual admiration society?"

Nonetheless, Quintero had no easy task in convincing Jennifer to make a firm commitment. "We spent days, literally, talking about Henry James and his books and what kind of a girl this particular heroine, Isabel Archer from Albany, really was," recalled Jennifer, but she was intrigued. Isabel was full of ideals and eager to meet life. Then comes disillusionment when she becomes enmeshed with decadent expatriates in Europe. "José made it all come alive," she said.

Quintero said he agreed with Selznick that the script needed work and promised that it would be rewritten, but according to David, the promise was never kept. Selznick later bemoaned the "semiprofessional setup of writing and direction and production and all manner of other things."

Despite Selznick's misgivings, or perhaps because of them, Jennifer forged ahead ("They argued and argued," recalled Anita Colby, "but Jennifer stood firm"). If codependency had been the overriding characteristic defining Jennifer's relationship with David, she'd finally reached the point of forcefully exercising her own will.

Her theater friends, including Constance Collier, Sanford Meisner, and Michael Chekhov, encouraged her. A highly distinguished cast was assembled, insuring Jennifer the finest professional support on stage. Costar Robert Fleming had starred in London's West End with Greer Garson and Gladys Cooper and in the United States with Jennifer's idol, Katharine Cornell, and in John Gielgud's Broadway production of *The Importance of Being Earnest*.

Cathleen Nesbitt had recently played Audrey Hepburn's aunt in the stage production of *Gigi* and had scored a great Broadway success as one of the leads in *Sabrina Fair*. She'd played in all the classics and was one of the finest actresses working in the theater.

Other cast members were equally highly regarded. Douglas Watson had starred on stage with Helen Hayes, Ruth Gordon, Shirley Booth, and Judith Anderson. Actress Barbara O'Neil boasted impeccable theater credentials, although she was best known to audiences for her portrayal of Scarlett O'Hara's mother in *Gone With the Wind*.

The great Cecil Beaton was engaged to design Jennifer's costumes, ensuring a breathtaking wardrobe for the star.

Portrait of a Lady was scheduled to open first in Boston, with its Broadway debut scheduled to take place in late December in the newly refurbished ANTA Theater on Fifty-second Street between Broadway and Eighth Avenue. Jennifer hoped to to celebrate a brilliant Christmas and settle in for a long New York run (the baby, and her nurse, would be with her).

Jennifer implored David not to interfere, and the producer acquiesced, although he supervised her publicity for the show. Martin Schwartz, the production's press agent, discovered that his work was more than cut out for him. Jennifer's stage debut was an event of earth-shattering importance as far as her manager-husband was concerned, and Selznick was fanatical concerning the biographical material to be handed out to the press.

Jennifer's official bio included an outright lie, the statement that she had graduated from the American Academy of Dramatic Arts. It also claimed that she'd "initially suggested and fostered, and was one of the five players who organized, the Actors Company of La Jolla, California, for the purpose of giving to Hollywood players a living theater."

There were restrictions involved in working with Jennifer directly, dictated by her reluctance to give interviews. Reporter Emory Lewis, on meeting her, accurately isolated key elements of her personality: "An ever-changing combination of a fresh, almost childlike enthusiast and a reserved, worldly woman."

To David's chagrin, the press revealed the fact that Jennifer hadn't, as legend had it, made her screen debut a decade earlier in *Song of Bernadette* but had "already [previously] labored in the Hollywood sweat-shops. She had emoted in several Westerns as a gun-toting gal, and she had been imperiled regularly in a Republic serial, *Dick Tracy's G-Men*. . . . Obviously Miss Jones and her Hollywood mentors are most anxious to forget it."

To make matters worse, photographs of a "gun-totin' " Jennifer, as she'd appeared fifteen years earlier, found their way into print. Such "revelations," however, were hardly of major concern with the problems soon facing the production.

By the time of the Boston opening, the three-act, six-scene play hadn't jelled. Jennifer was familiar with the sickening feeling of a venture that wasn't working. Conflicts erupted. Everyone struggled to infuse the work with energy in a desperate attempt to make it work, although Jennifer fought to remain calm in the midst of the chaos.

"Jennifer was a lovely person." recalled Cathleen Nesbitt, "but perhaps a bit too sensitive. You have to have a spine of steel to survive in the theater."

Jennifer insisted the Boston tryout be extended.

The show then proceeded south, for fifteen performances in Washington and fourteen in Baltimore. Jennifer didn't leave her worries at the theater; she dreamed about the play nightly. Her anxiety was apparent to all.

Reporter Milton Bracker interviewed Jennifer twice, first in Boston and then in Baltimore: "In her dressing room . . . her legs tucked up under a red skirt and her hands restless—now above her head, now in her lap or fretting each other and a wooden pencil— she seemed vividly and tensely aware that her Broadway debut posed problems apart from and beyond those she had solved, often with distinction, in Hollywood."

She had plenty to lose if the play bombed. It was her name going above the title. ("The smartest actor in the business is Bing Crosby," David Selznick once noted, observing how Crosby always insisted "that they costar somebody, even if it was a bit player, so that he couldn't be blamed alone if the picture failed.")

Selznick kept his promise and stayed away, although he repeatedly suggested that they either remain on the road and get the production in shape, or close the show.

The play proceeded to New York. Associated Press correspondent Hal Boyle was in the audience on opening night. "She was a beautiful-looking gal and a very good actress," recalled Boyle. "It wasn't her fault that the play was god-awful. She had stage presence. If she'd chosen a good vehicle, she'd have been the toast of the town."

Backstage, after the show, Quintero embraced Jennifer and told her how wonderful she'd been. "Was it okay? You *really* liked it?" she repeated over and over, her complexion flushed with excitement. "The adrenaline was flowing," recalled Quintero, "as well as the champagne. We all thought we might have a hit. I'd thought Jennifer had done a good job, and one can never really predict how critics will react, you know."

Whitney Bolton, Selznick's publicity director back in the early forties when Phylis Isley first joined the fold, was now a theater critic for the *Morning Telegraph*. Interestingly, although one might have accused him of favoritism, Bolton's comments reflected Hal Boyle's: "Miss Jones does her level best to pump something besides gilly water and lavender flowers into this work, and it must be a tremendous task. She has life, she has color and warmth and desperation. But the vehicle burdens her."

The choice of vehicle had been Jennifer's, and her worst nightmares were realized. Walter Kerr, noted critic for the *New York Herald-Tribune,* had this to say about Jennifer's performance: "Miss Jones . . . moves with delicacy, smiles enchantingly, and looks like several million in Cecil Beaton's white, beige, and wine-red costumes. She is, however, technically immature. The lines are filtered softly and musically through a kind of dramatic hour-glass: each bit of dialogue passes at the same rate, and with pretty much the same intonation. The emotional reactions are limited, too: there is a kind of childlike gaiety, and there is a tight-lipped, drawn evasiveness— and the catalogue is complete. Though Miss Jones finds some dignity and a sudden trace of force in a troubled last-act scene, the performance as a whole is curiously light, unvaried, thin."

Jennifer was devastated by the reception. "I bled from every pore," she said later. "I wanted to run off to Tahiti and hide." To her credit, she didn't abandon ship. There were no lines at the box office, but with Jennifer's concurrence management made the decision to play out the week. Closing notice was posted for the following weekend (the play ran for seven performances).

Selznick was sad but not shocked. A decade earlier Vivien Leigh, over his objections, had appeared on Broadway opposite Laurence Olivier in Olivier's disastrous production of *Romeo and Juliet.* Even though Leigh was at the peak of her star power, directly after *Gone With the Wind,* as was Olivier after *Wuthering Heights,* the play didn't run. Selznick had permitted Leigh to do the play then for the same reason he'd permitted Jennifer to do this one—"To make her happy."

Ironically, the trade press blamed Selznick for "*not* interfering!" *Variety* ran a feature that asked why Selznick hadn't somehow salvaged the wreck. "Apparently I can't win, either by interfering or not interfering," moaned Selznick.

And apparently, from a career standpoint, Jennifer was better off with David than without him.

Chapter

25

*F*or Jennifer, one venue was absolutely
out of the question as far as her manager/husband was concerned:
television. Top movie stars were now appearing regularly on the
medium. Loretta Young had scored a spectacular success only the
previous year. Young, at thirty-nine, had debuted in a weekly filmed
anthology series (produced by her husband, Tom Lewis) and become an even bigger star than she'd been on the silver screen. As far
as Jennifer and other dedicated actresses were concerned, the
Young series offered an actress the ultimate luxury of casting herself
in a wide variety of roles "other producers," in Young's words, "would
never have given me."

There was a heavy price, of course. The work schedule was so
grueling that an exhausted Loretta often slept at the studio and
went for long periods without seeing her family. This was a situation
Selznick would not have tolerated for Jennifer, especially now that
they had a new baby to consider (not to mention her two sons, now
fifteen and sixteen, currently away at boarding schools).

One didn't have to do a series, of course. Other top-level actors,
like Jennifer's pal Joseph Cotten, Claudette Colbert, Rosalind Russell, Helen Hayes, Noel Coward, Merle Oberon, Barbara Stanwyck,
Teresa Wright, Ginger Rogers, Edward G. Robinson, and Charlton
Heston, were appearing selectively on television. Even twenty-eight-

year-old Marilyn Monroe, currently the biggest movie star in the world, had made an excursion onto the small screen (as a guest on Jack Benny's show).

Not Jennifer. Selznick even tried to discourage their pal Lauren Bacall from doing TV, telling her that she was crazy to do a live show. "If you make a mistake, you make it in front of three million people."

But Bacall forged ahead. The Bogarts were slated to costar in a "live" TV version of *The Petrified Forest* (with another newcomer to the medium, Henry Fonda).

While she had no plans to appear on TV, Jennifer (and everyone else in Hollywood) gossiped about how television had launched the careers of actresses and actors who'd never been top level in Hollywood, particularly Lucille Ball. "Lucy," at forty-three, was very "old" by Hollywood standards. Yet she'd become a national institution. And promising younger talents, such as Paul Newman and Joanne Woodward (Newman was only six years younger than Jennifer), were noticed by Hollywood only after they'd been showcased on television.

Jennifer and David watched plenty of television. One day Don Keefer, Jennifer's old pal from American Academy days, was walking down Madison Avenue and spotted Jennifer and David across the street. To Keefer's surprise Jennifer waved and exclaimed, "We saw you on TV last night!"

During this period Selznick of course continued to support Jennifer in the style to which she'd been accustomed. He derived fresh income from an old contractee who'd struck gold on television: Alfred Hitchcock. Hitchcock's weekly series had dramatically enhanced the director's box office value, and Selznick cashed in on it. He'd retained rights to the director's movies made for the old Selznick studio. David edited several of them down to a running time of about one hour each, combined them into one three-hour package, and rereleased them abroad.

Meanwhile it was crucial to Jennifer's professional future that the Selznicks remain front and center on the New York and Hollywood social scenes and maintain that all-important image of wealth and success. As 1955 began Jennifer was represented by leading power broker Charles Feldman (who'd expanded his horizons from superagent to producer, having packaged and produced the hit film version of *A Streetcar Named Desire*). Both Feldman and Selznick networked Hollywood's executive suites, on the lookout for a suitable situation for Jennifer.

The studio earning the most money and in the best overall shape was 20th Century–Fox, born again thanks to the public's enthusiastic acceptance of CinemaScope. Darryl Zanuck was a personal client of Feldman's, and a three-picture deal for Jennifer was negotiated that would reportedly earn the actress close to $500,000.

A variety of other factors now fell into place in Jennifer's favor, including the presence of two important executives at 20th Century–Fox. David Brown had been hired by Zanuck to be Fox's executive story editor, a vitally important position in those days. Among the many properties Brown acquired for Fox was a best-selling novel, *A Many Splendored Thing*. "It was an actual memoir by Han Suyin," recalls Brown, "about her romance with a British journalist, and we Americanized it [*Love Is* was added to the title for the movie version].

"I acquired the property (when I say 'I,' of course I mean Darryl Zanuck and I and my colleagues in the story department, who recommended properties to me) for a producer named Sol Siegel, a very good producer who eventually left to become head of MGM." Brown underscores an important point: "Don't forget, in those days, producers were surrogates of the front office. *We* bought the material and interested *them* in producing the movies, not vice versa."

As it happened, Sol Siegel's departure from Fox was fortuitous for Jennifer; the executive who replaced him was a unique individual indeed. David Brown fondly recalls forty-six-year-old Buddy Adler. "He was an elegant New Yorker, kind of a Mississippi River boat captain. Let me say a Hudson River boat captain. He loved the races, he loved baseball, and he was certainly one of the most elegantly dressed producers, and in those days dress was important in Hollywood."

Adler had something to prove. "Buddy was *exceedingly* ambitious," recalls Brown. Before joining Fox, Adler had been executive producer at Columbia Pictures, where Harry Cohn was undisputed despot. Buddy Adler's expertise and ability as an executive was proven by the fact that he'd been able to deal successfully, for an extended period of time, with the autocratic Cohn. Cohn respected Adler's ability to deliver prestigious, money-making films at reasonable budgets. And he liked Adler personally. Although Cohn some-times taunted Adler, the two men maintained a strong working rela-tionship.

Ironically, the honeymoon fizzled after the record-shattering success of *From Here to Eternity*, produced by Adler. Via a carefully-or-chestrated-by-Adler public relations campaign, the film became known throughout the industry as one Adler had been largely re-sponsible for. Cohn resented the tactic and, at the expiration of Adler's contract, refused to meet terms necessary for Adler to re-main (by this time every studio in town was after him).

At Fox "Buddy Adler was determined to set a record for high-quality productions," recalls David Brown, "and he ended up doing so well that when Darryl Zanuck decided to go to Europe and form an independent production company, he nominated Buddy to be head of production, over the protestations of many of his longtime, long-term producers who knew him well. Buddy Adler was an ex-tremely skillful and commercial producer, with more than a touch of class."

From Jennifer and David's point of view, having Buddy Adler on the scene was an incredible stroke of good fortune. "Buddy liked Jennifer, and David knew he would cast her well," says David Brown.

While Selznick and Darryl Zanuck, in David Brown's diplomatic words, "were not close," Brown recalls that "David felt comfortable with Buddy and liked him very much."

Adler was highly enthusiastic about producing *A Many Splen-dored Thing*. "He loved the book, was instantly attracted to it, and it became one of the many pictures he made in the first eighteen months of his arrival, first as a producer and later as head of the stu-dio," states Brown.

At this time Henry King was the senior director on the Fox lot. Now seventy-four years old, he'd of course proven his ability to draw stunning results from Jennifer in *The Song of Bernadette*. In ensuing years King had directed many of Fox's biggest hits, most recently *The Snows of Kilimanjaro*. King was assigned to direct *Love Is a Many Splendored Thing*, from a screenplay by John Patrick.

Those who were skeptical that Jennifer was held in highest re-gard by her new studio were convinced when Buddy Adler signed William Holden as her leading man.

Holden, only one year older than Jennifer, was one of the very top young leading men in films. He'd actually been in films longer than Jennifer and was virtually at the apex of his career (he'd recently won the Best Actor Oscar for *Stalag 17*). As far as Selznick was concerned, her new leading man was a coup. However, from a more personal point of view, the virile Holden, although married with two children, nonetheless represented a hazard that Selznick had always feared—a well-known womanizer who always made a play for his leading ladies.

Holden had fallen madly in love with Audrey Hepburn during the filming of *Sabrina,* and wanted to marry her (she rejected him). Grace Kelly had an affair with him during production of their recent films together, *The Bridges at Toko-Ri* and *The Country Girl* (Kelly had even taken Holden home to Philadelphia to meet her father). Shelley Winters and Holden, who never made a film together, were having an ongoing affair. The list of Holden conquests was formidable.

Gossips watched and waited to see what would happen between Holden and Jennifer. Production was slated to begin in March, with Jennifer's makeup, hair, and wardrobe tests scheduled for early that month (it was also the month that Jennifer would celebrate her thirty-sixth birthday).

The tests were a disaster, and Jennifer was highly distressed. She complained to David. "I'll handle it," he assured her.

Adler and Henry King had apparently decided that although Jennifer would be portraying a Eurasian, her features were not to be altered in any way by makeup. Selznick now pointed out how Jennifer faced an "extraordinary burden" in having to impart an Oriental flavor via her characterization alone.

The hairdo the studio had devised for her was another burden. Although Oriental in appearance, the coiffure was not only unflattering, it made Jennifer appear older (it gave her an "unnecessarily mature appearance," was how Selznick diplomatically phrased it).

He pointed out to Adler how this would harm the love story "and . . . [regarding Jennifer] instead of it being a good performance, the reaction will simply be, 'My, how old Jennifer Jones has gotten!' . . ." Selznick astutely observed that an actress could easily add twenty-five years or more to her appearance and play an old lady, "but it is terribly dangerous to both the actress and to the love story to have her appear ten or twelve years older, for no reason. . . ."

Selznick also expressed his concern over the fact that although

Jennifer's character was supposed to have been educated in England, she was expected to play the part without a British accent. Selznick summed up her dilemma by appealing to Adler's "dreams and expectations" for the picture and pleaded eloquently with him to make the necessary changes.

Selznick made the point that he was discussing these matters with Adler "without . . . Jennifer's knowledge," but this seems unlikely. How would David have known of her discontent with the studio's plans if she hadn't told him? Nonetheless, he asked Buddy Adler not to discuss any of his (Selznick's) comments with Jennifer (subsequently most of Selznick's suggestions to Adler were implemented).

Arrangements were finalized for principal cast members to travel to Hong Kong for two weeks of location shooting. Jennifer was totally embroiled in the details of creating her character, who she felt represented everything she admired: the woman was a doctor and a humanitarian, but one who kept her distance. This duality of personality mirrored Jennifer's own.

David was suddenly obsessed with what would happen to six-month-old Mary Jennifer if he and Jennifer were killed in a plane crash. Without Jennifer's knowledge, he took the infant to visit Irene. He expected his former wife to be so charmed by the child that she'd promise to raise the baby if Mary Jennifer were orphaned. Irene was nonplussed by the proposal, which Selznick considered totally "reasonable." "All he had to do was sell the idea to Jennifer!" recalled Irene Selznick.

As far as anyone knows, Jennifer was never informed of David's proposition. Immersed in preparations for the picture, she soon departed for Hong Kong.

"Fox sent Jennifer and Bill Holden to Hong Kong for background shots before I had even finished the screenplay," recalled screenwriter John Patrick. "I then had to write my screenplay to include as many of these shots as possible."

Selznick was up to his old tricks. "The only problems with Jennifer," recalls David Brown, "were that David sent endless memos to the point that, on *A Many Splendored Thing*, Henry King finally said,

'I will stop shooting and read the memos, but I will not read them on my own time.' "

Did Selznick, as reported, actually spend time on the set? "I don't recall David Selznick coming on the set, because Henry King certainly wouldn't permit it," states David Brown. "King was a very pragmatic kind of director, a brilliant director, but he brooked no interference in those days when most directors *were* interfered with. Selznick was not able to interfere—King stood his ground, and Selznick backed off. The last thing he wanted to do was impede his wife's career."

William Holden, an easygoing, fun-loving, and hard-drinking man, was completely turned off by Jennifer's obsessive involvement with her performance. "The film was a rare instance when [Holden] lacked affection for his leading lady," reported Associated Press correspondent/author Bob Thomas. When Jennifer's complaints about her makeup, costumes, and dialogue failed to evoke sympathy from Holden, "she complained about *him*," noted Thomas. " 'I'm going to tell David about this,' she said repeatedly." The studio, in turn, was deluged with more memos.

Soon, off camera, Jennifer and Holden were barely speaking to each other. Holden subsequently attempted to mend broken fences by presenting Jennifer with white roses. "She threw them in his face," said Bob Thomas.

Holden harbored another complaint. Many years later—he claimed he never knew why—Holden said that Jennifer had chewed garlic cloves before their love scenes. One theory was that this had been her way of totally discouraging Bill from becoming too involved in the love scenes. (Alfred Hitchcock often described how love scenes which began in front of the camera usually concluded behind closed doors in the stars' dressing rooms.) If so, the ploy certainly worked. It was ironic that Holden, the leading man David feared the most, turned out to have the least personal chemistry with Jennifer off camera.

Garlic cloves and petty disagreements aside, on screen the passion between Jennifer and Holden photographed as absolutely genuine.

When production was completed (it had taken less than three months, and there had been no delays), the picture was quickly assembled. But studio brass weren't ecstatic and were uncertain about the film. "We were uncertain about *all* movies," states David Brown. "In the case of *Love Is a Many Splendored Thing*, it was a very fragile flower of a story. In the end she lost him, he was killed, and Han Suyin had to move on."

John Patrick recalls, "Han Suyin hated what I had done to her book and even refused to see me when I was in Hong Kong. Her daughter, however, was more gracious, and we met for a drink." (Later Han Suyin wanted Patrick to adapt her second novel. "I refused," recalls Patrick.)

David Brown makes an amusing but valid point. "In those days, when we were uncertain about a movie, we wrote a theme song that we hoped would become very popular." This had worked with phenomenal success in the case of the recent *Three Coins in the Fountain*. "For *Love Is a Many Splendored Thing*, Sammy Fain and Paul Francis Webster wrote the theme song," recalls Brown. However:

"The song at first was only background music," remembers John Patrick. "The film was recalled, and the producer had the words sung to make it eligible for the Academy Award."

In its initial version, even the song wasn't well received by studio brass. "The first lyrics were dreadful, about temple bells tinkling, et cetera," recalls David Brown. "So Sammy went back and wrote an elegant set of lyrics."

The film was scheduled for an August release.

Jennifer's obsession for work was for the moment well satisfied. She immediately began a new film based on another best-selling novel, Frances Gray Patton's *Good Morning, Miss Dove*. Jennifer would portray a schoolteacher who ages from a young girl to an old lady (she'd now have the opportunity to add those twenty-five years to her appearance).

Veteran Fox producer Samuel G. Engel, a buddy of Darryl Zanuck, and director Henry Koster were in charge. The fifty-year-old, German-born Koster was currently highly regarded at Fox (he'd directed *The Robe*) and was adept at filming sentimental, heart-tugging stories. Koster had also directed *The Bishop's Wife* and *Come to the Stable*, two of Loretta Young's most successful films.

Jennifer's parents visited the set during production. Jennifer made certain they weren't on hand on the days she was wearing her "age" makeup (a gray wig and rubber appliances on her face).

Dove costar Robert Stack recalled an amusing incident during shooting. "Jennifer was very shy. In one scene, as the doctor, I was supposed to give her the knee-reflex test. She kept looking at me, saying, 'Do you have to do that?' (In other words, did I have to put my hand on her knee?) I laughed and finally said, 'Jennifer, I'm the doctor, you're the patient, and it's in the script.' She was the only really shy actress I've ever worked with."

David Selznick was confronting (to use a phrase coined by David Brown) his own "crisis of confidence." Managing the career of his wife was not exactly a full-time or totally fulfilling occupation.

At a personal crossroads, he confided in Irene that he was cautiously deciding what his next career move would be, although he was fully aware that not all that much "is left of my career." And whatever was left of it was irrevocably attached to Jennifer's career.

In early August *Love Is a Many Splendored Thing* opened at the Roxy Theater in New York and at first-run theaters throughout the rest of the country (the picture had been filmed, edited, scored, and released within a period of six months). The advertising campaign featured Holden, in bathing trunks, clutching a kneeling Jennifer in an intense embrace. The copy read: "She was Han Suyin, the fascinating Eurasian. . . . He was Mark Elliott, American correspondent. . . . In each other's arms . . . they found a love that defied 5,000 years of tradition!"

The film, in David Brown's words, "was a roaring success," eventually making it into the magic circle: $4 million in domestic box office rentals. The public considered *Love Is . . .* one of the most romantic movies ever produced, but the critics were considerably less enthusiastic. Most agreed, though, that it was an achievement for its leading lady:

"It is Miss Jones's picture," wrote the *Los Angeles Times.*

The New York Times noted, "Miss Jones is lovely and intense. Her dark beauty reflects sunshine and sadness. She could be a piece of delicately carved stone." (The film, however, was dismissed as a "dew-dappled romance.")

"It's hard to believe that [Jennifer's] measured steps, practiced speech, and other Oriental characteristics are not her real personality," observed *Film Daily. Variety* declared the movie "one of the best woman's pictures made in some years" and raved that "Miss Jones is pure delight as the beautiful Han, who looks European, yet feels strongly Chinese. . . . Miss Jones's accomplishment in a very difficult part is quite remarkable and contributes greatly to the film's success. Her love scenes with Holden sizzle without ever being cheap or awkward. In her, the spirit of the book is caught completely."

Jennifer and David finally had the hit they'd been looking for.

"People don't realize how difficult it is to maintain momentum in a career," said Henry Willson, former Selznick talent executive turned very successful agent and manager (of Rock Hudson, Tony Curtis, Tab Hunter, Rory Calhoun, and many others). "So many factors are at play in a career. It's not like putting together an automobile, where you can be fairly sure of the results."

If Jennifer, as Selznick later claimed, was next scheduled to star with Tyrone Power in Darryl Zanuck's first independent production, *The Sun Also Rises,* David Brown wasn't aware of it (and there were few casting decisions of this magnitude at Fox that Brown wasn't aware of).

Selznick, however, said that both he and Jennifer (who very much wanted to portray Lady Brett) hated the *Sun* script, "a very bad adaptation of Hemingway." They were assured the script would be rewritten; and if Jennifer wanted to play Lady Brett, first she'd have to agree to step into another Zanuck production, his final one on the studio lot, that was ready to go.

Brown offers another possible explanation. "If Jennifer didn't want to do *Sun Also Rises,* it might have been because she didn't want to go to Europe to work on the film. It was to be filmed on location in Spain and in Paris."

The Man in the Gray Flannel Suit, to be filmed in Hollywood, was based on Sloan Wilson's huge best-selling novel, a 1950s epic on the order of *The Best Years of Our Lives.* The story dealt with a man trying to find himself and define the values in his life, and took a look at how the lives of the men who'd been GIs had developed since the end of World War II.

There was a highly controversial plot twist: the married all-American, leading man has fathered an illegitimate child, and the revelation wreaks havoc on his private life.

The novel had fascinated David Brown, who acquired it, and

Zanuck earmarked it as one of his personal productions, envisioning it as a groundbreaking cinematic statement on the order of *Gentleman's Agreement* seven years earlier.

Gregory Peck was cast in the title role. Filming began in Connecticut before the role of Peck's wife was cast. Christine Linn, an extra, was chosen as stand-in for "the wife." Ms. Linn, wearing a kerchief so that she could pass for either a blonde or brunette, was photographed from afar. Her scenes appear in the final film.

By the time the company returned to Hollywood, a reluctant Jennifer had signed to portray Peck's wife. The publicity department went to town trumpeting the reunion of Peck and his *Duel in the Sun* leading lady. This time, however, Jennifer's role was quite different. The wife in *Suit* was a middle-class shrew, hardly a femme fatale. Nor was she romantic or noble (Jennifer said she'd known women like that).

Since Jennifer's on-screen persona totally reflected the talents of a film's producer and director, on this shoot she was in trouble. Zanuck may have been a genius, but his forte had never been the presentation of actresses (although he'd successfully launched and featured many female stars).

Fifty-eight-year-old Nunnally Johnson, the director, was one of Zanuck's fair-haired boys. A journalist before coming to Hollywood in the thirties, Johnson had first developed into one of the industry's top screenwriters with *The Grapes of Wrath, Tobacco Road, Woman in the Window,* and *How to Marry a Millionaire.* But he had begun directing only recently, and *Man in the Gray Flannel Suit* was his fourth effort.

He'd also written the screenplay for *Suit,* although it was with reluctance that he'd tackled the project in the first place, since he felt no empathy for the material. David Brown recalls, "Nunnally—he was a Southerner and talked with a Georgia accent—said, 'I don't know these Madison Avenue people!' I said, 'Read the book.' He said, 'I like to write a screenplay of a book where I can cut out the dialogue and just paste it in the script.' That was Nunnally Johnson—he was a marvelous scriptwriter and very self-effacing."

But Johnson's efforts focused on Gregory Peck's character, not Jennifer's, and David was in no position to help her. She met personally with Darryl Zanuck to argue in favor of rewrites of certain of her scenes and won her points. Nonetheless, during shooting, Jennifer's portrayal was emerging as shrill and abrasive. Furthermore, the cameraman, Charles G. Clarke, wasn't particularly adept at photographing Jones.

Nunnally Johnson nonetheless appreciated Jennifer's efforts. He was moved by her performance in the scene where she becomes hysterical after discovering that her husband has fathered an illegitimate child. Johnson put it in writing: "In case your wife is too modest to tell you," he informed Selznick, "I want you to know that she did a scene today that was absolutely marvelous." He added: "P.S. Don't answer this!"

Johnson had, of course, been besieged by memos from Selznick about Jennifer. He'd replied: "Thank you very much, David. I passed your notes on to Mr. Zanuck."

Jennifer's reviews for *Good Morning, Miss Dove* (released in November, after she had begun filming *Man in the Gray Flannel Suit*) were excellent: "Miss Dove, in the person of Jennifer Jones, is a remarkable but believable character out of Dickens; her carefully etched portrait of the genuinely dedicated geography teacher is a neat blend of pride, genuine gentility, and humor," wrote *The New York Times*.

"Jennifer Jones gives a moving, throat-catching portrait of a dedicated, no-nonsense schoolteacher," wrote *Variety*.

Overseas reaction to the film was also upbeat. "Jennifer Jones brings such a fury of correctness to the role of the schoolmarm . . . that you'll be hard-hearted indeed if she doesn't leave you damp-eyed," wrote the British *Picturegoer*.

The film was another winner. The annual movie audience poll, in which ticket buyers were asked to vote for their favorite films and performances, was conducted throughout theater chains across the country. The winners received impressive statuettes (dubbed "Audie's") and lots of publicity. In effect, these were the "People's Choice" awards of the 1950s.

Jennifer was delighted to learn she'd been voted best actress for *Love Is a Many Splendored Thing* but was terrified at the prospect of attending the awards festivities. "Let someone accept for me," she suggested, but her husband insisted she go. She was front and center at the banquet at the Beverly Hilton Hotel on December 6, 1955, to receive the award (James Dean was posthumously awarded best actor).

Jennifer ascended the podium to accept her statuette. She'd

memorized her speech, which had been written by Selznick. "This award means more than the Academy Award because the people who see the movies do the voting, and not the people who make the movies," said Jennifer, her voice quivering. The audience was warmly receptive. Jennifer posed with other winners, including teen idol Tab Hunter and singer Peggy Lee (who'd made her screen acting debut in *Pete Kelly's Blues*).

Jennifer also won *Photoplay* magazine's "Most Popular Actress of the Year" award and received the California Federation of Women's Clubs Motion Picture Award for her performance as Miss Dove. Her impact in *Love Is a Many Splendored Thing* had extended to women's fashions. Jennifer's Charles LeMaire wardrobe in the film, mostly simple, high-necked, sleeveless, fitted sheaths (adapted from the classic Chinese cheongsam), won nationwide popularity and was copied and marketed by leading dress manufacturers.

But Jennifer's self-confidence didn't flourish with the adulation. On the contrary, she seemed to grow even more introspective. While other top stars on the Fox lot ate lunch daily at the studio commissary, there were two notable exceptions. "You didn't see Jennifer Jones or Marilyn Monroe around the commissary," recalls David Brown. "The chances were that if Jennifer was working, she would have lunch [alone] in her dressing room."

Jennifer and Marilyn (who'd filmed *The Seven-Year Itch* on a neighboring soundstage while Jennifer was working on *Love Is a Many Splendored Thing*) had other traits in common. Both women chose to rely completely on a key man in their personal lives (Jennifer's choice remaining constant, Marilyn's constantly changing); both women were devout believers in psychotherapy. Each lady nurtured an obsessive desire to perfect her craft, and both relocated to New York to place themselves under the tutelage of the same renowned actors' guru.

Selznick, meanwhile, had arrived at a decision. Despite the false start and emotional letdown after failing to launch *War and Peace,* he'd try again with another independent production starring Jennifer. Ignoring warnings and pleas from Sam Goldwyn and other friends, he negotiated for rights to the Hemingway classic *A Farewell to Arms.* It had been filmed successfully twenty-five years earlier ("It's a mistake to remake a great picture," Goldwyn advised), and most people didn't realize that *Farewell* had recently been remade, in 1951, as *Force of Arms.* William Holden and Nancy Olson had starred in the tale, which had been updated from World War I to the Korean War. The movie wasn't a notable success.

However, *Farewell* offered Jennifer the opportunity to portray one of the most fascinating fictional females, although preparing a brilliant script based on Hemingway would be no less formidable a task for David Selznick than it had been for Darryl Zanuck.

Early 1956 brought sad and shocking news from abroad of the death of Alexander Korda. In adapting to changing times, Korda had proven a far shrewder businessman than his peers. Instead of turning up his nose at television, he was the first to have made millions by leasing his old films to the new medium.

On Korda's death, Vivien Leigh, now forty-three, her film career and personal life in sad decline, suddenly faced a terrifying reality that would one day confront Jennifer—the demise of an irreplaceable ally/protector/adviser at an extremely vulnerable point in her life.

David Selznick, hardly in the best of health, proceeded full tilt to pull together the superproduction that had the potential to extract a harrowing cost, physically, emotionally, and financially, from both David and Jennifer. Negotiations to acquire rights to *A Farewell to Arms* were complicated. Once again Selznick had to anticipate the specter of going into deep debt as he faced the formidable task of arranging for financing and distribution for the picture.

Meanwhile Jennifer was nominated for the Academy Award, an honor that had eluded her for almost a decade, as Best Actress for *Love Is a Many Splendored Thing*. Alternating feelings of exhilaration and anxiety were her constant companions over the next few weeks. She spent hours talking on the phone with Anita Colby, who constantly told her how proud she should be of herself and how grateful that all the efforts Jennifer had poured into her career were once again paying fabulous dividends. "Try and enjoy it for a change, honey," advised Anita.

It was an unusually exciting race. Susan Hayward, on loan-out from Fox, had delivered a tour-de-force portrayal of singer Lillian Roth in *I'll Cry Tomorrow;* Katharine Hepburn was magnificent as an old maid in *Summertime;* Eleanor Parker was poignant and moving as opera singer Marjorie Lawrence in *Interrupted Melody;* and Anna Magnani, "Italy's Bette Davis," had exploded on screen in her first American picture, *The Rose Tattoo* (which Tennessee Williams had initially written for Magnani as a stage vehicle, but which the actress had been too terrified to attempt).

Love Is a Many Splendored Thing was also one of the five films nominated for Best Picture, along with *Mister Roberts, Picnic, The Rose Tattoo,* and a low-budget black-and-white movie, *Marty,* based on an original Paddy Chayefsky play produced initially on television.

Insiders assumed, with no Best Director or Best Screenplay nomination, that *Love Is a Many Splendored Thing* wasn't likely to win Best Picture, but the battle for Best Actress was another story. However, Magnani had taken the media by storm; never had a foreign actress so totally lacking in the two attributes Hollywood valued most—youth and physical beauty—so completely captured the imagination of the press and public.

Jennifer and David were royally feted by the town's power elite as Fox's campaign to lure Oscar votes clicked into gear. But whether Jennifer won or lost the Oscar, she was for the moment back at the top, placing Selznick in a strong position for financing *A Farewell to Arms.* He was close to an agreement with Nick Schenck at MGM when Schenck's power and influence at the studio suddenly collapsed, so Selznick began meeting with Spyros Skouras, president of Fox.

At this time Jennifer fervently wished to play the compassionate, loving heroine in *Tea and Sympathy,* currently a hit Broadway play starring Deborah Kerr and John Kerr (no relation to the actress). MGM had bought the film rights, and Vincente Minnelli was set to direct.

It's revealing of Jennifer's view of herself that she considered herself perfect casting for this role (as she had, years earlier, for *Claudia*). Deborah Kerr perfectly described the requirements for the character: a woman who demonstrates "compassion and pity and love of one human being for another in a crisis."

The plot concerns a young man at a boys' school falsely accused of being gay because he's interested in music and poetry rather than "manly" pursuits like football. The headmaster's wife—the character Jennifer hoped to portray—shares the boy's interests. To prove to him he's not homosexual, she "generously gives herself to him" (in 1956 this was considered extremely difficult and provocative material).

Despite Jennifer's reborn career, Deborah Kerr's agent, Bert Allenberg, successfully secured the film role for his titian-tressed client. Jennifer learned the news one afternoon at a tea party at Jean Howard Feldman's beautiful home. The disappointed actress proceeded to jump into the swimming pool with all her clothes on.

Jennifer sailed for Europe before the Oscar ceremonies. She'd been scheduled to present the Best Director award and intended to film a lead-in abroad that would be telecast on the Oscar show. She was also set to travel to England to portray poet Elizabeth Barrett Browning in MGM's remake of their 1934 picture *The Barretts of Wimpole Street*.

John Gielgud—the English superstar whose performance on Broadway in Shakespeare's *Richard II* had thrilled Jennifer in her American Academy days—was to be her costar (portraying her father), with Jennifer receiving top billing. Hot young British actor Bill Travers was cast as Robert Browning, with Travers's real-life wife, actress Virginia McKenna, in the role of Henrietta.

There was logic behind Metro's attempt to remake *Barretts*. The old film's history gave current executives, many of them dating back to Irving Thalberg's day, hope that lightning would strike twice. The original *Barretts* had been responsible for the famous *Variety* headline STIX NIX HIX PIX. Released at the height of the Depression, the film had been expected to bomb. The reigning powers assumed that the public would prefer films about "common folk"—boys and girls next door, farmers, et al. To the shock of the industry, the big hit of the season turned out to be the sophisticated love story of a famous English poetess.

The role of Elizabeth offered Jennifer the opportunity to play both subtly and with great inner strength. The love affair between Elizabeth Barrett and Robert Browning develops through an exchange of correspondence, despite Elizabeth's father's strong objections to Browning as a suitable suitor. But love conquers all, and there's even a happy ending, as Elizabeth marries Robert and they settle in Italy, where climate and a felicitous marriage restore her failing health. To quote Norma Shearer, the screen's original Elizabeth Barrett Browning, with this role an actress could "spread her wings and fly!" The new version, of course, would "open up" the story, in wide screen and color, with location photography at actual sites where Barrett and Browning had lived the tale.

Meanwhile, back in the States in late March, Jennifer, on film and sitting on a director's chair, announced the preamble to naming the winner of the year's Best Director award—Delbert Mann for *Marty,* which also won Best Picture.

Jennifer lost the Best Actress award to Anna Magnani. *Love Is a Many Splendored Thing* won in two categories, for Best Song and Best Costume Design.

Fox wasted no time releasing *The Man in the Gray Flannel Suit.* In April, only six months after production had begun, the film premiered at the Roxy Theater in New York and opened to blockbuster grosses. For a person who read her reviews, however, the news for Jennifer was indeed a mixed bag:

"Miss Jones allows almost no feeling of any real relationship between her and Peck. She alternates between being the nagging wife and the frustrated lover, except that she rarely conveys the impression of being in love with her husband in the first place," wrote *Variety. The New York Times* found the picture "a mature, fascinating and often quite tender and touching film . . . all the actors are excellent." In *Saturday Review,* critic Arthur Knight wrote that director Nunnally Johnson "permits Jennifer Jones . . . to overplay." And *The New Yorker* announced, "As played by Jennifer Jones, [the wife] is so persistently surly that it's hard to imagine why the fellow [Peck] does not clear out."

Peck himself wasn't enthusiastic about the movie, feeling that it didn't live up to the potential he'd seen in the book. "It was spotted," he said, "with some good sequences."

Jennifer and David, without mentioning Zanuck, later bluntly characterized the picture as "a bad film."

At this time, big plans were in the works to restore a "fallen star" to proper Hollywood orbit. Jennifer's old friend Ingrid Bergman was at work in Europe. David Selznick's prediction, several years earlier, that with the right film Ingrid could return bigger than ever, was soon to prove accurate.

David Brown recalls that Fox had bought the rights to the hit Broadway play *Anastasia.* According to some accounts, it was Buddy Adler who had the idea to cast Bergman in the title role, while other sources credit director Anatole Litvak.

"I think Buddy had the idea, but who knows?" says Brown. "It might have been an agent. Anything that worked, a lot of people took credit for. Buddy was no exception."

Whoever had the idea—and David Selznick was one of the few who didn't claim to have something to do with it—the *Anastasia* contracts were signed, over the objections of Ingrid's husband, Roberto Rossellini, who told his wife the script was "lousy." The couple's stormy marriage was finally on the rocks (they'd not collaborated on a single successful film), and Ingrid was desperate to get her career back on track (she'd end up paying Rossellini to accede to her wishes for a divorce).

Ingrid signed a multiple-picture contract with Fox, and if the gamble paid off, Buddy Adler (who'd produce *Anastasia*) would have another top star of a certain age (Bergman had recently turned forty-three) to consider when casting major productions. Jennifer and Ingrid were once again, in effect, vying for key roles.

"Obviously, with Jennifer getting older, she had fewer and fewer opportunities," notes David Brown.

Selznick finally secured from Warner Brothers the rights to A Farewell to Arms. During this period, Selznick's lawyer, Barry Brannen, urged him to produce a TV version of *Gone With the Wind*. Selznick's experience in the medium, with "Light's Diamond Jubilee," had not warmed him to the prospect of television production, although he'd received offers from his friend Bill Paley and RCA's David Sarnoff. But the possibility of remaking *Gone With the Wind* for TV, he told Brannen, "is too ridiculous even to contemplate."

He'd almost closed the deal with Fox president Spyros Skouras to finance and distribute *A Farewell to Arms*. Skouras, however, listening to complaints from theater exhibitors, was leery that the film was a remake and had an unhappy ending. Selznick convinced him "that generalizations never apply in this business" and pointed out that Cecil B. De Mille's current blockbuster *The Ten Commandments* was a remake, as were recent hits like *A Place in the Sun*, *The Prisoner of Zenda*, *The Three Musketeers*, Disney's *Robin Hood*, *Magnificent Obsession*, and the upcoming Bing Crosby–Grace Kelly–Frank Sinatra musical, *High Society*, a remake of *The Philadelphia Story*.

Selznick made an irrefutable point: "Remakes of very good

films . . . fail because they have not been remade by people as talented as those who made the first versions."

The first version of *A Farewell to Arms,* released in 1932, had starred Gary Cooper and Helen Hayes. It was both a hit and a critical success (although Hemingway's tragic ending, with the heroine dying in childbirth, had been altered so that she lived). Selznick bypassed mention of the 1951 remake and predicted that his version would certainly, at the very least, match the first. The clincher to the deal was Jennifer as the star.

Selznick was disappointed with the press coverage on the official announcement of the deal, and complained angrily to his press agent, Arthur Jacobs. Jacobs pointed out that many other projects announced by Selznick never got off the ground, and the press was dubious. As to Selznick's heated objections that reports referred to *Farewell* as a remake, Jacobs bluntly told his boss that it *was* a remake.

Producing *A Farewell to Arms,* a property that Selznick said he'd dreamed of making since his days at MGM, was to turn out to be, in Selznick's words, "the toughest job of my entire life." For Jennifer, having to contend with a production that her husband would eventually describe as encompassing "the most agonizing combination of problems I have ever been up against," the outlook for an artistically thrilling experience was, it seems, bleak from the outset.

Throughout the spring and summer Jennifer worked hard on Barretts of Wimpole Street. Madame Tussaud's Wax Museum in London unveiled a figure of Jennifer as Elizabeth Barrett Browning, and the actress was present for the dedication of a plaque at 50 Wimpole Street, the address where the Barretts had lived.

There were discussions with the duke and duchess of Windsor over a film version of the duchess's memoirs. The duchess was pleased by the prospect of Jennifer portraying her, but the project never materialized.

Back in the States, Jones was considered for the title role in Nunnally Johnson's next film, *Three Faces of Eve,* a harrowing drama of a woman with multiple personalities. When newcomer Joanne Woodward finally landed it, Woodward said she'd lucked out "because everyone they'd wanted had turned it down."

• • •

Jennifer was on guard and wary. "*Are you going to ask me any horrible* questions?" She was in period costume in her dressing room at MGM's Elstree Studios in London and was face-to-face with attractive young Joe Hyams, the Harvard graduate with a master's degree in sociology who'd become a major Hollywood columnist. A protegé of Humphrey Bogart's, Hyams had turned out newspaper pieces on Hollywood personalities that were groundbreakers, the first to reveal the sometime unflattering but always entertaining truth about what the stars were really like. He'd recently written a series of articles on Ava Gardner for *Look* magazine that had infuriated Ava and her estranged husband, Frank Sinatra.

For the moment it was prestigious for a movie star to be interviewed by Hyams, and Jennifer had allowed herself to be talked into it.

Hyams replied to Jennifer's initial question with a question of his own: "What's a horrible question?"

"Any question is a horrible question," she replied. "I just don't have any answers."

Throughout the interview, noted Hyams, Jennifer nervously twisted a scarf. When he began taking notes, she eyed him apprehensively. "What are you writing?" she asked.

"That you look like a cameo come to life in your costume."

Jennifer brightened. "How nice. You know, you're a very nice man." She stopped wringing her scarf.

Hyams wanted to know why Jennifer didn't often give interviews. He received a straightforward and self-revealing reply. "I'm a difficult subject and always have been," Jennifer admitted, and she began wringing her scarf again. "There's not much to be said by me or about me one way or the other," she said. "My work should speak for itself."

Hyams observed this beautiful woman who'd won the Academy Award, been nominated for several others, and been a top star for thirteen years to date, with no end in sight. Even at this sophisticated stage of the game, however, she seemed, to Hyams, "trapped." To break the ice he told her how much he'd enjoyed *Good Morning, Miss Dove, The Man in the Gray Flannel Suit,* and *Love Is a Many Splendored Thing.* Jennifer was appreciative but "horrified" when Hyams characterized her performance in *Splendored* as "very sexy."

"She didn't like the word *sexy* applied to her," noted Hyams. "The word she preferred was 'interesting.' "

Hyams discussed her characterization in *Man in the Gray Flannel Suit*. "You were so good that I disliked the character you portrayed, as I was supposed to!" Jennifer's reply was "a harmless but clever comment about housewives, such as the one she played in the film." Hyams was delighted with the quote.

"That's off the record," Jennifer admonished him. So was the story she told him about how she'd gotten the part, at which point she again began wringing her scarf.

Hyams pressed on. "Does criticism upset you?" he asked.

"Yes, to the point of tears," she admitted bluntly. "When someone writes unkind things about me I want to go off somewhere and be alone."

The contrast between Jennifer and the publicity-hungry stars he was accustomed to interviewing was dramatic. When their session was finally over, a relieved Jennifer took Hyams's hand "and [like a true Barrett of Wimpole Street] steered us aristocratically to the door."

A director wasn't yet signed for A Farewell to Arms, but Selznick, despite Jennifer's unpleasant experience with John Huston on *Beat the Devil*, had his sights set on Huston (whose troubled multimillion-dollar production of *Moby Dick* was a major disappointment at the box office). Selznick pointed out to Jennifer that she'd have no problems with Huston on this picture, since David would be in control. Huston was just completing direction on *Heaven Knows, Mr. Allison* and was one of the few important directors who'd consider working with Selznick.

Selznick, working with Ben Hecht, had labored intensely on the *Farewell* script. The plot of Hemingway's book concerns the relationship between a lieutenant in the ambulance corps of the Italian army during World War I and Catherine Barkley, an English nurse. When she becomes pregnant, the lieutenant deserts the army and flees to Switzerland with Catherine. They live an idyllic life for a few months until Catherine and the child die in childbirth. The lieutenant is left stunned by the disaster.

The character of Catherine was supposed to be around twenty years old, and as far as David was concerned, Jennifer was perfect casting (although she had expressed doubts). Selznick and Hecht had fashioned a "final" script (after five drafts, completed in six weeks) that was, in their veteran opinions, high quality; not only was Huston (a Hemingway friend) interested, but, in a spectacular coup for Selznick and Jennifer, Universal-International seemed agreeable to lending out their premier contract star, Rock Hudson, for the male lead.

Every top female star wanted to play opposite Rock Hudson, and Jennifer Jones was once again about to become the envy of her peers. After the recent release of *Giant*, the thirty-one-year-old Hudson was the hottest name in the business, and every studio was eager to borrow him. Hudson said he "liked *Farewell* best," because all the elements for success seemed to be present: Selznick, Jennifer, Hemingway, and Huston (who hadn't actually signed yet).

Selznick, around this time, quietly sold additional company assets for cash. William Paley of CBS acquired the Selznick studio's library of stock film and its files of story synopses (David tried unsuccessfully to interest him in also purchasing the studio's old special effects equipment). The deal brought the Selznick company close to $100,000 (around $1.2 million in today's terms).

Jennifer completed *Barretts* in late August, and the studio was happy with the results. The picture was scheduled for release early in 1957. In the tradition of current studio product, a title song, *Wilt Thou Be My Love*, was composed.

Meanwhile John Huston signed to direct *A Farewell to Arms* for $250,000. Soon after, negotiations were completed for the loan-out of Rock Hudson. Vittorio De Sica was secured as the third star of the film, ideally insuring a strong European gross.

Oscar Levant once noted that "starring in a major motion picture can be as much fun as walking through a field of cow dung with glue on your shoes."

Jennifer's ordeal was about to begin.

s the excitement surrounding the pro-
ject gained momentum. Jennifer insisted that David make some
financial arrangement with Hemingway, whom she considered a
friend, whereby the author would benefit from the film's success.

Selznick's reply to Jennifer's suggestion: "You're not a business-
woman. You don't understand these things." He explained that
Hemingway had sold the rights to the book decades earlier and
been well paid for them. If a farmer sells his land, and years later oil
is discovered on it, you don't negotiate a new deal, especially if you
got a fair price in the first place.

Jennifer kept after him. Hemingway, although always cordial to
Jennifer, didn't like David Selznick. The renowned author was con-
temptuous of virtually all of Hollywood's previous efforts to transfer
his novels to the screen, including *The Snows of Kilimanjaro.* He had
no confidence that Selznick could or would do any better. Back in
the early 1940s, the relationship between Hemingway and Selznick
had been fruitful. At Selznick's urging, "Papa" had played an important role in securing the role of Maria for Ingrid Bergman in *For
Whom the Bell Tolls,* and Hemingway never regretted it.

However, several incidents with Selznick in ensuing years antagonized Hemingway, including a personal incident involving Selznick's
behavior toward Hemingway's wife, Mary. When Hemingway pal Pe-

ter Viertel and Mary Hemingway once visited Selznick in his hotel suite in Cuba, supposedly Selznick hadn't stood up when they entered the room. On hearing the story, Hemingway was appalled at Selznick's bad manners. (With Hemingway, "good manners" was a relative term. He was notorious for using foul language.)

In any event, Selznick's version of the hotel suite story was that he hadn't stood up because it had been a very hot day, and he was playing canasta in his underwear (these were days before air-conditioning). To have stood would have been truly embarrassing for all concerned.

"You have always been exceedingly gracious to Jennifer," acknowledged Selznick, and he strongly denied ever being rude to Mrs. Hemingway, an explanation which ostensibly was never forwarded to Hemingway.

Hemingway was also miffed because Selznick had supposedly not contacted him after acquiring the rights to *A Farewell to Arms,* a charge Selznick denied. He *had* cabled him, he claimed, and was hurt that Hemingway hadn't replied to his cable and interpreted Hemingway's silence as a rebuff.

Jennifer was caught in the middle. "Do what you think best," she told her husband regarding the subject of Ernest Hemingway.

Back in the States, 20th Century–Fox released a film of little interest to Jennifer, Selznick, or most of their glittering peers, but it nevertheless foreshadowed the imminent onslaught of the next generation. The film was *Love Me Tender,* and in it Elvis Presley made his big-screen debut.

A far more significant and exciting event for Hollywood's elite occurred shortly afterward when *Anastasia* was released to tremendous critical acclaim and was a smash hit at the box office. Ingrid Bergman was once again America's darling.

The party that welcomed Bergman back to Hollywood is still talked about even today. David Brown was there. "I remember the crush of people in the Crystal Room at the Beverly Hills Hotel." If Jennifer and David were on hand, Brown doesn't recall seeing them, "although it was so crowded you could barely see two feet in front of you."

There were no crowds at the beautiful home of Humphrey Bogart and Lauren Bacall, where Bogart was gravely ill. A concerned

Jennifer and David had commissioned photographer John Engstead to shoot a special sitting of Bacall and her young children, Leslie and Steve, as a surprise Christmas present for Bogie. "Could you rush them through?" the Selznicks asked Engstead. The photographs were all they could think of to give "the couple who already has everything." (Jennifer was delighted with the sitting Engstead had just done of her own family. The photographs, taken at the Tower Grove estate, presented a fanciful portrait of family life, complete with perfect wife Jennifer and a pipe-smoking Selznick.)

"Jennifer and David came over one afternoon," recalled Lauren Bacall, "David very concerned whether everything that could be done for Bogie was being done. Shouldn't I maybe call in another doctor? Get another opinion? . . . He was sweet and loving, and I was grateful."

It was still a shock to Jennifer and David, and many others, when, on January 14, 1957, Bogart passed away.

The following month, however, held some good news for Jennifer when she received a very warm critical reception for *Barretts of Wimpole Street*.

"That rarity—a remake of an established Hollywood classic that is exceptionally fine in every respect," noted *The New York Times*.

The *Los Angeles Mirror-News* noted, "Jennifer has the ability to look more like a woman completely in love than almost any other actress I can think of."

The most perceptive critique on Jennifer appeared in *The Hollywood Reporter*. "Miss Jones has what looks like an easy role. . . . But it has its dangers. The performance must be muted through much of the story, and the character can be shown only gradually emerging from the icy chrysalis her illness and her father have put her in. Finally she must show—without shocking us too much—that she realizes her father's protective love . . . is potentially incestuous and her only hope is to risk her life and flee with the man she loves. Miss Jones does all this with great warmth and skill. Her supreme achievement is the conviction that she is a person capable of having conceived Elizabeth Barrett's piercing sonnets."

The film was a commercial success and Jennifer's fourth consecutive hit.

In Italy for *Farewell*, Jennifer and David were housed in a lavish Roman villa, complete with a non-English-speaking staff guaranteed to create havoc and confusion. Jennifer's trunkloads of clothes filled one entire room, and her lavish boudoir and marble dressing room and bath, complete with solid gold fixtures, were breathtakingly beautiful.

A Farewell to Arms, budgeted initially at a reported $4 million, was being produced abroad for purposes of spectacular locations, the availability of thousands of "extra" players at an affordable cost, and lower overall costs on the soundstage (the picture would have cost 50 percent more if produced in Hollywood).

However, an irresistible force was about to collide with an immovable object, with Jennifer trapped helplessly in the wreckage. At Cinecittà studios, in early March, Jennifer, Rock Hudson, Selznick, and John Huston posed together for publicity photographs. All appeared happy. Jennifer and Rock got along famously. The previous month, Hudson had been nominated for the Academy Award as Best Actor for *Giant;* Ingrid Bergman, in *Anastasia,* was front-runner in the Best Actress category. But Hudson was disappointed that he wouldn't be able to attend the Oscar ceremonies, since there were no breaks scheduled this early in the *Farewell* shooting schedule.

David, of course, was looking forward to the Oscars next year, when Jennifer and perhaps even Rock would surely be shoo-ins for *A Farewell to Arms.* The actress had just turned thirty-eight, and the greatest birthday gift David could give her was this classic movie showcasing her talents.

She was particularly apprehensive about the film, and with good reason. An unexpected and potentially catastrophic break in shooting suddenly loomed on the horizon. Huston had promised Hemingway that he'd be faithful to the book; to Selznick and Jennifer's horror, the director was rewriting the carefully wrought script, not only causing delays in planning, but wreaking havoc on Selznick's concept of the film and Jennifer's concept of her character.

Friends had predicted such an eventuality. Former Selznick production manager Ray Klune had warned David, "You'll kill each other." Huston had always controlled all aspects of his films and was well-known for writing and filming new material on the spot; Selznick was famous for abhorring screening room surprises.

As far as David was concerned, *Farewell* was first and foremost a love story for Jennifer, with a military background. Huston, however, was intrigued with the military aspects of the tale and felt the focus of the story had been shifted solely to provide a vehicle for Jennifer.

"Even your best friends thought I was out of my mind to cast you on a romantic love story of this kind," stated an angry Selznick.

By mid-March the harried producer was "desperately unhappy" about the way things were going (an understatement as far as Jennifer's feelings were concerned). Director of photography Oswald ("Ossie") Morris (he'd photographed *Beat the Devil*) recalled: "One thing John didn't like to do was rehearse ahead of time. But David wanted [rehearsals], so John said yes. David said eleven A.M. tomorrow with Rock and Jennifer, and at eleven there was no sign of John. They waited an hour, and then it would all be abandoned. Obviously John was taking no notice of what David was saying."

Jennifer was distraught, "She kept saying, 'I knew something like this would happen, I knew it!' " recalled Hudson. "I told her things would work out, she shouldn't get so upset. But her instincts were obviously signaling her frantically, and they were right!" Jennifer and Rock attempted to function as peacemakers as the rift between Selznick and Huston widened. At meeting after meeting, the two giants clashed. Each tried to bring the other around to his point of view.

Selznick was not embarrassed to challenge the director with the painful fact that Huston's attempt to be faithful to Melville's *Moby Dick* had failed dismally, not only alienating lovers of the novel, but attracting only small audiences. The producer was leaving Huston little room to maneuver, but David didn't seem perturbed. He told close associates that he knew exactly what he was doing, and it seemed apparent by his actions that he wanted Huston "to walk."

Huston was hardly a minnow in a shark tank and not a man to cringe before the onslaught of a talent-crunching producer; he'd crunched quite a few of his own! "There was [an] element about John, a little bit of the snake-oil salesman," noted Huston's *Moby Dick* star Gregory Peck.

There were no compromises on the horizon—final decisions, decreed Selznick, were his and his alone. Huston countered that, in that case, he felt like "a prostitute."

Selznick laid it on the line. "I would rather face the awful consequences of your not directing [the picture] . . . than sacrifice my health and my future [with my family] to this kind of picture making." History was repeating itself—Selznick had fired George Cukor after only two weeks of shooting on *Gone With the Wind.*

By the third week in March, Huston resigned. (Although publicly he soft-pedaled his anger, he remained bitter for years. He felt he'd been used by Selznick to finance the picture and then discarded when Selznick no longer needed him. One of Huston's associates said that Huston was ready to punch Selznick in the nose.)

With Huston out, Jennifer became hysterical. The actress, weeping and disheveled, accompanied by a sullen-looking David, departed from Rome's Ciampino Airport on a flight to New York. The couple had arrived secretly at the airport only a half hour before departure, with Jennifer so overwrought that airline officials had to usher her into a small private room used in cases of emergency illness.

John Huston made no secret of the fact he'd been fired and stated that his quarrels with Selznick "had nothing to do with Jennifer." Reports circulated widely, however, that Huston's clashes with Selznick "concerned the scope of Jennifer's role," with Selznick insisting "that Jennifer dominate the movie."

Selznick's official comment: "In Mr. Huston, I asked for a first violinist and instead got a soloist."

It seemed likely that the picture would be canceled. But five thousand Italian troops were already assembled for the filming of battle scenes at alpine locations at Misurnia. If filming were canceled, a fortune in heavy indemnities would be incurred. With Huston out, production manager Arthur Fellows and Andrew Marton directed the scenes.

Two days after arriving in New York, Jennifer and David departed for Hollywood, where Selznick's seventy-eight-year-old mother was scheduled for surgery. To counteract reports of Jennifer's frantic behavior at Ciampino Airport, damage control was in effect. Prior to takeoff, a beautifully groomed and smiling Jennifer posed graciously with David for photographers at Idlewild Airport.

Rumors continued hot and heavy that the split between Huston and Selznick "involved Miss Jones." Charles Vidor, a longtime veteran of the studio system, was Huston's replacement.

Vidor, a nervous, nail-biting man of fifty-seven, was explicitly told by Selznick to permit Jennifer to play a scene her way first, and then he could feel free "to redirect it as you see fit." Vidor was also informed by Selznick that Jennifer was so "disciplined as an actress [that] if you direct her before getting her conceptions, I am fearful that you will lose the benefits of the intense and very lengthy study that she always gives."

Jennifer, for the first time ever, had to make a business appointment to see her husband, who was drowning in the mire of problems engulfing the picture. David's office was a beehive of activity, full of people coming and going and telephones ringing. "Darling, this is ridiculous—you didn't have to make an appointment to see me!" he exclaimed as Jennifer, script in hand, sat down and prepared to discuss the voluminous notes she'd made.

Charles Vidor expected to be fired. According to "Ossie" Morris, the director seemed "terrified of the actors, of David. . . . He became a total nervous wreck." Vidor was accustomed, or so one would have thought, to working with strong producers and sensitive female stars. He'd recently directed Doris Day in her best performance, as singer Ruth Etting in *Love Me or Leave Me.* Ten years earlier he'd directed Rita Hayworth in *Gilda.* And Vidor had shocked Hollywood when he'd battled studio chief Harry Cohn in court. (The judge subsequently decreed that the litigants in the Vidor-Cohn case "inhabit a fictitious, fabulous, topsy-turvy, temperamental world that is peculiar to their way of life. Their standards are not my standards. Let them be judged by those people of decency who inhabit their world of fantasy and fiction.")

The fantastic, fictional world of *A Farewell to Arms* lurched along. It was reported that Vidor didn't get along with Jennifer. The director continued to have his own ideas about script and performances, but Jennifer always took her complaints directly to David, who never failed to recognize the logic in her arguments.

Friends of Rock Hudson's described the months of production on the film as difficult and strained. Hudson described Selznick as having "an air of confusion about him. Nothing was clear and set, as with George Stevens [producer-director of *Giant*]. This dynamo of a man was in constant confusion. He was so intense . . . always scribbling his memos. He wanted everything better than perfect. He never let up."

Selznick's obsession with Jennifer's physical appearance on screen finally resulted in the exit of "Ossie" Morris, who quit after receiving one Selznick memo too many "accusing me of sacrificing

Jennifer's looks for the sake of Rock Hudson." (A twenty-page, sin-
gle-spaced missive had outlined, at the start of the film, how
Selznick wanted Jennifer photographed.)

Selznick's fetish for perfection included Hudson, whose Adam's
apple was too prominent as far as Selznick was concerned. "I'd say
to him, 'Good morning, David,' " recalled Hudson, "and he'd never
say good morning. He'd say, 'Your Adam's apple isn't made up.' He
was such an intense man that it never occurred to him to say good
morning."

Jennifer retreated ever deeper into her cocoon of privacy, even
on the set. John Springer, today a leading public relations mogul
and master film historian, back then was in charge of national magazine publicity for 20th Century–Fox.

"Jennifer was like a frightened doe," he recalls. "At one point
she insisted that they put up huge black canvas screens on the set,
blocking her off from the view of all but the cameraman, the director, and other actors in the scene." Springer also recalls, "Even
Selznick had to peep through an opening."

While Springer had an excellent professional relationship with
Selznick and Rock Hudson, "Jennifer kept to herself."

For the most part Jennifer was delivering a mannered and self-
conscious performance, her face twitching visibly at times (a habit
King Vidor had noted that Jennifer's directors must watch out for).
Hudson was definitely more at ease in front of the camera, and it
was obvious Vittorio De Sica was speaking his role phonetically.

The script borrowed blatantly from *Gone With the Wind,* including the memorable scene in which Rhett and Scarlett observe soldiers of the South in retreat. In *A Farewell to Arms* it's De Sica and
Rock Hudson who do the observing, but the setup and dialogue virtually duplicate *GWTW*'s. However, without a Victor Fleming—or a
John Huston—to make it work, the *Farewell* version had no impact
or energy.

Jennifer's best moments occurred in the film's final scenes. "I
won't die, will I, darling?" she asks, suffering agonizing pain during
childbirth. When the baby emerges, stillborn, Jennifer, with exactly
the right nuance, asks, "Is he all right?" The emotion was disturbingly real. Jennifer's death scene impressed all on the set as simple, unmannered, and powerful.

Selznick was usually on the set, but out of Jennifer's view. Once, in the midst of an intimate love scene between Jennifer and Rock Hudson, Hudson spotted Selznick behind the camera, whispering in Vidor's ear. "David!" exclaimed the rattled actor. Selznick apologized "absentmindedly."

Jennifer, of course, wasn't available to be interviewed by the press, but Selznick often was. He made no apologies when confronted with tales of his being a tough executive. "Sure I am," he admitted. "Who the hell doesn't insist on having his own way if he is in charge? Why is this a criticism? I have a different concept of producing from other producers. . . . To me to produce is to *make* a picture."

And Jennifer knew what that meant. Veteran correspondent Lloyd Shearer visited the set and wanted to know what Jennifer was really like. Selznick was blunt: "It's nobody's business what sort of woman my wife is." But David's desire to publicize the picture overrode his desire to protect Jennifer's sensibilities. "If I didn't think [Jennifer] was a fascinating woman, I wouldn't have married her and remained married to her for eight years," he said. "Jennifer is extraordinarily sensitive. I have a feeling that she was born out of her time. She has nothing in common with modern women. . . . She has a strange mystical sixth sense about things. She is extremely ambitious, but for reasons completely different from those of other actresses."

How exactly did Jennifer's ambition differ from that of other actresses? "She has no interest in fame or money," explained Selznick. "All her awards, including the Oscar, have mysteriously disappeared from our house. She acts because she must act. It's a compulsion."

Jennifer's well-known preference for avoiding the press was easily interpreted by her husband: "She has a deep, ingrained feeling that the press wants to talk about her personal life. She just doesn't like being probed. Members of the press who stick to professional topics have no problems with Jennifer."

Columnist Art Buchwald asked David if he was "protecting" Jennifer in the film. "Ask Ingrid Bergman and Vivien Leigh that question," he replied. "I have always protected my stars, and I make no difference between her and any other star."

The saga of filming *A Farewell to Arms* was not to conclude on a happy note. "Several friends of mine told me how tense things were on the picture," recalled publicity man Bob Ungerfeld, "and Jennifer was virtually unapproachable toward the end. [It was] a publicist's worst nightmare, and that picture needed all the good publicity it could get."

After thirty grueling weeks in Italy, the last day of shooting finally arrived. It was mid-August. Jennifer, David, Rock Hudson, and the rest of the company were on location on beautiful Lake Maggiore. It was chilly and damp aboard the production boat, and everyone was exhausted and on edge.

Jennifer had been late in arriving. Production manager Arthur Fellows began arguing with Selznick over the producer's sudden plan to shut down the picture while new love scenes for Jennifer and Rock were conceived (Selznick subsequently abandoned the idea).

Meanwhile, for the scene at hand, the action called for Hudson (in a small boat with Jennifer, fleeing from Hudson's "enemies") to row Jennifer and himself to safety. A disagreement arose between Fellows and Selznick as to when to photograph the scene. Fellows favored twilight, when conditions would be best; however, the big searchlight scanning the waters for the escaping Hudson and Jennifer would not cast a photographic beam at that hour. Selznick favored shooting the scene at night, with the action illuminated by many searchlights.

Fellows pointed out that no multiple searchlights were on hand since they hadn't been called for. Selznick replied angrily that Fellows must immediately contact the army, which would provide them. Selznick's attitude was abrasive and hostile, and Fellows retorted: "David, why don't *you* call the army?"

Selznick supposedly slapped Fellows across the face (another witness related that Selznick "pushed Fellows"), and Fellows struck back, his fist jabbing David's face and shattering his glasses.

Jennifer—and everyone else—was momentarily stunned. "David, don't open your eyes!" shouted an onlooker. Selznick was bleeding. According to onlookers, Jennifer screamed and jumped to his defense as Fellows departed hurriedly.

An emotional Jennifer assisted David to an ambulance, which sped the couple to a hospital in Milan. The producer had sustained no serious injuries, except perhaps to his reputation. Rumors circulated wildly that *A Farewell to Arms* most likely was not only a fiasco, but a jinxed enterprise to boot.

As far as Selznick was concerned, the only real trouble he'd encountered on *Farewell* came from certain factions of the Italian press—namely, the communists, who hated him because he'd refused to employ communist labor, and the fascists, who regarded Hemingway's novel as anti-Italian. Together they'd caused Selznick production delays in hiring personnel and had forced the picture over budget by over three-quarters of a million dollars (which Selznick would have to pay).

Three-year-old Mary Jennifer had been brought over to Italy to be with her parents toward the end of shooting, and it was with a great sigh of relief that the Selznicks and entourage finally booked passage on the luxury liner *Queen Elizabeth* for their return to the States.

The leisurely voyage seemed to restore Jennifer's spirits. By the time the ship docked in New York in late August, she was rested and radiant. Wearing a very becoming beige suit and picture hat, she posed for photographers waiting at the pier. She cheerfully held Mary Jennifer in her arms as the child clutched an oversize Raggedy Ann doll. A huge smile lit up the little girl's face as she gazed adoringly at her mother, who in turn was smiling dazzlingly into the cameras.

Good news awaited the Selznicks. The Fox sales department, having seen footage on *Farewell,* claimed to be wildly enthusiastic about the picture. They wanted to rush it into release by the end of the year so it could qualify for both the New York Film Critics Awards and the Oscars.

Selznick usually took as much time with postproduction as he did with actual filming, which would mean, under ordinary circumstances, a release date perhaps a year hence. But Selznick was strapped for cash and anxious for Jennifer to win her next Academy Award. In addition, both Selznick and Fox wanted to cash in on Rock Hudson's box office appeal while still at its peak. Selznick began a round-the-clock effort to put *Farewell* together.

A personal tragedy intruded on the producer's concentration when Louis B. Mayer died of leukemia. Jennifer was once again the outsider as Selznick and Irene, both devastated by the loss, drew close together to commiserate and grieve.

Selznick wrote the eulogy for his former father-in-law and mourned the passing not only of the estimable Louis B., but of all that Mayer had represented in David's life and in the industry.

• • •

With a heavy heart Selznick returned to A Farewell to Arms. The film had its first preview in Burlingame on November 18. The next night it previewed at the Fox Theater in San Francisco. On both nights screams of delight welcomed the appearance of the renowned Selznick Studios logo on the huge CinemaScope screen. Near pandemonium erupted when the names of Rock Hudson and Jennifer Jones appeared, followed by Vittorio De Sica.

Oddly enough, the title treatment for *A Farewell to Arms* was almost an exact duplicate of that for *Gone With the Wind,* a very un-Selznick-like touch of avoidable self-plagiarism and a peculiar way to set up the picture.

As the audience settled down, there was a feeling of anticipation—people wanted to like the film, featuring the stars of *Giant* and *Love Is a Many Splendored Thing* together for the first time in a production from the creator of the greatest epic of them all.

Jennifer's first close-up, however, despite countless retakes, still wasn't perfect (there was a slight "turkey gobble" perceivable under her chin). As breathtaking as the actress's beauty was in person, it was impossible in sharp-focus CinemaScope for one to look twenty when one was thirty-eight. There were moments later in the film—especially a sequence in a sleigh—when Jennifer did photograph like a radiant young woman. And at no time was her pairing with Rock Hudson unbelievable.

"Picture too *talky!*" complained many *Farewell* preview cards. Other griped: "Too *long!*" (The film was over three hours.) The overall reaction, however, seemed good, and Selznick felt the movie would be a money-maker. One of the major cuts in the film would involve Jennifer's harrowing "childbirth" sequence, over thirty minutes long and too strong for audiences of the day (one wag described it as "an obstetric orgy").

The film world-premiered in New York and Los Angeles a week before Christmas. Gorgeous and glamorous in white mink and diamonds, Jennifer attended the Los Angeles opening, escorted by David and Rock Hudson. She was atypically gregarious and vivacious, and the evening was a brilliant success. Then the reviews came out, and it was a dismal replay of the terrible letdown all had suffered after *Duel in the Sun.*

To Jennifer and Selznick's horror, critics singled Jennifer out for damnation. If, as she'd told Joe Hyams, criticism drove her to tears and made her want to "go off somewhere and be alone," poor Jennifer must have thought of heading for a cave in Pago Pago.

Variety wrote, "Miss Jones imbues the nurse with a sense of neurosis and foreboding, but she only sporadically rises to the full challenge of this superdifficult role. As Miss Jones plays her, she frequently lacks warmth."

"Miss Jones plays the famous Catherine Barkley with bewildering nervous moves and grimaces. The show of devotion between two people is intensely acted, not realized," wrote *The New York Times.*

"Miss Jones as the nurse in love never quite seems to make it," was the opinion of *Cue* magazine. One of the very few positive reviews was expressed by the *Hollywood Citizen News:* "The acting is most commendable. Jennifer Jones will unquestionably win an Oscar nomination for her brilliant characterization . . . a masterpiece."

More typical was William K. Zinsser's evaluation, in the *New York Herald-Tribune:* "If there were a supreme Bad Taste Award for movies, *A Farewell to Arms* would win it hands down. This smutty version of Ernest Hemingway's novel will set thousands of stomachs to turning."

Zinsser and many others were obviously greatly upset with the liberties the screenplay had taken, none worse than at the very end of the picture. Catherine is about to die, and Lieutenant Henry offers the lament: "Maybe this is the price for sleeping together?"

How does one not take it all personally? The worst was yet to come. In a desperate attempt to win Ernest Hemingway's endorsement of the film, Selznick made what he considered to be an extremely generous gesture—he offered "Papa" a $50,000 bonus from the film's profits (he'd done the same with Margaret Mitchell almost two decades earlier on release of *Gone With the Wind,* when $50,000 was worth considerably more).

John Huston knew of Selznick's proposal (he said it had been his [Huston's] idea at the outset) and enjoyed a bit of revenge by going public with it, deliberately altering a key detail. Huston announced Selznick was intending "to give Mr. Hemingway the first $100,000 out of the proceeds."

Selznick could hardly deny the story, but it didn't matter. "Papa" was enraged, and his response was devastating. Hemingway said it wasn't likely there'd be any profits from the unfortunate production starring David's forty-one-year-old wife (Hemingway had prematurely aged Jennifer by three years), and he added that if, miraculously, the film did turn a profit, David "could change the [cash] into nickels at the local bank and shove them up his ass until they came out his ears."

Hemingway later told his biographer, A. E. Hotchner, "You know, you write a book like [*A Farewell to Arms*] that you're fond of over the years, then you see that happen to it, and it's like pissing in your father's beer."

Chapter

27

*A*s the full impact of the abysmal critical
reception of her *Farewell* performance sank in, Jennifer became even
warier and more cautious of any and all people outside her immediate, very small circle.

The good news for Jennifer and David, in those first weeks of
1958, was that *Farewell* was doing business. In retrospect, when
queried if *Farewell* was regarded as a hit, David Brown reflects and
replies, "Not especially. . . ." His recollections obviously reflect all
the troubles that plagued the film, its very high cost, and Brown offers an understated personal observation on the angst of bringing
the story to the screen: "I'm happy I wasn't there [in Italy during
filming]."

Jennifer was invited to appear with Rock Hudson on that year's
Academy Awards telecast to present the award for Best Short Subject. She accepted but withdrew at the last moment.

There were no Audie awards for Jennifer this year, nor were
there any exciting new offers for the actress's services. On the other
hand, ex–Selznick brother-in-law Bill Goetz had produced one of
the season's big critical and box office successes, *Sayonara.* Irene was
dismayed that David wasn't producing similar blockbusters while
leaving Jennifer to score her own successes in other producers'
movies, as she'd done so successfully in the recent past.

John Huston summed it up with this comment: "I'm afraid that none of the pictures David and Jennifer made together after their marriage amounted to much. One must certainly be sympathetic. There's even a kind of grandeur to the way David laid everything on the line for her." And, he might have added, to the way Jennifer strove never to disappoint David.

David was no longer the unabashed optimist—the disappointment of *Farewell* had hit him hard. Jennifer traveled to India, and rumors floated back to the States suggesting a relationship with a diplomat from South America.

David was now having an affair with one of his secretaries. Mary Jennifer, four years old, seemed the only great joy in her father's life, and he lavished incredible attention on her. Those on the scene have stated that Mary Jennifer had replaced Jennifer as the obsession in David's life—and that Jennifer was resentful. Nonetheless it was obvious, from correspondence and telephone conversations, that when separated from her daughter, Jennifer missed her—and David—a great deal.

The couple's next project was to be either *Mary Magdalene* or *Tender Is the Night.* Jennifer was in the same predicament as a world-class boxing champion who must keep in peak form despite huge gaps of time between matches. She seemed to benefit from acting lessons from Lee Strasberg in New York and had entered the sealed-tight environment of Strasberg's private classes.

In the past couple of years Marilyn Monroe had put Strasberg and his acting technique, called "the Method," on the map. Monroe had walked out on her 20th Century–Fox contract, demanding more money and control over what pictures she was cast in and who directed them. Highly dissatisfied with her image as the world's most desirable "dumb blonde," Marilyn sought to be "a fine actress" and enrolled in the Actors Studio, where, among others, James Dean and Marlon Brando had learned their craft.

Actor Gerald Gordon, soon to become the leading heartthrob on daytime television soap operas, was in Strasberg's private classes with Jennifer and Marilyn. "Jennifer was so fucking good-looking, she looked like a kid!" he recalls. Marilyn, on the other hand, was often unrecognizable, with hair pulled back under a scarf and, to quote Laurence Olivier, "bad skin with no makeup."

Gordon recalls Jennifer wearing a beautiful plaid outfit and a boyish bob haircut. "She was so vulnerable, so open, so unmannered in terms of appreciating the classes. She wasn't standoffish, but she was very, very shy.

"She seemed very lonely. It was an effort for her to talk to anyone. She was never introduced in class, and neither was Marilyn. Jennifer didn't want to be noticed at all. Her shyness surprised me. Marilyn seemed just as shy and vulnerable, but I thought Jennifer Jones one of the loneliest people I've ever seen.

"You could see she felt uneasy walking out of class, not unlike Marilyn. It was surprising—both shared a certain shyness and insecurity. They couldn't quite relate to the other students or the teacher, and Jennifer usually seemed ill at ease. Here was a woman who was a respected movie star [who'd] won the Academy Award. You'd think she would be comfortable, [but] she wasn't."

One would think that Jennifer and Marilyn, two women who'd experienced the pitfalls of fame, who'd had to contend with the studio system and who yearned to do quality work—and who were in such close proximity in acting class—would become friends. As far as anyone knew, it never happened; each remained totally absorbed by her own concerns.

Lee Strasberg's daughter, Susan, has recalled her father's fondness for both Jennifer and Marilyn. "My [physical] type is Jennifer Jones," he admitted, "that dark-haired, fair-skinned beauty." (However, in his youth, Alice Faye—a blonde—had been Strasberg's ideal.)

Lee Strasberg admitted to his biographer, Cindy Adams, that he'd had a crush on Jennifer, "except I don't think Jennifer crushed back," noted Cindy.

Susan Strasberg, then sixteen years old, was inspired to please her father by emulating Jennifer's dark hair and eyebrows. "When I saw photos of myself," recalled Susan, "I realized with a shock that I resembled a young Jennifer Jones."

Gerald Gordon recalls Jennifer's work in class: "She did private moments where you sit in front of the class and get involved in a very personal moment—a very sad event in your life—and re-create the circumstances that created the moment you're experiencing. She was very poignant, there was real expression on her face."

It would seem this type of exercise, dredging up extremely agonizing memories, could be psychologically damaging to the individual, especially someone as highly strung as Jennifer. With the torment of her years with Robert Walker, his untimely and mysterious death, and her complex relationship with Selznick to draw on for the purposes of "private moments," Jennifer was trodding a hazardous road.

"Yes and no," comments Gordon. "[Lee's method] *can* be harmful. It depends on your frame of reference. The technique, called 'spotlighting,' has been used by Lee's actors for years. 'Spotlighting' can be very deep, and it can become quite disproportionate," admits Gordon. "That can be the danger in that kind of work—in that kind of emotional pool you can go way, way down. Nonetheless, I give that kind of work its due. It can produce extraordinary moments. The trick is to keep perspective of scene and not let it get out of hand."

In Gordon's opinion Jennifer was "strangely enigmatic—as though there were a part of her that had never really surfaced. An unplumbed depth. A brilliant bottle of wine that had been opened before its time."

Gordon would encounter Jennifer in the future.

Laurence Olivier, in New York starring on Broadway in *The Entertainer*, shook his head in dismay on learning that Jennifer was in Strasberg's hands. "Oh, God, exactly what the poor darling *doesn't* need!" he exclaimed. Olivier detested Strasberg, personally and professionally, and had even less respect for Strasberg's wife, Paula, a woman who became an adjunct in Jennifer's career as she had in Marilyn Monroe's.

"Paula knew nothing," said Olivier (many others who worked with Paula disagreed). "She was no actress, no director, no teacher, no adviser. . . . She had one talent," stated Olivier, drawing on his personal experience with Paula on the set with Marilyn Monroe. "She could butter Marilyn up." And Paula was well paid for it, having been placed on the studio payroll for $1,500 per week.

What kind of an influence was Lee Strasberg on Jennifer at this vulnerable stage of her life? Arthur Miller (not an admirer of Strasberg's) considered Strasberg a negative influence on most actors. "He made people dependent on him," stated Miller. Olivier provided further insight. Thanks to Lee and Paula Strasberg, he said, directing Marilyn in *The Prince and the Showgirl* had been a traumatic experience.

Olivier observed that in the case of important stars, "the Strasbergs stood to make much capital" by being hired to "coach" the star during production. But Jennifer was well protected by David O. Selznick, and access to her was hardly unlimited.

In Los Angeles, Jennifer and David continued to give lavish parties for the town's elite, a deliberate and successful attempt to boost Jennifer's career. Invitations to the gatherings were highly sought after ("David and Jennifer's parties were great fun," recalled David Niven). On certain occasions there were unexpected developments, and Jennifer's insecurities became screamingly evident. One day, at home, Jennifer's phone rang. The caller was a beautiful newcomer to Hollywood's social scene, the sophisticated young wife of a major producer, who'd been invited, along with her husband, to a formal dinner party at Jennifer and David's.

"I phoned to ask Jennifer if I might bring along David Lean and his wife, Lela [Lean was the renowned British director of *The Bridge on the River Kwai*]," she recalls. "There was a hesitation from Jennifer—suddenly Jennifer's secretary got on the line and said, 'Let me get back to you.' Can you imagine Jennifer hesitating over David Lean?! The secretary got back to me and said it would be all right.

"Well, my dear, that dinner party turned out to be one of the strangest dinner parties I've ever been to in my entire life!

"I remember when we first walked in and I was introduced to Jennifer, my feeling was that she was a strange woman. When she said hello you didn't think she was really looking at you; it was as though she were kind of—drifting off. She seemed like a frightened little bird—excruciatingly shy and basically frightened.

"Now Lela Lean was from India, and the minute Jennifer spotted her, her eyes lit up and she was instantly drawn to her. They went off in a corner to talk, and Jennifer sat on the floor the whole time (she was dressed in something very pretty, a harem-style pants outfit, all metallic and shiny with silver-and-gold highlights).

"Well, Jennifer and Lela soon disappeared, and nobody saw them the rest of the evening. The hostess never reappeared—she was gone! I mean, she never appeared at her own dinner party, not even when dinner was served.

"I cannot, by the way, conceive of her running a major household, not at that time, anyway. She wasn't unkind, but she certainly didn't communicate well.

"During the evening, I managed to get through to Lela and asked her, 'Aren't you hungry?' She said, 'I'm starved!' I said, 'Well, why don't you come out and eat dinner?' She said, 'Jennifer won't let me go!'

"Lela also told me that she thought Jennifer was so totally involved [with yoga and spiritualism] that it was to the point where it wasn't healthy, do you know what I mean? It was a total, total obsession—it was almost as though if she came down to earth, she'd go totally mad."

There were many beautiful women at the dinner party that evening. "It was very strange," the newcomer recalls. "Jennifer didn't seem to mind that David was surrounded by beauties. She was only interested in what Lela Lean had to say that evening.

"Jennifer and Lela became friends," she recalls, "although Lela, who lived in England, was never deeply into yoga, and unlike Jennifer, she was not drawn to the spiritual."

The "newcomer" also offered this description of Jennifer on that long-ago evening: "Jennifer looked tortured, as though her sanity were ready to snap at any moment. I cannot imagine her being a cruel person—you can tell when someone has the capacity to be deliberately cruel. To me Jennifer seemed frightened and helpless."

Blue-eyed, chestnut-haired Betty Spiegel totally understood Jennifer's ongoing plight vis-à-vis David Selznick. Betty was a beautiful, fun-loving young woman from Virginia who'd married powerful producer Sam Spiegel (he'd come a long way since producing Jennifer's *We Were Strangers*). Spiegel was considerably older than Betty, and her life with him, on a personal level, in many ways paralleled Jennifer's with Selznick.

"Those men wanted total control, they were control freaks," explains Betty. "For example, Sam wouldn't let me organize 'our' parties. 'You wouldn't know how to place the guests, who likes and dislikes who,' he told me." Spiegel's attitude extended far beyond organizing the couple's social life: "Sam, Selznick, and men like them wanted control over everything! In the case of our parties, Sam controlled the guest list, the menu, the seating arrangements—but *I* controlled the flowers," Betty laughs. " 'You know about a lot of things, Sam,' I told him, 'but not about flowers!' I took over that aspect of our parties.

"Frankly, I didn't care. In those days I wasn't into running a household. I'm certain [from firsthand observation] Jennifer's situation ran along the same lines." And Jennifer's ego apparently didn't require an independent public or private identity. Her stationery revealed her perspective—the letterhead read: "Mrs. David O. Selznick," although she signed her correspondence "Jennifer Jones Selznick."

Tinseltown opinion makers were particularly impressed with a fabulous soiree the Selznicks tossed that summer. Katharine Hepburn, who usually never went to such affairs, showed up for this one. The next day it was the talk of the town. Hepburn had spent much of the evening deep in conversation with "her biggest fan," Louis Jourdan. *Gigi*, in which Jourdan starred with Leslie Caron and Maurice Chevalier, had recently been released, and Jourdan was the hottest leading man in town. Everyone wanted to cast him in a film, including Selznick, who wanted him for *Tender Is the Night*. Selznick was working feverishly to line up the elements for the project, in which Jennifer's character, Nicole, aged from nineteen to thirty (Jennifer had turned thirty-nine in March).

Romaine Gary was currently working on a script, and Selznick was cautiously hopeful he could come up with a version that was cinematically exciting yet would "preserve every Fitzgerald value."

It was again Selznick's duty not to disappoint Jennifer. Playing Nicole was yet another longtime dream of Jennifer's. "I have seen too many other dreams of yours come very close to realization, only to be spoiled," he told her. "I shall always feel sad that, despite the very substantial success of *Farewell to Arms*, it was not what you wanted. . . ."

Jennifer received countless intimate notes, letters and poems from David. He always wrote that he loved and adored her and thought of her all the time and that when they were separated he missed her more than he could have believed possible. Selznick's way with words had always found a welcome audience in Jennifer.

• • •

Considered "the Laureate of the Jazz Age," F. Scott Fitzgerald authored novels that were among the most evocative of life in the Roaring Twenties. *Tender Is the Night,* originally published in 1934, was a fictionalized account of Fitzgerald's young wife, Zelda, who'd suffered a mental breakdown. (Although Fitzgerald based the character on his wife, he called her "Nicole" in the novel.) Jennifer Jones realized she was about to tackle a legend. She wasn't without a sense of humor about her situation: "Everyone tells me I'm perfectly cast," she later noted, "but Nicole is such a tortured, neurotic person, it's a dubious compliment."

Selznick faced a formidable challenge in getting the picture made—Fox was wary of him after *Farewell* and not excited at the prospect of another David-Jennifer collaboration. For the next two years there would be a definite pattern regarding the studio's relationship with the producer and his star: indecision.

A major concern was casting the role of Dick Diver (Scott Fitzgerald). In this regard Jennifer's thoughts proved far more commercially minded than her husband's. David consulted closely with her on his plans for the picture. He told her they were "partners in everything, and doubly so, certainly, in your own films with me. . . ." In his correspondence to her it was almost as though Selznick were writing to an incredibly naive and sensitive adolescent. ("For David, Jennifer was like porcelain," notes David Brown, "very fragile and very much in that house up in Beverly Hills.")

While Jennifer insisted that Selznick do what he thought best in casting *Tender Is the Night,* he told her that he wanted to accomplish what *she* wanted, "in this above all cases. . . ."

She wanted none other than William Holden as her leading man and noted accurately and astutely that their teaming had proven very successful in *Love Is a Many Splendored Thing.*

Selznick said he agreed with Jennifer's choice, but he wasn't overly enthusiastic and pointed out that "despite [Holden's] neuroses," the actor wasn't nearly neurotic enough to portray Scott Fitzgerald/Dick Diver. In any event, Holden was not immediately available, and Selznick wasn't prepared to wait (a great mistake, it seemed, since there would be many long delays before the picture was finally given the green light).

Jennifer learned that the leading men currently available to be her costars (as of January 1959, and the list would change) included Henry Fonda, Robert Mitchum, Gregory Peck (who, according to

Selznick, "hated the book"), and a quartet of much older stars, each of whom would have been ludicrously miscast: Clark Gable, Gary Cooper, Bing Crosby, and John Wayne (Selznick liked none of them for the role, although the studio, and perhaps even Jennifer, would have accepted any one of them).

Laurence Olivier was another possibility, but Selznick considered him too old for the part. Montgomery Clift was available, but Selznick bluntly told Jennifer, "I am afraid he would throw you higher than a kite." Clift had survived a near fatal automobile accident a couple of years earlier, and the calamity had not only permanently damaged his face but had altered his entire persona.

Two candidates Selznick did like weren't movie stars, but young Broadway actors with promising futures—Christopher Plummer and Jason Robards, Jr. ("I must say that I find [Robards] unprepossessing physically for Dick Diver," said Selznick).

David told Jennifer to take her time and mull over his suggestions. "Then make your notes on a separate piece of paper. . . ."

Frances Fuller, director of the American Academy of Dramatic Arts, personally invited Jennifer to present an award at AADA in New York. The actress declined—she was off to Zurich. There she'd be spending several months undergoing analysis with Dr. Meier, before (she hoped) beginning the new picture. David, Mary Jennifer, and her nurse would join her (along with Ivan Moffat, who was working with David on the script).

Selznick's initial choice for director of *Tender* had been John Frankenheimer, an exciting young talent who'd scored spectacularly on TV. But Selznick grew "nervous" about hiring Frankenheimer, and the studio wasn't enthusiastic, so he opted instead for a man Jennifer was familiar with, the redoubtable Henry King. Now in his late seventies, King was a proven entity as far as Jennifer was concerned (the "inexperienced" Frankenheimer subsequently directed *The Manchurian Candidate*).

It was symbolic of Selznick's fortunes that during this period "Tara," or what was left of the famous but now crumbling outdoor set, Scarlett's home in *Gone With the Wind*, was dismantled for shipment to Atlanta, where it was scheduled to become a tourist attraction.

In New York David encountered John Huston in the lobby of

the St. Regis Hotel. "He smiled at me," recalled Huston, "began to put out his hand, and then hesitated, as if he were afraid I might not take it. I immediately took his hand. [Later on] I was out in California and Jennifer phoned. 'John, we're giving a party. Won't you come?'

"I said, 'No, I won't come. I'm still mad at him. But I'll get over it one of these days. Then, if you still want me, I'll come.' "

David was determined that Jennifer look breathtakingly young and beautiful in Tender is the Night. As a result of a discussion he had with Anita Colby, Jennifer was introduced to a dynamic, handsome, high-strung young man who'd assume enormous importance in her life. "He was a genius," said Colby. "He had the talent and ability to make women more youthful looking, beautiful, and glamorous than anyone I'd ever met."

George Masters had become the most sought after and innovative hairstylist/makeup artist on the New York–Hollywood scene. Elizabeth Arden had hired Masters for her New York salon. There was a network of well-heeled and well-known ladies on both coasts who made up the George Club—from millionairess Marion Davies (former silent film star and paramour of William Randolph Hearst) to Arlene Dahl, Cyd Charisse, and, later, Audrey Hepburn, Ann-Margret, and Marilyn Monroe (who happily paid Masters $2,000 for a haircut and white-blond hair color he'd created for her. She inscribed a photo to him: "To Killer George—Thanks for what you did for me!").

However, "Jennifer Jones was my first important movie star client," said Masters, "and the most beautiful woman I ever worked on." He recalled their first encounter. "She came to my salon soon after I started at Saks. She came only once. After that, I went to her. The one time she did come was quite a concession on her part. The salon was on the third floor, and she walked up rather than riding the elevator. She couldn't stand being boxed in with people staring at her."

On meeting him, Jones realized immediately that Masters knew what he was doing, and she attempted to commandeer the young stylist's services on a full-time, "on call twenty-four hours" basis. "George," she told him, "from here up I'd like to look like a—well, somebody a truck driver will whistle at."

While he refused to quit his job at Saks, "the Selznicks semiofficially adopted me as a member of the family. They gave me a key to the house. I was there almost full-time after my working hours at Saks—from about four P.M. until midnight on most nights, as well as weekends."

Masters was astonished at Jennifer's opulent lifestyle. In her bathroom, there were crystal chandeliers, a working fireplace, wall-to-wall carpeting, and, over the tub, several Renoirs.

Her personal quarters included a makeup room, a massage room, a sitting room, and closets the size of bedrooms.

"Beside her bed was an end table with a panel of push buttons—buttons for opening and closing doors, windows, drapes, and for switching lights and music on or off," recalled Masters. There was a button that switched on "a tumbling waterfall outside her window, filling the air with the soft romantic murmur of water cascading over a rock ledge."

Jennifer was, without question, "the most extravagant creature God and David O. Selznick ever created," said Masters.

Her extravagance extended to virtually all areas of her personal grooming. Jennifer wore stockings and gloves only once, then discarded them. "She would try on at least a dozen pairs of brand-new hose before finding one pair that suited her," recalled Masters, "then toss the rest to her personal maid to take out to the trash can. She was always imagining little defects in them."

Brassieres received the same scrutiny. She'd purchase dozens of them, then, according to Masters, "have her maid wash them in sections—cups and straps separately—and lay them out in rows to be tried on. It was a fascinating ritual. Certain bras felt better than others. Jennifer would try them all on, over and over again, until she decided on the one she was most comfortable in. The others went out with the garbage."

Face creams, too, required Jennifer's special attention. "She spent thousands of dollars a year on her creams, had them all de-perfumed at the factories and then tested by top dermatologists before putting one dab on her face." A jar would be discarded after it had been used once. "This is not an exaggeration. She had a storeroom for her cosmetics approximately twice the size of the average person's living room."

As for Jennifer's perfume collection: "She used perfume like crazy, but in the most surprising way," recalled Masters—she'd spray it on light bulbs, "then turned on the lights to warm the scent as it wafted over the house."

The flawless Jones complexion was maintained with far more than a quick soap scrub and pat dry with a towel. "At her home I used to watch wide-eyed as she cooked rose petals on a hot-plate burner, holding a towel over her head and steaming her face with rose water. And at other times she stirred up a batch of heavy whipping cream and honey, lathering it all over her face and leaving it on for twenty minutes so the vitamin D could soak into her skin."

While Masters worked on her, she'd change her bathrobe several times and took endless showers, after which Masters restyled her hair "from scratch—from shampoo to comb-out—two or three times a day." Even when Jennifer was finally "put together," Masters wasn't necessarily through with his chores. "She would look up at herself in the mirror and notice something not quite right. Then I'd start over again."

And then there was Selznick to please. "Mr. Selznick sometimes would come in for a final inspection and suggest a minor change here and there.

"He was the king of Hollywood, and she was his queen. It was their Grand Illusion and they lived it off screen as well as on." It seemed apparent that both Jennifer and David were happiest when playing roles. To paraphrase Tennessee Williams, they were like birds staying aloft on flights of fancy—but they could never land, for once they touched ground they would die.

George Masters liked David Selznick. "I learned as much from [him] as I did from Jennifer. He entrusted her to me completely, as he'd once entrusted her to Anita Colby."

Masters was impressed by Jennifer and David's extravagant devotion to each other. "[David] was completely enslaved by her beauty, and she was enslaved by sustaining the illusion for him both as an actress and as a wife." Masters doubted that "any woman was ever more involved in sustaining the illusion of beauty for her husband, or any man more devoted to continually perfecting and enhancing that illusion."

In Masters's opinion, "the Selznicks had an idyllic marriage." George recognized, however, that Jennifer was "an extreme case" in her pursuit of physical perfection.

The Sunday parties hosted by Jennifer and David during this period usually began at eleven A.M. and continued all through the day and night. "Doing Jennifer for these parties was almost as big a production as doing her for a movie," said Masters. He'd arrive before ten, to begin to prepare her. "I tried to get her upstairs to greet her guests by around one o'clock; she was always late for her own parties. Then I would go home and come back around four o'clock for the second beauty go-round.

"She would sneak downstairs to our beauty quarters, take a shower, and then we'd do another shampoo, set, and face makeup. Then she would rest [and change into a duplicate] of everything from bra and hose to her party gown. She would put on a dress identical to the one she had just taken off so no one would know she had changed clothes. Then she would go back upstairs to her guests, and they would all marvel at the way she still looked so fresh and beautiful."

They did it all over again around ten o'clock in the evening: "shampoo, shower, new makeup, hairdo, dress change. Again everything was identical. She'd put on the third dress, then go back upstairs looking as though she'd worn the same dress all day.

"That's what I call the ultimate effort in sustaining the illusion." And the "effort" was expended "every Sunday, like clockwork," recalled Masters. It never occurred to anyone that there might be an underlying physical condition that necessitated Jennifer's constantly changing clothes, a condition that one of Jennifer's contemporaries would shortly identify.

Masters noted that while Jennifer was usually late for her own parties, "she never liked for me to be late." He compared Jennifer to Marilyn Monroe, "who was notorious for being late. Jennifer was almost as bad."

Masters recalled how, when he once arrived late, Jennifer "came running out of the house with her hair soaking wet and made a dash for her car. I caught her and apologized. 'Let's go in and I'll do you very fast,' I promised.

"She was in one of her petulant Piscean moods. 'There is nothing you can do to help me now,' she said, pouting. 'Do you realize that my guests are due to arrive in five minutes?' "

Masters wanted to remind her that she often kept guests waiting for hours, but he didn't. "Her ego was bruised," he said, "because for once I had failed her when she needed me—or thought she did. She was so piqued that she refused to let me do her for the party.

" 'So what are you going to do?' I asked.

" 'I'm going to ride around all night until the party is over,' she said, and that is exactly what she did. She jumped in her car with her soaking wet hair and drove off in a huff. She didn't speak to me for three weeks. Pisces people are very emotional."

No matter what the cost—and it would involve a battle royal with the studio, because Masters wasn't a member of the necessary unions and had no intention of joining—Jennifer and David were determined to enlist Masters as her beauty guru for *Tender Is the Night*.

Masters thoroughly researched the fashions, makeup, and hairstyles of the 1920s for over a year and worked with Jennifer "until midnight almost every night, trying to perfect her look for this movie." (Jennifer would be forty-two by the time the picture finally went into production, and Masters was impressed. "Not many forty-two-year-old women can be made up to look like nineteen.")

Meanwhile studio decisions regarding the picture dragged interminably. There were renewed talks among Selznick, Jennifer, and the duke and duchess of Windsor regarding the proposed film of their lives (possibly for television). The royal couple needed the cash but lacked the courage to proceed with the project. While in Europe, Jennifer and David visited Lourdes for the first time, an emotional occasion for the actress.

Selznick's health was deteriorating, and signs of heart disease were surfacing. He chose not to alert Jennifer and continued to spend happy hours with their daughter. To Jennifer's chagrin, it was up to her to be disciplinarian with the child, a role she loathed. She complained to friends, but the situation didn't change. David acquiesced to Mary Jennifer on virtually any and all matters.

There was a major shake-up at 20th Century–Fox when Buddy Adler was diagnosed with cancer and was not expected to survive. "I think it was a blow to all of us when Buddy died," states David Brown (Adler died in July 1960). "The studio never fully recovered, until Darryl Zanuck came back."

As Selznick navigated the new corridors of power at Fox, Jennifer busied herself with personal concerns. She spent time with Anita Colby. The two women were as fascinated as everyone else in town with the headlined antics of twenty-seven-year-old Elizabeth Taylor. (The future debacle of Liz's *Cleopatra* would cause Fox to siphon off funds from its other projects, including *Tender Is the Night.*)

One afternoon Jennifer and Anita Colby quietly went to a local theater to see Elizabeth's current film, *Butterfield 8.* It wasn't Taylor's portrayal of Gloria Wondrous, however, but the characters of her middle-aged mother (played by Mildred Dunnock) and Mama's best friend (portrayed by equally matronly Betty Field) that Jennifer commented on wryly. The Field character had two small Yorkshire terrier dogs whom she adored (Yorkies were Colby's favorite animal—"I'd often take my Yorkies when I visited Jennifer," she recalled), and Jennifer turned to her old friend and, referring to Dunnock and Field, said: "If that's the way we're going to end up, we'd better stop now!"

"I'll kill you!" Colby laughed.

Selznick, always scrambling for funds, was negotiating to sell remake rights to Rebecca and *Intermezzo.* He envisioned the latter, the film that had introduced Ingrid Bergman to American audiences back in 1938, as a vehicle for Leonard Bernstein (Leslie Howard had played the part in the original). Selznick suggested to Elliott Hyman, of the Seven-Arts Corporation, that in the remake "the girl" should be played by Jennifer.

A major decision involving Jennifer faced Selznick. In order to be certain Jones was retained as star of *Tender* (the studio had been showing strong signs of casting Elizabeth Taylor), he now withdrew as producer (which was what they wanted him to do) and sold the package—Jennifer and the property—to Fox. Selznick's contract seemingly protected his creative control of the enterprise. However, he continued to encounter major stumbling blocks in attempting to confirm important details for the film.

A start date for *Tender Is the Night* finally appeared on the horizon (slated for early spring of 1961). Selznick fought successfully to get at least part of the film made abroad and barraged director Henry King with memos. This time the ploy backfired. King was highly resentful of Selznick's interference, and Selznick feared he would withdraw from the picture, a potential catastrophe from Selznick's point of view because King "gets a better result [from Jennifer] than any other director she has ever worked with."

King remained on the film, but Selznick's heart sank as the studio made its final choices for important cast members. While David had envisioned (among others) twenty-four-year-old Jane Fonda, along with either Peter Ustinov or Joseph Schildkraut, Fred Astaire or Montgomery Clift, and either Louis Jourdan or Marcello Mastroianni, the key roles ultimately went to Fox contractees Jill St. John, Sanford Meisner, Tom Ewell, and Cesare Danova. And while he'd finally decided on Richard Burton or Peter O'Toole for Dick Diver, the studio rejected Burton as box office poison (and soon after signed him to replace Stephen Boyd in *Cleopatra*) and turned down O'Toole because he was an unknown (the actor was subsequently cast as *Lawrence of Arabia*). Therefore the role of Dick Diver went to Jason Robards, Jr.

Selznick strove to keep up Jennifer's spirits. Paula Strasberg was to be hired, at considerable expense, to coach the actress throughout the shoot, but privately David faced the grim possibility that the venture could turn out to be the most disappointing and disheartening experience of his professional life. It was yet another agonizing case of his having failed Jennifer, but once again his dazzling past beckoned. MGM was pulling out all stops for a lavish premiere, on March 10, 1961, in Atlanta, for the latest rerelease of *Gone With the Wind*.

Although Clark Gable had recently died (three months short of his sixtieth birthday), the studio was proceeding with its plans. Vivien Leigh and Olivia De Havilland were slated to be part of the hoopla. Selznick was of course invited, but Jennifer had no interest in or intention of accompanying him (those years of his life belonged to Irene).

Selznick told MGM he wouldn't be attending, either. Unknown to Jennifer, David had suffered a heart attack. It's amazing how he was able to travel so extensively and maintain the illusion of good health. That winter, in Cuernavaca, Mexico, Selznick and Jennifer had been houseguests of Merle Oberon and her husband, multimillionaire Bruno Pagliai. The couple's extraordinary white marble home was a haven for leading members of the international jet set, a key place for movers and shakers to visit.

Selznick's old pal, publicity chief Howard Strickling, kept after David to revisit *GWTW*, and finally the producer relented, pointing out to Strickling that the festivities were sure to be more like a wake.

At first, for David, they were. He was depressed on seeing forty-eight-year-old Vivien Leigh, whose bouts with ill health and divorce from Olivier had taken a terrible physical toll. However, Olivia De Havilland was most concerned about Selznick; he looked terribly old (although only fifty-eight), and more disturbingly, his vitality seemed gone.

On the evening of the premiere, after the film was over, the audience (including many younger viewers who'd never seen the picture) roared its approval. Selznick was summoned to the stage to speak. The thunderous ovation he received appeared to puzzle him at first—then it galvanized him. Olivia De Havilland observed that he stood straighter and taller and seemed once again to be the David she'd known.

Selznick's latest journey into his past turned out to have a therapeutic effect and revived (temporarily, at least) his enthusiasm for the future. He optioned the Broadway rights to *Gone With the Wind* from the Margaret Mitchell estate, intending to turn it into the greatest musical stage spectacular ever produced.

Lauren Bacall accompanied Jason Robards to Zurich, where he was to film Tender Is the Night. Jennifer was pleased to have "Betty" along on the shoot. Bacall confided in Jennifer that she was planning to marry Robards (Betty was three months pregnant). The couple was in the second year of a volatile romantic relationship.

"[Jason] was quite dazzling—and a little crazy," recalled Bacall. "A remarkable actor and unlike any I've ever known." People said physically he resembled Bogart, but Bacall disagreed. "Jason was a drinker," she admitted. "He was unpredictable. There was an element of danger."

If the qualities Bacall had found so irresistible in Robards had transferred to film, *Tender Is the Night* would have benefited considerably. Potent chemistry between the leads—as it had existed on film between Jennifer and William Holden—was essential if Fitzgerald's tragic love story were to have impact and ring true.

Another key role in the film, "Baby," Nicole's manipulative, richer-than-Croesus sister, was played by Joan Fontaine.

By now Fontaine's career had encompassed television (she'd

been a partner with David Niven and Dick Powell in the successful Four-Star production company), and her interests extended far beyond the confines of a soundstage. Her experience on *Tender Is the Night* would prove to be a turning point for her, as well as for Jennifer.

Filming the picture was not a carefree picnic in the playgrounds of Europe. Paula Strasberg was Jennifer's overpaid hand-holder, as adept at buttering up Jennifer as she'd been with Marilyn Monroe. Jennifer and Paula spent long hours together alone in Jones's dressing room, Strasberg a rapt, attentive, and compassionate audience for Jennifer's unending litany on her life, her career, and her woes, real and imagined.

While in the past Jennifer had presented no problems during shooting, this picture was an exception. Joan Fontaine recalls, "Jennifer couldn't be found most of the time. They had to drag her onto the set, and then she had Paula Strasberg with her constantly when we were in Switzerland.

"I felt that acting was a torture to Jennifer."

Strasberg's technique with Jones on the set duplicated the one she'd used with Marilyn Monroe. "Paula sort of nodded to Jennifer when the take was right," recalls Joan Fontaine.

Fontaine also observed that "Jennifer was always sweating profusely—it was quite amazing." She offers an explanation that makes great sense: "It might have been menopausal—or," she adds, "fear. But it was copious.

"Getting Jennifer onto the set was such a chore for them. She would just disappear. They would find her in the shower or having her hair done again."

Jennifer kept in close touch with David via transatlantic telephone. "Once, our telephone lines got crossed, and I heard her talking to David in California, asking him to come on the set," recalls Fontaine. "I heard David ask, 'What kind of tablecloths are they using? What color?' and 'What was in the box?' and she was reporting all the details to him.

"Then I hung up, feeling guilty about what I'd heard, but evidently every night they would have business conversations while he masterminded things from California."

Fontaine realized early on the movie was in big trouble. Neither the script (in which Selznick later claimed there'd been unauthorized cuts) nor Henry King, at this stage of his career, was an asset.

"King, to me, was a very distant man," relates Fontaine. "He was of the 'know your lines and say them clearly' school, and that was about all the direction we got.

"The characters played by Jennifer and Jason Robards were supposed to have been sleeping together before their marriage, and Henry King said, 'Not in my picture they don't.' It changed the whole sense of the Fitzgerald book."

Fontaine experienced a moment of truth during filming. "I remember waiting for Jennifer on the set, on my marks, waiting, till they found her, and then I sat down and waited some more, and Jennifer finally came in and I heard the stage manager say frantically, 'Bring on the girl!' That was *me*, 'the girl,' and that's just about when I decided to leave Hollywood.

"Suddenly I perceived the whole picture and was hit with the impact of the terrible Hollywood class system. Jennifer had huge dressing rooms, with paintings by Impressionists, fresh flowers, and all that going on [thanks to] David, but I realized whether she had first billing or not, she was the lead and I was the supporting lead in the film. It was the first time I'd ever done that, and I realized the stigma. Terrible, isn't it?"

Production inched along. "How insecure Jennifer was," recalls Fontaine. "Mind you, I'm very fond of her and very sympathetic toward her and understanding of her doubts of herself.

"We were going to give a joint party together, for the crew, when we left Zurich, and I said, 'There's a wonderful restaurant, we can do it there and I'll see about a private room.' Jennifer called back several times about that, and it was finally arranged through the porter of the hotel, and she called me several times about what to wear.

"Since the party was for the crew, I told her to wear slacks. We'd all get together and drink a bunch of beer and have some wonderful goulash (or whatever it is that's Hungarian—Wiener schnitzel).

"And she kept calling about what to wear, and about the time, and the tables, the menu—finally I called down to the porter and said, 'I think Ms. Jones is changing the menu.' 'Don't discuss it with me!' he yelled. 'I wash my hands of the whole thing. She has called me too many times.'

"Nerves. Insecurity. She arrived late at the party, which should have been a most informal, jolly time with the crew. But she wore a rather fashionable black taffeta cocktail dress and was all coiffed. And, of course, with her was Paula Strasberg, who sat opposite me, unsmiling, tremendously strict, emanating a no-nonsense attitude, as though this party were an intellectual, artistic enterprise.

"It was supposed to have been just gay and fun and cozy, and that's the only kind of party to give anyway. But cozy, I would think, was simply not in Jennifer's understanding."

Fontaine comments on the fact that Jennifer required an "acting coach," drawing an obvious conclusion. "Jennifer simply didn't believe in herself. If you're over forty and have to have a coach on the set. . . ."

After filming on *Tender* concluded in Switzerland, Robards and Bacall planned to be married in Vienna. "Jennifer gave us a wedding dinner on the eve of our departure. She was a wonderful, caring friend," recalled Bacall.

Back in California, as *Tender* filming wrapped on soundstages at 20th Century–Fox, "There was the swimming pool incident," recalls Joan Fontaine. It occurred on a Sunday at the house on Tower Grove Drive. "Jennifer came down late, just before lunch was being served," recalls Fontaine. "After lunch she disappeared again, and we were playing pool with Romaine Gary and we were all having great fun.

"I must have wanted to go to the powder room, and as I passed the pool I saw George Masters swimming. I called out to him, 'What are you doing here?' and he said, 'Well, I did her hair before lunch, and she wore the same outfit—she has a duplicate—I've done her hair again and she's drying and she'll put on the duplicate and come out and say good-bye to you.' "

Bacall and Robards had decided to tie the knot in Las Vegas after Viennese authorities raised technical questions. "Jennifer would be my matron of honor," Bacall recalled, but again there were problems (regarding the Mexican divorce Robards had obtained from his second wife). A new game plan took the lovers to Mexico, where they were finally wed on July 4.

"David and Jennifer gave a large party," recalled Bacall, "which ended slightly disastrously with Jason drunk and all of us up until seven in the morning."

It was also the twentieth year since Jennifer and David first met, and their twelfth wedding anniversary.

Jennifer was the only actress of her generation still being cast as an ingenue, but that situation was fast approaching a finale. (The ingenue's twenty-one-year-old son, Robert Walker, Jr., was studying at the Actors Studio in New York and made his TV acting debut in a production of *The Picture of Dorian Gray*.)

Selznick was heartsick and outraged that all of his advice had been disregarded and his efforts to lift *Tender Is the Night* to the ranks of distinguished films had been thwarted at every turn.

Jennifer could do nothing, that summer and fall of 1961, but wait for the picture to open. She and David, for all practical purposes, led separate lives much of the time. Selznick was still a social animal, who loved parties and get-togethers. Jennifer, as always, preferred solitude and did much of her socializing on the telephone.

She did, on rare occasions, attend a Hollywood party. One was hosted by Debbie Reynolds and her new husband, shoe magnate Harry Karl. The guests of honor were Marge and Gower Champion (the couple was celebrating a wedding anniversary). As Debbie recalled the evening, "Lana Turner and Ricardo Montalban rhumbaed and Jennifer sat on the floor, observing."

With an opening date for *Tender* approaching, Jennifer, at David's urging, reluctantly granted several interviews. She met with Joe Hyams, and during their encounter Jennifer evolved, in Hyams's words, "from little girl to frightened woman." She sipped "a serenity cocktail [yeast and egg]" and held a silver-mounted teak "witch" cane with her other hand. "You're my weakness," She told Hyams. "You always get me to talk." She then proceeded to tell him virtually nothing.

She voiced a strong opinion on current actors in the public eye. "There are no more 'stars,' " she said wistfully. "There are only actors—good, bad, and mediocre. You meet attractive people socially, but it's the ones with talent you remember. You go to the movies to see talent, not just beauty. Personality plus talent is what makes an actor. Good looks is the bonus."

With other reporters she discussed the fact that in creating her performance as Nicole, she'd taken a "new approach" to acting, an approach she compared to religion.

Her performance in *Tender Is the Night* was the result of intense, agonizing long-range preparation, and for her the results represented her key to future successes—or else, in her words, she'd be "finished in pictures."

Tender Is the Night had a disastrous preview in Riverside, California, and David tried to "steel" Jennifer—and himself—for the worst. He made a futile last attempt to convince Spyros Skouras to withdraw the picture from scheduled openings abroad so the picture could be reedited.

The film opened nationally in February 1962. Jennifer had attended the New York premiere, in January, at the ornate Paramount Theater on Broadway and Forty-third Street. Beautifully coiffed and formally gowned, she arrived two hours late, and the crowds lined up outside the theater, who'd been waiting impatiently for a peek at the star, screamed their approval as she stepped out of her gleaming black Cadillac limousine. She waved to the throng, and photographers' flashbulbs exploded like fireworks as publicists escorted her into the theater.

The movie palace itself, all marble, crystal, and velvet, was an appropriate setting for a film set in the twenties. The black-tie audience applauded the credits and shouted approval of Jennifer's first close-up. Cameraman Leon Shamroy had done his job well. All the incredible effort Jennifer and George Masters had poured into her appearance had produced a good result. ("Maybe Masters should have directed the picture," quipped columnist Louis Sobol.)

Henry King's direction was extremely slow paced, and although Jennifer's performance was solid (especially in the latter part of the picture), there were absolutely no sparks between her and Robards; the juice came from Joan Fontaine, who tackled the role of Baby with energy and wit.

Jennifer didn't fare badly with the critics. "Miss Jones, absent from the screen since *A Farewell to Arms* . . . emerges a crisply fresh, intriguing personality and creates a striking character as the schizophrenic Nicole," wrote *Variety*.

Time magazine appreciated Jennifer's efforts: ". . . . in recent films the lady has limited her expressions largely to a toneless hysterical laugh and an alarming tic. But in *Night* she is well cast as a neurotic and does her best work in a decade."

"Jennifer Jones is quite proficient as the mercurial Nicole, proceeding from a state of mental anguish to one of rigid and heartless self-control," wrote *The New York Times*.

But others lambasted her and the film. "Miss Jones works hard at being Nicole, but cannot embody her," wrote *The New Yorker.* "The cast in nearly every case is unsuitable. The chief objection to be made to them is that they're all too old. . . ."

The only element of the movie to win popular appeal and an Oscar nomination was the title song (which Selznick abhorred) by Sammy Fain and Paul Francis Webster.

Chapter
28

*O*nly *work could make Hollywood* endurable for Jennifer at this point. The Tower Grove estate was quietly on the market, if a suitable buyer could be found (one wasn't). With no roles in sight the disheartened actress, determined to maintain her sanity, kissed David good-bye and fled to India to practice yoga and meditate.

The results were in evidence. After her return to the States, "I met her in California, taking frequent walks on the beach," recalls Gerald Gordon. "They were long walks—ten miles, from Malibu to Santa Monica. She walked along the shore, and I remember she wore a large sunhat, white shirt, and rolled-up white pants.

"She seemed quite different from the way she'd been in New York. There was a strength about her now—something regal. She looked older and more movie star–like, but she looked as though she were already past the whole 'star' trip.

"I found the change in her quite a contradiction, an absolute contrast to how she'd been in New York, and in such a short span of time! In New York she'd been like a kid, ill at ease. In California there was a real inner beauty about her. There was a difference in her posture, she looked like she owned the ocean."

Jennifer and Selznick met with noted playwright/screenwriter

William Inge and Inge's associate, John R. Connolly, after Inge had won the Oscar for his screenplay of *Splendor in the Grass* (the picture, directed by Elia Kazan, had launched Inge protegé Warren Beatty as a screen star, and given twenty-two-year-old Natalie Wood the most powerful dramatic role of her career to date). The purpose of the get-together was to discuss upcoming projects for Jennifer.

Jennifer and Inge were instantly simpatico (the writer was leery of dogs; Jennifer had several, immediately saw Inge's discomfort, and without a word put them in another room). "I think one of the reasons Bill and Jennifer got along so well is that they had similar roots," recalled John Connolly. "Bill was from Kansas and reacted to Jennifer as 'hometown' people. She responded to him because he spun stories for her.

"Jennifer had a sense of humor," Connolly recalls. "She'd toss off little 'asides' about people and events. Bill and I knew Jennifer had been in the same acting class with Marilyn. We knew Marilyn well, and Jennifer was quite a different personality—Jennifer had a temper, and was not insecure in the same way Marilyn was.

"Bill told me he'd have loved to use Jennifer as the lead in a play he was writing [which he never finished] about a grande dame who married an older man, a wildcatter."

Connolly described the Selznicks' marriage as "tactile. For example, when David became upset after certain phone calls he received, she tried to calm him and massaged his head."

Connolly and Inge were impressed with Jennifer, "and she was really beautiful," recalls Connolly. "She had the most incredible skin."

The beautiful Jennifer Jones had also just become a grandmother. Bob junior's wife, Ellie, had recently given birth to a daughter, named Michelle, and the family was living in the cottage on the grounds of the Selznick estate.

Selznick continued to option properties for Jennifer. One unlikely prospect was *The Wall*, John Hersey's novel about the Warsaw ghetto uprising. Jack Garfein had discussions with Selznick about it, and Garfein recalled: "Selznick insisted that Jennifer Jones play the female lead. 'We'll put a Jewish nose on Jennifer,' he told me!"

Selznick himself was approached by Jack L. Warner, who offered him a two-picture deal, acceding to all of Selznick's concomitant demands. The contracts were drawn up, but Selznick suddenly backed down. "I can't bring myself to sign it," he said. He confided to John Houseman that he realized he could never surpass *Gone With the Wind* and said that producing for television now appealed to him.

To Jennifer's consternation, she was grist for the tabloids that summer of 1962. Marilyn Monroe's death at the age of thirty-six had inspired a rash of articles dealing with "mysterious Hollywood deaths," including, of course, Robert Walker's. Hedda Hopper wrote poignantly about her late friend and commented on how "Bob Walker, Jr. . . . looks exactly like his father. . . . Director George Seaton tells me Bob will be as fine an actor as his father," she said.

Hedda then focused on Jennifer. "Jennifer Jones is still a very beautiful woman, her face unlined by age," she noted. "She is very nervous while acting, hating to be watched at work by anybody . . . flinching at even routine questions when she's interviewed." Hopper offered her own opinion on Jennifer's feelings about Robert Walker—"It must be easy for Jennifer to remember and mighty hard to forget."

Selznick admitted to intimates that he was broke, but all agreed that David being broke "is not like the ordinary person's being broke." There was income from distribution of Selznick's films overseas, where *Duel in the Sun* had proven a reliable and consistent draw; there was cash from the sale of some of Jennifer's jewelry. Selznick was also cashing in life insurance policies and had other prospects for revenue.

The sorry fact that Jennifer was no longer generating a yearly six-figure income didn't help matters, but the family's lifestyle never altered. Once again, this time with David and Mary Jennifer, Jennifer spent the winter in Zurich. On trips with Jennifer to New York, David insisted on thousands of dollars' worth of fresh flowers throughout their suite every day.

Jennifer made no films in 1963. Almost two decades earlier, in reply to an inquiry to "borrow" Jennifer, Selznick had told RKO president Charles Koerner that "Miss Jones's career is mine to build and protect. . . . I should be very disappointed if she is not a very great star for the next ten or fifteen years."

Her career had lasted as long as Selznick had predicted and as long as his own energy had held out. Like Garbo, Jennifer had gone down without a struggle. "It could have happened to anyone—and frequently did," observed David Niven.

Selznick's former *Duel in the Sun* publicity chief, Paul Mac-Namara, brought Selznick together with wealthy investors to discuss producing a film on the life of Winston Churchill, with Jennifer as Jennie Churchill. It was another hot idea that cooled down and evaporated. Sam Goldwyn and Sam Spiegel tried to line up projects for David, to no avail.

Jennifer became a grandmother for the second time when daughter-in-law Ellie gave birth to a son, named David.

For the time being David was somehow able to withhold from Jennifer the fact that his health was failing (he'd suffered yet another heart attack). The couple's seventeen-year age difference suddenly weighed heavily indeed. Jennifer was a strong, healthy woman, while Selznick had physically become almost an old man (the early years of Benzedrine abuse had effected a heavy toll). However, he continued to play knight in shining armor for his wife and daughter, whom he called "Jennifer the first" and "Jennifer the second."

One afternoon Elia Kazan was a visitor to the Tower Grove mansion. Selznick was once again searching for a buyer for his files of story synopses and scripts. On subsequently perusing the material, Kazan noted ruefully that the dozens of properties had been intended as vehicles for Jennifer (Selznick's preoccupation with her career was now, in some Hollywood circles, a subject of ridicule).

For the moment, Jennifer seemed perfectly content not to have imminent film commitments, or the anxiety that went with them. Shirley MacLaine, Ann-Margret, Natalie Wood, Julie Andrews, Julie Christie, and, of course, Elizabeth Taylor were the actresses in demand and receiving tremendous attention.

To draw down the immense premiums on his remaining life insurance policies (Jennifer was beneficiary), early in 1964 David submitted, without Jennifer's knowledge, to a thorough physical examination. It came as no great surprise to the man "who knew himself very well" to discover how ill he might soon become.

He confided the news, not to Jennifer (he didn't want to appear a sick old man in her eyes), but to Irene only and sought her help in locating the best cardiologist.

• • •

Robert Walker, Jr., was apparently oblivious of Ben Jonson's observation, "Greatness of name in the father oft-times overwhelms the son" (Peter Fonda, who faced the same dilemma, was one of Walker Jr.'s best friends). It seemed Bob was on the verge of launching a highly successful career as an actor. "He was adorable looking," recalls Betty Spiegel, who met him socially. "It was eerie how much he looked like his father . . . except he was even more handsome."

Walker and Shelley Winters toured in *Days of the Dancing*, a play that the producers hoped to bring to Broadway; but the show closed on the road.

Walker was always being compared to his father, and at first he said that he considered it "a compliment. He was a fine, marvelous actor and did some good things." However, Bob shared with his mother an intrinsic dislike for publicity, along with Jennifer's lack of flair for it. He admitted bluntly, "Everything I've done so far has been pretty lousy," and he began expressing second thoughts on being compared to Walker, Sr. "Actually, I don't think actors can be compared unless they have played the same part."

To the countless actors who'd never get a foot in the door, the following complaint by Walker hardly won him either friends or sympathy. "I would like to be able to develop as an actor in obscurity. What success I've had is wonderful . . . but everything I do is under a spotlight. I'm really just getting born as an actor, and birth ought to be a more private affair."

Michael, a student majoring in geology at UCLA, suddenly switched gears. He, too, came to New York to pursue an acting career. Jennifer was disappointed. "Being an archaeologist sounded so glamorous," she said. "Acting is rough . . . there are so many heartbreaks, you don't want it for your children."

In Europe David Selznick suffered severe chest pains around the time of his sixty-second birthday. He didn't want Jennifer to know and told her he was in the hospital because he'd broken his ankle (which he had).

Jennifer and Mary Jennifer joined David and the Louis Jourdans in Antibes for the summer, where Selznick, ensconced at the Hotel du Câp, went through the motions of lining up deals. The myth, over the years, that even at this point Jennifer was somehow blissfully unaware of David's illness and that only Irene knew the truth (a tale Irene herself promulgated) is set straight by Anita Colby. Jennifer had asked Anita to join her and David overseas:

"Jennifer knew—and I knew—that David could die at any moment. I joined them because I wanted to see him. They were having a big summer, with Mary Jennifer celebrating her tenth birthday.

"In private Jennifer was despondent about David. 'I can wake up in the morning and he can be dead next to me,' Jennifer told me.

"I looked out the window, at David and Mary Jennifer playing together. 'And there he is,' I said, 'sitting outside with Mary Jennifer, a big grin on his face, playing *parapluie de ma tante*. (Mary Jennifer could speak better French than David!)

"Jennifer never gave up," Colby says softly, "and never told David she knew how ill he was."

Anxious to bolster his modest estate by selling remaining company assets, Selznick traveled to New York with Mary Jennifer. David was more devoted to the little girl than ever, and his final goal was to insure her financial future, along with Jennifer's. (Irene claims that during this period Jennifer only visited David and Mary Jennifer "from time to time.")

Selznick's twenty-seven-year-old son, Danny (Jeffrey was in Europe), was on hand to help his father through these trying days and often entertained half sister Mary Jennifer when David wasn't up to it or had business appointments.

Ill as David was, there was still a lot of traveling going on for both Selznick and Jennifer. Incredibly, Selznick found the energy and the desire to discreetly indulge in yet another personal relationship. The woman was attractive, not in "the business," and her unconditional adoration obviously provided a necessary boost to his ego.

Selznick had been sent the script of a new play, *Goddess on a Couch*, by Patricia Joudry, which inspired him to attempt one last burst of entrepreneurial activity. The play, about the wife of a psychiatrist, seemed a perfect vehicle for Jennifer, and she agreed. The prospect of collaborating with his wife on the project, a comedy, seemed to lift both their spirits. Selznick, naturally, was thinking big—if it proved successful in out-of-town tryouts, the play would return Jennifer to the Broadway stage (and bring in lots of income).

Irene was fearful the effort would prove too much, but David's mind was made up. Getting involved with production might be better than all the medicine prescribed by his doctors. It was soon evident, however, that he couldn't handle it, and Danny Selznick agreed to take over.

Jennifer plunged into the venture with her usual concentration and focus. It was a most welcome distraction from her worries about David, whom she continued to consult, ardently and frequently, about the play. Danny Selznick had suggested a new title for the work, *The Man with the Perfect Wife,* and both Jennifer and David were delighted.

On March 2, 1965, Jennifer celebrated her forty-sixth birthday. The play was booked at the Royal Poinciana Playhouse in Palm Beach from March 22 through March 27, and then from March 30 through the second week in April it would run at the Coconut Grove Playhouse in Miami.

George Masters accompanied her to Palm Beach. "In one big scene in a psychiatrist's office, she had to stand on her head in some sort of yoga position," recalled Masters. "I had to be on call backstage every night to do her touch-up after this scene. I did touch-ups for all her scenes, of course, but the long standing-on-her-head scene was especially important because her hair got so messed up."

Securing Masters's services had been no easy task: he'd turned down an appeal from, among others, Audrey Hepburn, who wanted Masters to do her makeup and hair for the Academy Awards. Masters had told Hepburn he'd be happy to fly back, but Jennifer had other ideas.

"Julius [Masters's assistant] could have done [Jennifer] just as well for one night," Masters recalled, "but the truth is that Jennifer Jones would have stood on her head forever to keep me from flying back to do Audrey Hepburn—or anyone else, for that matter. I could never tell Jennifer I had to do somebody else. She would accidentally on purpose put cold cream in her hair or anything to keep me there with her."

David Brown, in New York, received a call from David Selznick, telling him that Jennifer was appearing in a play, "and David convinced me with his enormous powers of persuasion that I '*must* come and see Jennifer in this play.' He was so proud of her! I said, 'I'm not going to Florida, David, I'm going to L.A.!' Selznick hadn't lost his sense of humor. He said, 'For twenty-five dollars more, you can go through Miami,' which was the big promotion the airlines were offering at that time. I laughed and said, 'Okay!'

"I flew down and saw the play and liked it very much. The last I saw of Jennifer and David, they were walking arm in arm, like lovers, into the night.

"The next thing I heard was that David had died."

*T*he end came only two months after
Jennifer's play had closed. Selznick had become ever more frail and
gaunt, robbed of his stamina and energy by his relentless illness.
But he'd refused to become an invalid, and Jennifer was determined to allow him to maintain his dignity. Both were playing a
poignant, painful game, and David had somehow found the physical wherewithal to keep on the move.

He'd just celebrated, to his surprise, his sixty-third birthday (his
father had died at the age of sixty-two). But at a dinner party in New
York, in considerable pain and discomfort, he collapsed. He recovered and returned to Los Angeles.

Jennifer did all that could be done to create an anxiety-free environment for David at home. She spent hours talking and joking with
him, holding his hand and tending to his every need. They talked
about the old days and the future, with Jennifer reassuring him that
the best was yet to come. If he didn't believe it, he pretended that he
did, and so did she.

Selznick, who'd returned to California while Jennifer was appearing in the play, had felt well enough to accept an invitation to
speak at a celebrity-packed black-tie dinner honoring Alfred Hitchcock, now an industry unto himself, steered to rarefied heights by

the man who now ran Hollywood: Lew Wasserman, chief stock-holder and president of MCA-Universal.

At the dinner, Selznick was greeted enthusiastically by the high-powered crowd, which included Sam Goldwyn and Jack Warner as well as the new young Turks of the industry. After getting his speech off to a strong start, decrying what was happening in the movie business, David rambled on and the audience grew bored and restless.

"It was very disturbing," said Hitchcock. "David had been one of the most dynamic men in Hollywood, but his vigor and passion seemed sadly dimmed."

Former Selznick publicity director Russell Birdwell, now a lead-ing independent PR executive, bought daily space in *The Hollywood Reporter* and wrote a colorful series of columns singing Selznick's praises. He recounted the producer's past accomplishments and urged Selznick to return to the business: "The industry needs you, David!"

Selznick thanked Birdwell but told him that he feared people would think that he (Selznick) had paid Birdwell to write the columns. Birdwell made it clear, in large type in the final column, on June 22, that the producer had had nothing to do with either the idea or its execution.

Selznick seemed in good spirits that day and in better physical shape than he'd been. He kissed Jennifer good-bye and went down-town for a midday business meeting with his attorney, Barry Brannen.

During the meeting in Brannen's office, Selznick grew suddenly pale, complained of chest pains, and asked to lie down. He said he felt dizzy. Brannen immediately summoned an ambulance and called Jennifer.

Shocked, she rushed to Cedars-Sinai Hospital. David arrived at one P.M., and Jennifer watched through a window as doctors strug-gled for an hour and a half to save David's life. A veteran nurses' aide, Jennifer was no stranger to hospitals. This time, however, the jarring wail of the emergency room alarm, summoning additional help and signifying a patient dying, was sounding for her hus-band. . . .

It seemed like an eternity waiting for the doctor to emerge from the room, but when he did it was clear that the end had come for the great David O. Selznick. "I'm sorry, Mrs. Selznick, we did all we could. He's gone." And with him went the strength on which Jennifer had relied for so many years.

Arrangements had to be made. Selznick had requested a simple funeral, but with Jennifer's blessings Jeffrey and Danny Selznick took over. An impressive memorial service was held at the Church of the Recessional at Forest Lawn Memorial Park (the Jewish temple could not accommodate the couple of hundred guests). Rabbi Max Nussbaum of Temple Israel officiated.

Many key figures from Selznick's past came together for the sad occasion, including Jock Whitney, William Paley, Katharine Hepburn, the Louis Jourdans, Lauren Bacall, Cary Grant, George Cukor, and Joseph Cotten. Paley, William Wyler, Sam Spiegel, Sam Goldwyn, Alfred Hitchcock, and Christopher Isherwood served as pallbearers.

Despite Jennifer's entreaties, Irene Selznick chose to remain in New York.

Katharine Hepburn, at Jennifer's request, read Kipling's "If." William Paley, too emotional to read the tribute he'd written, asked Cary Grant to do it. George Cukor read a moving tribute by Truman Capote, and Joseph Cotten spoke also.

Afterward intimate family friends gathered at the Tower Grove home to exchange remembrances of David, and all wondered silently what would become of Jennifer.

In the weeks following Selznick's death, in an attempt to rise above the suffocating feeling of loneliness surrounding her, Jennifer clung desperately to her former routine. She made every effort not to think about what had happened, dwelling instead on all the nice things she and David had done together and on the happy times.

But she was undeniably aware of the truth. A great part of her life, indeed her very self, had belonged to David Selznick. They had lived together so long and shared so much. For a time it had been difficult to ascertain where "Jennifer Jones" began and ended or where David began or ended.

George Masters recalled, "Jennifer went into a long period of depression and became almost like a hermit, a recluse. I had to be at her beck and call more than ever. She consumed a great deal of my time."

It was a terrible period of adjustment, and according to Anita

Colby, it was eleven-year-old Mary Jennifer who'd been irreparably affected by David's passing. For the present, the child seemed to settle into a normal routine as she continued her private schooling at Buckley.

Jennifer dutifully fulfilled her obligations as mother, but the birth of her children hadn't triggered a life-changing perspective on her priorities. Now she faced a questionable future. She hadn't made a film in four years. People she knew were becoming ill and growing older. Where had the time gone?

At forty-six she was at a most difficult age for an actress and was suddenly on her own for the first time in her adult life (one recalls Joan Fontaine's observation of Jennifer: "She was simply not a fighter"). Her champion was dead, a reality she didn't want to acknowledge but could not escape.

Betty Spiegel understood Jennifer's dilemma. "A man like David Selznick—and my late husband—these men were a life force! I think any relationship involving an older man and younger woman centers around the fact that the woman is his little girl, he takes care of and protects her, and the woman feels very protected. Jennifer was protected *from life!*"

George Masters claims that "Jennifer tried to commit suicide during her depression after Selznick's death."

Most obituaries on Selznick claimed he'd provided a "great fortune" in his will. The unfortunate truth was that while there was sufficient capital to provide Jennifer with a comfortable lifestyle, there hadn't even been ample funds to provide cash bequests for Jeffrey and Danny (who had, in any event, been amply provided for by their mother and grandparents).

Jennifer would soon have to make major decisions about her future. David wasn't there anymore to tell her what to do and how to do it.

She resumed her acting classes, but while she was at a standstill as to her personal and professional life, the world around her was in flux. Only a few miles from her secluded estate, the Watts riots had erupted. The 1960s, by mid-decade, had evolved into a time of assassinations, war, and youth rebellion. A powerful counterculture had sprouted. Contemporary movies reflected all that was happening, and in the new marketplace "Jennifer Jones" was an anachronism. This was a reality Phylis Isley Walker Selznick would have to contend with and confront; she was an actress on the edge of nowhere.

Fate, as always in Jennifer's case, threw her a life preserver, and she grabbed it.

Chapter

30

*S*he hadn't been the producer's first (or even second) choice for the role, although she later claimed that she was. "Do it, Jennifer. You *should* do it, you *must* do it," advised Colby and her other friends. Jennifer's analyst encouraged her, too, although stepping back in front of the cameras was a terrifying prospect.

The voice that'd made the difference in selecting Jennifer belonged to a young man who'd never met her but had appreciated her performances over the years. "There was always something about Jennifer," recalls actor Michael Parks. " 'Interesting' is not the right word. I remember liking her so much in *Duel in the Sun*. I have some American Indian in me, and when I saw *Duel* she just had that authentic look."

Parks, a young actor on the rise, was the exciting newcomer expected to replace the late James Dean ("Try and live with that," Dean had said when he was expected to "replace" Marlon Brando). Parks had been signed to star opposite Kim Stanley in the film drama *The Idol*, based on a script by Millard Lampell. Production had already begun in London.

"I always thought that Kim Stanley was our best American actress," states Parks, and he and Stanley had become friends. "Kim and I came to England on the boat together," he recalls, "and Kim, who had just separated from her husband, eventually withdrew from the film."

The producers searched frantically for a suitable replacement. "I remember Jennifer's name was thrown in with five or six [other actresses]. I said no, the one who will be the best will be Jennifer." Parks had "a simpatico feeling, a respect" for her. And a very specific reason for feeling Jennifer was perfect casting. The film's story line concerned a mother whose nineteen-year-old son's friend (Parks) seduces her. Park's felt that it would be more effective for his character to seduce someone like a Jennifer Jones ("someone with class, grace, and elegance") than a blatantly sexy actress.

Parks explains. "It just seemed to me that the whole denouement of *The Idol* is when I seduce her—and it's only an act of revenge," Parks states with emphasis, "it's not something that is passionate, or heartfelt, or physical, or anything else—it's just merely an insidious or obliquitous experience.

"So I jumped in at the mention of Jennifer's name, and thank God they bought it."

Back in the States, things moved fast. Jennifer had just three days to decide. She was totally unaccustomed to the lack of preparation she faced regarding the role.

Still reeling over David's death, she accepted the offer (and later admitted it had come not a moment too soon, although she also said, "From now on I'm not going to allow myself to be pressured"). Filming began in early November, and George Masters provided her with his expert services, creating a very contemporary haircut and makeup for her (similar to the look he gave Audrey Hepburn, the next year, for *Wait Until Dark*).

Without David to consult and complain to and lean on for support, Jennifer plunged nervously into the film and fortunately found in Michael Parks an empathetic, sympathetic colleague. Parks echoes sentiments voiced by previous key men in Jennifer's life. "There is a thing about Jennifer that you do want to protect. . . ."

Parks understood and appreciated Jennifer's peculiar, very personal dilemma. "There was not a stronger personality than David O. Selznick in Hollywood—as Frank Capra said, that was the epitome of your name above the title: 'David O. Selznick presents G-O-D.'

"While people in Des Moines or Blue Shit, Idaho, would probably know more of Jennifer than they would David Selznick, in Hollywood he'd been a king. Jennifer was more 'Mrs. Selznick' than she was 'Jennifer Jones' and had been for such a long time that when Selznick died, Hollywood felt the world might as well have known that Jennifer died with him. Furthermore, they didn't really care!

"From the minute [Selznick] was gone, the phone [stopped] ringing. [It was a] terribly, terribly hard, desperate thing to go through, and I felt great sympathy for her for that."

Stepping into a role that'd been earmarked for the brilliant Kim Stanley must have intimidated Jennifer to some extent.

"We never confronted that, and I certainly wouldn't bring it up and no one else did, thank God. But I'm sure that bothered her," says Parks. "She was nervous in the very beginning and preoccupied. She hadn't worked in a while. I do remember the first day's shooting. In front of Jennifer I said something to the director, Dan Petrie, that there was something in the scene that was just 'unadulterated horseshit,' and I remember Jennifer stiffening.

"A little later Petrie came up to me and said how she disliked vulgarity or something to that effect. So, with Jennifer, I did kind of watch my *p*'s and *q*'s in that way.

"I'll never forget, it was about two weeks later she came up to me and said, 'Well, this is just unadulterated horseshit.' She'd repeated what I'd said! She had relaxed, and I just laughed."

They became friends and found they'd shared a traumatic experience: working with John Huston. "Jennifer had suffered through it. I'd suffered through it. She was never resentful in recalling it, and I don't remember her even saying anything bad about Huston. But she would tremble just talking about it [climbing the mast for *Beat the Devil*]—she would start to shake."

On *The Idol*, Jennifer contended as best she could with the usual behind-the-scenes attention that surrounds a star. "She was shying away from that," recalls Michael Parks.

"I don't know how much attention one can get or one needs at that point in life," observes Parks. "I mean, my God, she'd had years of attention, and it never seemed to have gone to her head. I don't think it was the attention of fame that she needed—" Parks articulates a crucial point—"I think she needed personal attention."

In London she met handsome British actor Stephen Boyd, and gossip columnists implied a romance. Neither Jennifer nor Boyd commented on the reports.

At this point in her career, Jennifer was in no position to turn down requests for interviews. She'd been off the screen for years, and the producers of *The Idol* expected her cooperation. Jennifer compromised and agreed to selected sit-downs with the press.

She bristled when the term *comeback* was raised, pointing out to a reporter that in her particular case there'd always been years between projects. The actress had brought Mary Jennifer with her to London, and mother and daughter seemed to have a loving relationship. They were staying at the Savoy Hotel. "David and I always liked the river view," she told Sheilah Graham. "But I'm looking ahead, not back. I have many plans. There's a possibility that I'll film the life of Aimee Semple McPherson. I've had it in mind for a long time."

Graham had known Jennifer for many years and offered the opinion that Jennifer hadn't known the score in her early Hollywood days.

"I don't think I do now," Jones replied bluntly, adding, "We make our lives more complicated." *Duel in the Sun* was appearing on television for the first time, and Graham praised the picture. Jennifer then made a startling admission: "I didn't see any of my films until I'd waited ten years . . . I didn't have the courage. But then I sat down for two weeks and saw them all. It was pretty devastating. You see things you wish you'd not done, but you can't do anything about it." And as for *Tender Is the Night*—"As far as I'm concerned, *Tender Is the Night* was never made," she replied.

Regarding Jennifer's children, the actress complained about how producers had already typecast her sons. "Both of them are baby-faced killers," she said, "and [producers] will never see them as anything else on television. . . ."

Mary Jennifer, who'd dropped the "Mary" from her name, was, according to her mother, "like a Gypsy; she doesn't really care where she lives. My sons always felt put upon when they had to travel to Switzerland and Paris . . . but they now realize that they had a marvelous time as children. But [Mary] Jennifer enjoys it all now. She's got David's brain, thank goodness. She came on *The Idol* set and said, 'Why can't I be in the picture?' Perhaps she'll be an actress when she grows up. But I hope she'll finish school first."

Jennifer was relieved when she'd fulfilled her obligations and the intrusive interviews were over.

As filming on *The Idol* progressed. Jennifer brought a delicacy and poignance to her scenes that was very much her own and quite different from the approach another actress would have taken. "You could not only see it, you could *feel* the blush in Jennifer," says Michael Parks, echoing Charlton Heston's comments.

Jennifer was instrumental in launching an important relationship in Michael's life. "Jennifer did something for me for which I will be forever grateful," he says. "She introduced me to a man— Jean Renoir—who became my best friend in life and actually *saved* me from I don't know what, from not leaving the business for sure.

"My brother had died during [the making of] *The Idol,* and I was ready to just pack it in. I didn't think I was going to make it.

"I saw Renoir every day for a year and a half. He was my closest friend until his death."

Renoir, too, had loved Jennifer in films, and the three became close friends.

"To me, Jennifer was like a reed in the wind—an extremely sensitive hybrid of delicate flowers," says Michael Parks. "I really don't think you would want to yell 'boo' behind her—she was—is—a sweet, nice lady. A thoroughbred."

Jennifer's friendship with Parks continued after production was completed.

The Idol was to be released in the summer of 1966. Advance word on the film, however, didn't arouse the kind of excitement that inspired other producers to seek her out. The actress, throughout most of the year, was professionally and personally adrift.

"I used to see her," recalls Michael Parks. "I would call her or she'd call me . . . [and invite] me to some parties, but I've never been one for those."

Jennifer did manage to convince Parks to attend one or two, "and I was glad I did," he said. "I met interesting people—Christopher Isherwood, for one—people I would never have met were it not for Jennifer."

A stage revival of ⟨The Country Girl⟩ was to be produced by Jean Dalrymple at the City Center in New York. A source affiliated with the production recalls that Lee Strasberg, who controlled the rights to the play, initially rejected Jennifer when her name was mentioned as a suitable star for the play.

The idea to cast her in *The Country Girl* had originated with actor Franchot Tone. Strasberg was enthusiastic about Tone portraying

Frank Elgin (played in the film by Bing Crosby), not only because it was a great role for the actor, but because Tone had provided financing to launch the famous Group Theater.

Dalrymple was a legend in her own right, "a little girl from Morristown, New Jersey," who'd become a leading light on the Broadway scene. She was a woman with great spirit and drive, a former actress and publicist who'd been good friends with David and Myron Selznick when all were teenagers living in Manhattan only a few blocks apart. "They used to like to come over to my apartment to play gin," recalls Dalrymple. "The three of us would play like mad!

"I was in vaudeville at that time," she continues. "I was an actress, and both David and Myron said they were going to be great film producers. I said to David, 'And you will make me a star!' He looked at me and said, 'No, you're not pretty enough.' "

Dalrymple was currently director of the Light Opera and Drama Companies of the New York City Center. For years she had been searching for a vehicle she could produce for Franchot Tone. "I had a terrible time planning something Franchot would like to do." Now that Tone wanted to do *The Country Girl,* Dalrymple was determined to make it happen. A source on the scene recalls that when Dalrymple told Strasberg that Franchot had suggested casting Jennifer, Strasberg's reaction was, "I don't think Jennifer has had much stage experience."

Tone continued to campaign for Jennifer as his costar, and she was eventually signed for the part. "I approached her directly," recalls Dalrymple. "I deal with most everybody directly. An agent negotiated the contracts, but the contracts were very simple. Everybody at City Center worked at Actors Equity minimum, so there were never any arguments."

No sooner had rehearsals started than disaster struck. "We were right on top of the first rehearsal week when Franchot was taken ill," Dalrymple recalls. "He went to the hospital for tests. They discovered cancer of the lungs. . . ." Tone was replaced by Joseph Anthony. The role of the director, played on screen by William Holden, was to be performed by Rip Torn.

Dalrymple kept in close touch with Strasberg and invited him to the rehearsals. According to onlookers, Jennifer became "nervous" in his presence. Queried about Strasberg's cruel streak and how it could interfere with certain actors delivering a good performance, Dalrymple replies: "I never saw that side of him at all. He was always extremely nice to me." But, she concedes, "A lot of people told me they had hard times with him."

Dalrymple tried to reassure Jennifer. "Lee likes you very much," she told her. But Jennifer was scared of him. It was pointed out that Strasberg "scares the hell out of everybody."

"I was dying to see her give a great performance," says Jean Dalrymple. "A lot of people had said to me, 'Why Jennifer Jones, for God's sake?' that kind of thing, and I said, 'I think she's *good!* I'd always liked her very much, and I liked her work.

"I'd met her years earlier in California (and later in New York). She was a nice, unassuming person, rather on the quiet and shy side, and I was surprised at what a good actress she was.

"In California I saw her in a play in one of the little theaters. She was very good and handled herself very well. I've worked with Grace Kelly, too, and Jennifer reminds me a lot of Grace. They didn't look alike, of course, but they had a very similar quality. I hate to say it, but they had a 'ladylike' quality that I admired, and which was essential for certain parts. That's why both were perfect casting for *The Country Girl*."

Dalrymple soon recognized a major problem troubling the *Country Girl* production. "The whole company was never really a *company*. I never felt that they were all working together, they never all had the same 'pace,' and therefore the play didn't have a rhythm to it, which a good play always has."

Dalrymple states bluntly that "Jennifer held the show together. She was the only one, because the cast kind of fell apart when Franchot [had to drop out]. It was like they were all expecting him to be there, and when he wasn't, they just couldn't make it."

The revival might have worked, according to those on the scene, if Strasberg had left it alone. "As soon as the actors would get some pace, Strasberg would say, 'It's too fast,' and he would slow it right down," recalls another source. "Ms. Dalrymple would encourage the director to 'get it moving, for goodness' sake, it's dying on its feet,' and he would, but then Strasberg came in and said, 'It's all wrong,' and poor Jean was stymied. The director was afraid of Strasberg, too!

"The pace *was* quickened, but on the afternoon of opening night, Strasberg showed up during a run-through and slowed it down, and made Jennifer very nervous."

Dalrymple was heartbroken with the results. "I felt terrible about that production." She felt so bad that "I put it all out of my mind . . . the only good thing about that whole production for me personally was Jennifer."

The show opened on September 29, 1966. "Miss Jones read most of her lines in a dull, listless fashion and appeared to be unconscious of the fact that she was playing with other actors," wrote *Women's Wear Daily.*

Vincent Canby in *The New York Times* noted, "It's difficult to discern which has been more unkind—time or this production. There is no problem about Miss Jones's looks, but her performance is cool when it should be vital and petulant when it should be angry."

Jean Dalrymple was furious. "I thought the critics were crazy not to realize that it was Jennifer who kept the tempo of the whole show," she declares. "The critics were wrong, absolutely wrong, she was wonderful, and I was indignant with them all. Jennifer was the one who had the strength, who pulled it back where it belonged and got it going again when it looked as though it were going to drop dead. She gave a remarkable performance, a strong performance, she was the strongest person on the stage, and I am extremely critical of anything I do. . . ."

Dalrymple reflects, "She was so eager for me to have a hit, she didn't want me to be let down."

As it turned out, *The Country Girl* was both Jennifer's and Jean Dalrymple's Broadway swan song.

Chapter

31

*O*nce again the beleaguered actress had stumbled out of the limelight and into the cold. A month prior to the failure of *The Country Girl* there'd been an equally disastrous reception for *The Idol*. The film's distributing company had had no confidence in the picture and opened it with a very modest and lackluster advertising and publicity campaign. The critics struck the fatal blow with their blistering reviews:

"This maudlin tale of Mommy's romance with Sonny's beatnik pal doesn't even qualify for worst picture of the year, missing the perfection and purity of that category by the sheer ineptness of script, direction, and performance," said Judith Crist on the *Today* show.

The *New York Morning Telegraph* noted, "It's not the years that have exacted their toll. It's the lamentable choice of the vehicle in which Ms. Jones may now be seen."

The New York Times was slightly less negative: "Both Miss Jones, as a forty-ish American-born divorcée, and young John Leyton, as her seventeen-year-old son, give workmanlike performances."

By now Truman Capote had fulfilled David Selznick's prophecies and become a full-fledged superstar, both as author and media personality. *In Cold Blood*, Capote's recently published "nonfiction novel," had created a frenzy of interest in its creator. A master at generating and sustaining publicity, Capote capitalized on the incredible attention by planning "the party of the century," his famous Black and White Ball, scheduled for late November at the Plaza Hotel in New York.

Jennifer was invited, and while the invitation substantiated her social standing, it was hardly a panacea for her melancholy outlook. How was she to contend with the long vista of years to come with nobody looking out for her?

The kind of "personal attention" Jennifer required had so far eluded her. She didn't fall victim to the handsome hangers-on who were always part of the scene, ambitious young men with no visible talents who traveled in Hollywood's highest circles, entertaining the lonely, bored, vain women who found excitement and diversion in them as they would in a new toy.

Jennifer was instead a victim of her own perspective, the eternal little girl accustomed to depending on a strong man to keep her from falling—and, if she did fall, to put her back on her feet again and point her in the right direction.

During this period, in New York, Jennifer often frequented a world-famous beauty salon in a town house on Manhattan's East Side. According to another steady customer at the high-priced establishment—a woman who'd known Jennifer socially in Hollywood—the actress wasn't at all popular with the employees.

"She was universally disliked," states the lady, "hated, in fact, because her behavior was so bizarre. She'd come in to have her hair done and *had* to have those heat lamps, because she felt that the blow dryer dried out her hair.

"And the salon girls would have to place the heat lamps just so. If one little shadow from the lamp touched her forehead, she'd go crazy!

"And Jennifer insisted on being totally isolated. She didn't want to see anybody, talk to anybody, or have anybody see her. I only happened to catch a glimpse of her because somebody opened a curtain to see if [her hair] was dry, and I said, 'Wasn't that Jennifer?' And they said, '*Shhhh.*' I said, 'What's the matter?' They said, 'She doesn't want anybody to see her.' They explained how she always wore dark glasses when she came in and stared straight ahead, a ritual she repeated when she left.

"It was very strange. You'd think someone that heavily into yoga and meditation would be very kind to people around them. She evidently wasn't, which surprised me."

In March 1967 Jennifer turned forty-eight. Three months later came the second anniversary of Selznick's death and the month after that the sixteenth anniversary of Walker's demise. There were no films for Jennifer on the horizon, although son Michael made his big-screen debut in a forgettable movie directed by Ivan Tors.

But even if the Walker boys had become superstars, Jennifer was hardly a mother who lived vicariously through her children's accomplishments. Friends had observed that thirteen-year-old Mary Jennifer had learned not to rely on her mother beyond the basics; it wasn't that Jennifer was an uncaring or unkind parent, she simply had her own consuming interests and worries.

Jennifer was greatly concerned over the ill health of her dear friend Charles Bickford, now seventy-eight. The actor, suffering from emphysema, had been hospitalized with a heart attack and was in critical condition. On a Thursday in early November, Bickford died. Jennifer was intensely unsettled by the news, which only magnified her own feelings of despair.

She made a decision she'd been considering for a long while, the product of a mind distorted by depression. That evening, beautifully groomed, as always, in full makeup, and dressed in tan slacks and a white blouse, she drove her new Mercedes convertible from her Tower Grove retreat to Malibu, fifteen miles away.

She registered at a motel as Phylis Walker and asked the clerk if there was a telephone in her room. "No, ma'am," he answered. "But there's a public phone a couple of blocks away."

It was 8:45 P.M. Jennifer went to the phone and called her physician, Dr. William Molley. She told him that she was calling from a booth in the Malibu area and that she had taken an overdose of sleeping pills—she said she'd taken four already and intended to take more.

Molley immediately notified the Los Angeles Police Department, which phoned the Malibu sheriff's station. They traced Jennifer's call. Deputies Paul Piet and Eldon Loken located Jennifer's automobile, lights still on, parked near the telephone booth at the top of a four-hundred-foot cliff, Point Dume. The officers descended a rocky trail and spotted Jennifer at the water's edge, the surf washing over her seemingly lifeless body. She'd apparently walked into the water (and may have started walking down the path from the top and fallen partway).

Sergeant Loken at first thought she was dead. "She wasn't breathing, but when I turned her over to pump water from her, I heard a heartbeat through her back. There was blood on her mouth, and her lips were cut. She also had scratches on her leg."

The deputies worked frantically to revive her with mouth-to-mouth resuscitation. "I held my flashlight to her face so I could see any response. She was very quiet. Then her breath started to come," said Sergeant Loken.

Jennifer was rushed to an emergency hospital, where her stomach was pumped. The doctors found traces of Seconal, and there was evidence she'd been drinking (investigators found an empty champagne bottle in her car).

The actress, unconscious, was transferred to Mt. Sinai Hospital. She was placed in the intensive care unit and remained in a coma for six hours, at which point she regained consciousness and was pronounced out of danger. On Sunday, three days after being hospitalized, she was released and sent home. "The little girl inside had been desperately unhappy," said a friend in recalling the incident and trying to explain it. "Jennifer's safety net—David—was gone."

As far as the public was concerned, "No one could—or would—explain Jennifer's act," declared one front-page account. Another offered "rumors that she was in love with a twenty-four-year-old actor who was on location in South America."

Jennifer, in later years, was totally candid about her plight and said the suicide attempt had been "a cry for help." She had wanted attention so desperately, and had felt so needy, so abandoned, that if someone didn't notice, she was going to die. . . .

Dr. Milton Wexler, a psychoanalyst with many celebrity patients, now entered Jennifer's life. He was not simply a passive listener, but offered suggestions and advice. Meeting Wexler was to prove a turning point for Jennifer.

Ingrid Bergman, in Los Angeles appearing on stage in *Stately Mansions,* got together with Jennifer. The two old friends had long talks, with Bergman's very practical European outlook on life offering a welcome change of perspective for Jennifer. Ingrid had remarried, this time to a Scandinavian multimillionaire, Lars Schmidt, and she was happy. Ingrid's advice to Jennifer: Marry again. Jennifer's reply, in effect: "Find me the man."

• • •

Don Keefer, Jennifer's old acquaintance from American Academy days, encountered Jennifer during this period. "There was a movement afoot to start a West Coast branch of Actors Studio," he recalls. "Jack Garfein was instrumental in launching it. There was a meeting at Jack and Carroll's house [Garfein's wife was actress Carroll Baker] in Beverly Hills, and Jennifer was there. I still called her Phylis—I don't think she quite liked it. She didn't have much to say. She was very serious."

For a year Jennifer remained totally out of the public eye. She spent many hours with her analyst, searched deep within herself, and strove to abandon the fantasy world she'd chosen to inhabit for so long. To her surprise, she discovered she was stronger than she'd ever thought.

Early in 1969 Jennifer shocked her peers by signing for a new film. Initial reaction to the news was that it was a bizarre joke or a mistake. Jennifer had signed with American-International to portray a former porno movie queen in an "epic" titled *Angel, Angel, Down We Go.*

There are several theories as to why one of the screen's most serious and introspective stars was about to appear in a blatantly exploitative film. One is that Jennifer decided to shed her old image after the suicide attempt and present herself from a totally different and far less serious perspective; after all, it had worked for Bette Davis and Joan Crawford with *What Ever Happened to Baby Jane?* only several years earlier.

Another theory was that Jennifer was trying to appeal to both a contemporary audience and contemporary filmmakers. There was a certain cachet to the new project. Roddy McDowall and Jordan Christopher were her costars. McDowall, former child star, successful adult actor and photographer, and devoted pal of Hollywood's biggest stars (especially Elizabeth Taylor), was always where the action was, as was Jordan Christopher, an actor/rock musician who'd married Sybil Burton, Richard Burton's former wife.

There was a practical reason, of course, why Jennifer may have accepted the role in *Angel, Angel:* she needed the money. (Vincent Price was earning $12,500 per week as the star of American-International's highly successful horror pictures.)

American-International was the premier producer of topical films in this era of *Easy Rider* and *The Trip.* Sex, drugs, and rock and roll were part of the "trendy" *Angel* script. Jennifer was portraying

Astrid Steele, a legendary beauty paranoid about growing old, the mother of a "wild" eighteen-year-old (played by Holly Near). The daughter's character was named Tara. "You know," says Astrid, "Tara, from *Gone With the Wind*. I loved the movie." Astrid is seduced by a rock singer on the prowl (played by Jordan Christopher). Jennifer's character dies by falling out of a plane piloted by her out-of-control daughter.

The film's director-screenwriter was Robert Thom, who was married to actress Janice Rule. Thom, a playwright and novelist, had been under contract to MGM, where he'd adapted Jack Kerouac's best-selling novel *The Subterraneans* for the screen.

Thom spent time with Jennifer in analyzing and dissecting her role. He was often a visitor to the Tower Grove mansion and later described to reporter Harry Haun how, walking with Jennifer across the lawn of the estate, "there was a little house, and Jennifer offhandedly gestured to it: '*That's* where we keep the children.'"

Angel's shooting schedule coincided with a very privately observed milestone in Jennifer's life: her fiftieth birthday. She'd fantasized about it decades earlier when she'd declared that she looked forward to playing character roles at fifty. "You don't have to go through the time glamour girls do, when after your youth is gone, you have to spend years reeducating the public to accept you as an actress," the young Jennifer had said.

But now it was only after spending many hours on makeup and hair, of staring at her reflection in the mirror and working up the courage to venture onto the set, that she was ready (though still reluctant) to face the cameras. She memorized dialogue the likes of which, in real life, she would have forbidden anyone to use in her presence: "I've made thirty stag films and never faked an orgasm!"; "In my heart of hearts, I'm a sexual clam"; and at one point Astrid insults a masseuse by shouting at her, "You're a bloody, sadistic dyke!"

Not in his worst nightmares could David O. Selznick have imagined Jennifer Jones speaking such lines! But Jennifer was an actress, and she did her job. The film would at least look good—major photography was taking place in the incredibly luxurious Beverly Hills estate that had belonged to the late Marion Davies. Other interiors were filmed in a rented studio at MGM's facilities in Culver City (the site where Jennifer had filmed *Madame Bovary*).

Production unexpectedly dragged on for months. Sometime in May, Jennifer learned from her father (her parents lived in Dallas) that her mother had passed away. Phil Isley, at seventy-six, wasn't in the best of health himself. It was yet another piece of tragic news; but Jennifer swallowed her grief and carried on.

Production wrapped on *Angel* in July, with the studio planning to rush the picture into immediate release. But *Angel* had unfortunately turned out so poorly that only a few theaters ever showed the picture. Initial play dates, in August, were dismal, and after the film's devastating reviews all hopes for its future were shattered. The damage to Jennifer's career seemed irreparable, except for the fact that so few people saw the movie.

"Jennifer Jones—how did she ever get mixed up in such a weird production?" wondered the New York *Daily News*.

The *Los Angeles Times* noted, "All the principals give wildly uneven performances, with Jennifer Jones perhaps faring the best. (Her fear of aging rings with decided conviction)."

Variety wasn't exactly enthusiastic: "Miss Jones, apparently uncertain as to what her role is supposed to be, wavers between sensuality and matronliness." *The Hollywood Reporter* noted, "Miss Jones's once mannered twitch has become an unpleasant snarl, in no way softened by the lines she is forced to mouth."

Obviously, if something wasn't done to make an improvement in her life soon, Jennifer felt that she would go out of her mind. It was up to her to make the change.

Back in the early 1940s, when David Selznick was dramatically shaking up Jennifer's young life, she'd attempted to keep herself grounded and retain perspective by becoming a nurses' aide.

Jennifer reached out farther this time and embarked on a new role that promised even more personal satisfaction—she became involved with the Los Angeles–based Manhattan Project, a group that worked to rehabilitate drug addicts.

Undoubtedly recalling Robert Walker's addictions, as well as David's, Jennifer became more than a regular volunteer and opened up her luxurious home for weekly therapy sessions.

What on earth would David have thought? wondered disapproving and concerned friends. The spectacular swimming pool setting that had once entertained Hollywood's brightest luminaries would now be a gathering place for junkies and pill poppers.

But Jennifer was unconcerned with what people thought and actively raised funds for a new branch of the Manhattan Project to be erected in Salt Lake City, Robert Walker's birthplace. Totally unaccustomed to asking anyone for anything, she contacted the rich and famous she'd been socializing with for so many years and surprised them with her fervor. She proved to be a highly effective fund-raiser and found success in her new role gratifying. People close to her saw the change. She now wondered what kind of damn fool she'd been, insulating herself for so many years like some rare bird. And she'd apparently decided the hell with daydreams—that was how life got away from you.

Daughter Mary Jennifer, now fifteen years old, was determined to become an actress. And while Jennifer had no objections, Anita Colby viewed the young woman's ambitions skeptically. She recognized the girl's desire for a career, and her wish to emulate her mother, but Colby felt the adolescent didn't have the looks, nor did she display the temperament or talent necessary to succeed. All she had, it seemed, was a name that would open doors.

Jennifer, meantime, was opening her own doors. For an entire year she devoted much of her time and energy to the Manhattan Project. American-International attempted to resurrect *Angel, Angel* and retitled it *Cult of the Damned*. It was an abysmal flop even the second time around.

Jennifer remained immersed in her charity work, which involved occasional trips to Europe. At this stage of the game the odds of her embarking on a serious new relationship with a "suitable" man seemed as remote as garnering the title role in a remake of *The Song of Bernadette*.

Part IV

Part IV

*I*t had been many years since she'd seen that particular expression in a man's eyes—something between longing and lust, appearing unexpectedly, surfacing when she'd done nothing to evoke it. One assumes at this point in her life it was a most welcome development.

There have been varying accounts of how they met. The most popular and romantic is that initial introductions took place at a glittering dinner hosted by the megawealthy Walter Annenbergs.

However, a former high-level employee of billionaire Norton Simon recalls a different and far more mundane scenario. "Jennifer was doing volunteer work with a mental health group [the Manhattan Project] that Norton Simon had contributed to." Simon's interest in the group went beyond philanthropy—"Norton's younger son, Robert, had committed suicide," explains the source (Robert had been thirty-one years old).

"A director of [the Manhattan Project] said to Simon, 'Why don't you come down on an evening Jennifer will be here?' He knew that Simon's thirty-seven-year marriage [to Lucille Ellis] was already over."

The sixty-four-year-old Simon was not a bad-looking man. Over six feet tall, 180 pounds with short cropped hair, he had a lean and craggy face that usually wore a very serious expression. ("He worries, frets, and broods," noted an observer.) His eyes, set deep in his head, were penetrating and intense. He was a restless man who tweaked his ears, rubbed his eyes, pulled at his neck, and had a weakness for Italian caramels.

"What's new? What's new? Anything happen?" he'd want to know when contacting associates on the telephone. "Is that all? Is that all?" he'd exclaim after being brought up-to-date.

Simon was far removed from the world of show business (although his holdings included shares in American Broadcasting/Paramount Theaters), but he knew of Jennifer Jones—years before, he'd tried, unsuccessfully, to acquire for his world-class art collection the painting Robert Brackman had done of Jennifer for *Portrait of Jennie.*

But who, exactly, was Norton Simon? Like David Selznick, he was an overachiever of the first magnitude, a man who knew what he wanted and went after it. Simon, too, was Jewish (son of Meyer and Lillian Glickman of Portland, Oregon), a fact not publicized by the financier or his socially prominent family.

Simon, like Selznick, possessed a quixotic personality; he seemed always to be negotiating with someone, somewhere, over something; he was fiercely independent, a gutsy fighter, unpredictable, and highly secretive. Also, like Selznick, Simon hadn't had much formal education. He'd attended Lowell High School in San Francisco, where the family had moved after Norton's mother died, but had dropped out of college. "The university was involved with requirements, and I was interested in learning only what I wanted to learn," he later explained. The legend goes that at twenty-two Simon invested three thousand dollars in the stock market, worked it into $35,000 and got out just before the 1929 crash. Among his other natural gifts were a photographic memory and the ability to calculate figures in his brain at seemingly computerlike speed.

In 1931, at the age of twenty-four—the same year David Selznick became Hollywood's boy wonder and Jennifer was a twelve-year-old schoolgirl—Norton Simon invested $7,000 (a *lot* of cash in Depression-ravaged America) in a bankrupt orange juice–bottling company. Through a series of clever acquisitions and shrewd mergers over the years, he transformed his small company into the Hunt Foods and Industries empire, the basis of his fortune.

He was not, however, immune to falling in love. Lucille Ellis, a Wellesley-trained social worker, met Norton at a Thanksgiving party in 1932, long before he'd made his millions. Three months later they were married.

The honeymoon combined business and pleasure. Simon felt millions of dollars were to be made in the steel business, whose workers were in bad straits. His socially conscious wife didn't like the idea. "I hope you won't do that," she told him, "because I could never eat bread from your table."

"Don't worry," Simon told her. "I'll change things."

Simon's relationship with Lucille was a strong one; she was, said friends, his inspiration, a woman who read a great deal and whose intellectual interests and pursuits impressed Simon (and were responsible for his subsequent interest in education; he later became regent at the University of California at Los Angeles and a trustee at Reed College in Oregon).

Simon, however, was usually thinking only of business and was always on the lookout for poorly managed companies whose stock was undervalued. One fact is clear: Simon's "the bottom line is all that matters" style somewhat echoed David Selznick's "all that matters is the finished film" credo.

In the 1950s Simon began his career as an art collector, starting with three Impressionist paintings (a Bonnard, a Renoir, and a Gauguin). His hobby paid off when, in 1964, he acquired the entire inventory of the renowned Duveen Brothers of New York. But Simon, like Jennifer, didn't like the hot glare of publicity. He and Lucille traveled frequently but avoided cocktail parties and entertained on a relatively modest scale, usually with people from the worlds of art and education.

"They have all of the various Hunt products in different silver containers," noted Jean Fowler, whose husband, Edward, had sold the Duveen collection to Simon. "[On one occasion] Norton said to Edward, 'Won't you have some catsup?' Edward said, 'Indeed not, I wouldn't spoil good food with that stuff.' Simon's wife laughed and said, 'That's why I've never learned to cook. Norton always pours catsup over everything.' "

Simon was a workaholic, rising no later than seven A.M. (often as early as six A.M.), and spent seven days a week pursuing his goals. His study at home, an office on Wilshire Boulevard in Los Angeles, and his company headquarters in Fullerton were usually where he could be found (the building in Fullerton had been designed by none other than architect William Pereira, who'd worked for the Selznick studio in the 1940s and had designed the sets for *Since You Went Away*). Like Selznick, he had a reputation for being pretty rough on people who got in his way and for becoming "so impatient that he frequently pounds the table and yells."

There were weekends when Simon and Lucille traveled to their home by the Pacific Ocean at Lido Isle, where Simon loved being surrounded by his works of art. All of his art-filled residences had state-of-the-art alarm systems and professional security guards on duty at all times. To relax, Simon swam in his pool. "Norton is the only one I know who will swim around at night in the dark," said his wife.

Simon, while a brilliant administrator, also thought of himself as a creative person. His explanation of how he revitalized a company was not far removed from the approach Jennifer had learned from Lee Strasberg on how to create a role.

"Picasso says that creativity is a series of destructions," said Simon. "You really don't create anything until you knock something else out of the way . . . [but] you should tear down only so much before it's time to build anew, for excessive tearing down takes the destructive process beyond the realm of creativity. . . . The question is, how much destruction can be tolerated?"

Jennifer, even at this stage of her life, was apparently willing to tolerate such an autocrat. "My hostilities are usually showing," Simon admitted, "but I do get rid of my anger very rapidly. Some people are born with peace of mind. I was not. In the Dostoyevskian sense, I am the suffering man; I know this about myself. And I know now that working my way out of it is a very gratifying experience. I have gone through a process of reconciliation with myself. . . ."

Jennifer herself has certainly been described over the years as a "suffering woman" and has often, to her own gratification, worked her way out of it and gone through a process of self-reconciliation.

Not surprisingly, for over thirty years Simon had been plagued by ulcers. "When [my ulcers] were operated on, I took an introspective look at myself," he said. "I don't like to be rough; it has even been difficult being firm with people. But I feel a very constructive part of being firm. I feel a constructive part of being rough. I feel a constructive part of letting my anger express itself."

"[Norton] may go to bed at night intending to fly to New York in the morning, but by morning he has changed his mind," noted Lucille Simon. She tried to explain her husband's thinking processes.

"He is extremely flexible, and I think it is because he is constantly in the process 'of becoming.' "

Lucille was echoing Simon's complex theory "of becoming": "I am in the process of becoming," he'd explained. "I have a rigidity of flexibility [sic]." Those in Simon's circle didn't contest the boss's pronouncements, and the fact that these statements seemed contradictory was exactly Simon's point. "I believe in a paradoxical form of life. I don't believe anything is wholly right, but both right and wrong. There is a thin line between. There is a Chinese proverb that states, 'Life is a search for truth and there is no truth.' It is important to know that truth carried too far becomes destructive."

"I cannot imagine spending seven days a week with [Simon]," said Norton Simon aide Jack Clumeck. "After a three- or four-day trip with him, I have to take a few days off. He is just that intense and probing."

Simon's sons, Donald and Robert, and their families were frequent visitors to the Simon homes. Donald had graduated from the University of Southern California, and Robert, at twenty-six, was head of Hunt's vegetable procurement division.

By the late 1960s, close to the time Simon met Jennifer, his personal art collection was reportedly worth $35 million. His diverse business holdings had by then multiplied and become a $1 billion sales empire. He had also created the Norton Simon Foundation, which lent out works of art for public exhibitions at no charge. Through the amalgamation of Hunt-Wesson Foods, McCall Corporation (which included *McCall's, Saturday Review,* and *Redbook* magazines), and the Canada Dry Corporation, Simon formed Norton Simon Incorporated, then resigned as chairman at a time when he and his children owned at least 8 percent of the stock, worth over $40 million. Simon was recognized as one of the great American success stories.

However, there were certain personal traits of Simon's that would hardly appeal to a woman who had not only enjoyed the glamorous lifestyle of a Hollywood star, but whose late producer husband had spent money on her with prodigal abandon. Simon, said a friend, "will search the streets for a restaurant where he can eat for five dollars."

Apparently, for one thinking of linking up with Norton Simon, either professionally or personally, there were many pros and cons (especially the latter) to consider. But drive, ambition, and power were obviously traits Jennifer Jones found highly attractive and stimulating in a man. She wasn't at all intimidated, and experience had taught her how to handle such a difficult character.

Joan Fontaine recalls a story she was told regarding Simon's whirlwind courtship of Jennifer. "A mutual friend told me that evidently David's financial 'empire' had dissolved after his death," and Jennifer had found it necessary to sell off artwork and possessions. But at this point, according to this friend, Jennifer didn't have anything to sell.

"Our friend told me that he filled a wagon [from the prop department at the movie studio where he worked] with furniture and other items and went and set-dressed her home for her to meet Simon!"

Jennifer and Simon, in recounting the official version of their love story, said that it started at a black-tie gala hosted by the Annenbergs in Los Angeles. They were immediately attracted to each other. "There was . . . a great 'simpatico' between us from the start," said Simon. "I found her soul more beautiful than her face, and you've got to admit her face is pretty nice. . . .

"I fell in love immediately."

For Jennifer, the mirror that counted most was the look in a man's eyes. Still, she was frightened. She was soon to leave for Europe, recalled Simon, "to visit the head of the Manhattan Project," in Paris on vacation, and Simon was due to leave for the Caribbean. But he decided "not to go," and Jennifer and Simon "made up our minds on the spur of the moment to go to Paris together."

A week before the trip, Jennifer got together with George Masters in New York. "Her secretary had called," recalled Masters. "and asked me to meet Jennifer in her suite at the Pierre Hotel. I arrived at midnight, laden with bottles of Dom Pérignon."

Jennifer greeted Masters with a kiss "and said excitedly, 'George, I want you to take a look at this man in the next room and see what you think of him. I think I'm going to marry him, but I haven't known him very long. Only eight days.' "

According to Masters, Jennifer "gently knocked on the door to the adjoining suite and opened it slightly.

"She called in to him, 'I have someone here, darling. I'll be with you in a moment.'

"As I started giving her a fast touch-up, she asked breathlessly, 'What do you think of him?'

"How did I know? I could barely see him around the corner through the crack in the door.

" 'He looks okay to me,' I said, brushing on her eye shadow.

" 'I've just met him, but I think I'm going to marry him,' she repeated.

" 'Go ahead,' I said. I knew she wanted encouragement.

" 'We're going to London to see how it works out.' "

Masters wasn't the only person whose encouragement she'd sought. Early on she'd introduced her analyst, Dr. Wexler, to Simon. She later told reporter Phylis Battelle that she'd brought Wexler along on her second date with Norton, "to look him over. . . . I was gold-digging for a project I was working on [the Huntington's Disease Foundation, which had been founded by Wexler]."

Simon, in turn, had his own analyst look Jennifer over. (Simon's intense interest in psychotherapy—he'd been in analysis since the 1950s—was a vital link between the couple.)

Jennifer's resolve didn't waver. In Europe, "[Norton] walked me around Paris and London until I was so exhausted I couldn't resist him anymore. It was the most romantic thing that's ever happened to me," she said.

The romance had been preceded by a prenuptial agreement. Jennifer later recalled the discussion that had preceded it: "Norton said to me, 'I'm a crook and you're a crook—what do you want?' So he gave me a substantial sum for the Huntington's Disease Foundation and didn't get much from me but a dowry of chipped china and worn Porthaulдt sheets." (Simon went a step further: he added a painting by seventeenth-century master Francisco de Zubaran, valued at $3 million.)

Simon proposed to Jennifer in Paris. In London events progressed with lightning speed, almost as though any delay would ground the couple's romantic flight of fancy.

British residency requirements, however, and the British Whitsun holiday weekend made a regular wedding on land impossible, so Simon chartered a yacht outside territorial waters. The ceremony would take place on board the craft on Saturday, May 29, late at night.

But first, in the afternoon, Jennifer went on a no-holds-barred shopping spree (apparently those tight purse strings Simon held on to were loosened considerably when it came to his bride-to-be) and bought thousands of dollars' worth of clothing and accessories.

Afterward the couple drove to Folkestone and boarded their

fifty-foot chartered yacht, which sailed five miles out into the choppy English Channel.

"It was great fun," recalled Simon. "We were bobbing about in the sea, and in the early morning light I could just make out the white cliffs of Dover. It was very romantic." Friends noted that never before in his life had Simon ever described anything he'd done as "romantic."

The couple were wed by a Unitarian clergyman, Reverend Eirion Phillips, at four A.M. "The sea was so rough," the reverend recalled, "that one of the witnesses became seasick. The boat was lurching so much, I could hardly stand up to perform the ceremony."

The predawn ceremony took ten minutes. On returning to shore, "we came straight back [to the hotel]," recalled Simon, "and we slept all day."

It was no surprise to anyone who knew Jennifer that there'd been no advance notice of the nuptials. "We kept it quiet because we didn't want any publicity," said Simon.

What *was* a surprise was Jennifer's reaction to the appearance of the press the following day. Instead of running for her life, her new husband in tow, she welcomed the photographers with a smile on her face as wide as when she'd won her Oscar on that magical day twenty-seven years earlier (there was an atypically broad smile on Simon's face as well).

Back in the United States, George Masters looked at Jennifer's wedding pictures. "Her bridal costume was black leather pants and peau de soie blouse and a black leather hat. Jennifer had come full cycle in her fantasy world, from ethereal nymphet to Auntie Mame."

Jennifer Jones, a woman on a tightrope since David Selznick's death, had—at the age of fifty-two—again landed spectacularly on her feet.

"To me, it was the most incredible thing in the world that she wound up with Norton Simon," says one Hollywood social figure. "I don't know why he married her. I've never been able to figure that out."

The attraction the sad-eyed, widowed, emotionally needy actress and the successful older businessman felt for each other obviously came at a crucial point in both their lives. Simon's feelings of guilt and pain over his son's suicide, and the effect it had had on his family, were severe. Jennifer, having survived Robert Walker's tragic death, obviously understood it and related to it. They could give each other comfort. The new relationship apparently filled a deep void in both Jennifer's and Simon's lives.

Jennifer was the first to admit that the marriage had been very sudden. "Yes, we behaved impulsively. But, at our age, you're not exactly terrified of such things." She was convinced that "the older you get, the more risks you're willing to take."

"I remember Jules Stein saying to me, 'You will never be happily married until you marry [a Jewish man], because they are wonderfully protective and caring and wonderful family people,' " reflects Joan Fontaine. "Evidently Jennifer felt that and needed that from both of those men [David Selznick and Norton Simon], who made her feel like a jewel."

Simon was obviously delighted in taking on that role in Jennifer's life. And, as Joan Fontaine points out, Simon liked beautiful things, "and Jennifer was a very beautiful thing."

On returning to the States, Mr. and Mrs. Simon (technically speaking, she was now Phylis Glickman) flew directly to Salt Lake City so Jennifer could be present for the opening of the new branch of the Manhattan Project, which she'd been instrumental in funding. A "new," more relaxed Jennifer began to emerge on this trip. She wasn't being cautioned (or cautious) about what or what not to say (which had often been the case with David) and hadn't a care in the world regarding her finances.

She interacted comfortably and effectively with the people in Salt Lake. Her new husband was impressed and noted that Jennifer "was fabulously good talking with the people . . . about their problems." He was proud, he said, "to be simply the husband of Jennifer Jones Simon that night."

On the home front, Mary Jennifer, almost seventeen, was taken aback by her mother's marriage and all the attention it brought to "Jennifer Jones." She was jealous. Also, the nuptials had occurred close to the anniversary of David's death, and Mary Jennifer's memories of her adoring father had always remained painfully vivid (*"too* vivid," says Anita Colby).

"Jennifer the second" had never and would never recover from the loss of her father (as a child she'd sometimes referred to him as her husband). David's death had left his daughter an emotional cripple. The young woman chose this moment to relocate to the East Coast. (In Los Angeles at that time, "there were only three things to do," noted young producer Julia Phillips, "Work, do drugs, and have a nervous breakdown." Apparently Mary Jennifer would do them all.) With the help and influence of her half brother, Danny, Mary Jennifer enrolled in Uta Hagen's acting classes in New York.

"Jennifer the first" had moved into Simon's Malibu estate, and there he gave her carte blanche to redecorate. She was also embarking on a study program of her own by learning about her husband's obsession, the world of art. Whereas she'd previously viewed museums as "dreary, boring affairs," her perspective changed and she developed "quite a good eye." In time, "I learned to discuss the masters with an expertise I couldn't believe was mine," she said.

Norton accompanied Jennifer to many museums and art galleries, where she was anxious to learn about everything she saw. These were times when Norton was more entranced than ever with Jennifer, when she suddenly betrayed herself as a child whose complete trust made him feel like the ultimate protector. "Jennifer was able to merge her identity with the man she was with," notes a friend. "Her femininity was such that she allowed a man to feel *more* masculine, and men loved that."

Simon talked to Jennifer about the paintings' histories, told her the name of this artist and that sculptor. Many an evening she'd sit curled up on a chaise longue in her boudoir, studying art books.

The epiphany came in Sienna, Italy. "For the first time I looked at paintings of the Madonna and Child and saw them as abstracts, which Norton had been telling me they were all along," recalled Jennifer. "Suddenly the subject matter went away and I could see, for example, that Matisse had been here."

Jennifer had offered Selznick the challenge of transforming her from naif to sophisticated movie star; to Simon she offered the opportunity of making the movie star over yet again into an art patron and first lady of Southern California society. As always, she was a willing and pliable student and a most welcome companion for Simon. Like a neglected rose suddenly transplanted, Jennifer blossomed anew.

There were skeptics who suspected that the union was strictly another "marriage of convenience," rather than one filled with real passion. A former Simon insider theorizes that "it's true that on a certain level of New York or Los Angeles society, sex has nothing to do with it. The way it works is that a man marries a hostess (whereas a woman, in some cases, marries a stud).

"However, if you're Norton Simon, you're not looking for a Pia Zadora." In the case of Simon and Jennifer, the source states bluntly, "Yes, they were sleeping together."

One thing for sure was that Jennifer was certainly a "trophy wife." Here was an Academy Award winner whose film work had been in strictly top-quality productions (never mind the relatively recent embarrassment of *Angel, Angel, Down We Go,* which, fortunately for Jennifer, hadn't surfaced into the public's consciousness). "Jennifer Jones" still radiated the kind of aura men like Norton Simon respected, and she played her new role to the hilt.

Norton and Jennifer's life together assumed a pattern: "Certainly there were endless 'divine' dinner parties," comments the insider, "with rich people sitting around bullshitting each other. [Norton was] a rich windbag with answers to everything. [He] was extremely opinionated. I think [apparently] Jennifer needed that sort of man in her life. Selznick was a bulldozer, and Norton certainly got *his* way, and that may be what Jennifer has *always* needed—my God, her experience with Robert Walker, when things just fell apart. . . .

"Selznick and Simon were men who seemed to have control of life, of their own destinies. I think Jennifer needed that in *her* life. . . ."

With the aid of a social secretary and others working for the Simon empire, Jennifer eased into the role of billionaire's wife. At social gatherings with Norton, they were a striking couple on the dance floor. Afterward Jennifer would often sit quietly and listen to others talk about the places they'd all been and what they'd seen, things they'd done, how bad the service was at certain restaurants, and so on. She tended to slough off her own experiences, touching on them in some oblique manner so that without meaning to she gave the impression of being a woman to whom amazing things had happened, automatically and naturally. Which, of course, they had!

It appeared she'd long since made up her mind not to talk about David, for she was certain she'd hear something she wouldn't like. At first she felt a bit out of her element with Simon's crowd; they were primarily wealthy business people, self-confident and sophisticated, and she felt like an interloper.

Naturally, some of the wives and girlfriends of Simon's associates were overtly jealous and envious. "I simply never liked her in films," one woman was heard to say on one occasion. Jennifer, only a few feet away, missed the catty remark but not the nasty look.

But she could be tough when she had to; becoming Mrs. Norton Simon was her most challenging role to date, and she rose to the occasion. "You must remember that, for the most part, the women Jennifer had to contend with in her new circle weren't career women, as she'd been. They were what I'd call 'professional wives,' " states Anita Colby. "I'd had to deal with plenty of them over the years. Those women can be nasty, and wary of 'outsiders,' especially of a woman like Jennifer, whose looks and talent had been praised for years! She'd *accomplished* something. Jennifer would often call me and we'd talk for hours about her new life and how she should handle it."

As she had with Selznick, Jennifer derived supreme satisfaction through exercising the prerogatives of being Mrs. Norton Simon and was soon a well-liked and highly valued customer at the finest boutiques, department stores, and jewelry salons at home and abroad. She also learned that she could in effect always speak in a whisper yet be heard loud and clear. As Mrs. Norton Simon, her opinions carried great weight. "Money talks," a credo David Selznick had always respected, was never more evident than in Jennifer's new social circle.

In no time Jennifer was functioning beautifully. "She's nobody's fool," states a woman who served on a committee with her. "She's affable, but not really friendly until she's sized you up. A lot of people were after her to serve on committees and contribute to causes. She was very cautious about people, and I didn't blame her."

There were two other women in Simon's personal life, his socially prominent sisters, Marcia and Evelyn. If there was any resentment of Jennifer by Simon's immediate and highly competitive family, they never showed it in public. In her Selznick days Jennifer had had to contend with Irene Selznick as a formidable role model insofar as Hollywood's social scene was concerned; now it was Marcia Simon Weisman, who was a powerhouse and one of California's most prominent (and, like her brother, forceful and outspoken) art collectors (she was known as "Mrs. Art" in Los Angeles).

Marcia's pal, artist Andy Warhol, described Marcia as "a tough, bossy lady," one who was at ease in the bare-knuckled world of big-time art collecting. Marcia, not exactly a great beauty, wasn't particularly fond of Jennifer ("the shiksa"), and the two women according to associates, remained distant. But she was respectful of Jennifer, who was a vital new element in her brother's life that Marcia could do nothing about. She wasn't about to alienate her powerful sibling by alienating her new sister-in-law.

Another passion, other than art and Jennifer, existed in Norton Simon's life: politics. The year before he met Jennifer, he'd been an unsuccessful candidate against then Senator George Murphy in the 1970 Republican primary. Simon was thoroughly beaten in the race after having spent $2 million on a campaign that emphasized a capitalistic approach to government.

He worked to wrest control of the California Republican machinery from the party's conservatives, particularly one of its biggest money men, Henry Salvatori. Simon bankrolled liberal candidates and was an active opponent of then Governor Ronald Reagan's hard-line position on students and college administrators.

Simon sold part of his art collection for a then astronomical $6.5 million. He needed cash to finance his campaign for Representative Paul N. McCloskey, Jr., liberal Republican of California. Simon, with Jennifer by his side, planned for McCloskey to challenge President Nixon for the Republican presidential nomination in 1972 (the challenge was effectively routed).

Whatever activities she was involved in, the new Mrs. Simon could retreat, when necessary, into the insular lifestyle made possible by Simon's money. She now had the luxury of living the life of a movie star without having to go to the trouble of making the movies.

Jennifer introduced Norton to selected Hollywood friends, including John Huston. Huston and his latest amour, Cici, were the Simons' guests one evening for dinner. Admiring the Old Masters on the walls, the fine silver and spectacular table settings glimmering under the soft glow of rock-crystal chandeliers, Huston was nonetheless out of sorts. There was tension in the air, a result of the fact that Cici had been pressuring her aging lothario to marry her (which he subsequently did). Huston, by his own account, was "more than half drunk. It was an absolutely dreadful evening."

At the dinner table, Huston, in his cups, "fell forward, and his face landed in the soup."

It was an embarrassing scene. But nothing surprised or embarrassed Jennifer; she'd seen it all in the course of her Hollywood years. For Simon, however, one assumes that this inside view of Hollywood's legendary characters surely made him realize how wise he'd been to pursue a career in another field!

When the designer Halston and his business empire were "acquired" by Norton Simon Incorporated, Jennifer, along with Elizabeth Taylor, Liza Minnelli, Lucille Ball, and other luminaries, became a favored Halston customer, scooping up countless creations at a cost of four and five figures per garment. Jennifer, presiding over many a glittering soiree for her husband, was properly dazzling in her beaded Halstons. Unlike Liz, Liza, and others, however, Jennifer stayed far removed from Halston's drug-oriented party scene (which usually unfolded in the dark private rooms of New York's premier disco, Studio 54).

Around this time, Jennifer's eldest son, Robert Walker, Jr., now thirty-three years old, quit the movie business (in which he hadn't exactly caught fire) and took a job driving a limousine.

"For the first time I really feel like a useful person instead of a show business commodity, trying to make a fortune by whatever means possible," he said. (Within a couple of months, however, he was back in "the business.")

Brother Michael, thirty-two, was also out of the public eye. One report had him living in a kibbutz in Israel. "It wasn't much fun," he was quoted as saying. He moved to Paris, where he appeared occasionally on television and in independent films.

Jennifer's life continued on its gilded course. Her lifestyle with Norton was strictly formal. "With the Simons there were no casual visits," notes an insider. Jennifer was not a person who thrived on spontaneous socializing. " 'Open house' isn't everyone's way of life, and it certainly was never Jennifer's," states Anita Colby. "That doesn't make her any less of a good person or a good friend. She enjoys her privacy, while some people need lots of people around all the time! And there's been no shortage of friends in her life. Also, she was working on getting Norton to relax more."

One way Jennifer accomplished this was by attending intimate soirees with her husband, hosted by Ann Rutherford and her husband, producer William Dozier (who'd produced, among other TV fare, the *Batman* series). Ann Rutherford had been a popular film actress in the 1930s (she became famous as Andy Hardy's girlfriend, Polly Benedict, in MGM's *Andy Hardy* series and for portraying Scarlett O'Hara's younger sister Careen in *Gone With the Wind*). From the mid-1950s on, Ann Rutherford Dozier was one of Hollywood's leading hostesses.

Jennifer and Norton were regulars at the Doziers' for gourmet Chinese cuisine prepared by household chefs Tsai and Ah Yiang Tuck (whose family of five was domiciled at the Doziers' Beverly Hills mansion).

Those meals were not quickie affairs—dinner often lasted four or five hours, and each guest had his or her own particular course; for ten people, there would be ten main courses. "You learned to pace yourself, you learned to relax and just enjoy sitting at the table and eating," recalled Rutherford. A lazy Susan was placed on the table, and it was "almost like an audience participation show," she said. Jennifer, Norton, and the other guests "loved twirling the lazy Susan."

In these pre–Jane Fonda aerobics days, Jennifer and her friends kept their figures trim by hiring masseur Marvin Hart. Rutherford adored him, thought him "a marvelous man, a fabulous masseur, he was the 'in' masseur." Hart was the man who would "look at an Ann-Margret or a Jennifer Jones or someone else in impeccable shape and say, 'You need an eighth of an inch off your left thigh.' Then he'd give them punishing exercises," recalled Rutherford of this "personal trainer" regimen in place years before the term was coined.

But Jennifer could exercise, serve on committees and attend just so many dinner parties. She was becoming restless, although her interest in the field of mental health remained intense and her financial contributions to the cause were formidable. Her outspoken support of the mentally ill took courage; a tremendous negative attitude, fueled by ignorance, misunderstanding, and prejudice, prevailed during these days, and those who campaigned for the cause were often stigmatized. Jennifer was not deterred.

The Simons' relationship, like every spousal relationship, was an evolving one. They were emotionally accessible to each other. A friend of Jennifer's notes, "I remember Rex Harrison once saying, 'Never marry an actress. They never stop acting.' [All of Rex's wives were actresses!] But if Jennifer was acting, it was a flawless performance. I believe she was absolutely sincere. The marriage was a new beginning for her. Her inner hurricane was calm for the first time in a long, long while."

Actor Michael Parks was a visitor to the Simon home. "Jennifer wanted me to meet Norton, because Norton wanted her to get back into movies," recalls Parks. "But I wasn't working much at the time, and, as they say in Hollywood, I was persona non grata, I would assume because of [some] disagreements I'd had with Lew Wasserman and Sam Spiegel.

"I had dinner with Norton and Jennifer, and he said something like 'Well, I'd like Jennifer to do some more pictures and start working again, but we just can't have [her do] more terrible kinds of B-movies like *The Idol*. . . .

"And the next thing I know, there she was in *The Towering Inferno*."

Chapter

33

David Selznick would have cringed, at Jennifer's below-the-title costar billing and the lack of "perks" granted to her for *The Towering Inferno,* which starred Paul Newman, Steve McQueen, William Holden, and Faye Dunaway (how Selznick would have barraged the producer with phone calls and memos: "Dear Irwin, Jennifer is *perfect* for 'the girl . . . ' ").

Industry gossip claimed that Norton Simon, a 20th Century–Fox stockholder, had used his influence to secure the supporting role for his wife (a role that had reportedly been turned down by Olivia De Havilland), but he obviously wasn't wise in the ways of Hollywood. As Joan Fontaine has pointed out, it was Selznick who'd made sure Jennifer had the properly appointed dressing rooms and all the rest that signified the presence of "a star."

There was not even mention in the press that Jennifer and Holden, the lovers from *Love Is a Many Splendored Thing,* were appearing together for the first time since then. Such nostalgia had no place in the marketing scheme of these contemporary products.

The Towering Inferno was a multimillion-dollar "disaster" movie. Irwin Allen, the film's fifty-eight-year-old producer-director (the "Master of Disaster") had two years earlier scored a blockbuster success with *The Poseidon Adventure.* That epic thriller, about people trapped underwater in an overturned ocean liner, had earned costar Shelley Winters an Academy Award nomination as Best Supporting Actress.

Inferno was a similar thriller, this time about people trapped in a burning skyscraper. Jennifer was to portray a sympathetic widow falling prey to con man Fred Astaire (who at seventy-four was almost twenty years older than Jennifer and had already appeared in many character and cameo roles).

On the plus side, the film would bring Jennifer back to the screen without the burden of having in any way to carry the picture. (One is reminded of the four stages in the life of an actress: "Who's Jennifer Jones?"; "Get me Jennifer Jones!"; "Get me a young Jennifer Jones!"; "Who's Jennifer Jones?")

It was a "hot" property (so to speak) because 20th Century–Fox and Warner Brothers had separately purchased novels with the same plot and theme, and each was planning to produce a movie version. They joined forces to make one picture, with a then astronomical budget of $14 million.

Irwin Allen cast the film's other supporting roles with a variety of well-known names, including Robert Wagner, Richard Chamberlain, Susan Blakely, O. J. Simpson, and Susan Flannery. While Jennifer would be appearing in the picture, she was hardly being *presented* in it—she'd not be the recipient of the kind of careful attention that had characterized all aspects of her previous efforts.

The film's costume designer, Paul Zastupnevich, hadn't met Jennifer, he'd only talked with her on the telephone. But he was an admirer. "She was coming in for a consultation and fitting," he recalls. "I knew that in the old days Jennifer had had a special dressing room, a star bungalow on the Fox lot, where we were shooting the picture.

"She hadn't been on the lot in years, and when I walked into the dressing room that they'd rigged up for her, I was appalled! There was a tacky chocolate brown rug, ugly plaid upholstery on the furniture—it was gauche, impossible!

"I knew her taste. I'd done research. I'd dashed around and found out all about all her likes and dislikes. Many of her clothes over the years had been made by a woman at Magnin's; I also discovered that Jennifer loved to have an arrangement of lemons in her dressing room [rather than] flowers.

"I got hold of the man at Fox in charge of set decoration, and I said, 'You can't do this to someone like Jennifer Jones, she's been a star for years!' For her to walk into such a dressing room—it had been used as an office by Danny Thomas! I said, 'We just can't do this to Jennifer, you've got to help me out.'

"So we pulled out a French rug, some French furniture, we changed the drapes to gray satin, we fixed the lighting in the room, I got the arrangement of lemons, and made sure everything else was all arranged. In about two hours I'd switched her dressing room from a god-awful monstrosity to a worthy setting for Jennifer Jones.

"I had to disappear for some reason. In the meantime, she showed up, walked in, and said to her makeup man that she couldn't believe it. 'That the studio would do this for me!' She'd had trepidations about showing up at all, she was afraid it would bring back bad memories. . . .

"And she said, 'To walk in and to find the lemons!' The makeup man had told her that she should have seen the place about two hours earlier, she wouldn't have believed it was the same room! He told her, 'Your costume designer came in and blew his top; he said, "You can't do this, I won't let you do this to her," and he arranged all of this for you.' She was thrilled.

"And finally I met her. When I walked in she said, 'I understand I have you to thank for all this.' I said, 'Oh, no, I just made a little change here and there.' She said, 'That's not the way I heard it.'

"From then on I consulted her on all the details of her costumes. I'd send in one of my assistants to show her the materials and say, 'Now these are the beads we plan to use on your gown, which do you prefer?' She said, 'I leave it up to Paul, whatever he wants,' and from then on [I had] carte blanche."

Zastupnevich notes that while Jennifer appeared "very shy, very timid, she's very centered inside. She doesn't open up much to people, you have to gain her confidence, and it takes a long time.

"We became great friends because she became interested in my niece, who looks a great deal like her and who wanted to be an actress. So Jennifer was always inquiring about Marinka."

Jennifer was anxious about facing the cameras. "She'd been off the screen for a while and was leery of what was going to happen to her," recalls Zastupnevich. "The day that she had to shoot with Fred Astaire she said, 'Just think, I'm going to dance with Fred Astaire!' I think that was the secret ambition of everyone, even Jennifer Jones, to dance with Fred Astaire. I wanted to say that *my* ambition was to dance with Jennifer Jones!"

Jennifer was determined to look her best in the picture. "We were getting ready to make her important gown," recalls Zastupnevich. "Jennifer loved silk, and she said to me, 'I know they're not going to splurge, would you mind if I got the fabric myself?' I said, 'Certainly not.' She arranged for us to get some incredible silk. If I remember correctly, it cost $175 a yard. We needed about ten yards, so we're talking almost two thousand dollars' worth of fabric and beadwork.

"The poor little girl in the workroom was scared to death. 'I don't even want to cut into this,' she said. 'I'm *afraid* to cut into this! What if we make a mistake?' I said, 'So if we make a mistake, we'll correct it with a sewing machine.' "

Jennifer loved the gown, and Zastupnevich was pleased how she looked in it. "She wore it beautifully. She was so easy to work with. She knew how to wear clothes, knew how to wear something elegant. My credo has always been, 'Keep it simple.' If you're in doubt about a trim, or beadwork or anything else, leave it off."

The studio apparently regarded neither Jennifer nor Fred Astaire (also receiving below-the-title costar billing) as particularly valuable properties. Zastupnevich recalls, "Fox had arranged for dressing rooms on wheels for Jennifer and Fred and wheeled them *outside* the stage and practically into the gutter! They'd just hosed off the outside area, and that's when they began calling for Jennifer!

"She was all dressed in the silk gown, with matching shoes and all. Now she was supposed to come out of her dressing room and go on stage.

"I said, 'Look where you've got her dressing room. If she goes down those steps and walks onto that wet gutter, if she slips or something happens, we don't have another dress! This is the original, there isn't a standby or duplicate for it.' I blew my top. I said, 'No, I won't permit it.' They said, 'You're out of your mind.'

" 'How stupid you are,' I said. 'Wheel her dressing room onto the stage.' 'Oh, no, we're not allowed to put her dressing room on stage,' I was told. They had orders to have Jennifer's and Fred's dressing rooms off the stage.

"I said, 'Well, then she ain't going to work! *She's* not saying that, *I'm* saying that. I won't permit it.' And I didn't. They finally rolled the two dressing rooms onto the stage."

Zastupnevich adds, "It was easier for me to fight the battle for things like that, rather than have them figure Jennifer as being temperamental."

The good news was that Jennifer and Fred Astaire worked beautifully together. "It's amazing that she was paired off with Fred," recalls Zastupnevich. "I was amazed to discover that Fred, too, was so shy and reserved. Fred and Jennifer were so much alike! I suppose that's why they got along so well and blended so smoothly."

Astaire had another trait in common with Jennifer: discretion. "We got to talking," recalls Zastupnevich, "and I brought up Judy Garland's name [Astaire and Garland had starred in the smash hit *Easter Parade*, back when Jennifer was working on the MGM lot in *Madame Bovary*]. Fred would not say one harsh or nasty word about Judy, only what a remarkable talent she was and what a joy and delight she was to work with, but that she was 'troubled.' That was as far as he'd go."

In *Towering Inferno* Jennifer had an important sequence opposite Paul Newman (who was portraying the skyscraper's architect). The scenes involved the rescue of two little boys, and in her valiant attempts to save them, Jennifer's character falls to her death. Jennifer performed with power and dimension.

While making the picture, the actress traveled daily to the studio from her home in Malibu. Zastupnevich was a visitor. He was nonplussed at Jennifer's splendid lifestyle. "In Jennifer's bedroom were museum-quality paintings worth about half a million dollars!" he recalls. "They were French Impressionists, Monet and Renoir, I think."

Postproduction on <u>The Towering Inferno</u> *was rushed along so the film could* open in time for the Christmas holidays and to qualify for Academy Awards. On December 10, 1974, the film premiered and ultimately fulfilled the expectations of its producers (and had an effect on changing fire laws in hotels and office buildings. "We were all very proud of that," recalls Paul Zastupnevich).

Jennifer's reviews were good. "Jennifer Jones, looking fit and attractive, not only gets to play romantic scenes with a still charming Fred Astaire, but also struggles gamefully through tough physical ordeals," wrote *The Hollywood Reporter*. She was also nominated for a

Golden Globe as Best Supporting Actress. And in 1975, when Academy Award nominations were announced, Fred Astaire won a nomination as Best Supporting Actor, and *Towering Inferno* was up for Best Picture (along with *The Godfather, Part II, The Conversation, Lenny,* and *Chinatown*).

Jennifer's old pal Ingrid Bergman, nominated for Best Supporting Actress in *Murder on the Orient Express,* won in her category, with *Godfather II* sweeping most of the other major awards. *Inferno,* however, had done its job for Jennifer—Irwin Allen wanted her for his next epic, *The Day the World Ended,* again to star Paul Newman.

It would appear that Jennifer's life had at last assumed a satisfying rhythm—a blend of charitable, social, and now professional activity.

Jennifer's hard-won carefree days, however, were soon to come to a sudden and terrible halt. Anita Colby recalls that Mary Jennifer Selznick, now twenty-one, was experiencing serious, ongoing emotional distress. "The child didn't seem to be able to cope. As a girl, David had treated her like a fairy princess, complete with her own enchanted garden. My room, when I'd been a houseguest at Tower Road, overlooked the garden, and I'd often watch her play in it with her 'magic wand' and 'magic ring.' She was always playacting in later years, too. Make-believe stayed with her far too intensely."

An understatement. Colby was Mary Jennifer's godmother, and Mary Jennifer often visited her. Colby had married late in life (at age fifty-six, to businessman Palen Flagler), and the couple lived at Flagler's sprawling farm in upstate New York. "Mary Jennifer loved the place, and she loved to plant flowers and vegetables.

"I always took her into Manhattan," recalls Colby, "to the theater, to the '21' club. Once, Bill Howard got up from his table at '21' and introduced Mary Jennifer to the crowd as 'Jennifer's daughter.' "

It was hardly a description Mary Jennifer appreciated. Colby recalls how, when Norton Simon had entered Jennifer's life, "Mary Jennifer went out of her way to dress up when he was around. On one occasion she was dressed to the nines in an off-the-shoulder [and very provocative] red dress. 'One day I'm going to be famous and people will know me as they do you and Mother,' she told me."

Mary Jennifer became, as a young adult, "very emotional and mixed up. And her boyfriend was no good," Colby says, and draws a specific comparison: "Mary Jennifer was as naive as her mother."

As Mary Jennifer approached her twenty-second birthday, she

had to date survived an attempt at suicide, a stay in a mental hospital, and an abortion. She was undergoing analysis and was in group therapy. A fellow patient, reluctant today to discuss the matter on the record, nonetheless recalls sadly that "Mary Jennifer had problems relating to her mother. She felt her mother had done and said all the right things, but that a dimension was missing to their relationship; that 'something missing' could of course have been Mary's fault as well, but in her mind the fault was her mother's."

Jennifer had been under the impression that her daughter was finally doing well, that "the world [was becoming] her oyster." The girl had moved to Pasadena and was taking courses at Occidental College. However, a former classmate of Mary Jennifer's said that at that time Mary "had been a very strange, self-absorbed girl. A real loner." And she added, "She also had a substance abuse problem."

On April 26, Jennifer was front and center at a glittering fund-raiser, a fashion show held at the Beverly Wilshire Hotel. She'd been in charge of organizing the event, a benefit for Dr. Wexler's Hereditary Disease Foundation. It was a memorable evening, with an impressive turnout of Hollywood's old and new guard: Cary Grant, Jack Nicholson, Gregory Peck, Warren Beatty, Walter Matthau, Jack Lemmon, Kirk Douglas, Cher, Sally Kellerman, Carol Burnett, Diahann Carroll, Jacqueline Bisset, Anjelica Huston, Rosalind Russell, Candice Bergen, and Elizabeth Taylor. Barbara Walters and Alfred and Betsy Bloomingdale were also on hand.

Acknowledging the success of the evening, Dr. Wexler made a speech and warmly praised Jennifer as the dignified, caring, and generous woman "who brought all this together. . . ."

She appeared deeply moved. "Helping is just another form of loving," she said, "and I want to thank you all for being such great lovers."

Phil Isley, Jennifer's dad, was now eighty-three and in very ill health, living in Dallas. Jennifer was greatly concerned about him and, in mid-May, was by his side when she received the bloodcurdling news—Mary Jennifer had been found dead. She'd apparently plunged from the roof of 10701 Wilshire Boulevard, a twenty-two-story building in the Westwood section of Los Angeles. Police were able to identify her only because she'd left her purse on the roof.

"Can you imagine?" asks Anita Colby, shock and disbelief in her voice even today. "There was Jennifer with her father, who was dying of cancer but struggling to live, and Mary Jennifer just tosses her own life away. . . ."

Chapter

34

*J*ennifer was stricken to the core. Numbed by shock, she flew to Los Angeles to claim Mary Jennifer's body. Authorities didn't realize that the claimant, the expression on her face frozen and masklike, was Jennifer Jones.

Another tragedy was in store. Only two weeks later Jennifer's father succumbed after complications following surgery. It was a shock, but coming on the heels of the deep grief and feelings of guilt over Mary Jennifer's suicide, Jennifer was overwhelmed. There were rumors of another suicide attempt.

The ensuing year "was a very difficult one in Jennifer's life," recalled Anita Colby. Jennifer's access, as always, to the very best professional help and her apparently indomitable will to survive would somehow, hopefully, pull her through.

Actress Nanette Fabray, who suffered the loss of husband, mother, and brother all within a very short span of time, has explained how, under such emotionally shattering circumstances, one has little control over one's reactions. "You are who you are," she says. "You can retreat, feel sorry for yourself, or survive. In my own case, I discovered I was a very strong person."

Jennifer Jones once again discovered the same about herself. It broke her heart, but she withstood it. The prime element in her support system remained her husband. He'd lived through the anguish of his own son's suicide and didn't underestimate the impact of the aftershock.

"The death of a child is the very worst thing that can happen to a parent, the hardest to handle," says Dennis Wholey, author of *When the Worst That Can Happen Already Has.* "You can't forget—a piece of you isn't there anymore."

"You don't survive," declared singer Eydie Gormé, years after the death of her twenty-three-year-old son, Michael. "It's every day, every moment. It's right now. It doesn't get better, it gets worse."

In her mind and heart, Jennifer would never be the same. The tragedy had touched a deep chord within her. And there could be no satisfactory answer to the bizarre pattern that seemed to shadow Jennifer's life, whereby catastrophes befell those she loved—yet she always landed on her feet. "I was devastated when Mary died," she later said. "She had gone through treatment and, I thought, was at peace with herself. You never know . . . about the mind."

Jennifer emerged slowly from her depression. She displayed a resigned acceptance of her loss and became a woman with a mission. Her commitment to the cause of mental health loomed larger than ever.

"Many good purposes and intentions lie in the churchyard," observed Philip Henry, but this was not to prove the case with Jennifer Jones. She was in a position to accomplish plenty. While her pain was no less traumatic because there were million-dollar paintings hanging on her walls, her financial wherewithal and social contacts would prove invaluable in starting up programs and organizations to help others. But it is a sadly ironic fact that for all her wealth and social standing she'd been unable to help her own child.

Keeping Jennifer active was crucial to her recovery. Simon involved her more and more with his art empire (no less cutthroat a field than the world of filmmaking). He was devoting all his formidable energies to improving his extraordinary collection, and around this time he offered to pay off the debts of the Pasadena Museum of Modern Art, a private nonprofit museum built on public land by a group of wealthy donors. He subsequently gained control of the board of trustees and in September 1977 installed Jennifer Jones Simon as chairman and changed the name of the museum to the Norton Simon Museum.

The events leading up to Simon's complete takeover invoked a raging controversy, and the aftershocks are still being felt today in the art world of Southern California.

A civil suit was brought against the museum by several former board members, who charged Simon with "cannibalizing the permanent collection and manipulating the museum's assets for personal gain." Jennifer was hardly comfortable with this development. The lawsuit dragged on, charged with negative publicity. Although Simon was subsequently absolved of any impropriety, a feeling of bitterness and acrimony reportedly remains, on both sides, to the present day.

George Masters, regarding Jennifer's appointment as chairman of the Norton Simon Museum, observed wryly that while he didn't know if Jennifer still had her three Renoirs hanging over the bathtub, "at least she has a museum." And Masters noted that she finally had something "she always yearned for to complete her ultimate illusion, and which even David Selznick's money couldn't buy for her—a full-time, live-in hairdresser."

Masters's evaluation of Jennifer's life with Norton Simon was "a life of 'expanded consciousness,' as Jennifer calls it, almost exclusively in the world of art rather than movies."

Jennifer was a commissioner on the Huntington's Disease Council (Huntington's was a chronic mental illness) and narrated an eighteen-minute slide show for the Hereditary Disease Foundation. She traveled to Washington, D.C., where she screened the presentation for Senator Birch Bayh in the projection room where the Senate Appropriations Committee holds its hearings.

Jennifer's narration for the film was blunt in describing those afflicted with the disease, concluding, "They [the victims] are profoundly suicidal. It saps the person of dignity, it absolutely bares him." Jennifer's purpose was to plead for Congress to appropriate $53 million to fight the ailment. Senator Bayh's comment to Jennifer after the presentation: "Academy Award."

She consented to an interview with Nancy Collins, who was then reporting for *The Washington Post.*

Collins, a striking blonde, was impressed with how beautiful Jennifer still was. She was "the last of the big-time Hollywood glamour queens," said Collins, and described Jennifer as "gracious, upbeat, and self-effacing." Collins noted how unusual it was for Jones to meet the press. "I have spent my whole life resisting," conceded Jennifer. "Suddenly these last few years, I find myself doing everything I said I'd never do."

Collins was of course interested in Jennifer's Selznick days and his role as her Svengali. "Well, frankly, I have always had a belief in my own basic talent, but obviously I was very fortunate to find David Selznick or have David find me," she said. "Every actress discovered or nurtured by him—and God knows we all need nurturing—well, every actress David helped was very fortunate."

Jennifer's recollections of winning her Oscar, thirty-three stormy, tragedy-filled years after the fact, had altered drastically. Now she said that she'd "kind of expected it. . . . When you're very young . . . you expect everything. Of course this should be happening, I thought. What else? I came to New York to be an actress, and everything is going according to plan. And the same thing went for the Oscar."

Jennifer admitted, however, that if an Oscar came her way now, "I'd be overwhelmed, thrilled to death."

Incredibly, she didn't remember how she'd been christened "Jennifer Jones." She recalled that perhaps Selznick had taken the name from an old nursery rhyme. She was, in fact, remembering the old publicity handouts that had apparently assumed the ring of truth for her. And she "roared with laughter" when Collins asked her about accounts George Masters had related concerning Jennifer's fanatical beauty regimen.

"I love George dearly," said Jennifer, "but I'm afraid that was all fantasy on his part—a little poetic license. God, I would have been so tired I couldn't have enjoyed my own parties.

"Besides, that does sound awfully narcissistic, doesn't it? I must say I plead guilty to a certain degree of narcissism, but not to that extent. It's true, of course, that we did have people over on Sundays, but I didn't spend the day changing clothes, I assure you."

Regarding her late daughter ("clearly . . . the tragedy of her life," observed Nancy Collins), Jennifer replied that it was a subject she preferred not to discuss.

Jennifer was more than happy, however, to discuss her latest mental health project, the creation of "separation centers." She envisioned them as twenty-four-hour halfway houses for those "in the throes of some sort of separation, either from a marriage or relationship . . . [a place] where people can come to talk to people with similar problems. . . ." Obviously a group Jennifer would have taken advantage of herself in years past.

Jennifer declared that she wanted to continue acting. "It's what I do best," she said, and added that she was looking for a good script. She also said that she was a happy woman and realized that she'd already had a good run. "Actually, every time I stop to think about it, I'm really amazed. I think I've had an extraordinary life. And lots of times I can hardly believe it's me."

According to Jennifer, Norton Simon could hardly believe he was married to a movie star. "Sometimes I come home and catch Norton watching one of my old movies on television," she said. "He always seems kind of amazed that the woman he's watching is the same woman he's married to. But I just say to him, 'You're not really looking at that old thing, are you? Come on, Norton, you're looking at my past. Let's live in the moment.'"

Living in the moment was what she strove to do.

The twenty-five-year-old Jennifer Jones came on view in homes throughout the land when *Since You Went Away* was recirculated on television, the same year Jennifer turned sixty. "I'm glad I made it," she said.

Jones was determined to provide benefits for the mentally ill that would endure beyond her lifetime. She discussed the subject with Norton, who encouraged her to set up a foundation. There were numerous meetings with attorneys, and the details were swiftly finalized. Early in 1980 Jennifer donated $1 million to establish the Jennifer Jones Simon Foundation for Mental Health and Education. "Jennifer Jones's life has been an incredible ordeal, but one with a happy ending!" wrote medical columnist Ruth Nathan Anderson. Others noted that the foundation was Jennifer and Norton's way "of saying 'thanks' for their own good fortune in finding happiness after tragedy."

Simon stated that the foundation would "work to eradicate the public stigma of mental illness, improve care in mental institutions, and assist in all aspects of mental treatment."

Jennifer was often Simon's emissary to art auctions, empowered to spend millions of dollars. On one occasion, at Sotheby's in London, her assignment was to acquire the painting *Resurrection of Christ,* by the fifteenth-century Flemish master Dierik Bouts. The auctioneer's estimate was $440,000. Jennifer, in a fierce bidding war, went up to $3 million, with no end in sight. A hurried telephone call was placed, and then, by transatlantic telephone, her husband took over. He finally made the winning bid at $4.25 million.

On another occasion Jennifer was locked in a fierce bidding war over a painting with an anonymous competitor participating by telephone. Fortunately it was discovered in the nick of time that Jennifer and Simon were bidding against each other (both withdrew from that auction).

The stakes weren't always life-and-death. Jennifer placed the high bid—twenty thousand dollars—for a painting on sale at a celebrity auction. The still-life she acquired was by her friend, Henry Fonda.

These activities aside, Jennifer still nurtured a strong desire to resume her career. She immediately recognized a role she'd be perfect for. She told Norton how deeply moved she'd been by the plight of schoolmistress Jean Harris, who had shot her lover, "Scarsdale Diet" doctor Herman Tarnower, to death. It was far more than an ordinary crime of passion because Jean Harris was an outstanding member of the community, a well-bred, highly respectable woman whose irrational behavior made her actions all the more fascinating and incomprehensible, both to the media and to the public at large.

Jennifer apparently understood and empathized with the dilemma of this highly emotional woman who'd become the victim of her own passion. She was determined to portray her, and Simon financed Jennifer's aspirations.

The Simons had a meeting with David Brown (who by now had coproduced *Jaws* and *The Sting*), to discuss the project. "She was very interested in being cast as Jean Harris," recalls Brown. "I believe she'd even funded a script. She wanted to play the role very, very much, and we talked."

The project didn't come off, however, mainly because a TV version of the Harris story, starring Ellen Burstyn, swiftly hit the airwaves after transcripts of the trial became available.

Jennifer's instincts regarding another project were also on the money. *Terms of Endearment,* by Larry McMurtry, was the story of a totally self-absorbed woman named Aurora Greenway, who has to contend with a rebellious adult daughter. When the daughter suddenly discovers she has terminal cancer, the relationship between mother and daughter, and Aurora's entire life, is forever altered by the crisis.

Jennifer wasn't fearful of tackling a subject so close to her heart. The novel was optioned by Jennifer and Simon, and a screenplay was developed for her by James Brooks.

Jennifer excitedly confided her enthusiasm for the role to Anita Colby as the script slowly took shape. Brooks, however, eventually persuaded Jennifer and Simon to sell the movie rights to Paramount, because, according to Colby, Brooks told Jennifer she was "too old" for the part. "That hit her where she lived," recalled Colby. "So she gave [the property] up!"

"Once Jennifer Jones sold the film rights . . . there was not a single actress in auditioning distance who wasn't foaming to do *Terms*," wrote the *Los Angeles Times*. The film Brooks subsequently wrote and directed went on to win the Oscar as Best Picture, plus it garnered Oscars for Brooks as Best Director and writer, for Jack Nicholson as Best Supporting Actor, and for Shirley MacLaine as Best Actress.

Jennifer meanwhile had developed into a leading light on the West Coast social scene. Superagent Irving ("Swifty") Lazar, a long-time acquaintance of Jennifer's ("We were friendly . . . however, our relationship was always a very distant one," says Lazar), approached her to write a book about her parties.

"Lazar wanted her to do the book," recalls Anita Colby, "but Norton said to Jennifer, 'I thought you were a smart woman. . . . If that's the only book you can come up with, it's ridiculous!' "

Jennifer didn't write the book.

Despite her efforts, there'd be no imminent return to the screen for Jennifer Jones. There were far worse fates, of course. Her dear friend Ingrid Bergman, after a lifetime of abundant energy and good health, was stricken with cancer. While seriously ill, she delivered one of the outstanding performances of her career, portraying the title role in the life story of Israeli prime minister Golda Meir in a TV miniseries.

Ingrid won the Emmy for her efforts. But in the summer of 1982, at age sixty-seven, Bergman died. That same year Henry King, the man who'd guided Jennifer to stardom in *The Song of Bernadette*, passed away at age ninety-four.

The years went by. Jennifer was not oblivious of the rigors of advancing age, but she was holding up spectacularly well. So she looked none the worse for wear when, at age sixty-five, she made a brief appearance on a televised American Film Institute tribute to Lillian Gish.

Jennifer, for the broadcast, was seated in the audience. Sporting a very flattering, youthful haircut, from a distance she didn't look much different than in her heyday. She rose on cue and nervously voiced glowing comments about "my good friend Lillian." But despite her good looks and good health, filmmakers were still not clamoring for her services. And unfortunately, yet another personal crisis was about to surface.

*T*he *news made her go cold. Norton,* seventy-seven years old, had been diagnosed with Guillain-Barré syndrome, a rapidly progressive nerve disease characterized by muscle weakness. It was very serious, and how dramatically it would affect Simon, his life with Jennifer, and the quality of their life together remained to be seen.

Jennifer was fearful and apprehensive, although she never allowed Simon to see it. An intensive care unit was set up in the Simon home, with a round-the-clock team of ten nurses ("The nurses are like family to us," Jones said). Jennifer remained close by her husband, and his condition eventually improved.

In a most unusual move, Jennifer and the ailing Simon relocated their household to a complex of attached bungalows in the luxurious Beverly Hills Hotel. The hotel, long a haven for the world's millionaires, sits at the summit of glittering Rodeo Drive and provides a blissfully serene and rustic setting with its lush tropical gardens, exotic flowers, and private walkways through groves of orange blossoms, coconut palms, oleanders, and bougainvillea. The countrylike ambiance belies the fact that the hotel is located only minutes from central and downtown Los Angeles, Hollywood, Westwood, Century City, and Beverly Hills and is only minutes from the finest hospitals.

The Simon bungalows at the Beverly Hills were especially renovated to accommodate hospital equipment and a nursing staff. The Simons' "neighbors" were likely to be people Jennifer and Simon had known for years. (David Selznick had stayed at the hotel on many occasions. Back in 1970, after Simon had divorced Lucille but before he'd married Jennifer, he'd moved into the hotel for a year. At one time or another, everyone from the Walter Annenbergs to game show producer Mark Goodson and show business luminaries Johnny Carson and Elizabeth Taylor have been regular residents.)

Why had the Simons made this move? Betty Spiegel offers a likely explanation: It was a way for Jennifer to preserve her beloved privacy. "Round-the-clock medical people can take over [your own home]," states Betty, speaking from experience. When her mother became ill, "I turned my mother's house into a hospital for six months, with round-the-clock help. While all my attention was focused on my mother, I wasn't noticing what was going on in the kitchen [and elsewhere] and, in effect, [the medical people literally commandeered the house]. Do you see what I'm driving at? Keeping Norton at home, Jennifer would no longer have had any privacy in her own home."

Another reason Jennifer and Norton moved to the Beverly Hills Hotel was the fact that Simon's friend, financier Ivan Boesky, and his wife, Seema, had recently gained control of the hotel. The Simons knew that everything that could be done would be done to create an atmosphere conducive to Norton's recovery.

The entrance to the Simons' cluster of bungalows, which were pretty pink structures with Spanish-tiled roofs and white shutters on the windows, was on Crescent Drive. Although more luxurious bungalows were available, in the case of a medical emergency, Crescent Drive offered the swiftest route for an ambulance.

Jennifer, as one would have expected, maintained a low profile while living at the hotel. "She kept very much to herself," relates a hotel employee. "We rarely saw her, since she could exit from their bungalows directly onto the street."

"Certain Arab sheiks used to prefer these bungalows so they could make fast getaways," says a former resident of the hotel, laughing.

While Simon was physically still quite ill, he was very much in control of his mental faculties and therefore still in control of his business empire. However, the fate of his art collection became the hottest and most controversial issue amid Southern California's art aficionados, whose worst nightmare would be to see the collection broken up and sold to various individuals and institutions.

To Jennifer's (and the art world's) relief, early in 1987 Simon declared that he would donate his entire collection to UCLA. The university prematurely announced that "an agreement in principle" had been reached and that the collection would remain in Pasadena and be administered by both the university, the Simon Museum board, and the Norton Simon Foundation. A new building would be erected on campus to display part of the collection. (Regrettably, a few months later Simon decided not to donate the collection to the school.)

Jennifer again considered reactivating her career (there were still many Jennifer Jones "fans" out there, including Jack Kemp, a presidential candidate, who said that Jennifer was his favorite actress—he'd even named his daughter in her honor).

There had been reports of Jones being cast in *The Colbys,* the spin-off series spawned by the TV megahit *Dynasty.* Charlton Heston was the star, and he recalled, "Jennifer's name never came up. The role [of Heston's wife, a manipulative, conniving, bitchy character] wouldn't have been good casting for her—that's not the kind of thing she does well."

Jennifer agreed to appear on the upcoming Oscar telecast, scheduled for live broadcast in late March, to present the award for Best Cinematography.

The evening went well. Backstage Jennifer and Lauren Bacall, who was also presenting an award, greeted each other warmly. Bacall knew all too well what it was like to contend with a seriously ill spouse. "You look gorgeous!" enthused Bacall, whose flowing blond hair and up-to-the-minute chic contrasted sharply with Jennifer's lacquered coif and stiff-looking formal gown.

Bacall presented the Best Costume Design award with her usual flair, while actress Isabella Rossellini, one of Ingrid Bergman's daughters, presented the award for Best Art Direction.

Jennifer was up next. A brief film of highlights of her career preceded her appearance, and the audience gave her a warm reception. Visibly nervous, her voice trembling, she presented the Best Cinematography award to Chris Menges (for *The Mission*). On handing him the statuette, she shook his hand in businesslike fashion, but he managed a kiss.

• • •

Simon suffered another medical crisis the week Jennifer celebrated her seventieth birthday and was rushed to the hospital. Presently, an announcement was made that Simon was relinquishing his role as president of his museum and installing Jennifer in his place.

Considerable controversy erupted regarding Jennifer's qualifications and actual ability to run the museum. Henry Hopkins, director of former Simon brother-in-law Frederick R. Weisman's Art Foundation, voiced a rosy outlook: "Probably nobody's better versed than Jennifer as to what his [Norton's] wishes are."

Few others dared voice an opinion on the record. "Under [Jennifer]," said one cautious anonymous source, "I think we'll start to see the museum become a bit more friendly." Norton Simon had been "single-minded" about building his collection, claimed this expert, but Jennifer would "give the museum a higher profile than her husband had allowed by encouraging educational programs and attempting to make the collection, which is open only four days a week, more accessible to the public."

Others were not as generous in their opinions, claiming that in her role as a Simon Museum board member Jennifer "appeared at times to be working from a script prepared by her husband." Another well-placed source stated that Jennifer had been "sort of a passive participant" in her role as a member of the Getty Trust's board.

An official announcement from Simon himself seemed imminent, since he'd acknowledged for years that even he (Simon) could not afford to subsidize his museum in perpetuity and would have to make arrangements with another institution.

But the wily Simon was in no hurry, and he trusted Jennifer to make sure his wishes were carried out. People speculated that the J. Paul Getty Museum in Malibu would be the future home of the Simon collection, since Simon and Jennifer had a close relationship with Harold M. Williams, a former Simon employee who was now president of the Getty Trust's board.

Williams admitted that no talks were currently in progress, but he was highly optimistic about Jennifer. "Mrs. Simon will provide very responsible leadership. . . . She's not going to be another Norton Simon. She'll do it her way and do it very well."

Jennifer, needless to say, remained incommunicado. The art community remained abuzz with snide comments about her "credentials." Admittedly she'd known nothing about art "until Norton awakened me."

Ah, for the days when Jennifer's greatest worry (and for her it had been a great worry) was to ferret out the heart and soul of a fictional character and interpret a script.

For the moment, though, it was back to show business. Jennifer appeared on the American Film Institute's tribute to Gregory Peck. On the subject of kissing Peck in *Duel in the Sun,* she smiled and said, "It wasn't the hardest thing I've ever had to do."

A radiant and unusually chatty Jennifer, striking in a red ensemble, was one of thirty-five selected guests on hand for the wedding of Robert Wagner to actress Jill St. John in the spring of 1990. Wagner, like Jennifer, was a survivor. At sixty he looked twenty years younger, and his titian-haired forty-nine-year-old bride was also a Hollywood veteran (Jennifer had worked with Wagner in *The Towering Inferno* and with Jill in *Tender Is the Night*).

Jennifer wished the couple great good luck; she certainly empathized with "R.J." over the loss of his late wife, Natalie Wood, in a suspicious drowning incident, and the ghastly aftermath surrounding the tragedy (even worse than what Jennifer had experienced in the dark days after Robert Walker's death).

Meanwhile Norton Simon continued to keep everyone guessing on the fate of his art collection. Observers wondered whether the machinations weren't worthy of a dramatic miniseries, perhaps one with Jennifer Jones Simon portraying herself!

To calm the building tidal wave of gossip, Simon finally granted an interview to Suzanne Muchnic of the *Los Angeles Times,* which took place in the Simon bungalows at the Beverly Hills Hotel.

Simon, neatly groomed and snappily dressed in a suit and tie, was confined to a wheelchair. He was eighty-three years old and, considering his physical condition, looked quite good. More important, his mind was still sharp. Jennifer, by his side, was conservatively dressed and immaculately groomed, her hands often reaching up to touch the priceless pearls adorning her neck.

"Our desire is to keep going on our own, if we can, and we really think we can," said Simon, commenting on his plans for his collection. "I have a lot of faith in my wife," he noted. Simon said that he had seriously considered selling the collection, and he turned to Jennifer and remarked, "For a while I thought it might be better to get the dollars and put them into your foundation."

"But you didn't, and I'm glad you didn't," she replied. "You've put so much passion and love and energy into your collection, selling it or giving it up would be too sad." As sad, it would seem, as David Selznick's having relinquished all rights to *Gone With the Wind*. In this instance, however, there was absolutely no lure, financial or otherwise, great enough to convince Norton Simon to part with his beloved works of art.

One role Jennifer had gladly played over the years was that of best friend and, in effect, second sister to Anita Colby. Colby had approved of Jennifer's marriage to Simon. "Norton has done wonderful things for her," she said. "She's in charge. She's involved in so many worthy causes. If she loves you, she's very giving of herself (and loves to buy you presents). I remember her putting her arms around me and saying, 'I love you, Colby.' "

Colby, in later years, had developed serious health problems. Jennifer visited her often and kept in close touch but wasn't always able to fly east. "She said Norton wouldn't let her, and I understood," said Colby.

Yet another tragedy befell Jennifer when, in the spring of 1992, her dear friend and confidante Anita Colby died. It was yet another loss she braced herself to survive.

In Palm Springs, Jennifer often palled around with longtime friend Patricia Medina Cotten, wife of Joseph Cotten (years ago Jennifer had avidly encouraged their romance).

Jones was a frequent patron of the famous Polo Lounge in the Beverly Hills Hotel (only a two-minute walk from her bungalows). Hotel guests seated on couches in the adjoining foyer, or using the telephone booths, could not fail to notice her—heads always turned to observe the beautiful woman entering from the garden pathway through the double glass doors, striding past the jewelry showcase to the Polo Lounge entrance.

She was always greeted with broad smiles and immediately seated by the maître d' at the most desirable booth, number 503 (over the years the favorite spot of, among others, Charlie Chaplin). It was situated along the far wall, exactly opposite the entrance to the restaurant, its dark green upholstery and bright pink tablecloth and accessories a flattering setting for its occupant. "When people working in the Polo Lounge want to put someone in a choice spot, that's the booth," noted a "regular."

"Jennifer Jones is a very generous tipper," states a hotel employee, "and she helps a lot of people, many of them famous. She's generous helping people with problems. She's very well liked."

How did Jennifer look? "You'd swear it was thirty years ago," says the regular, smiling. "She's a bit heavier, very tall, still beautiful."

Jennifer's accessibility to the public, in this seemingly open situation, was deceiving. "The Polo Lounge is like a little club, but only the members know it.

"The public thinks they're part of it, but they're not," explains the regular. "They [the public] can look, but not touch. The staff looks after the regulars very carefully. One *can* be a recluse in the Polo Lounge!" he says with a laugh.

By the time the Beverly Hills Hotel closed for renovation, on December 29, 1992, the Simons had moved to a small house nearby, in Beverly Hills. Some of the hotel employees helped them move and decorate the new premises. Simon's strength had been ebbing steadily, and six months later, on the evening of June 1, 1993, at the age of eighty-six, he died in his sleep.

Time has proven Jennifer Jones to be no fragile morning glory (the beautiful blossom that blooms brilliantly but wilts by the end of the day). Henry Miller once described Jennifer by quoting Kazantzakis describing the geisha: "You look at her and your soul cools off."

While Jennifer lives in the moment, she's only human. In the wee small hours it would be surprising if memories of Robert Walker, David Selznick, and Mary Jennifer didn't flood her mind.

"I have seen it all," she once revealed to a reporter in a candid flashback on her life. Life has certainly taught her to understand people's suffering and pain. What has mattered most to Jennifer, according to the late Anita Colby, is that she has survived and constructed a productive life for herself that benefits others.

Today she is a faithful volunteer at the Southern California Counseling Center in Beverly Hills and has become a paraprofessional therapist. It is no longer the world of show business, but that of science and psychiatry that intrigues Jennifer the most.

• • •

"*What is success? . . . It is a toy balloon among children armed with sharp pins,*" noted veteran writer and Hollywood savant Gene Fowler.

Jennifer's solution to escaping the "sharp pins" has been to isolate herself from public scrutiny. To an extent, the approach has worked well. Her saga is not heading toward an unhappy ending. "I hear she is blossoming," says Joan Fontaine. "Now that Jennifer is in authority, she may actually have some confidence at last!" exclaims Fontaine.

As Jennifer's artist friends might phrase it, she's a work in progress. Unlike many of her peers, Jones has become a positive force in society, one to be reckoned with via her foundation for mental health and other charitable interests. She's light-years beyond a goal of merely creating a shrine to her past, of spending her days traveling to film retrospectives, talking about herself, her films, and her "fabulous" life.

Jennifer's impact on film endures. The prestigious Los Angeles County Museum ran a Jennifer Jones retrospective in the summer of 1992. Contemporary critics have praised Jennifer's screen persona, isolating her special quality as an ability to make one cry at unexpected moments, to envelop an audience in the thoughts and feelings her character is experiencing, and to make an audience respond. Jennifer had (and probably still has) the ability to make a sympathetic leap into a character and win our empathy; to embody a woman who can be easily hurt by the world. Her eyes seem always to be searching for an exit, for a little piece of sky. Cloud nine has been Jennifer's special residence on screen and, at times, even in her private life.

Jennifer Jones was both a victor in her pursuit of the American dream and a victim of it. For despite the fame, success, and wealth, despite her marriage to one of Hollywood's true legends of filmmaking, despite the awards, accolades, and applause of the public, the press, and the film industry, and despite her marriage to another man as equally powerful, brilliant, and wealthy as Selznick, Jennifer could not prevent the tragic loss of both a husband and a child to the ravages of drugs, alcohol, depression, and ultimately death; could not stop Norton Simon's debilitating illness, which forced her, who had been sheltered and protected most of her life, into the role of caretaker; and could not resurrect a brilliant career that had spanned almost four decades. Jennifer Jones has lived a life of supreme happiness and devastating sorrow. But whenever life threatened to knock her out, she always got back on her feet, stronger and more capable than before.

To a great extent, Jennifer Jones embodies a wise old proverb: "You don't know where you're going unless you know where you've been. . . ."

Acknowledgments

The author gratefully acknowledges the generous cooperation of Joan Fontaine, the late Anita Colby Flagler, Charlton Heston, David Brown, Gwen Verdon, the late Vincent Price, Phyllis Thaxter, Eddie Albert, Michael Parks, Patricia Lawford, Rhonda Fleming, the late Alfred Hitchcock, Tom King, Gerald Gordon, Jean Dalrymple, Don Keefer, John Patrick, Gladys Luckie, John Springer, John R. Connolly, Harry Haun, Mrs. Sam (Betty) Spiegel, Pat Gaston Manville, Sondra Lee, Mrs. George Sherman, Paul Zastupnevich, Sylvia Miles, Meg McSweeney; the late Henry Willson, Tay Garnett, George Seaton, Ava Gardner, Adela Rogers St. Johns, Rosalind Russell, Charles Walters, Joshua Logan, Dore Schary, Dore Freeman, Hal Boyle, Jerry Evans, Bob Ungerfeld, Wanda Hale, Earl Wilson, John Beck, John Griggs, Candy Jones, Hal Wallis, Irving Paul ("Swifty") Lazar. Thanks also to the individuals who, on condition of anonymity, graciously shared their thoughts and memories on the life and times of Jennifer Jones.

As public relations man for Universal Pictures in New York for well over a decade, I had the memorable and invaluable opportunity of meeting, working with, and spending many fascinating hours with people who were literally legends of the film industry (both in front of and behind the cameras, in the United States and abroad), and with legendary reporters as well. Their colorful recollections and reminiscences never failed to ignite my imagination and my desire to know all about what made the people who made the movies (and those who wrote about them, advertised, publicized, and promoted them) tick. To one and all, I shall be eternally grateful.

For their support and help, special thanks to Joan Perry, Chris Kachulis, Lou Valentino, Jean Napp, Phyllis Schwartz, Daniela Gioseffi, Johnny Madden, and Barbara and Larry Eisenberg.

For making this book possible, thank you to Michael Korda, Cheryl Weinstein, Charles ("Chuck") Adams, and Susan Ginsburg.

Select Bibliography

Bacall, Lauren. *By Myself.* Alfred A. Knopf, 1979.

Behlmer, Rudy. *Memo from David O. Selznick.* The Viking Press, 1972.

Berg, A. Scott. *Goldwyn.* Alfred A. Knopf, 1989.

Bergman, Ingrid, with Alan Burgess. *My Story.* Delacorte, 1980.

Black, Shirley Temple. *Child Star: An Autobiography.* McGraw-Hill Publishing Co., 1988.

Bosworth, Patricia. *Montgomery Clift.* Harcourt Brace Jovanovich, 1978.

Brown, David. *Let Me Entertain You.* Wm. Morrow & Co., Inc., 1990.

Clarke, Gerald. *Capote: A Biography.* Ballantine Books, 1989.

Cotten, Joseph. *Joseph Cotten, an Autobiography: Vanity Will Get You Somewhere.* Mercury House, 1987.

Farber, Stephen, and Marc Green. *Hollywood on the Couch.* Wm. Morrow & Co., Inc., 1993.

Fontaine, Joan. *No Bed of Roses.* Wm. Morrow & Co., Inc., 1978.

Garnett, Tay, with Fredda Dudley Balling. *Light Your Torches and Pull Up Your Tights.* Arlington House, 1973.

Griggs, John. *The Films of Gregory Peck.* Citadel Press, 1984.

Grobel, Lawrence. *The Hustons.* Charles Scribner's Sons, Macmillan, 1989.

Hackett, Pat. *The Andy Warhol Diaries.* Warner Books, 1989.

Harvey, Stephen. *Directed by Vincente Minnelli.* Harper & Row, 1989.

Haver, Ronald. *David O. Selznick's Hollywood.* Alfred A. Knopf, 1980.

Higham, Charles. *Kate.* W. W. Norton and Co., Inc., 1975.

Hopper, Hedda, and James Brough. *The Whole Truth and Nothing But.* Doubleday & Co., Inc., 1962.

Houseman, John. *Front and Center.* Simon & Schuster, 1979.

Hudson, Rock, and Sara Davidson. *Rock Hudson: His Story.* Wm. Morrow & Co., Inc., 1986.

Huston, John. *An Open Book.* Alfred A. Knopf, 1980.

Israel, Lee. *Kilgallen.* Delacorte Press, 1979.

Johnson, Nunnally. *The Letters of Nunnally Johnson.* Edited by Doris Johnson and Ellen Leventhal. Alfred A. Knopf, 1981.

Keith, Slim, with Annette Tapert. *Slim.* Simon & Schuster, 1990.

Keyes, Evelyn. *Scarlett O'Hara's Younger Sister*. Lyle Stuart, 1977.

Knef, Hildegard. *The Gift Horse*. McGraw-Hill, 1971.

Korda, Michael. *Charmed Lives: A Family Romance*. Random House, 1979.

LaGuardia, Robert. *Monty: A Biography of Montgomery Clift*. Arbor House, 1977.

Lambert, Gavin. *On Cukor*. G. P. Putnam's Sons, 1972.

Lawford, Patricia Seaton, and Ted Schwarz. *The Peter Lawford Story*. Carroll and Graf Publishers Inc., 1988.

Lindfors, Viveca. *Viveka . . . Viveca*. Everest House, 1980.

Linet, Beverly. *Star-Crossed: The Story of Robert Walker and Jennifer Jones*. G. P. Putnam's Sons, 1986.

McDowall, Roddy. *Double Exposure*. Delacorte Press, 1966.

Madsen, Axel. *William Wyler*. Thomas Y. Crowell, 1973.

Masters, George, and Norma Lee Browning. *The Masters Way to Beauty*. E. P. Dutton & Co., 1977.

Minnelli, Vincente, and Hector Arce. *I Remember It Well*. Doubleday & Co., Inc., 1974.

Moshier, W. Franklyn. *The Films of Jennifer Jones*. W. Franklyn Moshier, 1978.

Neal, Patricia. *As I Am*. G. K. Hall, 1988.

Niven, David. *Bring On the Empty Horses*. G. P. Putnam's Sons, 1975.

Nolan, William F. *John Huston: King Rebel*. Sherbourne Press, 1965.

Olivier, Laurence. *Confessions of an Actor: An Autobiography*. Simon & Schuster, 1982.

Parish, James Robert. *The Glamour Girls*. Arlington House, 1975.

Powell, Michael. *A Life in the Movies*. Alfred A. Knopf, 1987.

Quirk, Lawrence J. *Claudette Colbert: An Illustrated Biography*. Crown, 1985.

Schary, Dore. *Heyday*. Little, Brown & Co., 1979.

Selznick, Irene Mayer. *A Private View*. Alfred A. Knopf, 1983.

Stack, Robert, with Mark Evans. *Straight Shooting*. St. Martin's Press, 1980.

Strasberg, Susan. *Marilyn & Me*. Warner Books, 1992.

Thomas, Bob. *Golden Boy: The Untold Story of William Holden*. St. Martin's Press, 1983.

Thomas, Bob. *Selznick*. Doubleday & Co., Inc., 1970.

Thomson, David. *Showman: The Life of David O. Selznick*. Alfred A. Knopf, 1992.

Valentino, Lou. *The Films of Lana Turner*. Citadel Press, 1976.

Vidor, King. *A Tree Is a Tree*. Harcourt, Brace, 1953.

Wallis, Hal, and Charles Higham. *Starmaker*. Macmillan, 1980.

Wiley, Mason, and Damien Bona. *Inside Oscar*. Ballantine Books, 1986.

Wilkerson, Tichi, and Marcia Borie. *The Hollywood Reporter: The Golden Years*. Arlington House, 1984.

Filmography

Note: Release dates are domestic (USA).

New Frontier. Republic. August 1939. Director: George Sherman. Screenplay: Betty Burbridge and Luci Ward.
CAST INCLUDES: John Wayne, Ray Corrigan, Raymond Hatton, Phylis Isley [Jennifer Jones].

Dick Tracy's G-Men. A Republic Serial. September-December 1939. Directors: William Witney and John English. Screenplay: Barry Shipman, Franklyn Adreon, Rex Taylor, Ronald Davidson, and Sol Shor.
CAST INCLUDES: Ralph Byrd, Irving Pichel, Ted Pearson, Phylis Isley [Jennifer Jones].

The Song of Bernadette. 20th Century–Fox. December 1943. Producer: William Perlberg. Direction and screenplay: George Seaton.
CAST INCLUDES: Jennifer Jones, Charles Bickford, William Eythe, Vincent Price, Lee J. Cobb, Gladys Cooper, Anne Revere, Roman Bohnen, Mary Anderson, "The Lady"—Linda Darnell.

Since You Went Away. A Selznick International Picture released through United Artists. July 1944. Producer: David O. Selznick. Director: John Cromwell. Screenplay: David O. Selznick.
CAST INCLUDES: Claudette Colbert, Jennifer Jones, Joseph Cotten, Shirley Temple, Monty Woolley, Lionel Barrymore, Robert Walker, Hattie McDaniel, Agnes Moorehead, Nazimova, Albert Basserman, Keenan Wynn, Guy Madison, Craig Stevens, Lloyd Corrigan, Florence Bates, Helen Koford (Terry Moore), Dorothy Dandridge, Doodles Weaver, Ruth Roman, Rhonda Fleming.

Love Letters. Paramount. October 1945. A Hal Wallis Production. Director: William Dieterle. Screenplay: Ayn Rand.
CAST INCLUDES: Jennifer Jones, Joseph Cotten, Ann Richards, Cecil Kellaway, Gladys Cooper, Anita Louise, Reginald Denny, Ian Wolfe.

Cluny Brown. 20th Century–Fox. June 1946. Produced and directed by

Ernst Lubitsch. Screenplay: Samuel Hoffenstein and Elizabeth Rein-
hardt.
CAST INCLUDES: Charles Boyer, Jennifer Jones, Peter Lawford, Helen
Walker, Reginald Gardiner, Reginald Owen, Sir C. Aubrey Smith, Richard
Haydn, Sara Allgood, Florence Bates, Una O'Connor.

Duel in the Sun. Selznick Releasing Organization. December 1946. Pro-
ducer: David O. Selznick. Director: King Vidor. Screenplay: David O.
Selznick. Adaptation: Oliver H. P. Garrett.
CAST INCLUDES: Jennifer Jones, Joseph Cotten, Gregory Peck, Lionel Barry-
more, Lillian Gish, Walter Huston, Charles Bickford, Herbert Marshall,
Harry Carey, Joan Tetzel, Tilly Losch, Butterfly McQueen, Otto Kruger,
Sidney Blackmer.

Portrait of Jennie. Selznick Releasing Organization. April 1949. Producer:
David O. Selznick. Director: William Dieterle. Screenplay: Paul Osborn and
Peter Berneis. Adaptation: Leonardo Bercovici.
CAST INCLUDES: Jennifer Jones, Joseph Cotten, Ethel Barrymore, Cecil
Kellaway, Lillian Gish, David Wayne, Florence Bates, Felix Bressart, Anne
Francis.

We Were Strangers. Columbia. April 1949. An Horizon Production. Pro-
ducer: S. P. Eagle (Sam Spiegel). Director: John Huston. Screenplay: Peter
Viertel and John Huston.
CAST INCLUDES: Jennifer Jones, John Garfield, Pedro Armendariz, Gilbert
Roland, Ramon Novarro.

Madame Bovary. MGM. August 1949. Producer: Pandro S. Berman. Direc-
tor: Vincente Minnelli. Screenplay: Robert Ardrey.
CAST INCLUDES: Jennifer Jones, James Mason, Van Heflin, Louis Jourdan,
Christopher Kent (Alf Kjellin), Gene Lockhart, Gladys Cooper, Henry
Morgan, George Zucco, Ellen Corby, Eduard Franz.

The Wild Heart (in Britain, *Gone to Earth*). A Selznick Picture released in
the USA by RKO. May 1952. A Michael Powell–Emeric Pressburger Pro-
duction. Written, produced, and directed by Michael Powell and Emeric
Pressburger.
CAST INCLUDES: Jennifer Jones, David Farrar, Cyril Cusack, Sybil
Thorndike, Hugh Griffith.

Carrie. Paramount. June 1952. Produced and directed by William Wyler.
Screenplay: Ruth and Augustus Goetz.

CAST INCLUDES: Laurence Olivier, Jennifer Jones, Miriam Hopkins, Eddie Albert.

Ruby Gentry. A Bernhard-Vidor Production released through 20th Century–Fox. December 1952. Producer: John Bernhard. Director: King Vidor. Screenplay: Sylvia Richards.
CAST INCLUDES: Jennifer Jones, Charlton Heston, Karl Malden, Tom Tully, Josephine Hutchinson.

Beat the Devil. A Santana-Romulus Production released through United Artists. March 1954. Director: John Huston. Screenplay: Truman Capote and John Huston.
CAST INCLUDES: Humphrey Bogart, Jennifer Jones, Gina Lollobrigida, Robert Morley, Peter Lorre.

Indiscretion of an American Wife. Released in the USA by Columbia Pictures. July 1954. Producers: David O. Selznick and Vittorio De Sica. Director: Vittorio De Sica. Screenplay: Cesare Zavattini, Luigi Chiarini, and Giorgio Prosperi. Dialogue: Truman Capote.
CAST INCLUDES: Jennifer Jones, Montgomery Clift, Gino Cervi, Richard Beymer.

Love Is a Many Splendored Thing. 20th Century–Fox. August 1955. Producer: Buddy Adler. Director: Henry King. Screenplay: John Patrick.
CAST INCLUDES: William Holden, Jennifer Jones, Torin Thatcher, Isobel Elsom, Richard Loo, Philip Ahn.

Good Morning, Miss Dove. 20th Century–Fox. November 1955. Producer: Samuel G. Engel. Director: Henry Koster. Screenplay: Eleanore Griffin.
CAST INCLUDES: Jennifer Jones, Robert Stack, Kipp Hamilton, Peggy Knudsen, Marshall Thompson, Chuck Connors, Biff Elliot, Jerry Paris, Mary Wickes.

The Man in the Gray Flannel Suit. 20th Century–Fox. April 1956. A Darryl F. Zanuck Production. Direction and screenplay: Nunnally Johnson.
CAST INCLUDES: Gregory Peck, Jennifer Jones, Fredric March, Marisa Pavan, Lee J. Cobb, Ann Harding, Keenan Wynn, Gene Lockhart, Gigi Perreau, Portland Mason, Arthur O'Connell, Henry Daniell, Connie Gilchrist.

The Barretts of Wimpole Street. MGM. February 1957. Producer: Sam Zimbalist. Director: Sidney Franklin. Screenplay: John Dighton.

CAST INCLUDES: Jennifer Jones, John Gielgud, Bill Travers, Virginia MacKenna.

A Farewell to Arms. 20th Century–Fox. A David O. Selznick Production. December 1957. Director: Charles Vidor. Screenplay: Ben Hecht.
CAST INCLUDES: Rock Hudson, Jennifer Jones, Vittorio De Sica, Oscar Homolka, Mercedes McCambridge, Elaine Stritch, Kurt Kaznar, Alberto Sordi.

Tender Is the Night. 20th Century–Fox. January 1962. Producer: Henry T. Weinstein. Director: Henry King.
CAST INCLUDES: Jennifer Jones, Jason Robards, Jr., Joan Fontaine, Tom Ewell, Cesare Danova, Jill St. John, Paul Lukas, Bea Benadaret, Sanford Meisner, Alan Napier.

The Idol. An Embassy Picture released through Warner-Pathe. August 1966. Producer: Leonard Lightstone. Director: Daniel Petrie. Screenplay: Millard Lampell.
CAST INCLUDES: Jennifer Jones, Michael Parks, John Leyton.

Angel, Angel, Down We Go. American-International. August 1969. Producer: Jerome F. Katzman. Direction and screenplay: Robert Thom.
CAST INCLUDES: Jennifer Jones, Jordan Christopher, Roddy McDowall, Holly Near, Lou Rawls.

The Towering Inferno. 20th Century–Fox/Warner Brothers. December 1974. An Irwin Allen Production. Director: John Guillermin. Screenplay: Stirling Silliphant.
CAST INCLUDES: Steve McQueen, Paul Newman, William Holden, Faye Dunaway, Fred Astaire, Jennifer Jones, Richard Chamberlain, O. J. Simpson, Robert Vaughn, Robert Wagner, Susan Flannery.

Index

Index

460